FINNatics

The History and Techniques of Finn Sailing

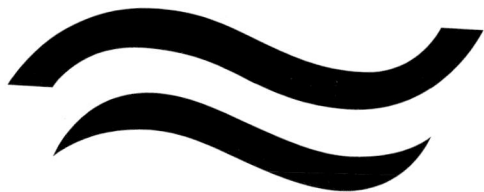

**Published by
the International
Finn Association**

Edited by Robert Deaves

With a Foreword by Paul Elvström

Published by the
International Finn Association

www.finnclass.org

First Edition 1999

Some material in this book was
originally published in
FINNLOG (published in 1986,
Edited by Peter Mohilla),
FINNFARE (the official
publication of the International
Finn Association) and various
other publications.

ISBN 0 9535504 0 0

Designed by Robert Deaves

Printed in Great Britain by
Lavenham Press, Water Street,
Lavenham, Sudbury, Suffolk
CO10 9RN.

Whilst every care was taken in
the preparation of this book to
ensure that the information
contained herein is correct,
neither the Editor nor the
publisher can accept any
responsibility for any errors or
inaccuracies which may be
present. If any reader has
additional information or is
aware of discrepancies, they
are invited to send this
information to the Editor.

Contents

	Foreword	*Paul Elvström*	5
1	Introduction: Fifty Years of the Finn	*Robert Deaves*	7
2	Report from the President	*Philippe Rogge*	10
3	The Birth of the Finn	*Rickard Sarby*	12
4	The Finnster	*David Leach*	16
5	Thoughts on Sailing to Windward	*Fred Miller*	17
6	Born to Win	*John Bertrand*	19
7	Finn Fundamentals	*Robert Deaves*	22
8	History of the IFA	*Peter Mohilla and Robert Deaves*	25
9	The Finn, a True Olympic Class	*David Leach*	41
10	Is There is Finn Specific Sports Injury?	*Frank Newton*	42
11	Paul Elvström on Singlehanded Sailing?	*Carl van Duyne and Dick Rose*	44
12	So You Want To Start Sailing The Finn	*Philippe Rogge*	46
13	The Finn - What Makes This Slow Boat So Fast?	*Jack Knights*	49
14	Finn Memories	*Vernon Stratton*	50
15	Psychology	*Paul Elvström*	53
16	John Bertrand on Boat Speed	*John Bertrand*	54
17	History of the Finn Gold Cup	*Peter Mohilla and Robert Deaves*	56
18	The 'Perfect' Mast	*Antonio Latini*	80
19	History of IFA Development Clinics and Camps	*Gus Miller*	82
20	From the Experts	*Pat Healy*	84
21	History of the Finn in the Olympics	*Richard Creagh-Osborne, David C Leach Georg Siebeck and Robert Deaves*	88
22	FINNFARE - History of a Magazine	*Robert Deaves*	107
23	History of the Finn Rules	*Peter Mohilla and Richard Hart*	114
24	Tacking the Finn	*Robert Deaves*	125
25	Hiking, Steering and Rig Control	*Ian Ainslie*	126
26	Regatta Preparation	*Sebastien Godefroid*	129
27	Gybe	*Garry Hoyt*	132
28	History of the Senior Europeans	*Peter Mohilla and Robert Deaves*	134
29	Technical Trends	*Peter Mohilla and Robert Deaves*	150
30	Downwind Finn Sailing	*Robert Deaves and Peter Mohilla*	156
31	Gybing the Finn	*Robert Deaves*	160
32	Plastic Fantastic	*Mickey Ickert*	162
33	Campaign Management	*Gus Miller*	164
34	History of the Junior Europeans	*Peter Mohilla and Robert Deaves*	167
35	Finn National Champions of the World		174
36	Planning your Sailing Season	*Mateusz Kusznierewicz*	180
37	Finn Racing Maxims		182
38	History of the Finn World Masters	*Peter Mohilla and Robert Deaves*	186
39	Major Finn Regatta Winners		192
40	The History and Evolution of the Finn Mast	*Gus Miller and Andy Zawieja*	197
41	Downwind Speed	*Larry Lemieux*	201
42	The Best Finn Sailors of all Time		202
	Index of Names		205
	Epilogue		208
	Index of Advertisers		208

Editorial

The fiftieth anniversary of the first ever Finn seems a suitable time to publish this collection of articles, race results and monologues written by those who made the class what it is. The Finn story has been going on now for over half a century and a massive amount of information has been published in that time and there was much more material suitable for inclusion in this book than could be fitted in. What has been attempted here is to bring together material that focuses on the important aspects of the class - the history and development, the race results and the techniques used to sail the Finn.

Most of the historical work herein was methodically researched and reported on by Peter Mohilla. In 1986 he published a book called FINNLOG, a monumental work covering the history of the Finn Class from its beginnings in 1949 up until 1985. This current book carries on from that work and brings the matter up to date. Grateful thanks are offered to Dr. Gertraud Mohilla for permission to republish much of her late husbands work.

The history of the Finn Class consists of a wide variety of interrelated aspects. Initially there is the human factor - who were the people that formed the class, held it together, drove it forward and dealt with the administrative problems? The pivotal chapter is therefore the 'History of the International Finn Association', dealing with the organisation of the Finn Class and the human forces that shaped it.

Of interest to others might be chapters on the technical development of the class: the development of the rules, construction and development of the hull and the way Finns were built and raced in the early days.

Others might be interested in the stories of the actual Finn racing - who were the fast people in the Finn during the last fifty years. There are separate chapters about each of the major sailing events: Olympics, Gold Cup, Europeans, Masters plus previously unpublished sections on National Champions and Major Regattas.

Of interest to some will be the wide diversity of opinions of authors within the book. No attempt has been made to remove contradictions between the various authors, which although may be confusing to some, it also shows the technological development of the class. Each article should be read whilst also bearing in mind the time that it was first published.

The common starting point of all the administrative, technical and sailing matters was the birth of the Finn, and Rickard Sarby himself wrote this chapter in 1975.

This book was designed to be many things. First and foremost it is a celebration of the first fifty years of the Finn, as a boat, as a class and as a sailing ideal. This book is also intended to be a nostalgic reminder to all those who have sailed the Finn over those fifty years - of the people, the events, the races, the technological development and the defining moments of one of the greatest classes ever. Thirdly, it is there as a reference for Finn sailors of the present and the future: a book of knowledge and instruction from which one can learn what the Finn is about, how it is sailed and what those who have sailed the class thought about it.

Finally, a publication of this kind would not be possible without the collaboration of a great many people all over the world. Thanks to them this book is a testimony to the people and the boats that make up the history of the Finn.

Acknowledgements

The editor wishes to thank the following people, whose help, encouragement, supply of photos, compilation of information and copyright permission was indispensable in the production of this book:

Richard Berg-Larsen, John Bertrand, Fabio Bodra, Michael Camps, Pierre le Chatelier, Luksa Cicarelli, Fritz Cordshagen, Paul Elvström, Dr. Gerhard Gfreiner, Sebastien Godefroid, Richard Hart, Pat Healy, Garry Hoyt, Mickey Ickert, Sarah Kingston, Mateusz Kusznierewicz, Antonio Latini, David Leach, John de Leeuw, Larry Lemieux, Richard Lott, Walter Mai, Paul McKenzie, Gus Miller, Dr Gertraud Mohilla, Dr Frank Newton, Jiri Outrata, Darrell Peck, Brian Porter, Philippe Rogge, Dick Rose, Francois Ruck, Otto Schlenka, Ali Serritslev, Georg Siebeck, Oleg Shilov, Srdjan Volarevic, John Skinner, Richard Stenhouse, Simon Stonehouse, Vernon Stratton, Imre Taveter, Mark Turner, Pablo Villar, Clifton Webb and anyone else who is not mentioned but who helped in any way.

Photo Credits

Ocean Images: Front cover (main photo), Back cover; Peter Bentley: 4, 6, 15, 149, 204; Antonio Latini: (Front cover - small photos - centre and right), 97, 101, 104, 105, 106, 111, 112; Sail Shots (www.sailshots.co.uk): inside cover photo, 79, 103, 184, 200; Francois Richard: Front Cover (lower left), 155; Dan Ager: 9, 157; Phil Cook: 20, 54; Jan Dominowski: 28, 136, 168; Robert Deaves: 80, 120, 123, 125, 152, 153, 155, 162; Bill Dotsch: 135; van Elst Archive: 66, 137; Paul Elvström Archive: 27, 59, 135; Jerzy Fijka: 16; Rolf Hamilton: 12; Maria Janko: 147, 173; David Leach Archive: 69; C.A. Marchaj: 62; Th. Martinez/Worlds 99: 79; Peter Montgomery: 70, 84; Curd Ochwadt Archive: 26, 27; Adriaan Pels: 141; Corinne Rolland-McKenzie: 79, 81, 95, 105, 127, 148; Rickard Sarby Archive: 12, 13, 14, 25, 26; Börge Schwarz; Georg Siebeck Archive: 119, 153, 198, 199; Vernon Stratton: 27, 52, 57, 116, 134, 136, 169; Vernon Stratton Archive: 2, 25, 30, 33, 50, 51, 52, 58, 64, 65, 117, 118, 138, 181; Andrew Wylam: 161; Zlatko Sunko: 102, 129, 148, 194; Yachts and Yachting: 56. All other photos by Josje Hofland-Dominicus and/or International Finn Association Archives.

Foreword

by Paul Elvström

It is a great honour for me to have the opportunity to write a foreword to this lovely book that holds so many wonderful memories.

During the 1948 Olympics in Torquay a warm friendship started between the father of the Finn and me and it lasted until Rickard passed away. I was very keen to defend my Gold medal from '48 so I followed the birth of the Finn with close interest. Rickard had the philosophy that everybody should build their own Finn. Even the sails should be made by the sailors themselves. He was a 100% amateur in the positive way and was not quite happy with those who made a living from building boats and making sails. He would turn in his grave if he could see what was going on in the sport of sailing today.

To me however it was with great happiness that in 1951 I received the first Finn from Borresens Boatyard. The same builder also built all the Finns for the Helsingfors Olympics. I had been sailing my brother's Dragon as this was the most competitive class where I lived. Our Dragon was not one of the best so it was shear happiness to get into a dinghy where economy was not the most important thing.

I had been doing hard physical training up to getting my first Finn so my body was OK, which is the basic for all dinghy sailing. I had learned in the Olympics in '48 that, in my opinion, most of the other competitors, if not all, were not sufficiently fit. Still, at the first Nordic Finn Championship in Stockholm the rest of us were taught a lesson on how to trim the mast with a plane. Rickard won and I had to fight hard to finish second. But I learned, so the next year when we sailed the Nordic Championship in Copenhagen I won with relative ease and my reserve for the Olympics Helmer Petersen came 2nd.

Shortly after at the Olympics in Helsingfors, I won sailing equally confidently. Rickard came 3rd and Charles Currey 2nd. During the next couple of years I got concerned over always winning. For this reason, and this reason alone, I decided to try other classes, and very competitive classes. It turned out that here I could also win so I ended up with 12 more World Championships in 8 different International Classes.

Later, other top Finn sailors have moved to other classes and gained top results, so the years have proved that a good Finn sailor can win in almost any other class.

I loved my first Finn. I felt that the dinghy and I were one and often I talked to it during races. For example when we did not quite perform to our expectations I would say "We have managed before so don't give up". Unfortunately it ended its days on a German Autobahn.

It's my hope to see the Finn in the Olympics in the future, but I think that the class should not be afraid of modernising it. The shape of the hull is perfect but I will not go into further details here. To replace the Finn in the Olympics would be the same as replacing the skis with snowboards in the alpine disciplines.

I would like still to sail a Finn today but my arthritis prohibits that. Börge Schwarz my old friend and reserve from the 1956 Olympics in Melbourne is still sailing the Finn today and I am very jealous that I cannot join him in the fun. Now I have to be satisfied with the joy of seeing the class still produce so many fine and good sailors to the benefit of our sport.

I wish the International Finn Class good luck in the future.

Paul Elvström

1. Introduction: Fifty Years of the Finn

by Robert Deaves

In 1999 the Finn became 50 years old. For over half a century this thoroughbred singlehanded dinghy has had an incalculable influence on the sailing world, being a blend of a popular club boat, Olympic legend and teacher of many top sailors. The dinghy that began life in the mind of a Swedish canoe designer has come of age.

The Finn is one of the survivors of the sailing world. It has survived 13 reselections as an Olympic class and 50 years of technical development, from the wooden hulls, wooden masts and cotton sails of the 1950's to the GRP hulls, carbon masts and kevlar sails of the 1990's. It has sustained criticism over the years for being hard to sail and expensive to campaign but it has always won through. And in spite of all this it has strengthened its position as the worlds premier dinghy for tactical as well as technical singlehanded sailing.

Quite how the Finn has retained its Olympic status for 50 years is a story all in itself, as every four years the class has to fight off challenges from other classes and those who think that it is time for change. But if the Finn has proved one thing, it is that change for the sake of change is rarely a good idea. The Finn is still providing the yachting world with top-calibre sailors who move onto greater things. It is perhaps no coincidence that the only two helmsmen to win the America's Cup off America are both Finn Olympic medalists (John Bertrand AUS - Bronze 1976; Russell Coutts NZL - Gold 1984).

But the Finn is so much more than just the Olympics - a pinnacle that many aspire to, that few reach but that all Finn sailors can

identify with and learn from. Sailing the Finn goes hand-in-hand with developing strength of character, perseverance, tenacity and the challenge of doing something difficult really well. To many, the Finn is the perfect embodiment of the Olympic ideal, wherever it is sailed, and perhaps this is the ultimate attraction of a dinghy that has thrived for half a century as a leading class on the world yachting scene.

Beginnings

It all began back in 1948 when the Finnish Yachting Association were considering which boats to use for the 1952 Olympic Games at Helsinki. With the lack of a suitable dinghy in Scandinavia, they instigated a design competition to find a single-handed dinghy which could be used primarily for inter-Scandanavian competition, but could also be used at the Olympics.

A Swedish canoe designer, Rickard Sarby, entered a design into this competition and although it was not initially selected, he was invited to take part in the trial races because he had already built a prototype. Several trial series were held and on May 15th 1950, the Finnish Yachting Association adopted the boat as an Olympic dinghy. This boat was the Finn and an Olympic legend was born.

First Olympics

So, in Helsinki in 1952 the Finn made its Olympic debut, and over the following years, names such as Paul Elvström, Willy Kuhweide, John Bertrand and Jochen Schümann sailed themselves into the record books. Elvström won three of his four Olympic Gold medals in the Finn (the other being in the Firefly), completely dominating the class in 1952, 1956 (Melbourne) and 1960 (Naples). The first Finn silver medal went to Charles Currey of Great Britain and the first Finn bronze medal went to her designer, Rickard Sarby.

Birth of the International Finn Association

After the 1952 Olympics interest in the Finn diminished, but the class was kept alive because in 1953 it was reselected for the 1956 Olympics in Melbourne, Australia. Control over the administration of the Finn was handed over to the IYRU in 1955, then in 1956, the first ever Finn Gold Cup (the Finn World Championship) was held at Burnham-on-Crouch after F.G. Mitchell of the Royal Burnham Yacht Club was persuaded by Vernon Stratton of the British Finn Association to present the class with a Gold Cup. Until this moment there was no real basis for the International Finn Class and it is believed that the firm footing of the class started here. Also in 1956 Henri Leten organised the first AGM of the class at the European Championships and the International Finn Association (IFA) was born. This gave the class a strong foundation for future growth and development.

In 1961, the first issue of the Finn international newsletter, FINNFARE, was published from the USA, bringing the separate corners of the class together. All these years later this publication is still going strong having been published from various parts of the globe at different times and in 1998 it celebrated its 100th issue.

Defining the Rules

The early wooden Finns gradually gave way to experiments in GRP after the IFA decided to free-up the construction material in 1961. At the Gold Cup that year (now an established event), the top three places were filled by GRP boats and many sailors then thought that their wooden boats were now obsolete. In fact the magically fast GRP boat that finished third in 1961 was found to have a secret distribution of lead in the hull (improving its gyration) when it was remeasured the following year! It was at this time that Richard Creagh-Osborne took over from Sarby as Chairman of the Technical Committee and he was given instructions to sort out these problems. However, wooden boats staged a comeback in 1964 when Hubert Raudaschl won the Finn Gold Cup with a home built wooden hull.

With the increasing strictness and changes in the class rules, measurement of the boats became easier to control with less manipulation of the rules taking place. Perhaps the biggest problem to overcome was controlling the weight distribution within the hull. It was soon realised that Finns with light ends were fast and, as proved by the matter of the illegal lead, the rules could be circumvented. After various attempts to control weight distribution by means of measuring the bow weight and tilting the hull on a gunwale (which were never satisfactory), a Frenchman named Gilbert Lamboley devised a pendulum test. The boat

was suspended and timed over a series of oscillations. For the first time this provided an accurate method of controlling the weight distribution within the hull. It was then possible to free-up construction methods and to allow double bottoms in the hulls. The day of the 'magic Finn' was over! This 'swing test' method was introduced into the Finn class in 1972 and has since become the standard method of weight-distribution testing for many other classes. In this, as in many other areas it is not unusual for the Finn class to lead the way.

Rig Development

Early rigs were of the telegraph pole variety - very stiff and also uncontrollable. Wedges were used to keep the boom down offwind; these went through a slot in the front of the mast, underneath the boom. When the wedge was pulled aft, the boom was forced down. Theoretically, it could be controlled by a control line, but in practice this did not always work!

During the 1950's, Elvström gradually moved away from the stiff mast and developed a bendy rig with a full sail that was progressively flattened in strong breezes. Throughout the early 1960's one of the most widespread rigs in general use was in fact Elvström's mast and sail combination. But by 1968 Jörg Bruder and Hubert Raudaschl had developed rigs still further, and masts once again became stiffer with flat sails. But the tops of these masts were very flexible sideways, allowing the rig to depower for lightweight skippers. This Bruder/Raudaschl combination completely dominated the class until the early seventies. However, the seeds of change were in the wind in 1969 when Jack Knights from Great Britain turned up at the Finn Gold Cup in Bermuda with a metal mast. He was the only competitor that did not have a wooden mast, and over the next few years use of wooden masts gradually declined to be replaced by aluminium.

When aluminium masts were organised for use in the 1972 Olympics at Kiel, (supplied of course as was all Finn gear at the time), some within the class tried to reverse this decision. However after much argument, all competitors were eventually supplied with the new aluminium mast made in the UK by Needlespar. The British did not have the advantage, as was feared by many, and the metal mast soon became commonplace. Various manufacturers built metal Finn masts over the years, but the Needlespar maintained market domination until 1993, when experiments in carbon resurfaced all the old arguments about change. By the eighties, North had a virtual monopoly on Finn sails and it wasn't until the early nineties that other lofts managed to break their stranglehold and produce race winning sails.

Nowadays carbon masts have penetrated to virtually all levels of Finn sailing, and aluminium masts are mostly regarded as obsolete, especially by the top sailors. They are still widely used in the lower ranks though, as an inexpensive, durable alternative. Carbon construction also allowed builders to exploit the full extent of the mast dimensions and produce wing masts. These masts have an aerodynamic fore and aft section which some sailors repute to be superior to the standard round section.

Hull Developments

Following the freeing up of the construction rules, due to the revolutionary Lamboley Test, double bottoms were permitted for the first time in 1974. UK Finn builder Peter Taylor was the first to take advantage of this new rule and for a few years Taylor glassfibre hulls were frequently at the front of international fleets. In fact at the 1976 Finn Gold Cup in Brisbane, Australia, his hulls finished in 1st, 2nd and 4th places.

In 1978, a group of ex-Laser sailors from the United States took up Finn sailing and a period of American dominance began with names such as John Bertrand, Cam Lewis and Carl Buchan figuring in many International regattas. They all sailed the US built Vanguard hull, which proved to be far superior to any other boat available at the time. They dominated the Finn class until 1980, but after the US boycott of the 1980 Olympics in Tallinn, US interest in the Finn waned slightly and the Europeans regained their former dominance. However by now the Europeans were also sailing the US Vanguard hulls. This hull together with a Needlespar mast and a North sail, was to be the standard equipment amongst Finn sailors right up until 1993. The Vanguard, which is an all GRP hull, has a fine bow to aid upwind performance and a broad transom to promote early planing. It is a remarkable credit to the Vanguard hull that it was used to

win the Finn Gold Cup during the fifteen years up to 1992 on no less than fourteen occasions.

The Class Today

The class these days is very different to the one Sarby created in 1949. The hull is almost exactly the same, with tight controls still in place to keep the boat as one-design as ever. What has changed is the technology available to the class. The modern hulls are now all optimised GRP with carbon masts and kevlar sails, something which in 1949 would have only been a figment of the imagination. Since the Vanguard domination, there have been a number of well thought out and highly developed hulls that have all but relegated the Vanguard to club sailing (Devoti, Lemieux, Pata . . .)

The Finn Gold Cup

The first Finn Gold Cup (the World Championship of the Finn class) was held at Burnham-on-Crouch in 1956 and forty-five competitors from twelve countries attended. The largest fleet ever gathered at Cascais in Portugal in 1970 where 180 boats from thirty-four countries competed for the cup. This event was won by the mast builder from Brazil, Jörg Bruder.

When the Gold Cup was first presented by F.G. Mitchell in 1956, the deed of gift for the cup stated that the event had to be staged in the UK in Olympic years, and so it was from 1956 to 1968, but after an unsuccessful event in 1968, the rules were changed so that the event could be held outside of Europe at least once every four years. Over the 43 year history of the Gold Cup, it has been staged in some very distant and remote locations from its origins in the UK: Bermuda in 1969, New Zealand in 1980, Australia in 1976, 1985 and

1999, Brazil in 1988 and Canada in 1971 and 1991. The Finn Gold Cup is the highlight of the Finn sailing calendar and is widely regarded as one of the foremost sailing events in the World. To win it is an exceptional achievement, to win it twice is remarkable, but to win it three times is quite outstanding. This has only been done on four occasions: Willy Kuhweide of Germany in 1963/1966/1967, Lasse Hjortnäs from Denmark in 1982/1984/1985, Fredrik Lööf from Sweden in 1994/1997/1999 and perhaps the most impressive of all Jörg Bruder of Brazil who won it three times consecutively in 1970/1971/1972. Fate decided he was to remain unbeaten forever as he was tragically killed in an air crash in 1973 on route to defend his title.

The Future

The Finn has remained at the forefront of International and Olympic dinghy sailing for the past 50 years. It has done so because it offers the opportunity for sailors to push themselves to their limits; because it offers technical education and development for sailors; and because of the love that thousands of sailors all over the world have for sailing a great boat. And this is why it should hopefully remain at the forefront for the next 50 years . . . and possibly beyond that!

Although born from inauspicious beginnings, this modern thoroughbred class was nearly scuppered before it was all started. Without the encouragement that Sarby received to take his prototype to the trials in May 1950, the sailing world may never have been treated to the boat that is now one of the most widespread and influential of all dinghy classes. 50 years and 12 Olympics later, the class is as strong as it ever was. With 50 years under her belt and with ever increasing numbers of young sailors finding out for themselves what Finn racing is all about, the future for the Finn looks rosy.

This Book

Throughout this book you will read more about the history of this great class, the people that made it so, the great races and battles that were held, the personalities and the determination that held it all together. You will read about the technological development of the most long lasting Olympic dinghy ever, the people who guided this development with understanding, with initiative and how they overcame problems with revolutionary ideas that have marked the Finn as a class which many other classes follow. You will read about how the boat itself has changed and how the sailors of today tackle the same problems that their predecessors did, only today the difference is that they are dealing with carbon and kevlar rather than wood and cotton. It is a remarkable journey, and one that will keep on going. As you turn the pages and the history, the development and the modern thinking become clear to you, remember that what we are talking about here is a boat - but a boat that has, over the years, brought people together from all nations and educated them in the ways of International competition and set them up for life.

2. Report from the President

by Philippe Rogge

On the verge of the new millennium, the International Finn Association has a special reason to look back at its past. Indeed, 1999 marks the 50th birthday of the FINN. This book, which was written for this occasion, will take us through the history of our class, with its driving forces and heroes, discovering the many developments the Finn has gone through along the way.

When Rickard Sarby designed the Finn 50 years ago as the men's single-handed dinghy for the 1952 Olympic Regatta in Helsinki, he certainly would not have expected it to have been selected for 13 consecutive Olympic Regattas. Indeed, the wooden hull with spruce mast and cotton sails of the time seem a long way away from glass reinforced plastic hulls, carbon fibre masts and laminated sails that are in use today. Still, there is something unique about the original design, which may be the key to the Finn's long lasting success: it was designed as a very robust, relatively slow, fast tacking, physically demanding and very technical boat.

Although the boat has gone through tremendous changes, these 'design elements' have always remained intact. They have made the Finn the choice for close tactical racing, with small speed differences to be obtained

by the many trimming options and physical fitness. Its inherent robustness has contributed to its longevity, making it cheap to sail and thus accessible to developing sailing nations.

The Finn class is not just about the Finn. It is about providing sailors with the best possible racing within a bracket of commonly accepted parameters. The resulting 'tool', which the sailors have cared to develop over the years to best suit those parameters, is what we have

always called the 'Finn'. Under the watchful eye of our Technical Committee, the sailors have carefully managed the technological change in such a way that 'evolution' never led to 'revolution'. More importantly they have ensured that the boat never became outdated. These changes, however, have always been in the spirit of what the Finn was originally designed to be, in disregard of certain commercially or politically attractive changes.

The Class can pride itself on an ever expanding base. In the different countries National Finn Associations set up their own Class associations to develop Finn sailing. From those sailors, the best are selected for Junior, Senior and Master's Continental and World Championships, Regional and Olympic Games. We rely on the National Finn Associations to keep supporting our class in their country and to recruit new Finn sailors.

The Finn class is about its sailors. Whether they sailed fifty years ago or are still active, they all share the unique experience of having mastered the Finn. Another privilege that Finn sailors enjoy is the lifetime friendships formed between their peers from all countries, at all levels. In a class that consists of a minority with Olympic ambitions, and a large base of Finn aficionados, it's this camaraderie amongst sailors at all levels that past and current Finn sailors will most remember.

The Finn is currently raced by sailors from 17 until over 60 years old. Both our Junior championships and Master championships are more than just 'one-off' events. They both represent part of our active sailing fleets which deserve separate recognition. Our 1996 Olympic Champion was still a Junior at 21. His predecessor was 36. With close to 200 Finns (Seniors and Masters), the 1996 Gold Cup in La Rochelle was a fantastic event. 'Old meets new' was more than a convenient gathering of Finn sailors. Both fleets were seriously impressed with each other's performance and new friendships were forged. The success of this event will spur us to put on similar 'joint world championships' in the future including the latest addition of a Junior world title.

Fifty years on from the first ever Finn, the class prides itself on the achievements of some of its sailors, both in and outside sailing. Some of the most prominent sports and business leaders have sailed the Finn. Others hold the record for most participations in the Olympics, all sports combined, have won Whitbread Round the World Races, the America's Cup or Olympic medals in other classes. With the help of its development program, over the years, the Class has allowed many sailors from developing sailing nations to successfully compete on a world level, winning world titles and Olympic medals along the way. Perhaps even more important is the camaraderie and great racing in the Class that all have enjoyed, truly all over the world.

Whilst we celebrate the last fifty years, we also look forward to the next fifty. The goals and ambitions have not changed from those envisaged by Rickard Sarby.

The International Finn Association will continue working to ensure that Finn sailing continues to expand and develop and serve the sport of sailing into the new millennium. We believe its sailors are a 'special breed' and

that the Finn dinghy continues to offer the best challenge in single-handed sailing.

None of this success would have been possible without the tireless commitment of rule makers, technical experts, builders, sailors, judges, past and present International and National Finn Association's Officers - all of whom have worked (voluntarily and for the love of their sport) to allow Finn sailors over the last 50 years to enjoy sailing at its finest . . . in the Finn Dinghy.

What better way to sum up than to quote some of our past and present Finn sailors . . .

Valentin Mankin (USSR), Finn Olympic Gold Medalist 1968, "The years between 1956 and 1970, when I was sailing the Finn, were the best and most unforgettable of my life. The Olympics are great to win, but that is not the main thing. Finn sailing has helped me in all aspects of life - through university and career. The experience has given me extra power, and led to racing success in three other boats. Thank you Finn!"

Jacques Rogge (Belgium), IFA Past President and Executive Board member of the IOC: "The unique spirit of the Finn class transcends generations. Finn sailors know what it takes to master this magnificent boat, being the most physical and tactical in the world. This bonds them together."

Peter Holmberg (Virgin Islands), Finn Olympic Silver Medalist 1988: "My relationship with the Finn started by digging an old boat from the weeds behind our club and ordering ten issues of FinnFare! I credit the Finn as the best class available, offering an individual a true platform to learn and compete in at the highest level. The knowledge and work ethics gained from my years of Finn sailing have benefited me in all aspects of sailing throughout my career."

Mateusz Kusznierewicz (Poland), Finn Olympic Gold Medalist 1996: "When I discovered International sailing all I dreamed about was staying with Finn fleet for as long as possible: to travel and compete wherever they go. When I was young Finn sailors were the best examples to follow: ideals of sportsmen and people of success."

John Bertrand (Australia), Finn Olympic Bronze Medalist 1976 and America's Cup Winner 1983: "The Finn Class is unique. I learnt about winning and losing against the world's best. I established life long friends around the world as I learnt how tough physically and mentally a sailboat could be. I learnt the finest details of tuning and balance, the painful difference between fast and slow. Of all the boats that I have raced, from Sabots to the America's Cup and all the classes in between, for me the tough little Finn is the most sacred of them all. This class is a classic."

Paul Henderson (Canada), ISAF President: "When asked what boat you sail it is sufficient to say 'Finn' to prove excellence."

3. The Birth of the Finn

by Rickard Sarby

Reprinted from FINNFARE October 1975 and July 1976

For the Finnish Yachting Association (FYA), organiser of the yachting events in the 1952 Olympic Games, selecting the keelboats may have been fairly easy. Not so for the singlehander. The Firefly, from 1948, did not appeal to many Scandinavians. Neither did the German Olympia Jolle.

Actually, Scandinavia lacked a dinghy for International, or even inter-Scandinavian competition. Finland had a fleet of Snipes, Denmark heaps of Pirates, Norway some Snipes and plenty of Oslojollen. Sweden, in the middle of the others, had a few Pirates to the south and some Snipes to the east, but vastly outnumbering them were 500 sailing canoes of a special Swedish breed, found nowhere else.

When the FYA decided on a design competition for an Olympic dinghy, their prime interest may have been to find an inter-Scandinavian dinghy, which also could be used for the Olympics. Not the reverse. The FYA left all technical details to the Swedish Yachting Authority, supposed to have more knowledge about designing and sailing small boats. A committee of 5 Swedes sat down to discuss size, shape, material and safety. You want to know what sort of people they were?

Sven Thorell - Olympic Gold in singlehander, Amsterdam 1928. Top designer of sailing and

The first Finn, first time afloat

paddling canoes; Arvid Laurin - Olympic Silver in Star, Kiel 1936. Well known designer of 5 m R-yachts or bigger; SYA secretary - keen on Folkboat racing, and generally working for youth sailing; SYA measurer - Previous Star helmsman; Rickard Sarby - Either because of a few canoe designs, or the freshest taste of Olympic water (capsized a Firefly in Torquay 1948).

January 1949

On January 1st 1949, they came out with the following description (shortened):

'The Finnish Yachting Association invites entries to a design competition for a single-handed dinghy to be used at the Olympic Games in 1952, and which is also suitable as an inter-Scandinavian dinghy. The dinghy shall give high class sport for well trained helmsmen, but shall also be usable for less tiring pleasure cruising in all conditions where sailing is done within the Nordic countries.

Building methods and materials are free. It should be possible to build hulls and rigs so equal that competitors taking part in inter-Scandinavian racing need only bring their own sails.

The following, not binding data, are set down for the design:

Hull: Round-bilged. LWL 4.5 m, Beam max. 1.5 m, floating without tanks. Sail: 10 m2 in one sail, not fully battened. Rig: Hollow mast, grooved for luff rope. Boom arranged for roll roofing and grooved for foot rope.

Designers should also provide a bundle of plans, predict a total weight, invent a name and a sail mark. Closing date for the competition, May 15th 1949.'

Designing, and building my prototype, was done early in 1949. At this time fate was a bit rough. An electric cutter snatched off a couple of digits from a finger, and I was plastered up as a real singlehander with plenty of time to kill. The plans were quickly drawn, in the usual canoe manner - full size. When the lines are finished in this manner, the building frames are almost finished simultaneously, without enlarging from scale.

**Designer of the Finn
Rickard Sarby**

One hand can build a mast, a boom and a rudder, but not a complete hull. Two of my brothers - also boat crazy - came to help. The shell was built in a sort of double diagonal strip planking, which proved to be a quick way of building. The two layers were of pine strips, 5 x 20 mm. The layers were glued to each other, glued and screwed to keel, floors, timbers etc. The prototype was launched the first week in May 1949. Total weight 150 kg.

One building frame for each pair of timbers

The first strip of planking is put in place

The shell freed from the frames

Deck beams and coaming

Everything was not quite finished, but every piece was on board. The ship appeared to mirror the intentions. And the plans could be sent to Finland, if only a name and a sail mark could be found. A brain pressed for time does not work properly. What it worked out was the name 'Fin', which in Swedish adds a positive sense to practically anything. And to fit this name a black shark fin resting on a blue beam. What a mess. And how bleak. Happily, this mark was never sewn to a sail. This prototype was still sailing in 1971, still fairly shipshape. Considering the glue quality of 1949, the building method must have been a hit. Anyhow, the shell was very rigid.

We kept track of time and money for building her: Working hours: 120. Remember, we were amateurs, with limited tools. Total material cost Skr. 670: (Dinghy 390, Sail 280). Money must have fallen badly ill later!

June 1949
A jury sat down by the FYA decided: First prize in the designing competition went to a Swede, Harry Carlsson for the design 'Pricken'. Second prize to Andersson, Finland. Third prize was split between Thorell, Sweden and Rehlander, Finland. The FYA intended to build some of the best designs and try them out sailing. Later I was told that my design was put aside, because the dinghy was too small. Maybe they were polite - somebody wrote somewhere that a good boat always looks small.

During Summer 1949 the first and second prizewinning designs were built in Finland. When the FYA got to know that my design had already been built, they invited me to take part in trial races. 'Fin' was brought to Finland in late September.

October 1949
We had a wonderful week - sailing and sunbathing in soft breezes, boiling in their steam-hot saunas - and what not. Two more dinghies entered the little fleet. Another Finnish design, by Kynzell, and the German Olympia Jolle. Kynzell was a well known designer of very big yachts.

The helmsmen changed dinghies every race. The final impression was that Pricken and Fin were just about equal as to speed. Fin may have had a slight plus, because she was roomier and easier to move about in, but also a small minus - some helmsmen thought the boom too low. But there was one more impression. In the prevailing light winds, the Olympia Jolle was just as fast, or slightly faster. She set an enormous looking sail though, the boom practically sweeping the deck.

After racing, the FYA had a meeting to discuss experiences. The FYA decided to ask the designer of Pricken to redesign her on the basis of the trial experiences. They intended to build the new dinghy, and arrange new trials in the beginning of May 1950. All prizewinners - and me - were invited to take part in these trial races at their own expense.

Quite naturally all Olympic visions were scrapped. But in Sweden something else happened. Yachting papers, always hungry for any stuff, presented the Fin plans less the shark fin and under the name 'Fint' which in Swedish means almost the same as Fin, (or the English 'fint'), but is a little easier to say

Winter 1949-1950
The simple building method appealed to amateurs. During winter 1949-1950 twenty five Fints were built. In spite of my warning everybody that the new Olympic dinghy should be very similar.

A Finn in autumn 1949 in Finland

All builders shouted for a sail mark. To teach them a lesson, I asked them to send suggestions for a sail mark; suggestions which I duplicated and returned to every builder. Everybody should vote for what he liked best. Twelve suggestions arrived, and the blue waves collected twice as many votes as the next best. Wasn't this a good idea? The present sail mark is absolutely 'right' for the Finn. The designer was a young enthusiast, - a 'finnatic' - living in the very heart of Sweden, at the big lake Siljan, where dinghy sailing was hardly heard of before.

By the way - when digging through a package of dias recently, I detected that the two mourning earthworms, too often allowed to mix with Finn insignias, edged in on one side of a sail, as early as 1951!

In March 1950, when asked about the trip to Finland, I plainly refused, because the new Pricken was built and put on show at an exhibition in Copenhagen as the new Olympic dinghy. Even the price was fixed. (Paul Elvström sent me pictures and cuttings from Danish papers). The FYA swore themselves free of the exhibition incident, blaming the builder. You know about builders - always at least one notch ahead of reality.

From left to right: Pricken II, Pricken I, the 'Anderson' dinghy, the 'Rehlander' dinghy

13

The new Pricken

SYA insisted that I should go, and in the end they coaxed me over once more; with the same dinghy, but a new sail. The leach was shortened 150 mm to lift the boom, and the cut-away area moved to the roach. This small alteration provided a much better profile - more 'speed' in it. When you have plenty of time to spare, sit down and try to estimate what this alteration meant economically, in mast breakage and sail experimentation - you will stagger at the figures. And yet, with the original sail the design may not have been so interesting, i. e. popular.

Trial Races 1950
The 1950 fleet was of a different consistency compared to 1949. There were Pricken I and Pricken II, the second prizewinner. Andersson, again, but also the two designs sharing third prize, Thorell and Rehlander, and finally Fint. Missing were the Kynzell dinghy and the Olympia Jolle. Thorell, at this time well over fifty years old, was accompanied by his son-in-law Edding, to sail his dinghy. A good helmsman - we fought many battles in canoe sailing.

Weather was close to horrible: rain, cold and strong wind. The whole situation was a little peculiar. Actually I hoped that somebody else should sail Fint, at least in the first race. But there seemed to be some resistance, so I had to take her. I also sailed Fint in the third race, which was sailed on the longest course, and went out where the Olympic course should be. I like to imagine that this race was the most decisive. After starting in sheltered water, the course took us between a couple of islands to open sea. The immediate problem was to find a special sea mark in a forest of marks. A motor launch was out - watching us, not guiding us. The mark I found was not the right one, so I had to go chasing the others, a nice lead lost.

The average wind speed was 5-6 m/sec with puffs to 8. You never called 5-8 m/sec a strong wind? Well, things have changed a little. Remember, there were no self bailers and no extra buoyancy but a very spacious cockpit. And I had to stay upright. There were no wet suits, no lead shirts, no bendy mast, no cat rig technique. Lacking all this 0 m/sec is plenty of wind!

But Fint really did her best on the long dead run. (You may have seen a picture from this run in the little booklet 'Finn Fibel' by Curd Ochwadt). Most of the others were broaching hither and thither, the Andersson and Rehlander dinghies capsized, the latter was damaged and out of the series, while Fint managed to sail an absolutely straight course. At this time I had developed a kneeling-sitting stance on the run, which looked very calm and comfortable. You know how calm you can be, in spite of today's safety and gadgetry, when wind is puffing to 8 on a dead run.

Three Finnish helmsmen sailed Fint in race 2, 4 and 5. In the 6th race Fint was sailed by Edding, while I sailed the Thorell dinghy. Very interesting. These two dinghies really matched each other. The same length beam, sail, boom slot, cockpit area and centreboard. Thorell was in 1916 the initiator of the club I belong to, and I had built and sailed canoes from his design. This may explain why our thoughts ran in the same grooves. Yet these two dinghies were very different from each other. Of the body shape, the T-dinghy was more or less a round-bilged Sharpie on a slender underwater body, which may have been 100 mm narrower than on Fint. However nicely she cut the waves, she was not one, but two handfuls to keep upright when worked to windward, and three when running. I did not use my usual downwind stance. The redesigned Pricken was not a 're', but a completely new design. In many ways looking and behaving like a negative of Pricken I.

As far as I have been able to reconstruct from notes and cuttings, the results looked like this:

Race	I	II	III	IV	V	VI
Fint	1	1	1	1	1	2
Thorell	2	3	2	3	3	1
Pricken I	3	5	4	4	4	5
Andersson	4	2	ret	2	ns	3
Pricken II	5	4	4	5	2	4
Rehlander	6	6	ret	ns	ns	ns

On May 15th, 1950, the FYA decided to adopt Fint as an Olympic dinghy, to change the name to 'Finn', and use the blue waves for a sail mark. Later the FYA acquired uninhibited right to the design.

On October 11th, 1953, the Scandinavian YA adopted the Finn as a Nordic class and a Nordic Championship was established. Legal right to the design was transferred to the ScYA.

4. The Finnster

by David Leach

Reprinted from FINN North American 1981 Directory

Throughout the world there is a dedicated group of the finest sailors in the world known as 'Finnsters'. They take pride in their class, their ability, their stamina, and their competitive spirit. They are trying to be the 'best' and want the tough competition in the Finn Class. There are classes which are sailed by many more people but there are no classes which have more devoted sailors.

A Finn sailor is self reliant, in good physical condition, and takes pride in himself. But he is the first one to help a newcomer and eager to discuss new ideas with other Finn sailors. There is a common bond of friendship between Finn sailors from all over the world that is not normally seen in other classes. In what other class do you see a top U.S. sailor 'arm wrestling' with the Russians for amusement during a regatta?

The Finn Class is not like most other classes. They do not want the most people sailing but they do want the 'best' people sailing. In some areas, you will find a Finn fleet racing regularly but in many other areas, you will find only one or two Finns and the Finn sailors travel great distances to get to regattas where they find the competition that is lacking locally.

You will hear people say that 'Finn sailing is too physical and demands too much strength'. But Finn sailing is like track and field events or other athletic sports. It demands conditioning, strength, coordination, and mental alertness. That is why the 'Finnster' is devoted to the Finn Class.

5. Thoughts on Sailing to Windward

by Fred Miller

Reprint from SOLO (c. 1963)

The first requisite to sailing to windward is having the proper instruments, and having them in optimum working order, e.g. the mast must be exactly right for your weight, and the sail must fit it exactly. You do not adjust the mast to fit the sail, but make the sail to fit the mast. Nowadays, your sailmaker can give you the best deflection data to get the mast right.

Most skippers basically sail their boats right to windward. As with anything else, it is fundamentals properly practised to the utmost degree which determines the placings - and the distances - between 1st, 2nd, 3rd, etc. And to lay bare the biggest ingredient between 1st place and also ran, it is the desire to practice these fundamentals to their utmost, because to do so means to win.

When a skipper has the same mast/sail combination, boat, number of kilo in all-up weight as given factors, yet he noticeably has 'hot' days and 'cold' days, it is painfully obvious what the variable quantity is - desire. His desire may not be so great because he is ill, or he is hung over (clearly devoting a greater desire for something else than sailing the past 24 hours, or something in addition to it) which means there had been a mental conflict of interests if not a substitution of interests. Ab initio, the desire to win would most likely have accounted for the fact that his mast/sail combination in relation to his

height/weight had been made as proper as humanly possible, to begin with.

The basis concept of a sail properly set for windward excellence in Finns is: a uniformly shallow curvature with maximum depth point slightly aft of the bisected angle of the leech/luff, without distortion. Therefore, both the tightness of the leech and the luff/mast relationship have most to do with the uniformity, shallowness, and location of the sail's draft.

Since a stiffer mast requires a flatter sail, and a more limber mast requires a fuller sail, it can be generally said that the use of the traveller is more to accommodate the 'cup' of the leech, or lack of it, more than to accommodate the number of kilos of righting moment exerted by various sized skippers. Assuming one has the right mast / sail / height & weight combination the lighter skipper must carry his boom a little further out, and the heavier skipper must carry his a little further inboard. The starting point is where the black band on the boom intersects the rub rail. Never judge by the position of the traveller itself; only where the tip of the boom is riding is what counts.

It goes without saying that some booms are stiffer sideways than others. Accordingly, the mast should be raked just enough so that you

do not have to actually make contact with the deck, but can have the boom 5 cm off the deck, when you are strapped in just short of the distort point of the sail. One, you can always use this little extra sheeting when you need it (to win a luffing match, to squeeze around a mark) and secondly, sails do stretch out while racing. Thirdly, with the boom free and not jammed snug to the deck, the tip can give with the puffs and absorb some of the shock when going through heavy seas.

Once this is all taken care of, one can 'ooker' properly. Proper ookering is very simple - just enough tension to pull the last tiny wrinkles out of the sail on both the foot and luff and no more for the particular velocity. If, in a good blow there are serious wrinkles even after you have ookered all you can, it is a good time to consider the mast / sail / height & weight combination from the beginning. There are, however, two things to always remember: a good looking sail is not necessarily a fast one, and vice versa. Also, do not be concerned if your rig shows weaknesses in extreme conditions (under 1 or over 6 Beaufort); most races aren't sailed then.

A heavy skipper (90 kg and better seems to be the dividing line here) will never be able to compete against lighter skippers in Force 3, especially in a sloppy seaway. Elvström was the first to discover there was virtually

nothing you could do about this rig-wise or sail-wise, and has long advocated two weight divisions to singlehanded sailing.

Sailing technique is divided into two schools: 1. 'Power' sailing & 2. Pointing. The heavy skippers usually are required to go the power school route, while the lighter skippers simply must rely on pointing. In the Finn a heavy skipper is seldom going to be able to point with a lightweight, and the lightweight can never hope to power with the heavy man. Yet, both can arrive at the weather mark at the same time remarkably often. The light skipper, of course, doesn't have to worry about being a little behind as he can make up fantastic distance off the wind. The heavy skipper must have sufficient yardage on the lightweight at the first mark in order to be within striking distance of him at the leeward mark as they start the final beat.

Whichever works best for a given skipper against a given competitor is the answer. And, it is perfectly true that some of the better skippers switch styles in the same race, to get past a certain boat, or because the wind velocity has changed. I'm a pointer for the most part, especially when the velocity is sufficient to enable it. But, most of the time I'm 50-50 on it and playing it by ear to suit the wind and waves combinations.

In flat water, no matter what the velocity, I have found most races are won by pointing. Since there are no waves to slow you down, you are so close to hull speed anyway driving off doesn't gain appreciably. On the other hand, in a good close chop or in slop or clean swells, you are constantly being slowed and accelerated, being kept far below hull speed, and the potential for additional relative boat speed is clearly existent, and the power sailors can win here with a great deal of physical effort.

You steer less in flat water, and a great deal in a sea. In fact, you should be steering each and every wave, trying to get the boat in a rhythm going over them. If you are doing this properly, keeping from being slowed by the wave as much as you can, and bearing off at the moment of 'shock' when the wave strikes and the helm comes over quicker and easier so that you can accelerate faster, you may find you can gain in both pointing and over-the-water speed. In heavy seas it is good not to cleat the main but to hold it. If a wave does slow you appreciably, it is going to jolt the flow of air right off the sail, and apparent wind goes right down to nothing. To get the boat going, you simply must let the sail off and then sheet in as speed picks up.

Keeping apparent wind up is the big secret, because when you have the boat 'in the groove' this is what is allowing you to feather up to windward, and keeping your stability, not to mention your real momentum.

When you see a wave is going to crash on you, it is good to let your sail out at the moment of impact. You would think this would never punch you through, but in fact this is what happens. Such a wave is going to stop you no matter what you do. By releasing the sheet at the impact, you have absorbed some of the shock on the rig and sail and avoided the wind being 'popped' out of it. Since you are stopped, your leech is already loose and ready to receive the flow of low-speed apparent wind much more quickly, hence you accelerate faster than a boat which went through the wave with everything strapped down all the time.

In smooth water it is obvious that you can ride gusts up higher than you can in a chop. There, most of your pointing gains are made in how you steer the waves, and because you are being jostled about so much the gust doesn't really

affect you with the force it could in smooth water. In short you head up only slightly for gusts in a chop, and not as quickly as in smooth water, because your 'stall-out' point is so much further away, and you need to get a full head of steam (wind) up to come up without killing way.

You are never going to be pointing well if you are hiking way out. One, because as your speed picks up the apparent wind gets above the optimum range, causes the sail to luff, hence you must bear off. Two, in order to keep the waves from hitting you, you have to heel the boat more, which takes it beyond its OAOH. It has been apparent to many that in many moderate-heavy winds, with typical waves accompanying, hiking may often hurt you as much as it might otherwise help you. However, if the seas are smooth or sufficiently spaced, so that you are closer to hull speed than the previous example, then hiking becomes important because the OAOH becomes more important. And when your hull speed is right up there, so is your apparent wind, and hiking is all that keeps you out of the stall-out zone. You can stall with half the sail luffing.

In the very highest velocities (above 6 Beaufort) I have found that it is wise to let the boom up a little to relieve the leech to an optimum point to avoid stalling out. You may think you aren't pointing as high, but if you are moving on the fleet don't think you ought to start heading higher or strapping it in. Most of the time, it will turn out the others are stalling with some frequency and duration. They are heading higher, but they are getting nowhere in these conditions. Don't let your traveller out all the way under any circumstances. It doesn't seem to do any good, yet it does allow your boom to catch the tips of waves, which leads to problems I won't go into here. Remember, your boom is going out a little when you let it up slightly, even though it never looks like it. Keep the boom out of the water.

Most of sailing to windward is by feel, and this feel is as much, if not more in the seat of the pants as in the hands. With fundamentals down pat, sailing a Finn is just like flying - the more hours you have in, the better you are. Practice may not make perfect - some people do have a gnawing, unquenchable desire to win, and others simply do not - but you can have a lot of fun trying.

6. Born To Win

by John Bertrand   Abridged and reprinted with permission from 'Born to Win' by John Bertrand. First published 1985

My friend Robbie Doyle introduced me to the highly competitive Finn racing class in 1971, and I sailed on the Charles River in Boston. Surprisingly, I very quickly mastered this little boat, which races in one of the most combative events in the Olympic Games. I got so good at it that I entered the U.S. National Finn Championships, held at Marion, Massachusetts. After a good regatta, I managed to finish seventh, which pleased me no end.

I next decided to go to Toronto for the Finn Gold Cup, which is the World Championship. In Canada I had a very fierce competitive regatta and finished fifth against the best Finn racing sailors. This was the highest any Australian had ever placed in World Championship Finn racing, so I decided to return home for the Australian National Championships and get myself selected for the 1972 Olympics in Munich.

1972 Australian Olympic Trials
However, I faced two fairly major problems. I had scarcely enough money for a bus ride over to the Charles River, never mind two air fares home to Melbourne. Also, I did not have a Finn Class boat. So, speaking as a hotshot America's Cup sailor, I decided to fire off a few letters to Melbourne businessmen to see whether I could raise some sponsorship. To my great delight, a Melbourne car dealer, whom I had never met, decided that I must have a lot of brass neck, if not talent, and he forwarded $2,000. Much later I found out that the Olympic manager, David Linacre, had a great deal to do with this heaven sent sponsorship.

When we returned to Australia, I went into strict training on behalf of myself, my young wife, my mum, and the saintly car dealer. For five weeks I prepared to take on the might of the Australian Finn fleet, many of whom had been racing in highly competitive European events for four months as preparation for the National Championships. And every one of them turned up at the Sandringham Yacht Club.

It was a wicked close struggle, at the end of which I narrowly brought my borrowed boat over the line in first place.

Preparation
I was now qualified to receive $20 a day from the Australian Yachting Federation to conduct a 31/2 month sailing campaign in Europe, culminating with the 1972 Olympic Games in Munich, in which I was my country's number one hope in the Finn Class. And once more we boarded a plane heading north, bound for the open seas and competition against the best in the world.

We set off for Kiel Regatta week in northern Germany, the site of the Olympic water-sports later that summer. I was nowhere near ready, and when the German event started, I was still screwing fittings onto the boat. I finished 35th, probably the worst performance of my entire career

Rasa and I packed up our few belongings and, with our list of hostels and cheap hotels, we set off for Medemblik, a little resort on the Zuider Zee, that great Dutch near-landlocked ocean due north of Amsterdam. I finished seventh in the European Finn Championships there; by now I had the boat properly tuned. Next, we turned south to Italy, crossing the Alps and driving down the coast to the port of Anzio, where the Finn World Championships were to be held. I sailed like a demon and finished second, beaten only by the great Jörg Bruder of Brazil, who, at his best, could be just about unbeatable in Finn Class sailing. He beat me decisively, but I was a very solid second.

We were beginning to enjoy this adventure. We did not have much money, but everyone was very kind to us and we were often invited to stay overnight and have meals with other sailing people. Remember, being a yacht racer is not like being a tennis player - where you wind up being wealthy by the time you attain my level of accomplishment. This is sailing. Your principal reward is the overpowering sense of achievement, a boost to your psyche, after defeating the opposition and doing it with style.

I felt very good as we headed north again for the National Championships of Finland. We took a long and picturesque car journey that was magical for Rasa and me. We arrived at the Little Island course and at last I was the

master of my little boat - I won the championship. We then turned our rented Peugeot south for the Olympics.

1972 Olympics - Kiel
In the Games I finished fourth, earning for myself the leather medal, an experience I wish never to have again. It is a very funny thing, but in most trades or professions, if you are the fourth-best practitioner in the world, you have at least fame and probably fortune. In our game it's different. There are first, second, and third: gold, silver, and bronze. Everyone else is last. Nothing is as tough as the Olympics. I packed up our Peugeot somewhat ruefully, a rookie Olympian who had just undergone what seemed like a fiery baptism in my first Games. At the closing ceremony in the great stadium, Jörg Bruder, who had beaten me in the World Championships in Anzio, came up and put his arm around me. He was a charming man, that Brazilian, but he just could never come out on top in the Olympics. He always froze up with nervousness. But he was very nice and always very generous to me. He had switched from the Finn Class to the Star Class, and he, too, had finished fourth. "John," he said, "now we have both done it. We've both won the leather medal."

By the time I was ready to leave the Olympic Village that summer, I had already been approached by the Sydney boat designer Ben Lexcen. He asked if I would assist in the preparation of a new assault on the America's

Cup in 1974. I accepted with some alacrity. I did not know where this new path would take me, but as usual, the prospect of a very fast boat was like an aphrodisiac to me, and I could not resist. The man who headed up the new syndicate was named Alan Bond.

Education

Before I joined Ben Lexcen and took part in the 1974 America's Cup, I received my masters degree in marine engineering from the Massachusetts Institute of Technology. (Incidentally, I had earlier studied at Melbourne's Monash University where my degree thesis had been a long treatise on the aerodynamics of the sails of 12-Meters - a subject that would more or less consume me until the 26th day of September 1983.) Although sometimes tempted away from my studies by sailing, my university study has been an essential building block for whatever I have successfully done since. I think that it is very important for aspiring young Finn sailors to understand that they should get a formal education as well as trying to sail fast and win medals. Otherwise, they may not have a decent career to fall back on when the Finn sailing is over, whether this is in launching into their own business career or in taking on the complexity of an America's Cup assault.

Working for North Sails

After the 1974 America's Cup, with great eagerness I had accepted a position with Lowell North, the famous American sailmaker, who was himself an Olympic gold medalist and one of the nicest and most knowledgeable men in the world of international yacht racing. Lowell had phoned me and suggested that I spend a couple of years in the States, working at one of his lofts, with a view to opening a franchise of North Sails in Melbourne. I was very excited about this all summer. We flew to Pewaukee, Wisconsin, which would be our home for two happy years.

Meanwhile, I had to have a major sailing goal - I always had one of those - and I chose the Olympics again. I would go to Montreal in two years and win the Olympic gold medal for the Finn Class. That seemed to be a suitable ambition. I would sail in Pewaukee, train on the lake, race throughout North America, and return to Australia for the Olympic selection trials. Life stretched out before me in a contented, comfortable journey, with just enough bite attached to that Olympic ambition to make it interesting.

At North Sails I had a marvellous time. I helped in the design of the Vanguard Finn Class yacht, built in Pewaukee and now the premier boat in this 16-foot class. I love the Finns - one sail, one man, the roughest class in all the Olympic sailing events - and at North I was also able to develop a sail that is still

the most popular in the world for that class. I designed and tested it, and that sail has won the World Finn Championships for the past five years. It is totally dominant in its class.

Designing sails and sailboats on the picturesque northern waters in the spring of 1975 confirmed my general view that Pewaukee was indeed paradise. I was in the heart of a fine group of American sailors and enjoying every moment. Shortly after winning the Canada's Cup [match racing in 2-tonners], we drove to New Orleans for the U.S. Finn Class Championship and took delivery of my brand-new Vanguard Finn. I summarily set sail and clobbered the 40 best Finn Class sailors in North America to win the national title.

1975 Finn Gold Cup

I was now prepared to go home to Australia for their national championship, in which I would attempt to gain Olympic selection. On the way home I went to Malmö, Sweden, for the Finn World Championships, a Gold Cup event. I hate 'if onlys', but I would have won that, if only . . . Unfortunately, I was disqualified for being two pounds overweight in the clothing I wore in one of the races, which I won. That cost me the championship, but no one could take away from me the fact that I had finished first - never mind the two pounds - and we returned to Melbourne feeling on top of the world. I next went off to Brisbane and sailed in the Australian Olympic trials, and I won that as well. So I was on my way to Montreal. After spending Christmas at home we flew back to Pewaukee to complete my preparation for the Montreal Olympics.

1976 Olympics - Kingston

After intense preparation throughout the spring of 1976, we left our charming lakeside home in Pewaukee and headed for the Olympic regatta site at Kingston, where I carried the Australian flag in the opening parade. I sailed better than I had ever sailed before, of that I am certain. I was having a terrific time - until the 11th hour, when something happened that I will never forget and that was to have a profound and lasting effect.

Five races had been sailed. It came down to a straight fight among Australia (me), East Germany (represented by Jochen Schümann). Russia (represented by Andre Balashov), and Brazil (represented by Claudio Biekarck). Conditions were perfect, with a 15-knot wind as we broke for the first windward leg. David Howlett from Great Britain was in the lead, but he had had two bad ones, and two victories would not get him a fourth overall. I was second, with not one bad race, tracked hard by the East German. He was almost on my transom as we headed down to the wing mark of the first triangle. Approaching the bottom mark I was planing at between 10 and 12 knots, and I kept glancing back at this impassive blond German about three feet behind, nearly touching my boat. Until the day I die, I will remember the feeling that rushed over me. Suddenly, from out of the blue, I thought, "Am I good enough?" It was my first moment of self-doubt in the entire competition. Defeatism is like a forest fire in a big international event. Quickly I thought, "Can I hold him off? Am I being pushed beyond my normal limitations?" These were

my first negative thoughts in the Olympics. And, seized by a need to make a positive move, I decided to take a chance that I would never have dreamed of taking in a normal race. I would not even have done this in practice. But I took the opportunity of transferring the mainsheet from the boom through the ratchet block in the floor of the boat. I was under total stress at the time, and I knew this particular manoeuvre would save one step, would save me precious time and inches, would stop the East German from gaining an inside overlap at that mark and from giving him the opportunity to pass me. I could not even bear to think about that possibility.

Then I lost control of the mainsheet, and the main boom shot out to leeward, beyond the position for stability control of the sail. The boat immediately flipped out of control and capsized to weather. I had gone from very nearly being in a control position to being totally out of control. If only I had had the presence of mind to do what I had been trained to do. I had fallen into the trap that nearly every Olympic competitor falls into. I had taken a stupid risk, losing the significance of the race and my position in it. I had done the opposite of everything I had been trained for. And now I was upside down. Puffing and gasping, I righted the boat, climbed back in, and finished seventh - which left me in an almost impossible position with regard to a gold medal. The East German finished second, very steady, very controlled. I have no idea why I suddenly was bothered by him. I had never even heard of him - it was not exactly like being locked in combat with Paul Elvström at his peak.

And so to the seventh race. I was in an equivocal position. If I match raced the Brazilian and beat him, I would be assured of a bronze medal. If I went for broke and sailed to win that final race, I could still win the gold as long as the East German was beaten for second place. However, in going for broke in this class, you have to take chances, and the prospect of capsizing again was personally unappealing. The dread of a second leather medal haunted me. Australia had finished fourth in this class in three of the last four Olympics, and I did not want to make it four. I decided to play it safe and to match race the Brazilian. After leading the entire field for some of the way, I finally found myself on the wrong end of a windshift on the opposite side of the course from the East German and the Russian. They went on to take the gold and silver medals. I stuck hard by the Brazilian and beat him easily for the bronze. (I might add as a footnote to those Olympics, that on the very same day the U.S. placed third in the Tempest Class. The helmsman who won the bronze medal was Dennis Conner.)

John Bertrand and David Howlett at the 1976 Gold Cup

I had achieved some of my ambition by winning a medal in the Olympic Games, and it was a very proud moment for me - very satisfying yet very thought provoking. My main regret was that I took that one chance - but for that, I could so easily have won.

Lessons

I suppose most beaten competitors have at least one regret - but I took that one negative moment deadly seriously. I reflected on it many times after the regatta because it had happened at a critical time, and it spurred me on to become a keen student of sports psychology, of the psychology of winning. I still felt I had what it takes, but it did give me some new insights into myself. It amazed me how cool, or at least apparently cool, that East German had been, even though he had never before won a European championship or any major regatta. He just kept doing what he had been trained to do, reproducing his training under extreme pressure. That East German just seemed to be enjoying the atmosphere and the competition, and that was what I should have been doing, achieving that same degree of self-control. I should have been able to step back and analyse the opposition, without allowing my performance to deteriorate. I wanted to find out more about myself and why I had reacted as I had in the heat of the moment. Was I afraid? If so, of what? Why should defeat hold such devils for me? How could I develop the perfect poise in these situations and summon the correct response for these moments? These were the questions I asked myself, and these were the questions I would have to cope with in the coming years. Winning America's Cup skippers cannot, after all, afford the kind of weakness that I had displayed so spectacularly on that Canadian lake.

Life is full of lessons, and the key is to use them as building blocks. That is a definition - my definition - of experience. And, like time, you cannot buy it. You just have to use it, to serve your apprenticeship. When I was very young, Mum would tell me that everything always happens for the best. I remember thinking that this could not possibly be so - setbacks, in my mind, being setbacks forever. Only in later years, especially after my reflective months beyond the 1976 Olympics, did I fully realise what a very positive attitude this is, to turn life's disasters into positive knowledge.

The trouble is that you need so many disasters in order to make yourself into the complete athlete, fighter, yachtsman, or whatever. You need years and years of trying, of serving your time. You just cannot say we will win because we will win because we will win. That will not do it. You have to catch every blow an opponent aims at you and store it up to develop an innate sense of wisdom. Yacht racing, like any big sport, has precedents, and you need total recall for these lessons learned in the past. Like statesmen and generals, an international sports competitor who does not understand the past will not be much of an authority on the present.

It is always the lessons that count. There is no question in my mind that without my defeat at the careful and emotionless hands of Herr Jochen Schümann, of the German Democratic Republic, on July 27, 1976, Australia II categorically would not have won the 1983 America's Cup.

7. Finn Fundamentals

by Robert Deaves

Although at first sight the Finn rig may seem to be a relatively simple piece of gear compared with other boats of a similar size, almost as many problems can be encountered in tuning it as in two-sailed boats. The first difference that a novice Finn sailor will notice is that the boom is sheeted at an angle to the centreline and never on the centreline. Because the Finn does not have a foresail, airflow is not directed onto the back of the mainsail. The airflow therefore breaks away from the lee side of the sail earlier than it would if a foresail were present.

To move this break point further aft the maximum draft is cut into a Finn sail at about half the chord length back from the mast. This produces a resultant forward-force which is angled further aft than it really should be. To overcome this, the traveller is positioned nearer to the gunwale to increase the angle of the boom to the centreline and hence shift this resultant force-angle to point further forwards so that the driving force is moving the boat forwards rather than sideways. (The further the boom is let out the further forward this force-angle points.)

As the wind increases the draft is pushed aft in the sail, so the boom should be let out more to compensate. The windier the conditions are, the further the boom is let out. It should

never really be sheeted further in than the inner sidedeck and the end can sometimes be a matter of several feet away from the gunwale in a strong breeze.

Mainsheet

Often overlooked in the finer points of sail control, the mainsheet has more effect on sail shape than all the other controls put together. Before you are fully powered up, (and the boom is on the deck anyway), mainsheet

tension is critical both to pointing ability and to power. When the mainsheet is pulled in, the sail is progressively flattened and the leach tensioned. This action causes the leach to hook, so some inhaul/outhaul tension may be needed to open it up again. Flattening the sail will help you to point higher although some power will be lost. Easing the sheet will have the reverse effect in that you will gain power but lose some of your pointing ability because of the lack of tension in the leach.

In all instances a compromise is necessary when deciding whether to go for power or pointing - you cannot always have both. Care should be taken when setting the sheet so that it is not under-sheeted (giving you lots of power but no pointing) or that it is over-sheeted (making you point very high but travelling very slowly) and it should be appreciated that the mainsheet should always be used in conjunction with the other sail controls to obtain the best shape for the conditions of the day.

When you are fully powered up and hiked out, the end of the boom will be strapped down onto the aft deck. The only thing that then controls the leach tension is the mast rake. If you move the mast forward, which decreases mast rake, you increase leach tension; move the mast aft, which increases mast rake, and you decrease leach tension. This is why mast

rake is so important on the Finn, because with the boom end on the deck in most wind strengths, it is the only thing that controls leach tension - the vital element in fast Finn sailing.

Mast Rake

Mast rake is measured by hauling up a tape measure on the halyard and measuring the distance to the centre of the transom. On the older boats this was easily done as the mast gate was fixed in the deck, so the measurement for one type of boat would generally be transferable.

Since the advent of the adjustable mast gate, sailors can now adjust both step and gate, allowing a wider range of measurements to be used (and a wider range of helm weights to sail the boat). On the old boats, a figure of 6800 mm mast rake would get you in the right vicinity, however the difference between fast and average speed can be as little as 10 mm difference in mast rake, so it needs to be fine tuned depending on your mast and sail.

Hulls

Perhaps one of the most important things to consider if you are buying a secondhand Finn is the centre of gravity numbers. In 1974 a test was introduced to the Finn class by Gilbert Lamboley that allowed the distribution of weight in the hull to be accurately determined and controlled. Early on in the Finn history it was found that boats with light ends were faster than those with heavy ends and before the introduction of the Lamboley test this fact could be exploited by centralising weight in the boat. Fast Finns will have the centre of gravity as far aft and as low as possible and will have a minimum radius of gyration (how light the ends are).

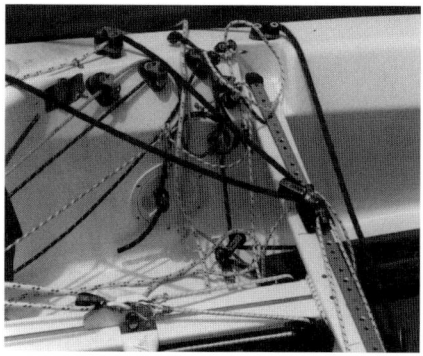

Rig Critique

Finding the correct mast/sail combination for you is arguably the most crucial consideration when preparing a Finn for racing. Without a matched rig you will never get the best out of your Finn. As a general rule the heavier you are the stiffer the mast that you can have, but you need a sail that matches that mast in order to reap the benefits of having the perfect mast. Having found what is a good mast for you, a sail must be found that has a luff curve that matches the bend characteristics of your mast. You can find out what these are by supporting the mast between the heel and the mast ring, bending it under a known load (say 20 kg) suspended from the mast head and measuring the deflection of the mast from the straight line between the upper and lower measurement bands. This needs to be done for fore-and-aft bend and for sideways bend. The figures that you arrive at will help the sailmaker build a sail to suit that mast. These figures do not give some ultimate reading, they only give static deflection characteristics which are only useful for comparing different masts. The luff of your sail can also be recut to suit the bend characteristics of your mast by making adjustments in the luff tape along its length. These alterations may be between 3-10 mm, which may seem small but this can make a large difference to boat speed and control of the sail.

Steering

After the mainsheet, the rudder is arguably the most effective control on the Finn, and incorrect use of it is probably a major reason for lack of boat speed. Upwind in a breeze, it needs to be used constantly and sometime aggressively to get the most out of the boat, steering hard through the gusts and around each wave. Offwind it needs to be used discriminately - too little and you miss waves and get nowhere, too much and it acts like a very large brake.

Watch what the top sailors do as they disappear off the start line and learn from them. When you learn that, watch how they steer offwind. It will probably appear that they are going significantly faster than you without much effort, but this is because they have perfected the technique and are at one with the boat and the waves. This can only come about after much practice and a lot of time in the boat.

Sail Control

The majority of sail setting sense will come from sailing the boat, getting experience and speaking to the experts. Perhaps the most important thing though is balance. With experience you will be able to judge what is the best balance. Is the mainsheet too tight or too loose? Is the sail too far out or too far in? After a while it should become apparent what is fast and what is slow. You will develop a

oneness with the boat and the rig. You will be able to squeeze that last bit of speed out of it just by feeling your way with the mainsheet, the tiller and use of your bodyweight. This won't be automatic or quick, it will only come about after you have spent a lot of time practising, practising, practising... This is often what separates the front from the middle of the fleet - just that little bit extra to pull out a lead and not get swallowed up in the pack.

Buying Secondhand

If you buy secondhand it is crucial to check certain areas to make sure you are buying a boat worth having. Check the mast step for wear into the hog and for lateral security to see whether it is likely to break. This is an area of very high stress. Also check that the mast gate is secure and tight fitting. Look also for damage to the deck around the gate. On GRP boats check the seal between the hull and the deck for signs of leakage. Check the toestraps and the fittings to see if these are secure, firmly bolted down and have not distorted the hull.

The hull needs to be fair and not damaged - especially along keel band area and transom. A badly scratched hull may indicate that the boat has not been too well looked after and may develop other faults later on. Likewise the double-bottom (if it has one) should be

checked for cracks and leakages. Lastly, if possible, weigh the hull (even get it swung for the Lamboley test). Figures which are way off could indicate a slow boat that might best be avoided.

Fitting Out

If you buy a new Finn, it will come fully fitted out and there is little need to make adjustments of any sort. If you are buying an older Finn that needs a refit then there are several things to consider that are quite important.

Many older boats had dual compasses, one on either sidedeck just forward of the hiking position. These were frequently damaged due to their vulnerable position. Modern boats normally have just one central fitted compass, just forward of the centreboard case and this is perfectly adequate providing it is big enough to read as you are crashing through waves covered in spray. Also make sure that the centreboard does not travel too far forward and smash it.

Rudder security is a must. If your rudder becomes detached from the boat, it can be a disaster. Make sure that it is securely tied on or use a strong rudder clip that will not fail - even if the boat is bouncing around in waves

upside down! Similarly, the mast must be secure in the boat. Some older metal masts had pegs at their base that slotted into a groove under the mast step. With modern shoe type mast steps this is not possible, so a piece of cord tied from the mast gate round the gooseneck is adequate - as long as it is tight enough.

Because the centreboard is heavy, a capsize will invariably result in the board disappearing up the case. Therefore an elastic shockcord arrangement is mounted from the centreboard and around the centreboard case so that the board is forever forced down. Thus when the boat is inverted, the board remains extended by the pull of the shockcord.

Get Well Padded

In the early days of Finn sailing, pain was a fact of life. These days you can have padding on your toestraps, padding on your sidedecks and even padded-battens on your legs. Removal of pain can generate the biggest increase in boat speed of them all. At the end of a long hard race, he who can hike hardest will inevitably win the battle. The more comfortable you are the better you will be able to concentrate on tactics, strategy and boat speed.

Fit for the Job

A control line system and any fitting is only good enough if you are happy using it and can get along with it. If you can't, then something has to be done to remedy the matter. Make sure that all lines can be reached with ease from wherever you might be sitting. Ensure that fittings are not going to be in the way of ropes or any part of you. Plan ahead in any fitting out process so that everything is logical and will function accordingly. Most of all use gear that you can trust not to fail when you need it most. To get the most out of them, Finns need to be pushed hard and gear failure should never be an excuse for not finishing a race. Make sure that whatever fittings and rope you finally decide on, they will not break in a windy race or fail to work effectively when used to the limit. If you are confident that the boat will stand up to the extremes of the weather, then in anything less than the extremes, you can push the boat as hard as you like without worrying about gear failure and damage.

Fitness

Being fit is as much a part of being a competitive Finn sailor as getting the right gear, and conversely having the best gear in the world is not going to do you any good if half way up the first beat you're already dead-beat with exhaustion. The best training for Finn sailing itself is really Finn sailing but other training can help supplement water based activities. You need to consider various aspects of getting fit, not just physically, but also mentally. Physically you need stamina (aerobic fitness - running, cycling swimming etc); you need strength (circuits or weight training); you need speed (anaerobic fitness - interval training); you need suppleness (flexibility and stretching) and you need skill (go sailing and train intensively). Mentally, use the techniques available, read the recommended books and do everything you can, so when it comes to the crunch you're not let down by your mind.

Commitment

Finn sailing offers some of the most rewarding sailing around. Those who sail the boat competitively and successfully know that in order to succeed they need to apply mind and body to all aspects of racing, tuning and fitness. To make it to the top in Finn sailing requires a dedication to your purpose and a single minded ambition to be the best. Nothing less will do. Train hard, work hard and give it your best, but remember to have fun along the way.

8. History of the International Finn Association

by Peter Mohilla and Robert Deaves

First published in FINNLOG

It is not easy to handle the different aspects of the history of the Finn. There are many different points of view upon the subject. It is possible to sort out some of them and to cover them in special chapters, like the technical development or the history of the most important regattas. However the administrative aspect turned out to be most central and interrelated with all other matters. It reflects in detail the motivation of the leading people in the Finn Class. Therefore this chapter might bear the subtitle of 'General History of the Finn'.

Also there were controversial periods in the history of the IFA. Different people had differing motivations for activities on behalf of the Class. It is understandable that these different people had and partly still have contradicting opinions about the subject matters at stake. Questionable viewpoints are therefore recorded in regard with the authors. The reader has to make up his own mind about these hot issues.

1950

In 1950, Rickard Sarby handed over all the rights of the 'FIN', 'FINT', 'FLINT', 'FINN' design to the Finnish Yachting Association. As the organiser of the Olympic regatta the Finnish Yachting Association published the plans and written description of the dinghy. In mid-1950 the Scandinavian Yachting Union adopted the Finn as a Scandinavian Monotype, but did not yet take over the administration of the Finn.

The Swedish sailing in the Nordics with reefed sails

Rickard Sarby felt burdened by the responsibility of being the designer of the Olympic monotype for 1952, and was afraid that his dinghy might turn out to be a similar failure as the 1948 'Firefly'. In a letter, Sarby wrote that he was not eager to become the designer of an Olympic dinghy. He would prefer to keep up friendships with all his friends from the 1948 Olympic Games in Torquay. Rickard was afraid it would not be possible to create a dinghy that would be accepted by all the Europeans.

1951

As a preparation for the 1952 Olympic Games a number of nations had asked for the plans and description of the Finn. In Germany 9 boats were built, which were strongly rejected by the majority of the former 1936 O-Jolle sailors.

In the UK Vernon Stratton, the later President of the IFA, Richard Creagh-Osborne, the later Chairman of the Technical Committee, and Charles Currey, the later Silver Medalist of 1952 had the first private Finns built. France built 5 Finns, Holland 5, Belgium 2, Austria 2. In Denmark Paul Elvström had his 'Bess' built, in order to compete in the first International Finn Regatta, the 1951 Nordic Championship. In a letter to a friend in South Africa (where the first Finns were also built as early as 1951), Rickard Sarby complained bitterly about the rough and unfair sailing technique of that Danish hotshot. Sarby won that event but Elvström eliminated two other competitors for second place by sudden tacks from port to starboard and causing collisions without warning. In those days windows in the sails were not allowed, so it was easy to allure your opponents into that trap. In the fifties Sarby was against any self bailing equipment. He felt that sailing dry was part of the game, and if you capsize it should be the end of that particular race.

1952

For the first time the Finn was the Olympic monotype. The races in Helsinki dominated the season completely. A number of nations had built or bought some Finn dinghies in order to give their top single handed helmsmen from other classes an opportunity to become

In order to promote the Finn, Rickard Sarby exhibited his boat in Uppsala

familiar with this boat. Because of certain initial shortcomings of the Finn in those days many sailors rejected the Finn and predicted only a short life for the class. In light air the primitive arrangement of the wooden mast on the wooden hog and the wooden boom in the mast slot caused a squeaking noise revealing

The first three Finns built privately in the UK in 1951

One of the Swedish Finns built in 1951

every manoeuvre. In heavy air every newcomer took his lessons on the reaches and runs with sudden death rolls to windward. Some even capsized when entering the Finn for the first time because Sarby had not included a word about the trick of how to get past the mast.

In contrast, Paul Elvström took a positive approach towards the peculiar characteristics of the Finn. He spent many hours in his boat practising, found out about his and her limits, and developed many new ideas to overcome shortcomings. This experience was the basis of his success at the Olympics. He attached hiking straps which allowed him to keep his boat more upright. While the Finns in Germany and England had the sheet attached to a horse at the transom - limiting the boom - Paul invented a short traveller on top of the thwart, which allowed him to keep his boom down

**Spectacular beaching
in Forte Dei Marmi**

and farther out. He went faster and pointed higher. He invented, improved and perfected the hiking and sailing technique which is customary nowadays in the Finn, not sitting on the sidedecks but hiking on the gunwale. But not only did he train hard to sail fast he also practised to keep his boat stationary at the favoured starboard end of the starting line which gave him a definite advantage at the start.

1953

After the 1952 Olympics interest in the Finn diminished in some countries. However in 1953 it was agreed between the IYRU and the Australian organisers of the 1956 Olympics, that the Finn would remain the monotype for Melbourne. In 1953 the Finnish Yachting Association handed over the administration of the Finn to the Scandinavian Yachting Union. The only international race of importance for the Finn in 1953 was the Scandinavian Championship in Oslo, won by Elvström with Rickard Sarby second. In the Scandinavian countries, in Holland and Belgium, and partly in France, South Africa and the UK the Finn remained alive and increased.

**Henri Leten, the driving force behind
the formation of the IFA, Secretary
1956-1957, President 1957-1960**

Charles Currey and Rickard Sarby acted as technical advisors to the Australian organisers of the 1956 Olympics. Some interesting considerations were not translated into reality at that time. Buoyancy bags and any self-bailing devices were refused, because it was accepted that a capsize should end the race. A reduction of the sail area to 9 or even 8 m2 was not adopted. However kicking straps were refused as well, since it would have prevented

**The international fleet gathering at
Rickard Sarby's home club in Uppsala**

reefing, frequently used in heavy air in the early days. Currey suggested and Sarby approved to move the centreboard bolt further aft but finally the Olympic Finns were built in accordance with the original plans. The Australian Yachting Federation requested permission to build the Olympic Finns in fibre glass construction, however the Scandinavian Yachting Union denied approval.

In November 1953 the IYRU agreed that it would be very desirable to retain the Finn Class as a single-handed class in Olympic regattas for some time. It was agreed that the grant of international status to the Finn Class would be favourably considered if a request for it was received at some time. The addressee of that message was the Scandinavian Yachting Union. However that body remained inactive to the disadvantage of the Finn Class.

1954

As a preparation for the 1956 Olympics the Dutch Sailing Federation heavily subsidised the construction of Finn Dinghies in 1954. Aside from Sweden, Belgium became the centre of Finn activities with French, British and Dutch participants in the international race at Zeebrugge. The 9 existing German Finns were not used in 1954.

Some new countries were interested in starting Finn sailing. However the development was handicapped by the fact, that the Scandinavian Yachting Union administered the Class. Requests for the delivery of building plans and instructions were answered very late or never. The problem with the Scandinavian Yachting Union was, that English is not the official language and that the administration rotates every other year between the four

Paul Elvström's Bess

**Rinze Koopmans, first President
of the IFA 1956-1957**

Scandinavian countries. Only the fact that it was decided that the Finn was to be the Olympic monotype for 1956 kept the Class alive.

1955

The Finn enjoyed the official support from the IYRU as the 1956 Olympic monotype and was already being considered for the 1960 Olympics as well. Newcomers to the Class interested in the construction of Finns were referred by the IYRU to the Scandinavian Yachting Union with limited success. Rickard Sarby gave valuable personal advice, but was unable to help since he had passed on all the rights for the design. Several countries developed differing measurement instructions. The IYRU regretted that no International Finn Association had yet been formed to which it would have been eager to grant international status.

The German speaking countries would have liked to see the Finn fade away again in favour

**Richard Murray, IFA secretary
1957-1961, sailing at Itchenor in 1958**

of the 1936 O-Jolle, and hoped secretly, that the Italians would select that old type as the Olympic monotype for 1960. However the Italian Sailing Federation with the present IYRU President Beppe Groce as the leading force supported the Finn and even organised with tremendous expenditure a big international Finn event in Forte Dei Marmi with 31 participants from 10 nations.

The Commodore of the Royal Belgium Sailing Club Henri Leten was the most active and powerful supporter of the Finn outside of the Scandinavian countries. He was well aware of the intention of the IYRU and the discontent of many other nations with the administration of the Finn by the Scandinavian Yachting Union. On behalf of the Belgium Yachting Federation Henri Leten invited all National Sailing Federations of countries with active Finn sailors to attend a conference in Brussels on November 12-13, 1955.

The agenda of that conference read:
1. Unification of the Finn rules.
2. Recognition of the Finn for the 1960 Olympic Games.
3. Choice of the Finn for the 1960 Olympic Games.

Point 1 of that agenda would have been the responsibility of the Scandinavian Yachting Union and points 2 and 3 of the International Yacht Racing Union. After the Scandinavian Yachting Union had not responded to the politely phrased request of the IYRU to unify the rules, to initiate an International Finn Association and to apply for the international status of the Finn Class, it questioned the legality of that conference in Brussels. The four Scandinavian countries boycotted the endeavours of Henri Leten, arguing that the organisation of such a meeting would be their sole responsibility. But the Scandinavian Yachting Union missed again the opportunity to hand in the proper application to the IYRU in 1955. Instead the IYRU itself decided at the 1955 November conference to adopt the Finn as the one design for singlehanded sailing as soon as the rules and plans were revised and given a clean English text, and an International Finn Dinghy Association could be founded.

Encouraging for the Finn Class was the donation of a Gold Cup by F.G. Mitchell by the end of 1955, to be sailed for the first time at Easter 1956 in Burnham-on-Crouch, England.

Paul Elvström, on far left, keeping his boat very flat at Kiel

1956

With the approval of the IYRU and under the protest of the Scandinavian Yachting Union Henri Leten claimed by January 1956 that the International Finn Association had been founded in November 1955 in Brussels. The IYRU approved that the European Championship with a crew of one (previously sailed in the 1936 O-Jolle) be organised by Belgium for 1956 in the Finn Class. Leten pushed to regard the newly created Finn Gold Cup as the world championship of the Finn Class. In addition, in early 1956 it was decided to select the Finn as the monotype for the 1960 Olympics as well. Many nations were preparing for the 1956 Olympics at the end of the year in Melbourne. Even the Germans took the old Finns out of storage (which had been lying idle for 3 years) to sail the selections.

Dr. Söderhjelm from Finland and Henri Leten revised the rules and J. Loeff from the Netherlands redrew the plans of the Finn. The Gold Cup in Burnham on Crouch turned out as a big success with 46 boats from 12 nations participating. Under these circumstances it was easy for Henri Leten to organise the first Annual General Meeting of the International Finn Association at the occasion of the European Championship on August 23, 1956. Disregarding the pending question, whether the meeting in Brussels in November 1955 was legal or not, the results of this conference were accepted, and the legal foundation of the International Finn Association was acknowledged. The Scandinavian Yachting Union had given up its opposition and transferred all the rights of administration and on the plans to the IFA. L.R. Koopmans from Holland was elected as the first president and

Fred Miller and Willy Kuhweide at the Finn Gold Cup in 1961

Henri Leten as secretary of the IFA. A Technical Committee with Rickard Sarby as chairman and Richard Murray (UK) and B. Dotsch (Belgium) as members was created for interpretation and advice on the rules.

The founding members of the IFA were the national Finn Associations of England, Holland, Belgium, South Africa, Finland as the only Scandinavian country, Argentina, France and Spain. Germany, Switzerland, Sweden, Turkey, Portugal, Norway, Ireland, and Poland had sent representatives to that first AGM in 1956. Since Paul Elvström considered the sailing conditions of the Loosdrecht lakes unacceptable for a European Championship, Denmark was not represented.

M. Skaugen (Norway) proposed Rules for the IFA, which are the first draft of a constitution. They include the suggestion to publish a Finn Bulletin to be sent to members free of charge (later to become FINNFARE).

In the fall of 1956 a national Finn association was founded in the Federal Republic of Germany with Curd Ochwadt as the driving force. In November 1956 the IYRU granted international status (category 1) to the Finn Class.

1957

Already in its second year the Gold Cup was generally accepted as the official World Championship of the Finn Class. In 1957 it was organised in Sweden on the huge inland Vänersee by the later third president of the IFA Bengt Hornevall. 70 boats from 13 nations participated which was a record by any standard for that time. The 1957 AGM was also organised at the occasion of the Gold Cup for the first time. Henri Leten was elevated from Secretary to President and Richard Murray from the UK became the new secretary because English was the official language of the IFA.

The national Finn associations of Portugal, Federal Republic of Germany, Norway, New Zealand, Sweden, United States, Poland and Denmark joined the IFA in 1957. As early as the 1957 AGM the countries which were to organise the Gold Cups up to 1967 were determined. Surprisingly that schedule was actually adhered to in the following 10 years. Dacron sails and fibreglass boats were considered but not yet accepted at the 1957 AGM.

Since the Kiel Week of 1957 was a great success for the Finn Dinghy the new Class bypassed the traditional O-Jolle in the German speaking countries after that date. Paul Elvström remained the leading force in the technical development of the Finn. He

constantly improved the bendy mast, longitudinally stiff boom and corresponding sail. After 1957 the so called 'Elvström bailers' became popular, which several people claim to have invented, including Elvström and Sarby.

1958

A number of new national Finn associations joined the IFA. Richard Murray collected the subscriptions and achieved such a good surplus, that he suggested that the fees should be reduced.

In local races in the US dacron sails were used on an experimental basis and proved to be superior, especially after a rain or a capsize. So the IYRU approved to allow the sail to be made of woven cloth of even thickness as from 1st Jan 1960. Pressure to built Finns from GRP increased. In Switzerland Airex built some experimental boats. The IYRU agreed to the new material in principle. The Finn Class had to face the first technical revolution. For the years to come the challenge was to remain the leading single handed boat without outdating the existing hulls. Rickard Sarby built an FD and partly lost interest in the Finn Class.

Bengt Hornevall
third President
1960-1962

Harald Bredo Eriksen
fourth President
1962-1964

Vernon Stratton
Secretary 1961-1964
President 1964-1971

1959

For the first time in the history of yachting more than 100 boats gathered for a regatta - at the 1959 Gold Cup in Hellerup, north of Copenhagen, in front of the home of Elvström. Paul was the host and dominator of the event. At the AGM it was decided not to collect any payments for one year, since there was no good use for the money already collected in the previous years. Everyone agreed that a Finn bulletin as required in the Finn rules would be a good thing. However nobody was prepared to be the Editor.

There was a basic discussion about the one-design status of the Finn Class. One view was, you may only do what the rules allow and nothing else, the other, you may not do what the rules specifically forbid, but you can do anything else. In the following years the Class adopted the latter option which allowed the Finn to remain the leading centreboard class. In order to allow more modern construction methods, the need was recognised to control the centre of gravity. By 1959 Richard Creagh-Osborne previously only known as a good helmsman started to help the IFA secretary Richard Murray on technical matters. On specific questions Rickard Sarby was asked for advice.

1960

The Finn was well established internationally by 1960, being the Olympic monotype for the third time. Participation at the Gold Cup in the UK suffered from the preparations of many nations for the Olympics in Italy only two months later. Also at the AGM only 8 nations were represented. Bengt Hornevall, the

representative of Sweden and organiser of the 1957 Gold Cup, was elected as the third president of the IFA. Richard Murray was reelected as secretary. Again a serious attempt was made to produce a Finn Bulletin. Richard Murray asked each nation to answer a sort of questionnaire. From the responses he hoped to be able to put together a Finn Bulletin. However he never received any replies.

A campaign resulted in the selection of the Finn as the Olympic monotype for 1964.

In about 1960 a double clew at the tack of the sail was developed in order to control the shape of the sail, later called the Cunningham.

1961

At the 1961 Gold Cup plastic boats were allowed to participate for the first time. Because the first three boats were made from GRP many owners felt that their old wooden hulls were inferior. The US built plastic boat of Fred. H. Miller jr. caused great concern because of superior speed. However Fred did not only bring a sensational boat but also a startling magazine 'FINNFARE'. Up to that time the official United States bulletin, it was adopted as the official IFA publication.

Richard Murray resigned as secretary and after some discussion Vernon Stratton agreed to take the job. Bengt Hornevall was reelected as President. In order to pay for an assistant to the Secretary and also for the publication of FINNFARE more money was needed. The dues remained at 5 shillings for each boat but was to be collected from each active Finn sailor. A proposal to hold the Gold Cup outside Europe in regular intervals was defeated.

After the Gold Cup many sailors ordered new GRP boats from HVM (Holland) or Elvström (Denmark). In addition to the irritation because of the superiority of the plastic boats over wooden hulls, Richard Creagh-Osborne discovered severe discrepancies between the official table of offsets and the official templates. The IYRU became concerned about the one-design status of the Finn Class.

1962

When the measurement committee at the 1962 Gold Cup discovered some hidden lead in the plastic boat which Arne Akerson had bought from Fred H. Miller the year before, the chaos was perfect and the Class about to fall apart. Bengt Hornevall resigned as president. The moral host of the Gold Cup Harald Bredo Eriksen, vernacular Big Apple, accepted the vacant position on the condition that a capable Technical Committee be formed to cope with the pending measurement problems. The Englishman Richard Creagh-Osborne was elected Chairman, Rickard Sarby and Ole With (Norway) members. The Technical Committee had to draft new rules for wooden and plastic boats alike in order to assure the one-design status of the Finn. The obsolete table of offsets had to be replaced by a new template-system. Uniform instructions for measurers had to be issued. The IYRU and the forthcoming Olympics in Tokyo put a tremendous time pressure upon the work of the honorary members including President Eriksen who actively participated in the drafting of the new control system.

Rickard Sarby was pessimistic that a workable set of rules could be enforced. Sarby had sailed against the ex-Miller Newport Finn in Sweden and observed that it responded twice as quickly to waves than a conventional wooden boat or a plastic boat with normal weight distribution. Rickard came up with the suggestion to control the location of the centre of gravity athwart by a leaning test and later also longitudinally by controlling the bow weight with the hull supported at station 3. We now know that these rules did not solve the problem technically: not until ten years later when Gilbert Lamboley provided the technically correct answer. However the centre of gravity rules coped with the situation psychologically. The owners of conventional boats felt that the one-design principle was secured. And the leading forces within the IYRU were put at ease and kept the Finn as the Olympic monotype. Rickard Sarby most likely had sensed these correlations intuitively but remained silent until the proper new rules were adopted in 1974.

While Paul himself had withdrawn from active Finn sailing by 1962, Elvström GRP boats, Elvström masts, and Elvström sails were the most common equipment in 1962. Andre Nelis remained also second behind Paul in the development of the HVM Finn. However the US built Newport Finns were said to be the fastest boats. Of the 133 boats at the Gold Cup 50 were made of plastic.

Aside of the problems with the Technical Committee, Big Apple Eriksen also had to cope with difficulties concerning the production of FINNFARE. Fred Miller was an idealistic enthusiast but unreliable and frequently entangled in fights with the US Finn Association. He constantly asked for money but never produced any receipts. To improve the situation the Secretary Vernon Stratton became European co-editor of FINNFARE.

A third problem plagued the Finn Class: pumping. The conservative sailors despised pumping, the young aggressive hot-shots practised it, and the responsible forces within the IFA and the IYRU could not agree upon an answer.

1963

The waves of the previous year were still heavily rocking the Finn. The Technical Committee was fighting a war on two fronts. Drafting the new set of rules and accompanying documents required tedious and attentive work in order to obtain the approval of the IYRU. At the same time eager boat builders urgently asked for instructions, and measurers asked for guidance in order to

satisfy the high demand for new boats. There were already more than 3000 boats registered in 39 nations. The Gold Cup in Medemblik had 162 entries from 22 nations. Fred Miller kept up with his tradition of causing trouble at the Gold Cup. He developed a new boat on the basis of the Newport Finn with Wesco

Fred Miller (left), Henry Sprague (right)

Marine in California and claimed it had such fabulous performance that it outmoded the existing 3000 Finns all over the world over night.

Then he talked young gifted Henry Sprague into the adventure to transport that dinghy to the Gold Cup where it was measured, found not to be a Finn (breaking several rules), and was refused entry. The story ended with Fred H. Miller jr. fighting with everybody: with the Dutch measurers for only pecking at the Wesco Finn and letting 161 other illegal Finns sail; with Richard Creagh-Osborne for drafting rules and issuing interpretations specifically biassed against the Wesco Finn; with Wesco Marine for not following his instructions; and Sprague sr. and jr. because of the scandal in Medemblik.

The Europeans with Big Apple Eriksen as president and Vernon Stratton as secretary transferred the editorship of FINNFARE to Jack Knights in the UK. At the 1963 AGM, rules for the conduct of the Gold Cup and major championships were issued.

By 1963 the flexible Finn rig was developed to such a degree that lighter helmsmen were also able to compete successfully. The light-weight skippers gained an advantage over the heavy-weight people on the reaches and runs where Finn sailing became more dynamic.

By 1963 the new Technical Committee with Richard Creagh-Osborne as the Chairman was about to get the template problem under control. The shape of the hull was redefined on a sheet of aluminium by Fairey Marine under the direction of Charles Currey, silver medalist of the 1952 Olympics, and new templates were made.

Vernon Stratton (K 144) leads Hubert Raudaschl (OE 31)

1964

While the basic proposals of the Technical Committee to control wooden and plastic boats alike were approved by the IYRU in November 1963, the most significant contribution to the one-design credibility of the Finn Class was accomplished by an active sailor. Hubert Raudaschl won the 1964 Gold Cup with a homemade wooden hull, his homemade mast, and a homemade sail. For about 10 years wooden boats proved to be at least equal if not superior to plastic hulls: Kuhweide won the Gold Cup twice and later Bruder won it three times in wooden boats. This was before the Lamboley test was introduced, and gave the Finn Class time to digest the shock of the early sixties after the approval of plastic for the construction of the hull.

1964 also brought a change in the leadership of the IFA. According to Heidi Auer the Secretary Vernon Stratton lobbied successfully against the President and managed to be elected. In accordance with Vernon Stratton and the minutes of the AGM, Big Apple was unable to continue, Mr. Stratton initially refused but was finally persuaded to take the burden and Dr. Fred Auer accepted the post of Honorary Secretary. This was the beginning of a new eventful chapter of the IFA, earmarked to end with an even more dramatic coup d'etat. In that same AGM Vernon Forster was elected to fill the newly created position of Class Measurer as a paralysing horror for ingenious builders and top competitors.

At the 1963 November meeting of the IYRU it had been decided to announce a vacancy for a new singlehander. However, soon after the 1964 Olympics it was decided to keep the Finn as the Olympic monotype for 1968. The prolific work of the Technical Committee under Richard Creagh-Osborne had convinced the IYRU just in time that the Finn was still the best international singlehander.

1965

The crisis was under control. Vernon Forster gave the old boats at the Gold Cup in Poland which did not measure in every little detail according to the new rules one last warning. Two wooden boats from the German Democratic Republic came first and second in the world championship proving the one-design character of the Finn Class.

Since the Finn Class was expanding rapidly the Honorary President and the Honorary Secretary, even with the help of his indefatigable wife Heidi, were not able to cope with the work load. Therefore four so called link-officers were elected to support the executive committee. The energy or interest of Jack Knights to produce FINNFARE had faded away and the Auers had to do most of the work. So a new editor was found in Belgium: Manfred Schiller.

1966

Willy Kuhweide won the Gold Cup with a wooden Raudaschl hull and Hubert the European Championship with guess what type of boat. Elvström still had 50% of the sail market. The Class had further expanded to 4000 sailors from 45 nations. A new rule book was issued as the climax of Richard Creagh-Osborne Technical Committee's endeavours. In order to create some trouble for the sake of excitement it was suggested to test new materials for making spars. The problems of the years to come were casting their shadows ahead.

The 1966 AGM acknowledged the actual power structure of the IFA by electing Dr. Fred and Heidi Auer as the Honorary Secretary. Vernon Stratton suggested to limit the duration of a presidency and remained president himself for another five years since no one wanted the job.

The first suggestions for the control of the distribution of matter in the hull were discussed already in 1966 which would allow for the further development of the Finn Class. In order to get hold of more financial support from eastern European countries the Junior European Championship was invented at the 1966 AGM.

1967

Publications about the Finn had a boom in 1967. Curd Ochwadt wrote his 'Finn Fibel' Elvström and Creagh-Osborne published the 'Expert Dinghy Racing' with many references to the Finn and the AGM decided to print an IFA Handbook 'as soon as possible', although nothing was published until Peter Mohilla's FINNLOG nearly twenty years later. Earlier it was not possible. Paul Miller from the US

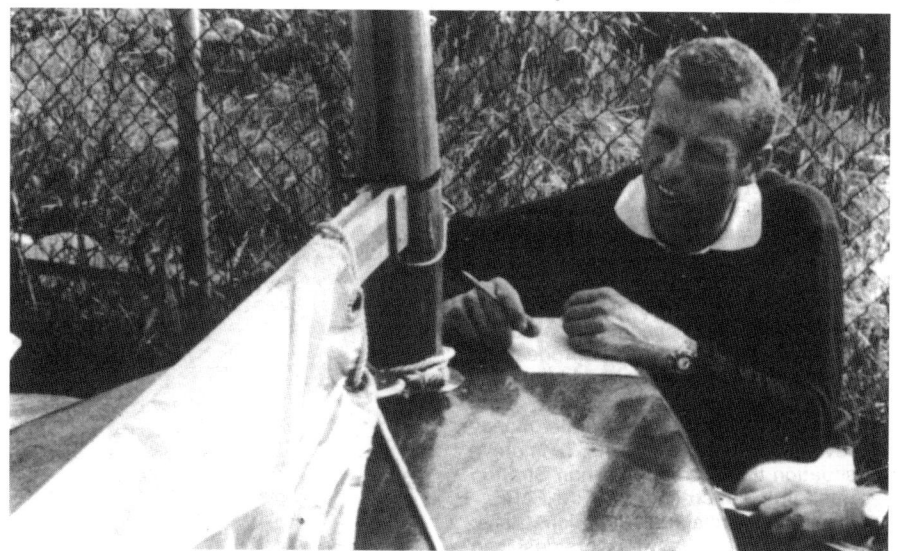

Hubert Raudaschl won the 1964 Gold Cup with a wooden boat

kindly agreed to become the Class Record Officer and to publish that IFA Handbook.

The 1967 Gold Cup was the climax of Chief Measurer Vernon Forster's rule of horror. He discovered the secret of the fast Raudaschl wooden hulls, ruling out a hollow keel section at station 1. Even Willy Kuhweide had to plane down the aft section of his 'Darling'. However this did not prevent him from winning the Gold Cup for the third time.

Acknowledging the world-wide distribution of the Finn it was agreed that the Gold Cup should be organised outside of Europe every four years. Centre of gravity, double bottoms, thickness of hulls, sandwich construction and

Heidi Auer, IFA secretary

basically the control of the distribution of matter were the burning yet unsolved problems of the Technical Committee under Richard Creagh-Osborne in 1967. Dr. Roland Langer (Austria) started to work on a new constitution for the IFA but did not get too far. The task was taken over by others in the years to come and was completed in 1971.

1968

High points of the season 1968 were the successful Olympics in Acapulco and a disastrous Gold Cup in Whitstable, UK. The poor organisation of that Gold Cup caused the IFA to adopt new rules for the Gold Cup and the European Championships.

Vernon Stratton and the Auers stayed in power with 9 link officers to support them. The Technical Committee still chaired by Richard Creagh-Osborne was reinforced by Gilbert Lamboley. Mr. Michael Gilchrist was elected Editor of Finnfare unanimously never to publish a single copy. Vernon Stratton himself continued to do all the work. Paul Miller USA claimed to make progress with the Class records and the IFA Year Book but never to burst into print either.

By 1968 Bruder and Raudaschl developed a new mast-sail concept. They went back 15 years to stiff masts with relatively flat sails going fast and pointing high in light to medium winds. By making the top of the mast very flexible sideways the leach was freed in heavy weather, thus not overpowering a normal size skipper. Successful tests with aluminium and fibreglass masts and Raudaschl sails made of different material in the top section (tracked down and prohibited at the Gold Cup) were pointing in the direction of future development.

1969

Although the rules permitted aluminium and plastic masts in 1969 only Jack Knights brought a strange non-wooden mast to the

Gold Cup in Bermuda. The AGM solved all the pending problems in regard with the constitution, the rules for the Gold Cup and the Major Championships, and the internal management of the IFA by referring the details to the subcommittee of the link officers. In accordance with the minutes of the AGM all the problems were solved: in reality hardly anything happened. The Auers suggested a Veterans Finn World Championship for sailors over 40 years of age.

Paul Elvström improved his Finn and turned up once again at the Gold Cup to take the cup for those over 40 years of age. By 1969 the old boom wedges were replaced by kicking straps between mast and boom. This resulted in a change of the sailing technique on the reaches and runs.

1970

By 1970 the Bruder mast and Raudaschl sail combination reached its climax. However David Hunt, with his star pilot Patrick Pym, was working hard to make the new aluminium Needlespar mast go fast. The big question mark of the time was which equipment would be used at the forthcoming 1972 Olympics in Kiel. The 1970 AGM was very concerned about the IFA accounts approaching bankruptcy.

Vernon Stratton was reelected president and Heidi Auer (for the first time not together with Dr. Fred) as secretary and treasurer. Richard Creagh-Osborne was not able to attend the AGM and Gilbert Lamboley was elected as the new Chairman of the Technical Committee. Dr. Fred Auer was elected as Chairman of the Link Officers. The proposed new constitution was rejected by the AGM. Dr. Fred Auer was asked to prepare a new suggestion with the help of two lawyers.

Rickard Sarby made a proposal to adopt a special smaller 'Storm Sail' for strong winds. Since the Contender was being considered as the monotype for the 1976 Olympics, suggestions were made to modernise the Finn

Gilbert Lamboley, Chairman of the Technical Committee 1970-1980

Hans van Elst
President 1971-1975

Carl van Duyne
first Vice President
Sailing

Andy Zaweija
first Vice President
Administration

Ken Ryan
Secretary 1971-1975

Rickard Sarby
attended his last IFA
AGM in 1971

with larger sails, longer masts, a shorter boom, and sliding seats. However the AGM refused all proposals to change the Finn dramatically and the boat remained in principle as designed in 1949.

1971

For the IFA, 1971 was a year of political unrest. The main issue was the question of which masts should be used at the 1972 Olympic regatta in Kiel. The President Vernon Stratton (from the UK) supported the notion to use the new aluminium Needlespar masts (made in the UK) because David Hunt said that they would be perfectly uniform. However most of the top helmsmen had no experience with the new material and wooden masts were still considered to be faster.

Jörg Bruder won the Gold Cup for the second time with a wooden spar. The IFA Honorary Secretary Heidi Auer was in favour of wooden masts. She claimed that aluminium masts would give the British sailors an unfair advantage.

The IYRU had agreed to use metal masts at the Olympics, upon request of the German organiser of the Olympics as suggested by

IFA President Vernon Stratton and the Chairman of the Technical Committee Gilbert Lamboley. However IFA secretary/treasurer Heidi Auer was fighting to have this decision cancelled again. A strange extraordinary AGM in Athens called too late on the spot by the Auers on the occasion of the European Championship elected Dr. Fred Auer as the new President of IFA and reversed the decision of the former president to use aluminium masts at the 1972 Olympics. Vernon Stratton declared that AGM to be illegal and insisted to remain the duly elected president of IFA.

The official AGM on the occasion of the Gold Cup in Toronto approved a new constitution and the selection of aluminium spars for the 1972 Olympics. Hans van Elst from Holland was elected the new president of IFA and a completely new team took over the helm. Ken Ryan from Ireland was elected Honorary Secretary to be supported by a paid assistant and a professional accountant. As Mr. Achermann from the Swiss Credit Bank in St. Moritz was already acquainted with the work, it was decided to have him carry on. Carl van Duyne (USA) was elected as the first Vice President (Sailing) and Andy Zawieja (Poland) as Vice president (Administration). Gilbert

Lamboley was the only member of the old team to survive the revolution as the Chairman of the Technical Committee. The father of Serge Maury (France), Mr. Raymond Maury kindly agreed to do FINNFARE in the future in form of a bimonthly bulletin, however not a single copy of that publication survived in any archive. Independent from these administrative scandals the Finn Class prospered and Jörg Bruder won his second Gold Cup in Toronto.

1972

When Jörg Bruder won his third Gold Cup with his own aluminium mast the former opposition of the top helmsmen against the new material melted. After several trials and errors the Needlespar M turned out to be the spar for the years to come.

By 1972 Gilbert Lamboley had introduced his revolutionary concept to control the distribution of matter in a Finn dinghy. For one year this system was used parallel to the old system to control the centre of gravity.

At the 1972 AGM the new Honorary Secretary Kenneth Ryan was not able to clarify the accounts he had inherited from the former executive officers of the IFA. It was felt that an additional position should be created to take care of the financial matters and Peter Roost from Switzerland was elected the first treasurer of IFA. Against the decision of the IFA AGM not to control the weight of wet clothing at all, the IYRU decided in November 1972 to limit the maximum to 20 kg.

4 of the 10 Finns that were provided for the 1968 UK Olympic Trials

Laszlo Zsindely
Treasurer 1973-1977

Mikos Nemeth
Vice President Admin.
1973-1977

Ed Bennett
Vice President Sailing
1974-1977

Nikos Kouklelis, secretary
1975-1991, elected Life
Honorary Member in 1991

Marino Barendson
seventh President
1975-1979

1973

When the Lamboley test finally became effective it caused a technical revolution. The new control methods allowed the abandonment of the former rules regarding the centre of gravity, the combined control of material and wall thickness, and the exclusion of unmeasurable constructions like double bottoms or sandwich. The new system controlled the basic elements of the boats performance in the waves and not the construction. So the IYRU agreed to allow any material for the construction of the hull and to introduce double bottoms. Therefore the Finn remained the most modern dinghy for top competitive sailing.

In 1973 the Finn Class suffered a severe loss from the human, sporting and technical point of view, when Jörg Bruder was killed in an airplane crash on route to the Gold Cup in Brest to defend his title.

Because of an increasing income from the sale of rule books and sail labels the financial situation of the IFA improved considerably. The IYRU put pressure on the IFA to limit the number of participants in the Gold Cup to about 60 boats. However the AGM voted clearly in favour of adhering to the established quotas and the entry system remained in principle unchanged, allowing for far more than 100 boats. In order to encourage organisational efforts in each country, national Finn secretaries were allowed to enter the Gold Cup above the quota of their country. This also increased the number of qualified delegates to the AGM.

1974

In accordance with the new rules a new rule book was printed in 1974. The first builder to take advantage of the new rules was Peter Taylor in Great Britain. He produced a good looking hull with a double bottom, which sailed very dry and turned out to be fast especially downwind. However after some time the majority of the Taylor boats started to leak at the joint of the hull with the deck. Gilbert Lamboley contributed further to the improvement of the IFA finances through the production and sale of new templates that he had produced with a computer controlled milling machine. The aluminium masts introduced in 1972 caused safety problems in

a capsize and it was agreed to require all masts to be watertight and float. However within two years it became obvious that this rule resulted in trapping water in the mast rather than keeping it out and therefore the rule was abandoned again in 1977.

1975

Four years after the turmoil of Toronto the turn of Hans von Elst from Holland as president was over and the AGM in Malmö, Sweden peacefully elected Marino Barendson from Italy as the new president and Nikos Kouklelis from Greece as Honorary Secretary. Barendson, who had never sailed a Finn in his life, thought to benefit the Class by making it more modern. He travelled on his expenses all over the world to push for a reduction of the hull weight and to support experiments. Barendson's well meant but uncoordinated actions were curbed by the Chairman of the Technical Committee Gilbert Lamboley, who successfully guarded the one-design character of the Finn Class. No substantial rule changes were even proposed to the IYRU.

Gilbert Lamboley also managed to obtain a new Gold Cup from Somms Marine, after the original Cup had been lost in that tragic air crash of Jörg Bruder in 1973. Another effort was made to control pumping. However it was not possible to bring the diverging opinions from sailors on flat and open waters closer together. In spite of that some countries included in their sailing instructions the requirement of a minimum three rope purchase through the floor block except when gybing.

1976

As a reaction to the difficulties with the selection of the Olympic masts in 1972, the participants in the 1976 Olympics in Kingston, Canada were allowed to bring their own spars and sails. The majority of the sailors would have preferred to use their own boats complete. A second edition of the new rule book was printed in 1976 with very little changes compared to the 1974 edition.

Jacques Rogge
eighth President
1979-1981

Peter Mohilla

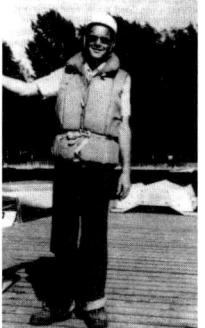

David Howlett
Vice President Admin.
1982-1983

Wolfgang Gerz
Vice President Sailing
1984-1986

José Luis Doreste
Vice President Sailing
1986-1987

Since the 1976 Gold Cup took place in January in Australia, the 1976 AGM was divided into two sessions, one at the Gold Cup the other at the European Championship in France in May. The Council of the IFA called the attention of all present and future IFA Executive Committees to the need to coordinate their individual efforts with the other members of the Executive Committee and the relevant committees.

By 1976 a negative side-effect of the Lamboley test upon the development of the Finn Class was observed. Some builders emphasised top speed too much and neglected seaworthiness by constructing extremely thin weak hulls and using more lead than plastic. Some boats sank to the bottom of the sea and sailors were in severe peril. However the problem solved itself inasmuch as the respective makes fell into discredit among the sailors despite the speed advantages. The Finn Class turned out to be rather reluctant to accept the recommendations of the IYRU regarding the old problem of pumping.

1977
The negative climax of that year was the withdrawal of the Gold Cup from competition when the Spanish authorities refused the participation of a sailor from South Africa. At the 1977 AGM some new people were elected members of the Executive Committee: Jacques Rogge (Belgium) as Vice-President (Sailing), Gerardo Seeliger (Spain) as Treasurer. The entry system for the Gold Cup and the European Championships was changed, but without reducing the potential for over 100 boats at the Gold Cup and 40-60 at the Continental Championships. Attempts of Fred Miller to produce fibreglass masts did not find a response among the top helmsmen.

1978
The 1978 Gold Cup was organised in Mexico and signalled the dawn of a new generation of sailors and winning boats. For the first time a group of former Laser sailors dominated the event using Vanguard hulls. Once again the

IFA successfully withstood pressure from the IYRU to reduce the number of participants at the Gold Cup to about 60 by changing the entry system.

The AGM considered several notions to keep only 30,000 sfr as a reserve and to spend the rest of the accumulated capital for the promotion of the class. It was considered to subsidise measurement at major events, sailors from other classes, the production of the Class magazine FINNFARE, stands of the Finn at boat show, or advertisements for the Finn in various yachting magazines. The Council passed an inconsistent judgment against some Spanish boats, which had an unusual bulb in the deck. There was no specific rule quoted to be infringed, however it was felt that the arrangement was not in conformity with the original design of the Finn by Rickard Sarby.

After Georg Siebeck had done an excellent job on FINNFARE in 1975-1977 he failed to publish any issues in 1978-1979, which caused considerable concern in the class.

1979
The dominance of former Laser sailors from the US was striking and in view of the 1980 Olympics in Tallinn alarming for the Europeans. Most successful on the European circuit was the 1978 Gold Cup winner John Bertrand (USA) - not to be confused with the John Bertrand from Australia who won the America's Cup for his country in 1983. However in the 1979 Gold Cup John Bertrand (USA) was only runner up behind Cameron Lewis.

After four years as president Marino Barendson did not attend the AGM 1979 and was replaced by former Vice-President (Sailing) Jacques Rogge from Belgium. In order to improve the finances of IFA the minimum number of IFA stickers per country was raised from 18 to 36. The minutes of the 1979 AGM mention problems with some boats not measuring at station 8, first discovered at the European Championship in Malcesine, Italy. The idea

of a portable jig is mentioned, to be taken to major regattas, since several boats had measured correctly once and were refused the next time by other experts.

The sailors were disconcerted because of the inaccuracy of the measurement procedure. A notion to curb pumping beyond the ruling of the IYRU was refused by the council and instead the delegates proposed to abandon the rule 60 (means of propulsion) altogether. Gilbert Lamboley did not attend the AGM but questioned the legality of the meeting because of the use of proxy-votes.

1980
The season was shaped by the Olympics in Tallinn. The Finn Class suffered severely from the boycott of the Olympics initiated by the US, which excluded many potential medalists from participation and discouraged them. The Gold Cup was staged in New Zealand in February where the US sailors continued their dominance. The 1980 AGM was organised in two sessions again, one at the Gold Cup and the second on the occasion of the European Championship in Finland in June.

At the AGM in New Zealand a new notion was considered to support third world countries in their endeavours to participate in the Olympics. The council was worried about the attitude of the Chairman of the Technical Committee. After Gilbert Lamboley had rendered extraordinary services to the Finn Class for almost ten years, it became more and more difficult to deal with him internally. For the second session of the AGM Gilbert Lamboley handed in his resignation and was replaced by David Howlett (UK) as Chairman of the Technical Committee.

After a long silence FINNFARE was published again by the new editor Shimon-Craig Van Collie from San Francisco. Former Laser sailors introduced a new dimension into the art of pumping. However the IFA decided against a proposal of the US and voted in favour of the IYRU ruling to ban pumping.

Robert Neilson
Vice President Administration
1983-1989

Andreas Müller
Treasurer 1984-1992

Chris Pratt
Vice-President Admin.
1989-1990

Gus Miller
Vice President
Sailing 1979-1981

John Hofland
Vice President
Sailing 1987-1990

1981

Since the glorious US team of 1979/80 had fallen apart after the disappointment of the Olympic boycott, the Europeans gained back their dominance in the Finn Class in 1981. The former Laser star Lasse Hjortnäs from Denmark won the majority of individual races in the 1981 Europeans and many other major events, but was beaten to runner up in the Gold Cup by the 'Veteran' Wolfgang Gerz.

After only two years on duty as president Jacques Rogge resigned and exchanged position with the Treasurer Gerardo Seeliger. The problems with station 8 remained and experiments with portable jigs brought to light difficulties of accuracy after reassembling. David Howlett suggested to hire an Executive Director to run the business of the IFA, a proposal which was refused at the AGM in 1982. A steady stream of rule changes ensured that the Finn Class remained modern without outdating existing boats. Shimon-Craig Van Collie resigned as editor of FINNFARE.

1982

What everybody had expected Lasse Hjortnäs to achieve in 1981, he managed in 1982 and won his first Gold Cup. Lasse also defended successfully his title as the European Champion.

Andrzej Ostrowski was elected new Chairman of the Technical Committee. The Executive Committee entrusted the editorship of FINNFARE to Peter Mohilla, who produced

controversial and much too expensive issues. He heated up once again the unsettled question of station 8, which many would have preferred to remain under the carpet. However he produced a measurement jig, which he managed to transport to the Gold Cup in Holland, where it caused amusement, but proved that the system of a portable measurement jig was workable. Mohilla caused further controversy by opposing poor behaviour at a formal dinner invitation and was replaced as Vice-President (Sailing) by Otto Pohlmann.

1983

For the 1983 Gold Cup in Milwaukee, USA John Christianson produced a very fine measurement jig. It was declared the prototype for all future major events and thus ended the controversy about station 8.

At the Gold Cup all the young aggressive sailors were beaten by the conservative US Navy officer Paul van Cleve. This made them so frantic, that they again started to throw food at the President Gerardo Seeliger on the occasion of prizegiving in a five star hotel at the end of the event. They simply disregarded the decision of the 1982 AGM, about Rule 1975, ensuring that the behaviour of Finn Class members remains within the limits of social acceptability.

To honour his past and present achievements the council unanimously voted to elect Gilbert Lamboley as Life Honorary Chairman of the

Technical Committee. To support Finn sailing in third world countries the IFA decided to subsidise these countries with 30 IFA membership dues.

1984

In the 1984 Olympic season many favourites exhausted themselves in the national trials in order to be nominated for the Games and failed in the event itself. An exception was the US, where the trials assumed heroic proportions because of a dazzling combination of sporting, legal and financial efforts between the three top contenders, and the final victor of that in-fight still managed to win the silver medal. A Finn clinic in Canada and a grant of the IOC supported the participation of sailors from third world countries in the 1984 Olympics. Lasse Hjortnäs managed to win the Gold Cup for the second time at the beginning of the season, was struck by bad-luck at the Europeans, when he capsized and broke his best mast while returning into the harbour, and performed poorly for his standards at the Olympics.

1985

After the Olympics in Long Beach a new group of sailors entered the Finn class. Lasse Hjortnäs regained his former dominance by winning the Gold Cup by 0.1 points and the European Championship by a safe margin. In the US Peter Quigley probably started a new chapter in Finn sailing by the development of a new carbon-fibre / s-glass / epoxy matrix mast. The IYRU decided to have the Finn dinghies for the Olympics in 1988 built in Korea. Again competitors would be allowed to bring their own spars but were forced to use the hulls supplied by the organiser. This has the advantage that the poorer countries are also able to participate with top equipment. For years the keenest helmsmen would prefer to use their own boats. Fred Miller, the founder of FINNFARE died on Jan 13th in California.

1986

Peter Mohilla published a book called FINNLOG in the spring of 1986. This book covered the entire history of the class up to 1985 and contained much material of interest

FINNLOG - Edited by Peter Mohilla

to new sailors. It was received with great acclaim and interest by everyone. A complementary copy was sent to many personalities of the world yachting community.

After missing out on the Gold Cup in 1985 by 0.1 points, Oleg Khoperski dominated the European Championships. Stig Westergaard won the Gold Cup without winning a race.

At the AGM of the class Wolfgang Gerz retired as Vice-President (Sailing) and was replaced by José Luis Doreste. Peter Mohilla published his last issue of FINNFARE at the end of the year. After many years of sporadic publishing dates before he took over, Peter Mohilla had managed to regulate publication to the extent that he had produced 4 outstanding issues every year for five years and turned the corner into the modern era of FINNFARE, where IFA members receive their bulletin on a regular basis three to four times a year.

1987

John Hofland (Holland) replaced José Luis Doreste as Vice President (Sailing). The Gold Cup was held at Kiel in conjunction with many others classes to celebrate the 100th anniversary of the KYC. The Gold Cup was dominated by José Luis Doreste while Stuart Childerley won a high scoring Europeans as well as the Pre-Olympics in Pusan, Korea.

The IFA Treasurer, Andreas Müller brought out a single issue of FINNFARE at the Kiel Gold Cup and in the Summer Inés Sagué from Spain became the new editor.

It was hoped that the Finns that were being built for the 1988 Olympics in Korea, would provide the class with a new builder in a new region of the world. However, although these

hulls turned out to be very consistent and similar, they were not proved to be competitive against the standard hulls of the day.

1988

The Gold Cup was early in the year in Brazil, the first time it had been held in South America. It was won by Thomas Schmid (Germany) in a much reduced fleet due to the long travelling distance. José Luis Doreste won the Europeans in Medemblik, Holland to add to his Gold Cup of the previous year.

The season was dominated by the Olympics in Korea. The 1987 World Champion, José Luis Doreste, won a very close series, while one of the favourites Stuart Childerley performed worse than expected after having his best masts broken in transit and another favourite, Lasse Hjortnäs broke his mast in the second race. Larry Lemieux was awarded a medal for giving up a second place in race 5 to go to the rescue of a Singapore 470 sailor who had lost contact with his boat. The IFA received a grant from the International Olympic Committee towards clinics throughout the year and prior to the Olympics which were run by Gus Miller and were very successful. The IFA was the only International Sailing Class which received money direct from the IOC. At the November IYRU meeting the Finn was again selected to be used in the 1992 Olympics Games.

At the Europeans Peter Mohilla brought with him his own personally designed and built portable station jig and computerised Lamboley test equipment for the measurement of the Finns present. It was generally agreed by those measured to be an accurate indicator of legal Finns. The IFA also published a new version of 'Major Championship Rules' which all organisers of Major IFA Championships have to follow.

1989

After 6 years in the post, Robert Neilson retired and was replaced as Vice President (Administration) by Chris Pratt (Australia) and Andrzej Ostrowski was replaced by Richard Hart (UK) as Chairman of the Technical Committee. The new Rule Book was published in 1989.

Stig Westergaard recaptured the Gold Cup whilst Hans Spitzauer from Austria won the Europeans. The dominant hull at this time was still the Vanguard from the US with a Needlespar mast and a North sail. The President, Gerardo Seeliger proposed at the AGM to add into the Rule Book a list of Olympic Medal Winners as well as a list of sailors who have made a significant contribution to the class. Peter Mohilla was named as the Chief Measurer of the Finn class. There were discussions to change some of the characteristics of the Finn: hull weight, length of boom, aspect ratio of the sail, although no radical changes were made.

1990

At the 1990 AGM Björn Westergaard replaced John Hofland as Vice President (Sailing) and Pat Healy became Vice President (Development) when Chris Pratt who was Vice President (Administration) retired. The Vanguard Finn was selected as the hull to be used in the 1992 Olympic Games in Barcelona. The Finn Veterans was renamed the Finn Masters. Robert Laban was appointed as the Chief Measurer of the Class. The discussions on improving the basic concept the Finn continued: making it easier to measure, easier to handle in strong winds, faster to sail and more attractive to a broader range of sailors. The class faced opposition for selection for the 1996 Olympics from the Laser Class who were making a strong bid to be part of the Olympic Games.

Bjørn Westergaard
Vice President Sailing
1990-1996

Pat Healy
Vice President
Development 1990-1997

Othmar Müller von
Blumencron
Treasurer 1992-1996

Jüri Saraskin
Chief Measurer
since 1992

Gerardo Seeliger

The reigning World Champion, Stig Westergaard, won the Europeans in the UK but performed poorly at the Gold Cup in Greece. Hank Lammens became the first Canadian to win an major Finn Championship when he won the Gold Cup after a close finish.

Inés Sagué published her last issue of FINNFARE in the spring and handed over the job to Josje Dominicus from Holland, who was to go on to produce more issues of FINNFARE than any of the previous editors (22 issues in all). At the end of the year, the contract that had been held with Emil Achermann, who had acted as the accountant of the IFA for two decades, expired and was not renewed.

1991
At the Gold Cup in Kingston, Canada, Hank Lammens retained his title in his home town while the distinctly non-European Larry Lemieux, also from Canada, finally won a major title by winning the European Championships in Anzio, Italy.

In 1991 the Finn class lost two of its most long standing and energetic supporters. On 13th May Peter Mohilla, former IFA Chief Measurer and former FINNFARE Editor and

Austrian Finn Association secretary died. On October 7th, the Chief Finn Measurer Robert Laban died.

In 1981 David Howlett had suggested that the IFA hire an Executive Director to run the business of the IFA. It was refused then but at the AGM in Kingston, Canada, the idea resurfaced and the current FINNFARE editor Josje Dominicus from Holland was elected to the post. That AGM also saw the retirement of Nikos Kouklelis who had been the class secretary since 1975. He was made a Life Honorary Member of the IFA. It was decided that the entry quota for the Europeans and the Gold Cup should be the same as from 1st Jan 1993.

1992
After a number of failed attempts, Mexican Eric Mergenthaler finally won the Gold Cup; a very windy one held in Cadiz in which 57 year old IFA Development Coach Gus Miller won the second race. About 20 sailors attended the pre-Gold Cup clinic for which the class received a $10,000 grant. Stuart Childerley again won the Europeans before achieving a 4th in the Olympics later that summer; the same result he achieved in the Olympics 4 years before.

Andreas Müller retired as IFA Treasurer after eight years service and was replaced by Othmar Müller von Blumencron. Jüri Saraskin from Estonia was appointed as the new Chief Measurer. After a long absence the South African Finns were back on the scene. Ian Ainslie was amongst a team of five South Africans at the Gold Cup in Cadiz.

The Olympics in Barcelona were won by José Maria van der Ploeg in one of the deepest Finn fleets ever. World Champion Mergenthaler could only manage 19th whilst co-favourite (and 3 times Laser World Champion) Glenn Bourke finished 20th. After the Olympics, the IFA President, Gerardo Seeliger, bought one of the Olympic Vanguard hulls and donated it to the class as a development boat.

Gus Miller was awarded an IYRU Silver Medal for his work with coaching and clinics. The change over to carbon masts was started. Kurt Andersen from Sweden started developing and testing composite masts with a number of top Finn sailors. The Finn was again selected as the men's singlehanded dinghy for the 1996 Olympics in Atlanta.

1993
1993 was a year of much technical development in the class. At the Gold Cup four different boat builders: Devoti, Lemieux,

Josje Dominicus
first IFA Executive Director 1991-1997
Editor FINNFARE 1990-1997

At the 1997 AGM, ISAF President Paul Henderson made a presentation to retiring IFA President Gerardo Seeliger after 20 years service, Treasurer 1977-1981, President 1981-1997

Pata and of course Vanguard all had boats in the top five. The Devoti hull had outstanding results in its first season. It won both the Gold Cup (with Philippe Presti helming) and the Europeans (with Stig Westergaard helming).

Many sailors were using and experimenting with the new carbon fibre masts which were starting to show good results. 1993 was also the year that much experimentation was done with courses and event formats, which did not prove too popular with the sailors (although the Gold Cup and Europeans were left alone).

At the IYRU conference it was again decided that the Finn hulls would be supplied at the 1996 Olympic Games, maintaining the tradition in the men's singlehanded event.

1994

After twice losing the Gold Cup on the final day, Fredrik Lööf finally fixed it and won it in Pärnu, Estonia, in what was described as one of the best Gold Cups ever. The Olympic Champion José Maria van der Ploeg won the Europeans in Turkey. The experimentation on courses and formats continued. The carbon

mast debate also continued with many fearing the lack of availability and the cost of the new masts.

The Devoti Finn was announced to be the supplied hull at the 1996 Olympics in Savannah.

The IFA development Finn was widely used all over Europe by sailors from Ukraine, New Zealand and Japan before being shipped to Australia for the 1995 Gold Cup. This provided developing sailors the opportunity to sail a Finn and compete at the highest level without the expense of transporting a boat.

1995

The season started off with the Gold Cup in Melbourne, Australia, the first Gold Cup in that region for 15 years. Hans Spitzauer won a very close series after the last race could not be started with the time limit. Almost everyone was now using the carbon masts, with Spitzauer using one of the first 'wing' masts that he had developed. At the AGM later in the year, the Technical Committee was directed to come up with recommendations to ensure that a financial arms races does not develop.

Many Finn sailors were involved in the America's Cup in the US. Russell Coutts, the 1980 Finn Olympic Gold Medalist won it convincingly.

On 25 April 1995, long time former IFA secretary Nikos Kouklelis died.

On Lake Balaton, José Maria van der Ploeg successfully defended his European Championship title. One of the favourites for the 1996 Olympics, Fredrik Lööf won the Pre-Olympics in Savannah.

1996

For the first time ever the Finn Gold Cup and the Finn World Masters were held together at the same venue and at the same time. The idea was to show everyone how big the Finn class really was. 192 Finns came together in May at La Rochelle, France for the biggest Finn event so far. Philippe Presti won his second Gold Cup and gained qualification for the Olympic regatta in the summer. Roland Balthasar won the equally competitive, if a bit older, Masters fleet.

Just before the Olympics, José Maria van der Ploeg won his third consecutive European title in fine form, becoming in the process only the third Finn sailor to win a major Finn regatta three times in succession. (The others being Paul Elvström, Olympics: 1952, 1956, 1960 and Jörg Bruder, Gold Cup: 1970, 1971, 1972.)

The four favourites for an Olympic Medal didn't win anything. Just after winning the Junior European title for the second time, Mateusz Kusznierewicz (Poland) won the Gold medal with a race to spare. The other two medal winners, Sebastien Godefroid (Belgium) and Roy Heiner (Holland) were ranked by coaches outside the top ten.

The Finn had to fight off perhaps its strongest challenge yet to Olympic Status. Many saw the Laser as a threat, but many also saw it as good for sailing, offering top quality singlehanded racing for helms of a different weight requirement to that of the Finn. At the ISAF (formerly IYRU) conference in Brighton, in the UK, the Finn argument won the day and the Finn was selected again for the 2000 Olympics in Sydney

1997

Luca Devoti had never won a major event, despite being one of the most experienced sailors in the Finn fleet, but in 1997 he won the Europeans in Split, Croatia. Fredrik Lööf won the Gold Cup for the second time, this time in Gdansk, Poland, winning the title from Luca in the final race. 1981 Gold Cup winner Wolfgang Gerz won the Masters event.

A 'rookie' place was introduced for the Gold Cup and Europeans for any sailor who had never before sailed in one of these events.

Paul McKenzie
IFA Treasurer since 1996

Marc Blees
Marketing Chairman
since 1997

Karlo Kuret
Vice President Sailing
since 1997

Philippe Rogge
tenth President
since 1997

Sarah Kingston
Executive Director since
1997

At the AGM in Gdansk, Gerardo Seeliger, who had been President of the IFA since 1981, retired and Philippe Rogge (whose father Jacques had been IFA President immediately before Gerardo) became the tenth President of the IFA. Gerardo was then presented with a model Finn by ISAF President Paul Henderson. The first thing Philippe Rogge did as the new IFA President was to appoint Gerardo as IFA President of Honour.

Also retiring at that AGM was Josje Dominicus after 6 years as Executive Director and 7 years as FINNFARE Editor. Josje's replacement as Executive Director was Sarah Kingston, while Robert Deaves who was the British Finn Secretary took over as FINNFARE Editor.

1998

The IFA Major Championship rules were altered to allow a minimum of 10 stickers to be paid for by a country (it had been 36). With the forthcoming 2000 Olympic Games in Sydney, the Southern hemisphere circuit in Australia and New Zealand attracted many European sailors. After looking forward to a Gold Cup in Durban, the South Africans had to withdraw at the last minute due to lack of funding. Fortunately, the IFA is always welcomed by yacht clubs around the world, so the Gold Cup was superbly organised in very short time in Athens, Greece.

After dominating most races early in the year, Sebastien Godefroid won the Europeans without winning a single race. The 1996 Olympic Gold Medal winner Mateusz Kusznierewicz won the Gold Cup. The last race in both these events was cancelled due

to lack of consistent wind. All year sailors were experimenting with hard cloth such as kevlar, mylar and vectran. Sails made of these materials were gradually gaining success and numbers during the season.

After being founded in 1961 by Fred Miller in the US, 1998 saw FINNFARE celebrate its 100th issue with a special issue with contributions from many of the sailors and personalities who had been part of its history.

1999

The 50th Year of the Finn started with the Gold Cup in Melbourne once again, with a massive combined World Championships in Port Philip together with 13 other classes. Fredrik Lööf won the Gold Cup for the third time and became the most successful Gold Cup participant of all time, having scored top three in the last seven Gold Cups.

It was decided to publish a new book on the history of the Finn, to bring the material in Peter Mohilla's FINNOG up to date.

Summary

This is the remarkable history of the Finn. For 50 years the Finn has remained the leading singlehander in yachting and hopefully will continue so in the future. In all these years the pivotal issue was to keep the boat modern and at the same time not to outclass the existing hulls. Changes were necessary, but the people in charge had to agree on the proper pace of development. Inevitably different characters had different opinions. There was quite a bit of controversy, but in total the history of the Finn Class was peaceful and productive. In this class everybody has enough trouble to negotiate the boat on the water. So you are glad if you have friends when returning to the harbour to get your craft out of the water. Studying the past of the Finn, it can be expected for the future, that this boat remains the most athletic, elite-conscious, rewarding, and the most Olympic class you can ask for.

9. The Finn, a True Olympic Class

by David Leach

Reprinted from FINN North American 1981 Directory

The International Sailing Federation (formerly IYRU) has chosen the Finn as the Olympic Singlehanded class consistently since it was first used in the 1952 Games. The reason is that the Finn is different from the other singlehanders and typifies what an Olympic class should be. The competition and requirements of the class are truly Olympic in nature.

Former Finn sailor and well-known British yachting writer, Jack Knights once wrote "The cult of the International Finn Monotype may seem strange to some people, uncomfortable, masochistically so to others. But to us devotees, there is nothing else remotely like it. The Finn probably offers the most purely athletic form of yacht racing and is, therefore, the most fundamentally competitive. The Finn gives thrills, frustration and pleasure in roughly equal measure. It offers the rewarding opportunity of doing a difficult thing well. There are lightnings and such for the rest, but there will always be those who aspire to be master of a Finn."

The Olympic Games are made up of many varied athletic events, each designed to test the athlete's ability to perform in his chosen field. The winners are the ones who have worked many years building up their strength, skills, stamina and mental competence. Events are not based upon luck or chance but on ability and hard work and are a test of the ability to perform.

Classes for the Olympic yachting events are not chosen on the basis of popularity or their design. The classes to be used in the Olympics are selected on the basis that the competition in those classes will best test the sailors in their ability, stamina, and competence to perform, based upon hard work and training. The Finn is just such a class.

The winner of the event is a person who knows how to best tune a boat and has the stamina and ability to sail it fastest, just like a track or field event. Notice that you will see a couple of Finn sailors pacing each other trying to adjust their boats to go faster and improve their stamina, much more often than you see them in a 'fun' race: just like a long-distance runner practising for a field event.

The Finn competition in the Olympics offers a true test of sailing skill, requiring stamina, mental competence, and long periods of hard training and practice. No other class demands more devotion, training, and stamina, like an athlete, than the Finn Class.

SAIL Magazine wrote, 'The Finn is the ultimate challenge and racing anything else, fun as it may be, is not just the same.' The competition in a true Olympic class should be the 'ultimate challenge'. The question is: Are you ready for the ultimate challenge?

10. Is There a Finn Specific Sports Injury?

by Frank Newton   Reprinted from 'The Finn Sailing Manual', published by the British Finn Association, 1996

Tennis Elbow, Jumper's Knee, Footballer's Ankle, Javelin Thrower's and Butterfly Swimmer's Shoulder and Hiker's Knee. Whose knee? Is this to do with long Sunday walks over the countryside? No. It is the condition of knee pain associated with the hiking position in dinghy sailing.

Finn sailing in the early days of the class was nothing like that of the present day because the rig was not comparable. Stiff masts, cotton sails without windows and poor control of the boom made life more difficult for the very early Finn sailor and probably more painful. The sails improved, visibility improved, but it was many years before the elevation of the boom could be controlled with anything like certainty. At that time 'Finn Sailor's Elbow' was the reward for a gybe when the wedge refused to adjust itself, and the boom struck the helm smartly on the not so 'funny bone'!

Todays Finn offers a Rolls Royce ride in comparison, and this better control of the rig also takes away some of the desperate last minute excursions outboard. When the sail was far too full, or rising skywards, rapid leaps outboard with consequent risk of hyperextension or excessive rotation of tilt of the lumbar spine, could result in back injury.

Hiking

The hiking position itself was always different in the Finn to those designs with minimal freeboard. The Laser has to be sailed semi straight-legged with the knees flexed by about 15°. The Finn offered the possibility of taking the knee joint to the gunwhale so that in the full hike the thigh bone lay against the hull side. In this posture knee flexion was about 90°.

In standing, the Centre of Gravity (CG) acts through a vertical line that passes by design close to the hip and knee joints. This results in the muscles working those joints having to do less work in maintaining the upright position. Evolution had sought the most energy effective system.

In most sports the athlete is erect. Fully 30% of young persons have a tendency towards a roughening of the under surface of the patella (knee cap) which tends to rub against the underlying lower end of the thigh bone (femur) when working under a load. This causes the most common 'sports injury' seen in young attenders at the Sports Injury Clinic.

In the hiking position, be it the full hike as in the early Finn helm, the Star crew or the Soling crew; or the semi-hike as in the 470 helm; or the near straight leg hike of the Laser; the line of action of the CG has moved well away from the knee. As a consequence the loading on the patella in pressing against the femoral surface below is altered.

The quadricep muscles, at the front of the thigh, pull strongly upon the upper edge of the patella to which they are fastened. This pull is equalled by the resultant pull on the patella tendon, which anchors the lower edge of the patella to the top of the shin below the knee. There is, because of the bent angle of the knee, a resultant force applying the patella strongly towards the knee joint.

In a relaxed standing position this force may be equal to body weight, at 30° knee bend from the straight position 2-4 times body weight, and at 40° 6 times, rising to 10 times at 70° of bend. With a roughened patella surface this will clearly cause pain in some persons.

Hiking Muscles

Whether there is discomfort does not entirely depend upon whether the patella articular surface is rough. More it depends upon whether the roughness gets into the wrong place, and this depends upon the tracking of the patella along the groove made for it on the lower articular end of the femur.

This tracking is determined by the balance in the action of the four component muscles of the quadriceps. Three of the four pull the knee straight but tend to take the patella too far towards the outside, or lateral side of the knee joint. The fourth, the medial quads muscle, also pulls the knee straight but takes the patella towards the inner side of the knee.

There should be a balance. If there is not it is usual for the outer three to win and for the patella to scrape along the outside of the groove and cause pain. In such circumstances the Finn sailor should perform specific physical exercises to improve the medial quads. Any qualified physiotherapist will teach these to you. At times a spell of sailing in the Laser dinghy with its more straight legged hike will be a more enjoyable form of therapy to enable you to return to the Finn with your medial quads in better shape, since they benefit from working in a less flexed position.

Knee Pain

Runners are also troubled by Hiker's Knee in which case it may be called 'Anterior Knee Pain' (AKP), or by the more old fashioned name of 'Chondromalacia Patella' (which is more correctly the name for the roughened patella surface). Biomechanics, the study of mechanical laws relating to body movement, has shown that runners who excessively 'pronate' the feet (flat footed) are helped by lifting the inner side of the foot with an

'orthotic' insert. For every degree the foot pronates the shin bone rotates inwards along its length by one degree. This adversely affects the biomechanics of the knee and the tracking of the patella.

It follows therefore, that in hiking, if the feet are crossed over one another in the toe straps, as when one is tired on a long beat, this effect will be the same as a weary runner pronating his feet and enjoying his AKP. The feet should therefore be alongside one another and the toe straps positioned so that the strap is over the ankle rather than the toe end of the foot. In the case of short persons there should be no element of the sailor straining to reach straps that are just out of reach. This will generate a 'pronation effect'. In particular the aft end of the toe strap should not be in the centreline of the floor. The straps should be parallel to the mid line of the boat if the sailor has AKP, and within easy reach.

Low Back Pain

The avoidance of Low Back Pain (LBP) associated with sailing is best achieved by the adoption of Proper Movement Patterns (PMP) within the dinghy. The lumbar spine (the spine relating to the low back below the ribs) is the origin of the most powerful of the muscles concerned with flexion of the hip joint. Ilios-psoas muscle arises from the five lumber vertebrae and from the inner rim of the pelvis. It is used to bring the body inboard from the hiking position, to hold it in the hiking position, and to lower it rapidly outboard into the hiking position. It will therefore be working concentrically, isometrically or eccentrically. It works in conjunction with Rectus Femoris (RF), which is only one of the quadriceps muscles to cross the hip joint. RF therefore is a knee extensor in holding the angle of the knee fixed in hiking, and also helps Ilios-psoas to move the body inboard and outboard.

If the abdominal muscles are not strong enough they fail in their duty in holding the body in a fixed position in relation to the pelvis. The body tends to arch backwards upon the pelvis by an increase in the hollowing of the lumbar area as a result of the strong pull of Ilios-psoas. This is the position of hyperextension. When combined with rotation of the lumbar spine associated with sheeting the sail, or tilting sideways in an effort to move weight fore and aft when going over waves, or worse a combination of all three movements under the stress of the heavy jacket, then this is a recipe for Low Back Pain. In older sailor the stress will be upon the front of the spine and discs, in those still growing upon the rear of the vertebrae causing stress fractures.

For maintaining a pain free back therefore, the sailor should avoid hyperextension of the lumbar spine, particularly combined with rotation and tilt. In other words there should be correct movement patterns within the boat. Plus a suitable programme of regular abdominal exercises for the low back.

Hiking Bench

During hiking the discomfort that increases over time is due to the muscles of the abdomen, and of the quads, being held constantly in a contracted state. This is 'isometric' contraction and is characterised by the muscle neither shortening nor lengthening as it works. The muscle becomes so tense that the circulating blood cannot enter the muscle, which therefore has to work anaerobically with local accumulation of lactic acid. Ischaemia causes pain.

Training to improve hiking therefore should be aimed at a lesser percentage of maximum effort. When they can do this the circulation can enter the muscle which then works aerobically. The best way to train these muscles is to construct a hiking bench to the Finn side

deck profile and to spend increasing time in the sit-out position. This will be more effective than spending all your time running, swimming or doing similar conventional endurance type training.

Fortunately since the Rectus Femoris muscle helps to control both the knee flexion and hip flexion it is not constantly acting isometrically. As it changes its length to help to alter the body position some fresh blood supply enters the muscle and relieves some of the quads discomfort.

The Fit Finn Sailor

The present day Finn sailor is fortunate that the configuration and length of Olympic Courses have changed. The early 2 mile windward leg at major championships with race durations of over two hours have changed. The fifteen minute windward leg now entails less long hikes on one tack. The overall race length of about fifty minutes is considerably shorter. The sailing technique may therefore become one in which a more 'semi hike' than 'full hike' position is adopted for longer portions of the race. Hiking bench training position should reflect this. The training effect is joint angle specific.

The avoidance of a Finn Specific Sports Injury will entail thought being given to the layout and accessibility of controls and of toestraps to give optimum race biomechanics. Also required are:

• The adoption of a good flexibility and muscle stretch programme.
• The adoption of Proper Movements Patterns within the dinghy.
• Time devoted to a structured Hiking Bench Training Programme to minimise isometric muscle discomfort, which will increase sitting out time.

If you do all these then take care when handling the Finn ashore that you do not sustain an injury before you launch! An injury is an injury, is an injury..........

11 . Paul Elvström on Singlehanded Sailing

by Carl van Duyne and Dick Rose

Reprinted with the permission of the author and Yachting magazine.

Sailors in the San Francisco Bay area had a chance to listen to the best sailor of them all when Paul Elvström visited St. Francis YC for a weekend seminar on singlehanded sailing. I'd like to pass on some of the comments Paul made in his lectures that weekend.

Elvström began by saying that because he had not sailed a dinghy for six years before arriving in San Francisco, "I will not be a teacher, but will give you a report of what I have done, and that way you can make up your mind if you will do the same thing, or go the other way. But should I teach you something, I would teach you to enjoy sailing, because if you forget all about the results in the regatta, then you will enjoy yourself more."

On training: "In 1948, I was selected to take part in the Olympics. In the Olympics, I realised how bad we all were in sailing small boats. Physiques were very bad, and I realised that if I went back and went into physical training I could win easily. So I ran five kilometres daily and made special exercises for training my legs and stomach.

My thinking was that if I could hang out without thinking about it or getting tired, my head would work better . . . I went through the rules once a week, and each time I got new ideas about tactics. I did not have to think of the rules during the race - I was always sure what was right . . . You can calculate tactics lying in bed, and in this way teach yourself what is best . . . In those days, I was very bad in school because I was concentrating on sailing. I was dreaming sailing, thinking rules, tactics and so on."

"Each day before I went sailing, I made a program of what I should do. If it was light wind, I would, for instance, concentrate on

going fast, feeling the boat. If it was strong wind, then perhaps I would gybe. Before I went out, I would think of the way to gybe, then I would practice. If it did not work properly, I would try a new technique. This way I would become better and better."

Two of the techniques Elvström used for on-the-water training I found particularly interesting. He used a mark rounding drill every day to sharpen his boat handling: first he would round a mark ten times to starboard, then ten times to port while trying to stay as close to the mark as possible.

When he was sailing alone, he would often dream that he was racing in a big fleet and he wouldn't always win. Buddy Melges used a similar technique when training for the 1972 Olympics in the Soling. He and his crew would race short, hard races against imaginary opponents because there were no other Solings on his lake. Whenever his crew became lax, he would start a vicious tacking duel with his imaginary but ruthless opponent. A fertile imagination just might be a prerequisite for racing success if you have no one else to practice with. Despite his emphasis on training, Elvström thinks sailors are born, not made: "You must have the talent to feel that you must continually make difficult decisions as

to how much it will pay to deviate from a straight line course to achieve this."

On windshifts: "When it is cloudy and then starts to clear in one place, then, in my experience, the wind will come from there. When it is cloudy everywhere, but darker in one place, usually the wind will come from there. When you see the darkness come closer, then you are sure."

Elvström suggests that smaller wind shifts can be detected by watching the water. "When the sun is shining from behind or from one side, you can see a lot on the water. You have to concentrate on seeing the patterns. When sailing has become routine, then you can practice seeing the wind on the water, the way the puffs hit the water and spread out." Of course, when you can see the shifts coming, you can make excellent decisions about when to tack, to foot off or to pinch up.

On lightweight boats and Olympic classes: When asked whether Quarter Ton boats are safe on the ocean, Elvström replied, "Very safe, because I think a lighter boat is safer in a sea than a heavy boat. When you put weight in a boat, you must put on a bigger mast, rig, and everything must be heavier. You make the whole thing worse in a sea."

Earlier, when speaking of the Olympic classes, he had stated, "the Olympics should be only for difficult dinghies sailed by young people. We should have more faster dinghy classes. Other sports do not change equipment so often as we do in yachting. We should have some classic dinghy classes, but we have not been clever enough to do it."

On nationalism in international competition: "In my boat I have never carried a flag because I think we are all one group, yachtsmen, and it should always be like that."

On steering and sail trim in different types of sea: When the sea is smooth and you are sailing to weather, Elvström advocates an average tiller position 4° to windward of the centre line. "If you move the tiller more than four degrees, then you slow the boat. But if your tiller is 4° to windward, the rudder gives you lift, and that way you use both the keel and the rudder to lift you. When it is flat water, you can adjust the sails to the rudder, but when it is rough you must compromise and adjust the course to suit the seas. Big changes will not help you, but if you can bear off or luff up just a little to avoid a collision with a big wave, then my experience is that this will help you."

With respect to sail trim, "the main principle is that the sail must be at right angles to the wind to get maximum power." Because you must be adjusting course to sail in a rough sea, you must settle for an average trim for these conditions. "When you sail in a heavy sea, if the mast is straight you will get maximum drive out of the main and jib. But when your bow goes down in a sea, the top of the sail will luff, and when you go up the back of a sea, the mast will bend back and flatten the sail. Therefore I give a great deal of attention to the seas when sailing upwind."

In a short chop, "the main thing is to keep the mast and sail quiet. The sail is the engine, and it is so important that the boat does not move too much in the seas. You must look for and find the flat water ahead. Sometimes you must point up or bear away to find less sea."

If you can't miss a big wave, then "go straight so that the sails keep maximum power. To windward in strong winds, you must have the right sail trim, Many people sheet too far outboard. It is better to sheet more lightly to windward to get the proper twist in the sails, both the jib and the main. The sails must have a certain amount of twist at the top. If there is no twist, there is no power at all. If you put telltales at the top you will find out how much it has to twist."

On gybing and rolling: In heavy winds in a Finn or a Laser, "the moment to gybe is when you have maximum speed and the wind goes down, but we are never able to gybe then. When the pressure on the mainsail is least, then gybe. You pull on the sheet and pull the sail across very fast. When you bear off to gybe, you must go far enough so that you are sure to gybe. The centreboard must only be down part way in the water, because otherwise, after gybing, there is a chance that the boat will not be able to slide sideways and you will capsize over the centreboard." He suggests that you can tell if you made a good gybe by observing your speed right after the gybe. "If the boat stops, that gybe was poor."

On sailing to windward in waves: Rather than using a technique for sailing over waves Elvström tries to sail around the waves to reduce pitching whenever possible. "The main thing is to keep the mast and sail quiet. The sail is the engine, and it is very important that the boat does not move (pitch) too much in a sea. You must find the flat water ahead-sometimes you must point up or bear away to find less sea but not too much. This way you

will get the maximum drive out of the sail."

Elvström uses essentially the same technique for sailing in waves when racing both dinghies and keelboats. But to sail around the waves, the skipper must sit to windward where he can see the waves. Even in keelboats, Elvström said, "I always sit where I can see the sea and the genny. Your head is in the right position, you can hear, you can feel the wind, and these are all important to give you the right feeling of a sailing boat." Sailing to leeward "is almost like sailing blind."

On sailing downwind: "First I find the lowest place in the water. If the water is higher to port, I go to starboard. If it is higher to starboard. I go to port. I use the tiller to follow the water. There is always a hole, and it is best if you always sail down. I don't use the mainsheet so much as the tiller because the tiller works so much faster while planing. I would use the mainsheet if I could. but I'm an old man Some people pump while planing. I have never done this and I think I gain more by concentrating on putting the boat in the right place in the water so that I can continue planing."

On seamanship: "Seamanship. I like that word very much, for to me it is to do everything correctly on the sea. Racing is pure seamanship." One little bit of seamanship Elvström handed out will be useful to every sailor at least once: "When you are sailing in a storm so strong that you cannot stay up even with the sails luffing, pull up your centreboard and just drift."

12. So You Want To Start Sailing The Finn?

by Philippe Rogge

It is good to see so many new sailors joining our class every year. Some of them make it to the top of their potential fairly quickly - while for others it takes a little longer to get right. Having been around for a while one quite easily picks out the good Finn campaigns from the bad. So, what do you do if you want to start sailing the Finn seriously?

Fitness

I am not going to spend a lot of time on this subject as it is covered elsewhere, but your first and foremost investment should be in your physical fitness. Whatever hull, mast or sail you have the differences in the Finn between first and second, and between the men and the boys, are made at the end of that last beat when you've been hiking for so long you can't even think straight anymore. So make sure you invest plenty of time in physical training.

Boat

Let's start at the beginning. You need a boat. Nowadays it's fairly easy to find a good second hand boat. When I started in 1990 it was all a bit of a mystery. Some of the old Vanguards were reputed to be softer and better than the others (as proven by regatta results), and the new ones were too stiff. So you kind of had to get lucky. Nowadays, the boats have changed a lot. A number of new builders have entered the market (Devoti, Lemieux, Mader, Pata). Their models keep changing every couple of years. To figure out what the best

boats are, check what the top guys are using. They will have tried all the boats, so there is no need for you to do it again. One rule of thumb: 'Don't outsmart the fleet'. You don't want your sailing skills to be overshadowed by question marks about your boat, which is different from the top guys. Sure, you can get a good deal and yes, it probably was fast at some point, but be sensible and buy a boat like (or from) one of the top guys. When buying a second hand boat do check for damage and general hull condition. It may also be wise to ask which mould or generation the boat is, as all builders do change moulds from time to time.

Old or New?

New is more fun, but you'll pay a lot more for that extra shine. The boat construction and the materials used are so good that a cheap secondhand boat will still win races and is a perfect compromise to get started. Talk to top sailors (who will swap boats regularly for no apparent reason to you), your national Finn secretary and the boat builders to find that good deal. If you maintain it well, it'll provide years of good service.

Booms

Booms are fairly straightforward. For decades now, there's only been one boom (Needlespar, UK). It's a bit heavier than the rules allow, but most guys will be using those. There are a number of lighter booms (we're talking about a difference of about the weight of a can of

Coca Cola) out there, like Holt in the UK (with the advantage of 'head friendly' rounded corners), but there's no need to get carried away by those small differences when you're starting out. Focus on the basics.

Mast

Masts are a different story altogether - but again, don't outsmart the rest. Your best strategy is to buy a second hand mast from one of the top guys. Because these guys try so many masts all year round, they will also have 'lemons' (the ones that leave a sour taste in your mouth). You must make sure it's a mast that has actually been used in a big regatta. Major Championship stickers or stamps on a mast are usually a good sign. At that time, the guy thought it was a good enough mast to use. Just make sure that it's not from a previous generation. A mast measured in 1995 would already be from a previous generation (although I expect major mast developments to slow down).

Wing or Round?

I don't believe there's a major difference between them, but since most builders only build wings, you'll probably end up with a wing mast anyway. You will want to try it out with your sail. We'll get to the sails later, but your mast choice must be linked to sails. He may want to sell you one of his sails to go on the mast, and that would be a good solution. Anyway, put it up, try it out and ask him (and some others) for advice. You can always get a new sail made to the same specifications from the sail maker.

Stiff or soft?

It is difficult to give accurate advice on stiffness, as everything is so relative to your boat, your weight, your sail and the conditions you're going to be sailing in. If you do want advice, though, here's my theory. Unless you're only going to be sailing on small lakes, you need a mast which is stiff in the bottom (fore and aft and sideways). Moving up your mast, it should start getting softer sooner (especially sideways) if you're light or higher up if you're heavy. Masts which are soft fore and aft will not give you a lot of power through waves. Masts which are stiff sideways will be great for pointing, but once the breeze or chop picks up, you won't be able to open that leech and go fast.

So in short: stiff fore and aft (minimum 'normal rake' should not be less than 6.70 meters or you'll lose too much downwind) and softer sideways, depending on your weight. If you're a pure lake sailor, you can afford a mast that's softer fore and aft (and stiffer sideways). ('Stiff' and 'soft' are obviously all very relative. With the appearance of plastic sails, most older masts will be too soft for a plastic sail.)

Buying a New Mast

If you can't buy a mast from a top sailor, you could buy a new one. However, do make sure you buy it off one of the reputed mast makers. Tell them your weight and skill level and those guys will know what a good 'all round' mast is. Sure, your first mast will not be perfect in all conditions. Different masts and mast/sail combinations are better in different conditions. You need to try it out in all conditions to see what its 'range' is. Try to buy something which

is fairly 'all-round'. As a general rule I'd say: if you're going to be sailing on flat waters a lot, buy a mast which is stiff fore and aft and a flat sail. If you're planing to do a lot of racing on the sea or large inland waters, buy a somewhat softer mast with a fuller sail. The key here is 'all-round'. You'll have to get to know your mast for a while, and only then will it work for you. Don't expect it to go automatically from the word go.

Sails

Sail choice is as complex as mast choice. Whether you buy a second hand mast from a top sailor or a new one from a builder or sailing shop, always ask them what sails go well with that type of mast (it's always better to have a look at a regatta yourself). Have them measure your mast (or even better, do it yourself if you know how to) and send those numbers (and

the method they used to measure it) to a sailmaker who's used to working with mast deflection numbers. With computer technology now having entered the sailmaking business, most sailmakers will be able to help you out.

Most of the top sailors now have a working relationship with a sailmaker. That means that the major Finn sailmakers will have at least one guy in his loft who knows the class and what's going on. Call him for advice.

What sailmaker to choose? Well, as before, it will depend on your choice of mast and what type of waters you'll be sailing on. What sailcloth to use? With the recent development of 'plastic' or laminated sails, cloth choice can be difficult. Ask your sailmaker to get you an 'all round' sail which will get you through light drifter, medium choppy conditions and a strong breeze. You won't be the fastest in any conditions, but on average you should be up there.

Simple really. If you buy a sail and it doesn't really fit the mast, you need at least to get the luff curve (i.e. the amount of bend in the front part of your sail - the luff - when you put the sail flat on the ground) to fit the mast. If you don't know how to do it, ask advice from another sailor or from a sailmaker with experience in dinghy sailing. It can be hard to

get it right, but it does matter a lot. The old style soft Dacron is not very 'all round' anymore. If you're going to buy one sail, buy a plastic (or laminated) one or a very light yarn tampered 'new style' Dacron sail.

Care

Take good care of your equipment. Make sure you get strong covers. You should at least get a cover for your mast and a bottom cover for the boat (a top cover will prevent the gel coat from losing its colour when exposed to the sun). Also get a decent dolley and a good road trailer with adequate suspension.

It's good practice to put some extra foam or a mattress underneath your boat when travelling. Remove salt water from your boat after each sail and make sure the boat doesn't stay wet for long periods. This way you'll enjoy your investment to the full.

Learning from Others

Talk to other, more experienced sailors. Most sailors will be open for questions, and you can learn a lot. If you have a coach, he may know another guy he used to sail against who's a coach in the Finn nowadays. If you don't ask, you'll never get an answer. When travelling abroad at regattas, make arrangements to stay with other Finn sailors during events. You'll learn a lot about sailing, but also about what they do before and after sailing, concentration, food, fitness and relaxation.

Finally, let me share with you the secret to most failed start-ups. It's the guy who has a special arrangement with his local mast builder or sailmaker. He gets the equipment for free if he only uses that one. Remember the rule of thumb? Right. If you don't know what the Finn is about, you won't be learning about the developments of the best gear around and your local mast (or sail) maker won't be learning

a lot either. Leave it to the top guys to experiment. Or you'll never know how good you could have been if it hadn't been for those masts.

The Finn class is not only about the boat. It's about the people. You'll enjoy your sailing and make friends for life. Good sailing and remember, Rome wasn't built in a day!

13. The Finn - What Makes this Slow Boat So Fast?

by Jack Knights

Reprinted from Yachts and Yachting (c. 1960)

May I ask you to be patient whilst I attempt to explain that what is puzzling in practise is explicable in theory. First to dispose of the less important contributory factors. Most Finns are sailed by Olympic aspirants and are, accordingly, well sailed. Their helmsmen are fairly heavy, fairly fit and anxious to do as well as possible.

Second, the Finn hull is a good shape for windward sailing. It has none of that exaggerated pigeon-chestedness, which makes so many British dinghies such a handful in heavy weather. It has a noticeably fine entry, yet with no hollows and a fine exit. The stability-giving sections are where they belong - abreast of where the helmsman sits. Third, and getting warmer, the Finn-cat rig, for all that the mast looks as it it has just been felled in the forest, and the sail similar to the old 'leg o' mutton', is extremely efficient. All the published findings of those who study these matters scientifically, whether in theory or practise, bear this out.

It has been proved that any rigging increases the drag and hence the heeling moment of a rig. Also a revolving mast is demonstrably better than a fixed one because it brings the luff slot down to leeward and enables the all important wind, which blows over the lee side of the sail, to journey more smoothly around the mast and on to the sail. Now the Finn has no rigging and the mast revolves, if only a short way. This is why they seem so stiff and sail so upright when they are jammed hard up against the wind

Fourth, and most important of all - in fact, the raison d'etre for this article - is the cut of the sail, the lead of the sheet and the flexibility of mast and boom. These are grouped together because, as I shall show, they are interrelated. I used to think that the effectiveness of the bending mast for certain boats had never been proved in racing. Now I am willing to admit that the Finn has changed this view, for, without a doubt, any Finn with a stiff mast is at a disadvantage against the others.

The sheet of a Finn is arranged in such a way that it exerts a purely downward pull on the sail when on the wind. There is no inward pull at all. This fetches the head of the sail aft and

with it the mast truck. This, in turn, throws a deep bow into the whole mast and of course, flattens the sail. In this it is abetted by the behaviour of the boom. The mainsheet is led to the centre of the boom so that its pull tends to put a downward bend in the middle, so pulling out the fullness in the foot of the sail. As the boom is much deeper than it is wide, having the sheet in the middle means that the after-most end is allowed to fall off to leeward. Naturally it takes the clew and the leach of the sail with it. Now if you can visualise this sail in plan for a moment you will understand that this tendency has the effect of flattening the sail still further and feathering it more into the eye of the wind. The Finn sail is fuller than any other made for any other boat, particularly at the foot, where it forms a deep pocket just above the boom and so helps to prevent that efficiency sapping escape of wind from one side to the other. Yet, although it is so full, its sheet and spars enable it to be flattened so much that, eventually, it resembles almost completely, a flat plane.

Incidentally, it is worth mentioning in passing that it has been found that the most successful Finn sails are those which are very full at the bottom, but quite flat from mid-height upwards. There is a logical reason for this, which makes me feel that other dinghy classes could profit from it, particularly heavily canvassed classes. If one makes the top flat and the bottom full, the power of the sail is concentrated low down, where it is easiest to use. The boat is all the stiffer for it and the sail can be used in a much wider range of wind speeds.

Because of the sheet arrangement described, now universal in Finns, with a midships horse running the full width of the cockpit, the sail can be allowed to go much further out than is is normal in other craft when on the wind, without having to ease the sheet at all. This means that mast and boom stay bent and the sail flat, and in almost one plane This is the perfect set-up for controlled sailing to windward because it means that the sail can be set at a very fine angle to the apparent wind. It can be feathered, so to speak, so that in heavy weather the wind slips past it with a minimum of resistance and, hence, without causing very much heeling. Because the Finn is not forced over on her ear in these conditions,

she can retain a good grip of the water and preserve a fair underwater hull shape. Thus she foots fast and goes where she points, in spite of a small and inefficiently shaped centreplate.

Several things follow obviously from these observations. If one eases the sheet at any time when sailing to windward - and this becomes more important as the wind blows the harder - the whole system is spoilt. The boom is able to lift, the top of the mast is released and springs forward, and the fullness is thrown back into the sail. Thus a jamb cleat of some sort for the sheet is a great help, one by which one can really force down the boom until it is only just above the deck. It should only be necessary to release the sheet from its clutches when going about, and then only for safety and to enable the traveller to slide across and one's head to get under the boom.

Paul Elvström, it is true, did not use a cleat of any description, but he was exceptionally strong in hand and wrist, and anyway he said that the only reason he dispenses with one is in case his toestraps should break and he should be precipitated overboard. If this happens when the sheet is cleated, a capsize naturally follows. Few, however, would be prepared to put up with so much extra labour for the sake of a contingency so remote.

Naturally, a sharp look out has to be kept ahead for freeing puffs, so that the boat can be pointed into them and weaved away as they pass. This is why one seems to waggle the tiller so much in a Finn. Another point is that the mast should be able to begin bending from as low down as possible. This is because the fullness is mainly in the lower half of the sail.

14. Finn Memories

by Vernon Stratton

Looking back fifty years and trying to remember stories that haven't been written is not easy. I can't remember how many years I was Secretary or President of IFA let alone how long I looked after the production, advertising, photography and editorial of FINNFARE. Luckily I don't need a lot of sleep.

The one thing I do know is that the Finn, like the Star class, has always had a fantastic organisation that is prepared to move with the times and keep ahead. It is this that has kept it as an Olympic Class for so long. I also think it has something to do with going up the last beat of a Gold Cup course. Finn sailors never give up till it's over. At seventy one I still race all the winter in an Illusion (mini Twelve). I don't win anymore but I race against some the world's best sailors. What more can you ask for?

Memories
In 1950 I sailed in my first single handed open meeting in a Firefly, the 12 foot dinghy that was used for the 1948 Olympics at Torquay in England - the Class in which Paul Elvström won his first Gold Medal. He was really a Dragon sailor but was put in the Firefly Class because he was the youngest!

Martin Beale, the winner of that Firefly race, held in very strong conditions, came up to me afterwards and suggested that I bought a Finn. I think that this must have been because I had survived the race (by bailing with a saucepan on the end of a broomstick!) as most of the 48 entries were wiped out! So I bought one!

This was to change my life. I met Charles Currey one of the World's best dinghy sailors at the time and I met my wife Pepe. We all practised in Finns throughout the winter of '51, something that was unheard of at the time. Charles won the Silver medal and Pepe beat Stewart Morris, the Swallow Class gold medalist in the '48 Olympics, in the Olympic trials. Not a bad result for a girl and that was in the days before the bendy mast. Pepe and I were engaged by the Olympic Trials and were married in 1952.

The Finn that I bought was one of four built by the Tormentor Yacht Station and cost £150

Vernon Stratton sailing in the Solent in 1951

complete. Charles exploited the tolerances to the maximum, making them very fast boats rather like the Raudaschls in the sixties. Jack Knights eventually bought Charles' Finn and took it to the USA where he raced it very successfully. I believe it was used as the mould for the Newport Finns of Fred Miller fame. They were unbeatable until the measurer found lead in the floor!

Elvström at Zeebrugge
In the early fifties we used to race in Belgium at Zeebrugge, which was organised by the Commodore of the Royal Belgium Sailing Club. Travel was quite expensive and I used to pay for my trip by selling the latest invention made by a man called Mr Lewrie who worked out of an old wooden shed near the sea at Emsworth on the south coast of England. In those days he would make one offs for

dinghies. Who would have thought that that would have been the start of Lewmar the international company that now supplies the best yachts in the world.

I remember one year at Zeebrugge in early May it was freezing cold and blowing a gale from the north (it nearly always did). The course was set inside the harbour mole which gave us a beat in very hairy conditions then a reach along under the harbour wall and back for the jibe and run to a turning mark by the lock gates. This was the last race I ever reefed a Finn. It was quite easy in those days. All you had to do was pull the boom out of the slot in the mast roll up the sail on the boom and put it back using a claw for the main sheet and then stuff in the wedge, Charles Currey's invention, instead of a kicking strap.

Paul capsized before the start gun. I breathed a sigh of relief as I then only had Börge Schwarz to contend with. We had a great race. I was quicker on the wind and he flew on the run. The turning mark was his undoing because he got out of control and nearly went up the harbour wall by the lock gates. I survived the next round to win the race.

I came ashore full of confidence thinking that I would win the regatta, but not a bit of it. The super human Paul who was never beaten, swam his boat ashore, pulled it up the Harbour wall and emptied the boat. He went to his car and got out a dry mainsail, launched it again single handed and calmly sailed round the course under full sail while I was in the shower thinking I was the Regatta winner! He finished sixth and as so few boats had completed the course he thus got enough points to hold onto his lead. Elvström was unbeatable in those days to such a extent that he used to get angry with himself if he only won six of a seven race series. Go home and train so that he was better!

I did beat him once! That was on the Lymington river when he took a short cut and didn't notice the ferry coming in so he was blanketed and had to wait until it had gone. Hardly a glorious win for me, but I did beat him. In those days one had to clutch at anything to boost one's morale.

Finn Gold Cup Starts
In 1956 I thought the class should have a World Championship and we were lucky enough to have in England a man of incredible generosity. Tiny Mitchell was a big man in every sense. He had built ten Finns for our Olympic Trials so that the top twenty dinghy sailors in the country could practice. I felt that he was the man to approach. I felt that we should give the type of hospitality that we were given when abroad. The net result was that all overseas entries were given financial help to come to this country, free transport when the boat arrived, and a trip to the Palladium in London to the best show in town.

The only snag was that the racing had to be held at his favourite Club at Burnham-on-Crouch at Easter. This was not the ideal venue as it was impossible to get an Olympic course. Andre Nelis won the regatta, Paul was second, it snowed, Pepe got locked out of the Hotel in her night dress walking the dog and I remember sitting on my boat upside down with the mast stuck in the mud. It was a great start to one of the most difficult Cups to win in sailing.

Elvström in Copenhagen
The Finn Gold Cup in 1959 was the biggest entry on record to that date, we also held a record number of starts for the Regatta - twenty nine! You don't have to ask who won, Paul of course with his secret weapon. I remember

UK Finns gather at Cowes in 1952

it so well before the start of the practice race (Oh yes, he had to win that too!) I was watching Paul, when suddenly I thought he had fallen out of the boat backwards he then surfaced shook his head and went in to the start. That was the start of heavy jackets. Once we realised what he was up to we all went mad with more and more layers of towelling to try and get heavier than Paul's sweaters.

1960 Gold Cup
I still have the string sweater that I used to help win the 1960 Gold Cup in Torquay against the Norwegian giant Harold Bredo Eriksen. The other reason why I won was because I had a new mitre cut Dacron sail from Hans Fogh. Andre Nelis was using a cotton sail. In those days the deed of gift was that the Gold Cup should be held in the UK in the Olympic year to give us an advantage and save travel costs.

1968 Gold Cup
That was the year the tide went out! It was also the year I started my business so sailing was out. I was however on the International Race Committee as President of IFA. I was sent for and hastily motored down from London to hear the protests against the day's race. There had been delays because of lack of wind and the race had gone on a long time. I listened to reports of Finns getting caught the wrong side of sandbanks and helmsmen having to take off their fixed rudders to cross the finishing line. The final straw was when the linesman on the far end of the finishing line reported that he stepped over the side and walked back to the Committee boat. Those were the days! and that was the end of Gold Cups in Britain every four years.

UK Olympic Trials in 1952
John Oakley (left) and Vernon Stratton (right)

Gilbert Lamboley

Gilbert will go down in the history of yacht racing as the man who invented the method of measuring weight distribution and thus keep a one design class equal. It is the pure simplicity that shows a man's genius and simple it is. Anyone who has helped measure a Finn at a World Championship will agree. Gilbert was running his own business and gave up too much time to the Finn class. He completely rewrote the rules of the class and it is through his work that we are still an Olympic Class.

A funny story. We went to the Finn Veterans in the South of France in 1974. Both Gilbert and I were surprised by the speed of one of the French sailors. We discovered that he had got his mast from the National Team and it was very fast. We then heard that the team coach had been to Needlespar and tested 200 masts to select six. We had to find out why they were different, so in the middle of the night after a good dinner we did the weight test on the mast.

Sure enough it was different, so when Gilbert was next in England we bought a new Needlespar, measured it and then proceeded to make it perform to the magic measurements. We found two large planks of wood and proceeded to hammer them with a sledge hammer until the figures were the same! A test race proved the French knew what they were doing - it was fast! 'Don't try this at home' as the TV programme says, as it

Richard Creagh-Osborne (K 7) and Jeremy Rogers (K 77)
Photo by Vernon Stratton

wouldn't get you very far with carbon fibre. It does prove however that the correct mast bend is what makes the boat go.

Jörg Bruder had a magic wooden mast. He tested 250 of his own masts against it, it was always faster. After two Gold Cups he sold it to Patrick de Barros.

This story is what inspired me to recommend to the German Olympic organisers in 1971 that a metal mast was the most likely innovation to give the fairest racing as they were more likely to be all the same.

1973 Gold Cup
I remember driving to Brest and passing the Brazilian Finns being double trailed along the road. It was moments later that I heard on the radio that a Brazilian plane had just crashed coming into Paris. I immediately said to Pepe that I pray to God that Jörg Bruder is not on that plane. He was and with the Gold Cup. What a tragedy. He was one of the finest sailors I'll ever know. He was so modest so kind and helpful to everyone and a brilliant sailor. I shall never forget him. That was the year that I was allowed to sail with a new double bottom Finn as a test to see if they should be allowed into the class. It passed the Lamboley test and it didn't seem to make a difference to performance. Now we all have double bottoms, a long way from the original Finns with no buoyancy at all.

1977 Weymouth Olympic Week
Still racing and just about to be fifty. I can't remember where I finished the week but I wasn't doing too badly for an old man till one day I capsized with my heavy jacket on. I had always been against them and had persuaded Gilbert Lamboley to do a paper for the IYRU (ISAF now). They had listened and put on a

weight limit, but not enough in my view. Well I couldn't get back in the boat even after taking it off. As there were quite a lot of capsizes that day I had to wait. This gave me time to think about what I was doing at my age, especially as I was Chairman of the Olympic Committee and manager of the team. It is one thing capsizing when you are young; old men should realise that they can be a liability. It was at this moment that I decided to give up racing a Finn - my love for twenty six years. Pepe could see that I was very upset by my decision so decided that I should have an early fiftieth birthday present, a Star. So I started a new love affair that lead to a Gold Medal in Korea - not for me but for Bryn Vaile my Star crew and ex Finn sailor.

15. Psychology

by Paul Elvström   Reprinted from 'Expert Dinghy Racing'

You must take great pains to keep clear and calm during racing. Psychological upsets can cause you great trouble and may make you do stupid things which you know you ought not to have done.

If you are racing against another competitor whom you believe to be better than yourself, then you must try to force yourself not to think of this. If he is sailing just a little bit faster you must say to yourself. "Ah well! This is just happening at this moment; shortly it will be my turn to go faster." You should concentrate on this. It is quite clear, however, that if he is sailing twice as fast then there is nothing much that you can do. Even if you have heard that this helmsman sails very fast and has won a great many races, you must still never think about it. You must concentrate only on the race which you are in, and you must always think what is the right thing to do and not consider that the other competitor might eventually beat you. I have too often had an easy victory when an opponent has allowed me to pass through an inferiority complex and without giving me a battle.

When you enter for a points series it is very important to show your worth during the previous practice races. When you are entering for an important series of races you ought to arrive two days in advance, sail round the course, tune up your boat and mast so that everything is ready for the start. Whilst you are practising and if you are sailing in company with some of the other top class competitors, you must try to sail as fast as you possibly can. This will look impressive to the others and they may finally get a complex about you.

My cleverest and most dangerous opponent, Andre Nelis, and I trained together for the Olympics in Melbourne, and I did everything I could to pass him all the time, and I was able to do this quite easily. He was so shaken by this that one day when we were at the Stadium he came and spoke to me saying. "Paul, I think that you will win your third Gold Medal." As soon as he said that I realised that he had got an inferiority complex about me and I said to myself, "Now I know I can win." I am sure that when a man has an inferiority complex his sailing will immediately suffer. There is another very important psychological fact in

hard racing. You must keep up your spirits and I always say to myself when I am getting to the end of a very long beat and am very sore in the legs through hanging out. "The others are just as sore as I am and the sooner I reach the mark the shorter time I will have to hang out. I must hold out for as long as I possibly can." If you are behind in the fleet and are very tired you must think that the others are also tired and say to yourself, "Hold on! Hold on! There is a chance that the others will give up, if they see that I am still holding out."

If your boat is travelling well you must never give up, however much bad luck you may have during the race. If you are unlucky at the start you must say to yourself, "I must still do absolutely the right thing, and go the way that I know is fastest." You must under no circumstances get flustered or take a chance, or make a hundred short tacks in order to try to gain a small amount - never do the opposite of what the leading boats are doing in the hope that you might pick up a little distance. If you are sure the leading boats are going the right way, and by this I am particularly thinking of beating to windward, then all you have to do is to follow them.

Should there come a moment when the leading boats take a wrong course, then you should go in the direction which you know to be right. By this means in a long race you may be able to get closer and closer to the leading boats and eventually have a chance to pass them.

It is very important to train yourself to recognise the difference between good and bad luck, and also skill and good fortune. If competitors in front of you have been lucky, for instance, with favourable windshifts, you must be very careful not to allow this to influence you in future races. On the other hand, if this happened to you, you must tell yourself that you won by good fortune and do not start the second race saying to yourself, "I won the previous race and therefore I ought to win this one." Instead, say to yourself, "The last race was a washout. I won by luck. Now I must concentrate 100% on the new race in order to prove to myself that I am faster than the others." When going to windward you often see another competitor going off on his own hoping that he can pick up a lucky windshift in order to take the lead - this is pure chance-racing. In 99.9 % of cases he will lose.

On the run it often happens that the bad sailors keep clear of the better sailors, in order not to interfere with them. To the bad sailors I would say they should never do such a thing. You should always do everything you possibly can, and this is the only way to improve.

16. John Bertrand on Boat Speed

by John Bertrand

Reprinted from FINNFARE April 1977

We have discovered on the Finn that outhaul tension is critical to pointing ability. I first observed it when my friend Thomas Jungblut and I were testing some new Finn sails in Milwaukee. As with all momentous discoveries we came across it purely by accident. After developing a sail which proved to be very good in winds above 15 mph we were about to give up hoping it would succeed in being versatile, and therefore fast in the 8-15 mph range.

Sailing back to harbour after a solid day of sail testing with another boat, my outhaul came untied and the sail slipped in about 5". We did a final test on the wind and discovered that the sail which had previously lacked speed and pointing ability through the chop had excellent characteristics. The rig literally came alive and for the first time this fast heavy air sail was able to hang in there in the light winds and choppy water.

We subsequently took photographs of the resulting sail shapes at different outhaul settings and then began to appreciate how significant an outhaul can be. By easing the outhaul, the sail particularly in the bottom half, increases in depth in a circular fashion up to 50 % The whole secret was to start off with a sail relatively flat in the bottom, i.e. a heavy wind type sail and progressively ease in when more power was required. Easing the outhaul on an already full sail will make the sail over full, set up too much drag and the result is slow.

So we essentially discovered that by starting off with a heavy air type sail, by playing with the outhaul we were able to be very competitive in the medium air. This was significant because it seems impossible to go the other way and make a good medium air sail highly competitive in fresh winds. We then increased the foot mound to such an extent that we essentially had a loose footed sail except we retained the end plate effect.

Gus Miller, the then 42 year old Finn sailor from Ann Arbor/Michigan took it one step

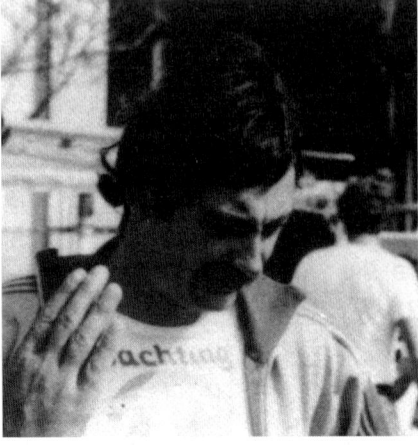

further and started to have a good hard look at the other sail shape controls on the Finn rig. He discovered that the inhaul was also a critical adjustment as well, although not so obvious at first. By designing the tack with a cut away of about 3 inches and having a control line attached to the tack leading forward to the gooseneck and back to the side tank, the position of the tack could be easily adjusted.

wind	smooth water			rough water		
Beaufort	**outhaul**	**inhaul**	**cunningham**	**outhaul**	**inhaul**	**Cunningham**
0-1	5.0 cm	off	off	7.5 cm	off	off
1-2	5.0 cm	off	off	10.0 cm	neutral	neutral
2	7.5 cm	neutral	off	12.5 cm	neutral	neutral
3-4	5.0 cm	neutral	neutral	12.5 cm	on	neural
4-5	2.5 cm	neutral	on	5.0 cm	on	on
+ 5	0	on	on	2.5 cm	on	on

Again it seems there is nothing new in sailing, it only remains for us to discover them over again and indeed the great Paul Elvström had cut away tacks back in the late 50's. But unfortunately he didn't tell me or Gus anything about them, so it was up to Gus to lead the way. Anyway Gus found that by pulling the tack towards the mast the bottom batten angle in particular was changed. We call this the lower exhaust angle of the sail and if we know one thing, the lower batten angle really has a large effect on weather helm. Have the bottom batten closed and the rig develops helm, open the batten and the helm goes neutral. So when Gus wanted more weather helm to point he would immediately ease off the tack inhaul. If he wanted more speed or had trouble steering he would pull the tack closer to the mast to neutralise his helm.

He then had a good hard look at what the cunningham did. Any book will tell you that increased cunningham tension will move the draft forward in the sail and open the leech. We found, however, that it has a huge effect particularly in the upper half. That is, cunningham tension opened up the upper batten area but did not alter very significantly the lower batten angle.

Because the upper part of the leech is relatively close to the pivot axis of the boat, the exhaust angle of the leech does not change the helm all that much. However it has a huge influence on heeling moment, so when Gus' legs would give out (he is 42 you know) he would pull down on his cunningham which would free the upper leech, and therefore reduce heeling moment. If he then had pointing problems, he would ease the tack out away from the mast to close the lower battens and inject more weather helm into the boat. Let me say Gus was fast and it was obvious he was onto something. A couple of Finn parties later, I had all the information I needed. Gus was never one for keeping secrets anyway.

Summary

Outhaul: changes curvature particularly in lower half. For smooth water, the lower camber can be on the flat side, but in rough water more curvature is required, therefore the outhaul is eased in. The outhaul adjustment was used just as much as mainsheet tension and traveller on the Finn.

Inhaul: If pointing ability was lacking the tack is eased away from the mast. This closes the lower batten plus it makes the leading edge of the sail finer off the mast.

Cunningham: If heeling moment was no problem, very little cunningham was used - just to clear up excess wrinkles off the mast. As soon as the boat became overpowered excessive cunningham is used to open the upper leech.

17. History of the Finn Gold Cup

by Peter Mohilla and Robert Deaves

Reprint from FINNLOG

Until 1956, the centre of Finn sailing was in the Scandinavian countries, mainly Sweden. Other countries introduced a few Finn dinghies only because it was used at the Olympic Games in order to give their top single-handed helmsmen an opportunity to become familiar with the peculiarities of the Finn. One of these nations was the United Kingdom where the first privately owned Finns were built as early as 1951. The driving force were the Stratton brothers Vernon and Desmond.

In 1956 Vernon Stratton, later to become editor of Finnfare, secretary and finally president of the IFA, induced F.G. Mitchell of the Royal Corinthian Yacht Club, Burnham-on-Crouch (Great Britain) to present a Gold Cup to the Finn Class. This Gold Cup was to be held for one year by the winner of a competition that quickly turned into the World Championship of the Finn Class. Originally the Gold Cup was intended by the donor to be organised once every four years in Great Britain.

The first Gold Cup took place in Burnham at the club of F.G. Mitchell in 1956. Four and eight years later it was sailed in Torquay UK. In 1968 it was organised in Kent UK, an unsuitable area with very strong tide and currents, which caused strong opposition by many nations to organise it once every four years in Great Britain any more. Instead it was decided to have it at least once every four years outside of Europe. Thus the event was staged in Bermuda in 1969, in Toronto, Canada in 1971, in Long Beach, USA in 1974, in Brisbane, Australia in 1976. Manzanillo, Mexico 1978, Auckland, New Zealand 1980, Milwaukee, USA 1983, Ilha Bela, Brazil 1988, Kingston, Canada 1991 and Melbourne, Australia in 1995 and 1999.

In 1970 at Cascais, Portugal, Jörg Bruder of Brazil won the Cup over the largest Finn fleet ever gathered (180 boats) and defended it successfully in 1971 at Toronto, Canada and Anzio, Italy in 1972. On his way to Brest, France where he was to defend the Cup once more, fate decided that he would remain unbeaten forever. Bruder died in an air crash on July 11th, 1973 and the original Gold Cup was lost.

In 1975 Gilbert Lamboley induced Somms Marine, a French Company which is well known for its support of Yachting, to donate a replica of the Cup. The contract that passed between this company and the representative of the Class, created only discrete obligations on the Class. It was approved by the IYRU. The rules for the championship and for the final destiny of the Cup remained unchanged.

The Gold Cup is the most important part of the history of the Finn Class. The formation of the IFA on August 23, 1956 in Loosdrecht, Holland was strongly influenced by the first Gold Cup in March/April 1956 at Burnham-on-Crouch, England. From then on the Annual General Meeting of the IFA was generally held at the time and place of the Gold Cup. Therefore the sporting and administrative climax of each year coincided at the Gold Cups. Also the Gold Cup races, together with the European Championships, turned out to be the best indicator for any new technical development of the Finn Class.

In the beginning there was no limitation of numbers of entries to the Gold Cup. Because of the difficulties at the starting lines in 1961 and 1962, the number of participants in the

1963 Gold Cup in Medemblik was limited to 15 boats per nation. In 1964 at Torquay there were 10 entries per nation allowed. In 1964 the idea was considered to have the Gold Cup divided into two weeks of racing, one week of eliminations and a second week with those qualified, but the idea was finally rejected. By 1965 it was agreed to allow again 15 boats per nation. In 1969 in Bermuda a new regulation was decided upon. A basic quota of 3 boats was granted to each member country, plus 1 entry for each 25 paid IFA dues, up to a maximum of 15 boats per nation. In 1971 this system was altered, the minimum being 2 boats per nation.

In 1973 the IYRU tried to reduce the number of entries to 60 boats but the IFA refused. The system remained unchanged and national secretaries were allowed to enter above the national quota in addition. By 1974 it was agreed, that the top 10 individual finishers of the previous Gold Cup are allowed to enter above the national quota. The proportional system, relating number of paid IFA dues to the number of entries to the Gold Cup and the European Championship was changed again in 1977. By 1978 the IYRU tried again to enforce a limitation of 60 boats, but the IFA decided it would try to find a way to circumvent this rule.

The Finn Gold Cup

The boats at the 1956 Gold Cup. In the centre, Paul Elvström's Bess

In 1980 the proportions between number of IFA fees paid and number of entries allowed was changed once again. In 1982 it was decided that the number of places should be linked to the average number of the fees paid for in the last three years. Later this was changed back to the fees paid in the current year only. In 1997 a 'Rookie' place was introduced, available to any helm from a paid up nation who had never competed in a Gold Cup or Europeans before.

In the first 5 Gold Cups 1956-1960 only wooden boats were allowed. When GRP was permitted in 1961 and plastic boats ended up 1st, 2nd and 3rd, the Finn class ran into a severe crisis. Many owners of older wooden boats were afraid that their equipment had been totally outmoded. In addition Arne Akerson won the 1962 event with the boat of Fred Miller jr., which Rickard Sarby found to behave very different from an ordinary Finn dinghy in waves. The measurement committee of the 1962 Gold Cup found several kilos of hidden lead in that magic boat, a fact which raised further objections against plastic boats. It was felt, that it was too easy to cheat in GRP. Then in 1964 Hubert Raudaschl won the Gold Cup in his home made wooden boat and thus turned back the wheel of Finn development for almost a decade. After two years of experimenting with his own GRP development, Willy Kuhweide bought back his old wooden Finn and won the Gold Cup twice. After Raudaschl and Kuhweide, the late Jörg Bruder also used wooden hulls to demonstrate the qualities of this traditional material.

In the mid seventies GRP hulls with soft wooden decks proved to be most successful. Then from the late seventies, full GRP hulls, mainly Vanguards, were dominant in Gold Cups. In the early nineties, the arrival of a variety of modern well thought out hulls broke the Vanguard monopoly. Lawrence Lemieux developed his own hulls (which Hans Spitzauer won the 1995 Gold Cup in), Pata Boats from Hungary also brought out a new hull, but the most dominant numerically was the Devoti, which first won the Gold Cup in 1993 with Philippe Presti helming. Developed by Tim Tavinor and Luca Devoti, the hull was chosen for the 1996 Olympics in Savannah and has virtually dominated the Finn fleet ever since.

With regard to masts the development was less confusing. The traditional wooden masts

F. R. 'Tiny' Mitchell

were outmoded by special wooden Bruder spars by 1969. In that same year Jack Knights showed up with an aluminium spar at the Gold Cup in Bermuda for the first time. In 1972 Jörg Bruder himself won the Gold Cup with his own aluminium mast. From then on only aluminium masts were used by the winners of the Gold Cup, and Needlespar masts gained a complete domination of the Finn market. When carbon was first allowed in 1993, masts made from this new material soon found popularity as well as boatspeed. Within a short time virtually all competitors were using carbon masts. In 1995 Hans Spitzauer was the first sailor to win the Gold Cup with a wing mast.

With regard to sails, up to 1959 only cotton was allowed. Thereafter Dacron was used exclusively. In the late sixties Raudaschl sails dominated Finn events in combination with Bruder masts. In the late seventies early eighties North sails gained a similar dominance which lasted through to the nineties. In 1998, modern materials such as Kevlar, Mylar, polyester and even monofilm were starting to be used and it wasn't long before sails made from these new 'hard' cloths were dominant on the water as well as in numbers.

Outstanding individuals in the history of the Gold Cup are:
Jörg Bruder of Brazil won the Cup three times consecutively in 1970/1971/1972 and was second in 1966 and 1969, Willy Kuhweide of FRG three times in 1963/1966/1967, Lasse Hjortnäs three times in 1982/1984/1985. Andre Nelis of Belgium won the Cup twice in 1956/1961, was second three times in 1958/1959/1960, and third twice in 1957/1962, thus he finished seven years among the top three. Fredrik Lööf has so far won the Gold Cup three times, in 1994/1997/1999, was second in 1993/1995/1998 and was third in 1996, and therefore is the most successful participant in the Finn Gold Cup up to the present time.

F.R. 'Tiny' Mitchell, donor of the Finn Gold Cup, died in England during November, 1962. Until he presented the Gold Cup, in 1956, upon the suggestion of Vernon Stratton, there was no real basis for the International Finn Class although many boats existed in several countries. There is no question that the Cup and its deed of gift were the first instruments which in fact created the IFA, as it brought all nations together for a week of meeting and racing. Without 'Tiny' Mitchell, it is not believed that Finn racing would be on such a firm footing internationally as it is now.

1. Gold Cup 1956

Burnham, England, March 29-April 2
45 entries from 12 countries

The first Gold Cup was sailed over Easter 1956 in Burnham-on-Crouch in Great Britain. It already attracted 45 entries from 12 countries. This first Gold Cup was won by the Belgian, Andre Nelis with 7343 points in accordance with the old Olympic scoring system, who was thus able to beat by 1491 points the great Paul Elvström who had 5852. Third was Brian Roswell from Great Britain with 4597 points. Nelis had won 2 races, Elvström 1, and another Englishman Bruce Banks 2 more. A sixth race was not counted, because the time limit had expired.

Final Results Gold Cup 1956

1.	Andre Nelis	B	7343
2.	Paul Elvström	D	5852
3.	Brian Roswell	K	4597
4.	Börge Schwarz	D	4546
5.	A. Svenson	S	4229
6.	J. M. de Yong	H	4065
7	Richard Murray	K	3681
8.	Bruce Banks	K	3555
9.	Vernon Stratton	K	3433
10.	Jack Knights	K	3257
11.	Richard Creagh-Osborne	K	3199
12.	Dijkors	H	2919
13.	Bengt Hornevall	S	2799
14.	Rinze Koopmans	H	2758
15.	Jerome Harinkouck	F	2678

Above: Winner in 1956, Andre Nelis from Belgium

Below: Racing in 1956 Runner-up, Paul Elvström in D 6

2. Gold Cup 1957

Karlstad, Sweden, July 3 -August 4
78 entries from 13 countries

The second event was organised on the huge Lake Vänersee in western Sweden by the later president of the IFA Bengt Hornevall of the Karlstads Kanotförening. The sailing area with many little islands offered a beautiful unique setting but caused extremely shifty wind conditions. 13 nations had sent 78 participants, which was exceptionally high for the standards of the fifties. But to the surprise of the experts in yachting in those days the Finn Class exposed a high performance level, developing special skills at the starts. Since there was no limitation of participants in those days, every nation sent all its best sailors and the mood was exceptionally friendly. Not a single protest was lodged. The winner Jürgen Vogler was lucky, because Andre Nelis, winner in 1956, broke his mast step in the fourth race while leading. Harald Bredo Eriksen of Norway, later president of the IFA, scored two firsts and was leading the last race, when an unpredictable wind shift caused him to finish third and therefore second overall. In addition the second participant from the German Democratic Republic, Wegener, gave another 126 points to Jorgen Vogler as a gift, by waiting for his team mate at the finishing line. Defender Nelis was finally third. Bert Sarby, nephew of the designer Rickard Sarby finished 8th as the best Swedish sailor and the designer of the Finn finished 11th. The British performed surprisingly well on the reaches.

Final Results Gold Cup 1957

1.	Jürgen Vogler	DDR 16	7650
2.	Harald Bredo Eriksen	N 25	7350
3.	Andre Nelis	B 24	7270
4.	Karel Warburg	H 30	5948
5.	K.H. Källström	L 45	5852
6.	Wim Maarse	H 33	5235
7.	Börge Schwarz	D 6	5192
8.	Bert Sarby	S 101	5191
9.	Richard Murray	K 18	5181
10.	Erik Rundström	N 23	5024
11.	Rickard Sarby	S 118	4916
12.	R. Frändestam	S 100	4635
13.	H. Andersson	S 97	4453
14.	Bjorn Rosen	S 90	4257
15.	Derrick Pitts-Pitts	K 6	4250
16.	Leo Gerhards	H 37	4232
17.	K.H. Wegener	DDR 6	4052
18.	E. Stadig	L 13	3984
19.	Hans Sleeswijk	H 35	3976
20.	Arne Baltscheffsky	L 51	3796
21.	A. Svensson	S 39	3698
22.	Rinze Koopmans	H 45	3454
23.	Jerome Harinkouck	F 41	3268
24.	Curd Ochwadt	G 11	3077
25.	S. Lückner	S 111	2988

Left: Close racing at the 1957 Gold Cup

3. Gold Cup 1958

Zeebrugge, Belgium, May 1-4
84 entries from 15 countries

As all participants were invited for food and lodging, 94 entries from 15 countries reached the organiser. 84 boats finally started. The conditions were extremely tough. The harbour was covered by a thick layer of oil and tides of six meters created strong currents. A start at low tide resulted in a water depth of 50 cm. Winds varied from Beaufort 0 to 6. Once, in extremely light winds only 17 boats reached the finishing line within the time limit, while the rest drifted up to 4 kilometres away from the finishing line in the strong ebb stream. Even Andre Nelis, leading up to the last race overall, drifted away, finished 65th, and lost the Gold Cup. Paul Elvström, 11th after 3 races, won the last 3 races and thus the title. In the 4th race more than 40 boats capsized, most of them at the gybe mark. Many of them were unable to right their boat, had to abandon it, and found it back on the shore wrecked for good. Nevertheless the mood among the participants was excellent.

Final Results Gold Cup 1958

1.	Paul Elvström	D	8432
2.	Andre Nelis	B	7315
3.	Adelchi Pelaschier	I	7072
4.	Karel Warburg	H	6638
5.	Richard Creagh-Osborne	K	6088
6.	Jürgen Vogler	DDR	5652
7.	Lemoine	F	5285
8.	Erik Rudström	N	5197
9.	de Jong	H	4991
10.	Peter Danby	K	4921
11.	Hans Sleeswijk	H	4747
12.	P. Gorelikov	SR	4437
13.	Barton	K	4251
14.	Philippe Harinkouck	F	4194
15.	Bert Sarby	S	4123
16.	Auclair	F	3764
17.	Nielsen	B	3650
18.	Jacques Gillard	B	3642
19.	Börge Schwarz	D	3617
20.	Bernhard Straubinger	G	3449
21.	Jannich	G	
22.	Kammerer	G	
23.	Jerome Harinkouck	F	
24.	Eriksen	N	
25.	Bill Dotsch	B	
26.	Prost	F	
27.	Roger	K	
28.	Wim Maarse	H	

4. Gold Cup 1959

Hellerup, Denmark, August 4-9
109 entries from 18 countries

Paul Elvström had taken the Gold Cup home to Denmark and organised the 1959 event in Hellerup. 119 boats from 18 countries entered, 109 started in the first race, and caused up to 8 General Recalls. Elvström won the practice race, races 1, 3, 4 (with 4 minutes over the next boat) and 6, and was second in race 5 arriving 10 seconds after Andre Nelis. Finally Paul had a lead of 2600 points over Nelis in second place. In race 6 for the first time in the history of the Gold Cup the strict 5 minute rule was in force. There was not a single premature starter, but after only 12 seconds the entire fleet was across the line, proving the extremely high standard of Finn sailing only 10 years after the design of the boat. The final results reflect the division of the Class into one superhuman and a bunch of tough but ordinary sailors. Nevertheless Paul was angry, that he had not won all the individual races but only four of them.

Final Results Gold Cup 1959

1.	Paul Elvström	D	10579
2.	Andre Nelis	B	7972
3.	Pierre Poullain	F	7216
4.	Jürgen Vogler	DDR	6826
5.	R. Frändestam	S	6494
6.	Hans Sleeswijk	H	6462
7.	Alexander Chuchelov	SR	6444
8.	Jan Olov Stork		6393
9.	Yves-Louis Pinaud	F	6232
10.	Borge Schwarz	D	5802
11.	Henning Wind	D	5700
12.	Leo Gerhards	H	5603
13.	Erik Rüdstrom	N	5106
14.	Richard Creagh-Osborne	K	5076
15.	Harald Bredo Eriksen	N	5041
16.	Keith Musto	K	4941
17.	Vernon Stratton	K	4917
18.	Wim Maarse	H	4865
19.	Hans Gerhard Flint	G	4723
20.	Adelchi Pelaschier	I	4652

Paul Elvström's perfect start in the 5th race of the 1959 Gold Cup

5. Gold Cup 1960

Torquay, England, June 4-10
38 entries from 7 countries

In accordance with the sponsor's wishes the event had to be staged in Great Britain in 1960. The date was in conflict with Kiel Week and the preparation of many nations for the Olympics. Vernon Stratton took advantage of the circumstances and won the Cup against 19 foreigners from 6 nations and 18 British competitors. Elvström did not defend his title but concentrated upon his preparations for the Olympics.

Gold Cup Winner 1960 Vernon Stratton

Final Results Gold Cup 1960

1.	Vernon Stratton	K	7979
2.	Andre Nelis	B	7132
3.	Desmond Stratton	K	6060
4.	Harald Bredo Eriksen	N	5935
5.	R. Creagh-Osborne	K	5591
6.	Hans Sleeswijk	H	5046
7.	Keith Musto	K	4834
8.	Richard Murray	K	4673
9.	Per Jordbakke	N	
10.	Peter Danby	K	

Andre Nelis   **Fred Miller**

Gold Cup Winner 1962 Arne Akerson

6. Gold Cup 1961

Travemünde, Federal Republic of Germany
August 14-19, 109 entries from 17 countries

Wind conditions in the Bay of Lübeck were excellent but the political climate frosty. The organiser did not allow the participants from the German Democratic Republic to fly their flag and therefore they remained ashore. The Russians took advantage of that misery and borrowed the unused boats, because their own crafts had gone astray somewhere between east and west. With Paul Elvström absent, the victory of Andre Nelis was certain by the end of the 4th race. Hans Fogh, silver medalist in the FD in Naples, established himself by winning the practice race. He convinced the fleet, that he had no intention to leave without the cup. Fred Miller, the first editor of FINNFARE, was the first participant in any Gold Cup from the US and finished third. He had the best equipment and speed of the entire fleet but poor tactics. Andre Nelis used a very simple plastic boat, the first plastic boat to win the Gold Cup. The fact, that the first three boats were made from GRP shocked the Class.

Final Results Gold Cup 1961

1.	Andre Nelis	B 24	10088
2.	Hans Fogh	D 11	8093
3.	Fred Miller	US 90	7444
4.	Vernon Stratton	K 44	7261
5.	Bjorn Rosen	S 250	6682
6.	Goran Andersson	S 144	6583
7.	Willy Kuhweide	G 303	6261
8.	Herbert Reich	G 142	6138
9.	B. Straubinger	G 16	5988
10.	Bernt Andersson	S 225	5900
11.	H.B. Reist	Z 99	5357
12.	Bruce McCurrach	SA 50	5314
13.	Per Jordbakke	N 19	5219
14.	Lennart Wallin	S 276	5046
15.	Peter Stulcken	G 235	5041
16.	Wim Maarse	H 115	4800
17.	Hans Sleeswijk	H 125	4652
18.	Jacqui Rogge	B 13	4648
19.	Per Werenskiold	N 25	4648
20.	Gerald Leverland	H 80	4574
21.	U. Jornmark	N	4318
22.	P. Josephsen	D	4274
23.	Kurt Ladendorf	G	4122
24.	Rudolf Ugelstad	N	3980
25.	D. Wayboer	H	3970
26.	Jouki Valli	L	3859
27.	H. Schuldt	G	3852
28.	H. Andersson	S	3696
29.	Dirdira	SR	3642
30.	P. Gorelikov	SR	3474
31.	Nicolino Fago	I	3386
32.	Peter Canham	K	3297
33.	O.M. Johannussen	N	3285
34.	I. R.W. van Noordt	H	3238
35.	Arne Akerson	S	3229

7. Gold Cup 1962

Tonsberg, Norway, August 6-11
133 entries from 16 countries

In 1962 the Finns gathered once again in Sweden for a Gold Cup. 133 actual starters from 16 countries lined up, the biggest fleet up to that time in any yachting event. The Swedish dominated the fleet, winning four of the five races. Arne Akerson had bought the plastic Newport which Fred Miller had brought from the US and sailed to 3rd place in Travemünde in 1961. Arne even used Fred's sail, mast and boom. Measuring that boat the committee had found several kilos of lead built into the bottom and forced Arne to take it out and place it under the deck. For the rest the top positions were dominated by Elvström boats. The Finn fleet was shocked by the outstanding performance of the GRP hulls. As a result the newly elected president of the IFA Harald Bredo Eriksen of Norway initiated a Technical Committee, which was supposed to work out a new set of rules, controlling wooden boats as well as plastic GRP hulls. The winds at the Gold Cup were strong, the waves tremendous, the committee boat not anchored, the starts a battlefield, but the racing great. The winner was not decided until the last beat of the last race.

The fleet in 1963

**Top three in 1962 - Andre Nelis,
Arne Akerson, Boris Jabobsson**

Final Results Gold Cup 1962

1.	Arne Akerson	S	7415
2.	Boris Jacobsson	S	6570
3.	Andre Nelis	B	6555
4.	Henning Wind	D	6142
5.	Hans Fogh	D	5774
6.	Bernt Andersson	S	5581
7.	Jouki Valli	L	5482
8.	Richard Creagh-Osborne	K	5348
9.	Roar Larsen	N	5211
10.	Harald Bredo Eriksen	N	4968
11.	A. Chuchelov	SR	4 731
12.	Rudolf Uglestad	N	4 730
13.	J.C. Jammes	F	4721
14.	Bernhard Reist	Z	4535
15.	Ulrich Libor	G	4306
16.	Bjorn Rosen	S	4215
17.	Gunnar Dahlgaard	D	4044
18.	Adelchi Pelaschier	I	4044
19.	Vernon Stratton	K	4039
20.	H. Willems	H	4024
21.	Hakan Kellner	S	3866
22.	Glen Foster	US	3853
23.	Lennart Lindahl	S	3802
24.	Ole Petersen	D	3738
25.	Hubert Raudaschl	OE	3669
26.	Brian Saffery-Cooper	K	3604
27.	Igor Moshkvin	SR	3588
28.	Per Werenskiold	N	3548
29.	Ulrich Hagan	G	3434
30.	Chr. Hansen	D	3395
31.	Mats Larsson	S	3372
32.	Hans G. Flint	G	3359
33.	Gunnar Andersson	S	3336
34.	Lennart Wallin	S	3312
35.	Bruno Trani	I	3257
36.	Dieter Mayr	G	3207
37.	Werner Werenskiold	N	3187
38.	Uwe Mares	G	3 121
39.	Desmond Stratton	K	3074
40.	Gerhard Huska	OE	3062
41.	Robin Webb	K	3024
42.	Hans Asklund	S	2968
43.	Gerald Leverland	H	2888
44.	J.B. de Jong	H	2880
45.	Arnold van Grünewaldt	S	2836

8. Gold Cup 1963

Medemblik, Holland, August 12-19
162 entries from 22 countries

The Gold Cup in 1963 brought another record with 162 boats from 22 nations. The weather was wet and the wind was always very shifty. All the five races suffered from a constant change of speed and direction of the wind. Success was mainly a question of a good start in front of the crowd and an instinct for the next windshift. Many of the old favourites ended up low down in the final results and some new faces appeared in top positions. Hardly anybody managed to sail consistently. The measurement was poor and the newly created Technical Committee was not yet in control of the situation. Twenty year old Willy Kuhweide became the young winner of the Gold Cup. He had acquired a brand new Elvström boat just before the event. But generally results were so topsy-turvy, that no general pattern emerged. All sorts of boats, masts, sails and people turned out to he successful.

Above: Andre Nelis
Right: Wim Maarse, Yves-Louis Pinaud,
Boris Jacobsson, Bengt Hornevall,
Goran Andersson

Final Results Gold Cup 1963

1.	Willy Kuhweide	G	6387
2.	Boris Jacobson	S	6211
3.	Hans Willems	H	5974
4.	Bernhard Straubinger	G	5699
5.	Valentin Mankin	SR	5651
6.	Ralph Roberts	KZ	5434
7.	Hubert Raudaschl	OE	5297
8.	G. Devillard	F	5282
9.	Per Werenskiold	N	5223
10.	Uwe Mares	G	5186
11.	Arnold von Grünewaldt	S	5178
12.	Per Jordbakke	N	5076
13.	Hans Fogh	D	5069
14.	Andre Nelis	B	4899
15.	G. Andersson	S	4869
16.	Peter Canham	K	4431
17.	Richard Creagh-Osborne	K	4410
18.	Hakan Kellner	S	4361
19.	M. Kojima	J	4349
20.	G. Andersson	S	4335
21.	A. Remien	G	4191
22.	M. Skalisz	PZ	4156
23.	Richard Hart	K	4071
24.	Alexander Chuchelov	SR	4023
25.	Bernt Andersson	S	4019
26.	Lennart Lindahl	S	3972
27.	D. Newell	KZ	3908
28.	M. Fletcher	KA	3684
29.	Lennart Wallin	S	3630

9.Gold Cup 1964

Torquay, England, July 18-26
65 entries from 20 countries

In 1964 the Cup had to be organised again in Great Britain. Because of the transport problems and a new entry system - in response to the problems at the starting line the previous year - only 65 participants entered. For the entire series there was hardly enough wind for gunwhale sitting, let alone leaning out. Every race suffered from big wind shifts, Sometimes these were so sudden and at such a magnitude that they turned the race into a game of chance. But whenever there was some rhyme and reason to them, there was Austria's 21 year old skipper Hubert Raudaschl in his homemade 1961 wooden boat with his homemade sail to take cool advantage of them. He even had the Cup in his bag before the last race and came out on the last day as a spectator. He had won the first and sixth race, placed sixth, fifth and fourth and finished only once with a two digit result. The measurement under chief measurer Vernon Forster was very strict. A newcomer from Brazil named Jörg Bruder ended up fifth.

Right: Jörg Bruder in his first Gold Cup in 1964. He would go on to win it three times in 1970, 1971 and 1972

Final Results Gold Cup 1964

1.	Hubert Raudaschl	OE	8275
2.	Hakan Kellner	S	7296
3.	Richard Creagh-Osborne	K	6838
4.	Peter Canham	K	6746
5.	Jörg Bruder	BL	6574
6.	Henning Wind	D	5787
7.	Alexander Chuchelov	SR	5609
8.	Mike Astley	K	5236
9.	Arne Akerson	S	5129
10.	Valentin Mankin	SR	5065
11.	Jack Knights	K	4989
12.	Gilbert Lamboley	F	4950
13.	Van Gelder	H	
14.	M. Kojima	J	
15.	Brain Saffery-Cooper	K	
16.	Wim Maarse	H	
17.	Per Jordbakke	N	
18.	Adelchi Pelaschier	I	
19.	F. Pampaloni	I	
20.	S. Golser	I	
21.	Ricardo Boneo	A	
22.	T. Yamada	J	

10. Gold Cup 1965

Gdynia, Poland, July 22-29
93 entries from 21 countries

For the first time in its history the Gold Cup was held in an East European country The racing was held in Danzig Bay. World measurer Vernon Forster took care of the strict measurement of 93 Finns. In the practice race a gate start proved to be unsatisfactory and the real racing was conducted with conventional starts. The wind was generally very strong causing many capsizes and much gear failure. The event was won by Jürgen Mier from the German Democratic Republic by consistent sailing in the difficult conditions. His countryman Bernd Dehmel won two races and finished second. Richard Hart from the UK won two other races. But the moral winner was Miroslav Vejvoda from the CSSR who had won one race, abandoned one whilst leading because of a minor collision and capsized twice in the windy last race after twice regaining the lead.

Final Results Gold Cup 1965

1.	Jürgen Mier	DDR 232	7587
2.	Bernd Dehmel	DDR 98	7152
3.	Richard Hart	K 131	6860
4.	Valentin Mankin	SR 636	6231
5.	Miroslav Vejvoda	CZ 111	6205
6.	Hans Fogh	D 84	6131
7.	Hubert Raudaschl	OE 31	5802
8.	Arne Akerson	S 321	5644
9.	G. Schwarz	DDR 27	5632
10.	Brian Saffery-Cooper	K 214	5432
11.	H. Hermann	DDR 113	5271
12.	György Finaczy	M 40	5090
13.	Arnold von Grünewaldt	S 366	4837
14.	P. Letcher	KZ 54	4724
15.	N. Everett	KZ 58	4635
16.	Phillipe Soria	F 374	4432
17.	F. Cordshagen	DDR 32	4428
18.	Bruce McCurrach	SA 272	4339
19.	Per Werenskiold	N 57	4296
20.	Miklos Tuss	M 50	4126
21.	Börge Sall	S 392	4061
22.	Boris Jacobsson	S 318	4002
23.	M. Skalisz	PZ 377	3869
24.	G. Dahlgard	D 80	3705
25.	P. Luttgart	G 584	3665
26.	B. O. Frimansson	S 328	3653
27.	H. Raben	DDR 72	3612
28.	Thomas Lundquist	S 438	3555
29.	Göran Andersson	S 365	3497
30.	Fabio Albarelli	I 306	3424

11. Gold Cup 1966

La Baule, France, August 21-29
150 entries from 26 countries

150 participants from a record 26 countries had to face a strict measurement in accordance under the new set of rules. This Gold Cup brought about a renaissance of wooden boats made by Raudaschl. Willy Kuhweide was a lucky winner followed by Jörg Bruder, both with boats, masts and sails from Hubert. There was general agreement that the Newport Finn of Ed Bennett from the USA was the finest plastic boat by far, but it was very close to tolerance at the sheer - extremely narrow. Willy Kuhweide did not win any races but always had fairly good results. In very difficult shifty wind conditions he proved to have an outstanding knowledge of meteorology. He was always looking around at the other boats, the sky and the weather and water conditions to gather information on which way to go. At the same time he sailed very fast while not giving boat speed his absolute attention. Germany with 1/3/4/5 dominated the fleet, but Jörg Bruder 2nd and Henry Sprague going top speed into the wrong direction indicated the awakening of a young continent for Finn sailing.

Final Results Gold Cup 1966

1.	Willy Kuhweide	G 711	48.7
2.	Jörg Bruder	BL 3	62.0
3.	Bernhard Straubinger	G 416	81.7
4.	Burghardt	G 341	82.0
5.	Uwe Mares	G 635	91.0
6.	V. Kozlov	SR 381	95.0
7.	G. Devillard	F 471	99.0
8.	Henry Sprague	US 707	101.0
9.	Valentin Mankin	SR 636	103.0
10.	Bernd Dehmel	DDR 9	108.7
11.	Bruce McCurrach	SA 272	132.0
12.	S. Golser	I 371	132.0
13.	Göran Andersson	S 516	134.7
14.	Arnold von Grünewaldt	S 366	135.4
15.	Richard Hart	K 231	141.0
16.	Miroslav Vejvoda	CZ 111	145.0
17.	Twist	US 532	148.7
18.	Pierre Poullain	F 430	163.0
19.	A. Bally	Z 145	166.7
20.	Hubert Raudaschl	OE 81	171.7
21.	Schwan	S 330	176.0
22.	Arne Akerson	S 321	183.0
23.	M. Skalisz	PZ 377	189.0
24.	B.O. Frimansson	S 328	194.0
25.	Peter Malm	D 51	196.7
26.	Baudouin Binkhorst	H 299	207.0
27.	Ed Bennett	US 534	209.0
28.	Lemanissier	F 424	211.0
29.	R. Bergsten	S 473	212.0
30.	Dick Tillman	US 419	214.0
33.	Hans Willems	H 75	217.0
34.	Jörgen Mier	DDR 3	218.7
35.	P. Lippert	DDR 6	222.0
36.	Lucian Christl	OE 70	223.0
37.	Burrows	IR 8	225.0

12. Gold Cup 1967

Hanko, Finland, August 6-12
130 entries from 22 countries

A force 9 gale on the first scheduled day of racing gave Vernon Forster one more day of telling 130 sailors what rules are made for. Hardly any boat had a rudder narrow enough to fit into the then 20 mm slot of Vernon's template. Most of the booms had hard wood extending further than 560 mm from the leading edge of the mast. The biggest deal however was the planing ceremony of the famous Raudaschl Finns (including those of Kuhweide, Mares and Bruder) at station 1 to get them straight and not concave. The event was dominated by wooden Raudaschl hulls, wooden Bruder masts and Raudaschl sails. The plastic GRP hulls had lost their glory which they had gained at the beginning of the sixties. The Germans Dehmel, Kuhweide, Mares and Mier lead 4 out of the 6 races from start to finish. The surprise was the Japanese sailor, Matsyuama, who won one race but was disqualified for a PMS and almost won another. After two races with light shifty wind the 3rd race was blessed with a steady force 5. Before the last race Mankin was leading by two points over Kuhweide. But Willy won because of his incredible speed and his steel

38.	Fabio Albarelli	I 306	226.0
39.	Gerhard Huska	OE 20	228.0
40.	Cole	K 245	232.0
41.	Ghiglia	F 436	236.0
42.	Miller	US 606	240.0
43.	F. Jammes	F 473	254.0
44.	Alain Maury	F 461	261.0
45.	Mike Astley	K 177	268.0
46.	H. Raben	DDR 7	269.0
47.	Wim Maarse	H 331	270.0
48.	B.E. Treleaven	KZ 62	270.0
49.	Appel	G 570	271.0
50.	Nilsson	S 384	275.0

Final Results Gold Cup 1967

1.	Willy Kuhweide	G 711	24.7
2.	Valentin Mankin	SR 636	34.4
3.	Uwe Mares	G 800	63.0
4.	Peter Tallberg	L 145	75.7
5.	Jörg Bruder	BL 3	80.7
6.	Robert Andre	US 618	89.0
7.	Börge Sall	S 392	95.7
8.	Miroslav Vejvoda	CZ 111	110.0
9.	Patrick Pym	K 174	110.0
10.	Hubert Raudaschl	OE 81	113.0
11.	V. Dordora	SR 1415	116.0
12.	G. Devillard	F 503	123.0
13.	Jürgen Mier	DDR 3	128.0
14.	Boris Jacobsson	S 318	132.0
15.	Per Werenskiold	N 57	134.0
16.	Arne Akerson	S 321	140.0
17.	S. Stork	S 543	141.0
18.	Fabio Albarelli	I 406	141.0
19.	Henning Wind	D 93	146.7
20.	G. Aasblom	S 521	168.0
21.	Jonty Farmer	KZ 9	173.7
22.	A. Bally	Z 145	177.0
23.	Hans Werner Zachariassen	G 635	177.0
24.	Bernd Dehmel	DDR 9	177.4
25.	Arnold von Grünewaldt	S 366	179.0
26.	John Maynard	K 154	179.0
27.	Lucian Christl	OE 70	181.0
28.	V. Kozlov	SR 381	183.0
29.	H. Tallberg	L 122	189.0
30.	Thomas Lundquist	S 532	194.0
31.	Hans van Elst	H 13	198.0
32.	Bernhard Straubinger	G 416	204.0
33.	F. Poullain	F 430	211.0
34.	S. Golser	I 371	212.0
35.	Walter Mai	G 614	213.0
36.	Clive Roberts	KZ 60	217.0
37.	Jan Winquist	L 119	218.0
38.	Carl van Duyne	US 245	227.0
39.	Baudouin Binkhorst	H 357	227.0
40.	H. Andersson	S 462	229.0
41.	Bernhard Reist	Z 224	230.0
42.	J. Brecht	G 603	232.0
43.	Kai Krüger	G 703	234.0
44.	D.C. Hardy	K 153	240.0
45.	A.A. Hofland	H 348	247.0

13. Gold Cup 1968

Whitstable, Kent, England July 8-13
138 entries from 38 countries

The commodore of Whitstable Yacht Club summed up the event in his speech at the prize giving by starting: "Companions in disaster, at least nobody was drowned". The regatta just didn't work out. By deed of gift the Gold Cup had to be organised every Olympic year in Great Britain. Many British Finn sailors themselves debated the wisdom of going to Whitstable. The small size of the Yacht Club, the crowded dinghy park, the lack of hotels, restaurants and mainly pubs, and the high tide were deplorable. Finally the actual racing was so unsatisfactory. At times some skippers had to sail with unshipped rudders. Others - less scrupulous - went overboard and dragged their boats towards the next mark. At the end of one race the crew of a rescue boat reported to have been able to walk across the finishing line without getting his knees wet. And the competitors had to pull back their boats over miles of mud because of the outgoing tide. At the end of the week only four races still stood and two of them had to survive protests to be abandoned. The best thing about this unhappy troubled week was that Henning Wind, the Danish Tokyo Bronze Medalist, was the best sailor and the winner. He won the first race, came fifth in the second and afterwards lost neither his hair nor his points average, though all about him were losing theirs. Raudaschl hulls, Bruder masts and Raudaschl sails dominated the fleet. But during the week it was found that Raudaschl's 1968 sails contravened the rules, inserting 4 oz cloth in the prevalent 3 oz sail.

Final Results Gold Cup 1968

1.	Henning Wind	D 93	35.0
2.	Uwe Mares	G 800	60.0
3.	Jörg Bruder	BL 3	64.7
4.	Bernd Dehmel	DDR 9	80.0
5.	Baudouin Binkhorst	H 369	88.0
6.	Börge Sall	S 392	108.0
7.	A. Hofland	H 382	119.4
8.	Patrick Pym	K 274	122.0
9.	Hans Werner Zachariassen	G 635	124.0
10.	Arne Akerson	S 321	127.7
11.	P.O. Gustavsson	S 546	137.0
12.	Walter Mai	G 875	137.7
13.	J. Stutterheim	G 904	139.0
14.	Willy Kuhweide	G 888	140.0
15.	B. Frimansson	S 328	143.0
16.	Thomas Lundquist	S 532	145.0
17.	Richard Hart	K 131	146.0
18.	Mauro Pelaschier	I 388	148.0
19.	Miroslav Vejvoda	CZ 111	148.0
20.	R. Bergsten	S 473	151.7
21.	Andreas van Eicken	G 567	153.0
22.	John Maynard	K 284	156.0
23.	G. Dahlstrom	S 156	163.0
24.	Valentin Mankin	SR 636	168.0
25.	Hans Joachim Fritze	G 711	168.0

14. Gold Cup 1969

Hamilton, Bermuda, October 2-10
132 entries from 27 countries

For the first time the Finn Gold Cup was organised outside Europe. A very generous invitation for food and lodging and vast support for transportation of the boats attracted a large number of entries. Even Paul Elvström decided to return to the Finn at age 41. All competitors agreed, that this was one at the best organised world championships ever. The only disruptions were Hurricanes Inga and Kara, pushing wind velocity as high as 30 to 40 knots. Because of Inga racing was postponed from October 3 to 7. Andy Zawieja was delivered by a crane from a Polish freighter, which did not enter Bermuda's territorial waters, and paddled with all his gear ashore, to be picked up again by the same freighter two weeks later in the middle of the ocean after he had cleared through customs. Lundquist, a 22 year old Student at Gothenburg

Above: Thomas Lundquist leads into the gybe
Right: Gold Cup Winner 1968 Henning Wind

26.	Serge Maury	F 496	171.0
27.	S. Golser	I 418	177.0
28.	Henry Sprague	US 707	181.0
29.	J. Liandier	F 552	182.0
30.	E. Quass	I 387	186.0
31.	Nigel Sharples	K 286	190.0
32.	V. Kozlov	SR 381	191.0
33.	L. Coccoloni	I 403	193.0
34.	Lucian Christl	OE 70	194.7
35.	Jürgen Mier	DDR 3	211.0
36.	Göran Andersson	S 516	217.0
37.	D. Hardy	K 153	229.0
38.	R. Ketelaar	H 199	234.0
39.	Desmond Stratton	K 200	236.0
40.	Tiemen Vries	H 367	239.0

University, won the Gold Cup. Jörg Bruder became runner up for the second time. Peter Barrett could have still won the trophy while leading in the last race, but capsized and ended up third. To any sane man the last race should not have been sailed with gusts up to 30 knots and above. But there is something mad about Finn sailors anyway. That last race Henry Sprague III was leading all the way but had a PMS. Finally Walter Mai got line honours, with Bruder second. Bruder masts with Raudaschl sails still dominated the fleet. Jack Knights introduced the first aluminium mast into the Gold Cup scenery.

Final Results Gold Cup 1969

1.	Thomas Lundquist	S 532	15.0
2.	Jörg Bruder	BL 3	21.4
3.	Peter Barrett	US 888	25.7
4.	Walter Mai	G 991	39.7
5.	Peter Conrad	US 530	51.7
6.	Uwe Mares	G 1041	53.7
7.	Bret de Thier	KZ 133	60.0
8.	Andy Zawieja	PZ 321	60.7
9.	Valentin Mankin	SR 36	64.0
10.	Willy Kuhweide	G 1044	69.0
11.	Fritz Beck	H 381	69.0
12.	Paul Elvström	D 106	70.0
13.	G. Aasblom	S 521	77.7
14.	Guy Liljegren	S 554	80.0
15.	Phillipe Soria	F 374	82.0
16.	Börge Sall	S 392	87.0
17.	Iain Macdonald-Smith	K 321	99.0
18.	Fabio Albarelli	I 433	101.0
19.	Andreas von Eicken	G 969	104.0
20.	Gordy Bowers	US 83	104.0
21.	Jürgen Mier	DDR 3	106.0
22.	Hubert Raudaschl	OE 110	107.0
23.	Arnold von Grünewaldt	S 366	114.0
24.	Baudouin Binkhorst	H 4	119.0
25.	Ernie Shaw	SA 182	120.0
26.	Hans Joachim Fritze	G 711	122.0
27.	Vernon Stratton	K 334	126.0
28.	Bjoern Ribbhagen	S 540	129.0
29.	Kim Weber	L 151	133.0
30.	Anthony Herrmann	US 225	140.0
31.	F. Huber	G 1014	144.0
32.	A. John Clarke	KC 78	150.0
33.	B.O. Frimansson	S 328	150.0
34.	Oleg Shilov	SR 4	154.0
35.	Bernhard Straubinger	G 916	155.0
36.	D. R. Kollock	US 780	157.0
37.	Jonty Farmer	KZ 137	161.0
38.	Kai Krüger	G 1003	165.0
39.	P. Kouligas	GR 122	166.0
40.	Peter Tallberg	L 145	175.0
41.	S. Golser	I 418	176.0
42.	Bernt Andersson	S 550	182.0
43.	Christian Schroeder	DDR 8	187.0
44.	Miroslav Vejvoda	CZ 111	191.0

15. Gold Cup 1970

Cascais, Portugal August 14-22
180 entries from 34 countries

The biggest fleet in any Finn Gold Cup most likely forever gathered in 1970 It was won and dominated by American sailors with Jörg Bruder winning for his first time, Sprague second and Andre third. After twice finishing as runner up, Bruder - already 37 - feared that this might be his last Gold Cup because of leg injuries. In the last race Bruder had to finish fifth or better in order to win the Cup, no matter what Sprague did. At the start Sprague used every match-race tactic he could in the huge fleet. Trying to hold Bruder back, Sprague luffed the Brazilian into the spectator fleet. But an the last beat Bruder was again leading. Sprague went up what he thought was the wrong side, but it turned out to be the right one. Now Sprague started a tacking duel until Bruder went head to wind because his rudder pintle broke. But Bruder lifted his centreboard in order to take off the pressure from his rudder and twisted the tiller with his bare but mighty hands. Sprague finished fourth and only could watch as the crippled Bruder crossing the line seconds before Andre and Mares, who had both overstood the line, crossed planing an a screaming reach. It was the most dramatic win of any Gold Cup.

Final Results Gold Cup 1970

1.	Jörg Bruder	BL 3	23.7
2.	Henry Sprague	US 868	24.0
3.	Robert Andre	US 830	44.0
4.	Thomas Lundquist	S 530	53.7
5.	Guy Liljegren	S 554	55.0
6.	Bernd Dehmel	DDR 9	57.7
7.	Per Werenskiold	N 83	58.7
8.	Baudouin Binkhorst	H 4	58.7
9.	Pieter Keyzer	H 404	62.7
10.	Magnus Olin	S 509	65.7

11.	Uwe Mares	G 6	69.4
12.	Iain Macdonald-Smith	K 341	73.0
13.	Peter Conrad	US 530	75.0
14.	Willy Kuhweide	G 711	83.7
15.	Jacques Rogge	B 87	86.0
16.	S. Golser	I 418	86.0
17.	Serge Maury	F 96	89.0
18.	Fabio Albarelli	I 3	98.0
19.	Kees Douze	H 7	99.0
20.	Fritz Beck	H 449	11.0
21.	Andy Zawieja	PZ 321	115.0
22.	Hubert Raudaschl	OE 121	120.0
23.	B. Frimansson	S 328	122.0
24.	Jürgen Mier	DDR 3	128.0
25.	P. Akerson	S 32	128.0
26.	Patrick Pym	K 274	134.0
27.	Miroslav Vejvoda	CZ 111	13.40
28.	Thomas Jungblut	G 1146	142.0
29.	Michael Hupin	B 90	150.0
30.	Uwe Heinzmann	G 1122	156.0
31.	Elias Hatzipavlis	GR 122	157.0
32.	Lennart Gustavsson	S 558	161.0
33.	Hans Werner Zachariassen	G 1133	161.0
34.	Paul Phelan	KC 61	163.0
35.	Phillipe Soria	F 6	172.0
36.	Ernie Shaw	SA 182	172.0
37.	A. Leenstra	SA 410	179.0
38.	Victor Potapov	SR 15	181.0
39.	D. Kollock	US 780	183.0
40.	J. Eggers	US 814	184.0
41.	Jamiz Knasiecki	PZ 335	185.0
42.	J. Leistikow	G 1050	186.0
43.	Börge Sall	S 392	192.0
44.	G. Ehlers	G 1102	195.0
45.	Chris Law	K 321	196.0
46.	Achim Türklitz	G 556	200.0
47.	Vernon Stratton	K 334	202.0
48.	Nitall Dirdira	SR 4	203.0
49.	Björn Ribbhagen	S 540	205.0
50.	Ian Brown	K 350	207.0
51.	J. P. Boumans	B 76	218.0
52.	B. Bergsten	S 557	218.0
53.	John Clarke	KC 78	223.0

Above: A packed leeward mark in 1970

Start line in Bermuda
Paul Elvström (D 106) leads away from
the starboard end

Below: Jörg Bruder wins

16. Gold Cup 1971

Toronto, Canada, October 1-9
87 entries from 21 countries

Because of new entry regulations and the poor reachability only 87 entries from 21 countries had arrived. Rickard Sarby was watching the races. After winning the North Americans just before the Gold Cup some misfortune in the first race (capsizing) made Jörg Bruder mad as a bull and he won by several hundred meters in the 20 knot wind. The next day Bruder was leading in a 20 knots wind again, when he tried to gybe with his boom vang still tight and capsized again. But he regained the lead and won again. A fierce duel between Carl van Duyne and Jörg in the next race ended with a narrow victory of Bruder after the lead changed 10 times. In the last race Bruder played it safe in the middle of the fleet, while Carl van Duyne gambled on a shift and won the race but not the Cup. On the last reach Carl tried all sort of tricks to slow down Bruder - overstanding the lay line and luffing like mad, but still had to finish ahead of Jörg. But finally Carl finished first and Bruder second, thus winning the Gold Cup for the second time.

Final Results Gold Cup 1971

1.	Jörg Bruder	BL 3	33.0
2.	Carl Van Dyne	US 245	34.0
3.	Serge Maury	F 7	51.7
4.	Ed Bennett	US 534	69.7
5.	Thomas Lundquist	S 532	74.0

6.	Thomas Jungblut	G 1146	77.0
7.	Göran Andersson	S 516	79.7
8.	Bret De Thier	KZ 133	89.7
9.	John Bertrand	KA 111	92.7
10.	G. Dahlstrom	S 156	99.7
11.	Arne Akerson	S 321	115.0
12.	Lennart Gustafsson	S 589	112.0
13.	Magnus Olin	S 509	116.7
14.	Henry Sprague	US 896	115.4
15.	Guy Liljegren	S 554	129.0
16.	Robbie Doyle	US 411	137.0
17.	Gordy Bowers	US 902	139.0
18.	P. Akerson	S 32	139.7
19.	Robert Andre	US 830	142.0
20.	John Clarke	KC 111	146.0
21.	Hubert Raudaschl	OE 131	149.0
22.	V. Neudoeffer	KC 93	155.0
23.	Richard Storer	KC 300	156.0
24.	Patrick Pym	K 274	163.0
25.	Hans Fogh	D 104	164.0
26.	Hans Werner Zachariassen	G 1160	164.0
27.	Chris Law	K 321	164.4
28.	Walter Mai	G 1171	196.4
29.	Andy Zawieja	PZ 321	171.0

17. Gold Cup 1972

Anzio, Italy, June 25-July 1
103 entries from 25 countries

For the first and perhaps last time in its 30 years of existence the Finn Gold Cup was won in three consecutive years by one man. Jörg Bruder from Brazil took the world championship again. This time Jörg used a new aluminium mast which he had developed similar to his successful wooden spars. He borrowed the Canadian '71 Raudaschl sail which had used to win the 1971 Gold Cup. Bruder's speed was normal however he pointed higher with the new mast which was more flexible sideways at the top than the Needlespar masts. Bruder's final score line of 2/3/2/1/4/6 is most impressive.

The 1972 Gold Cup was held in Anzio - 25 miles south of Rome - in typical Mediterranean weather. The winds were generally light at the beginning of the week but the last two races were sailed in a moderate westerly wind which produced a very big swell. These last two races were won in a most masterly manner by the Australian Olympic Finn helmsman John Bertrand, who was in front for the whole of the two races. He gradually moved further ahead, winning by over two minutes each race. Bertrand used the Olympic rig of a Needlespar mast and North sail on an Australian glassfibre hull. Certainly at the end of the week he was unbeatable in speed and tactics. But the lighter winds at the beginning showed a different winner each day and it was during this period that Bruder worked out an unassailable points lead, with consistent placings in the first three.

The first race of the regatta was led home by the former world champion and winner of Kiel Week in 1972, Thomas Lundquist of Sweden who desperately held off Bruder's last leg challenge. Fabio Albarelli of Italy, the bronze medalist at Acapulco, won the second race and the Swede, Lennart Gustafsson, the third. Finally in the light wind fourth race Bruder took the winner's gun and increased

his overall lead to an unassailable position. After his fifth race fourth place his only danger lay from Gustafsson, who could take the championship if he won and Bruder finished worse than fourth. In any event the last race was simple for Bruder as Gustafsson had a bad start and could never climb out of the pack. There had been little change on the fittings and gear side with one big exception; the universal acceptance of aluminium spars. A year previously the whole of the Finn class was against the introduction of aluminium; this year one third of the fleet sported metal masts and, to cap it all, aluminium masts finished first and second.

Final Results Gold Cup 1972

1.	Jörg Bruder	BL 3	19.7
2.	John Bertrand	KA 113	32.0
3.	Lennart Gustafsson	S 589	33.7
4.	Fabio Albarelli	I 465	50.4
5.	Thomas Lundquist	S 532	65.7
6.	Kim Weber	L 161	70.4
7.	Magnus Olin	S 509	75.0
8.	Elias Hatzipavlis	GR 164	84.7
9.	John Clarke	KC 111	93.7
10.	Bill Holmstrom	L 146	105.0
11.	Mikael Brandt	S 389	114.0
12.	Tom Sandberg	S 594	115.7
13.	Mauro Pelaschier	I 460	117.0
14.	Kent Carlsson	S 584	122.0
15.	A. Papaioannou	GR 165	125.0
16.	Baudouin Binkhorst	H 454	128.0
17.	Heilmut Duckeroff	G 1269	129.0
18.	Minski Fabris	Y 30	134.0
19.	Luciano Lievi	I 417	135.0
20.	Iain MacDonald-Smith	K 267	139.0
21.	Miroslav Vejvoda	CZ 111	141.0
22.	Torbjorn Ahlback	L 145	141.7
23.	Giorgio Gorla	I 435	146.0
24.	Fritz Gels	G 1100	147.0
25.	Guy Liljegren	S 4	152.0
26.	Rolf Beck	G 1268	167.0
27.	Kazuoki Matsyuama	J 15	168.0
28.	Bo Rogberg	S 398	172.0
29.	Claudio Biekarck	BL 10	174.0
30.	Christian Cuccurullo	F 651	176.0
31.	Magnus Lidholm	S 583	177.0
32.	Kevin MacLaverty	IR 21	182.0
33.	Sanford Riley	KC 143	183.0

Above: the fleet in 1972
Below: Serge Maury, winner in 1973

18. Gold Cup 1973
Brest, France, July 14-23
103 entries from 20 countries

Brest turned out to be unsuitable for a major international regatta and was certainly not within the rules laid down for the Gold Cup. The IFA had approved of Brest on the understanding that the course would be set on the open sea outside. But instead, sailing was organised inside the harbour. One side of the course was far too close to the maximum tidal stream through the harbour entrance. Vernon Stratton brought along a new double-bottom boat which received approval of the Measurement and Technical Committee. For the first time extensive Lamboley tests were used. The Lanaverres and Teels had the lowest permissible results, the Raudaschls performed mediocre. Almost all the front runners were using metal spars, Maury a Bruder-Alu mast, most others Needlespars. In the strongest winds wooden spars still proved to be superior. But the event was overshadowed by the death of Jörg Bruder who was killed in an air crash approaching Paris in order to defend the title. Nobody dominated as was the case in previous years and six different sailors look line honours. Before the last race Liljegren was leading in front of Olin and Maury. But Maury won the Cup by finishing second in front of Olin who was 4th and Liljegren who was 8th.

Final Results Gold Cup 1973

1.	Serge Maury	F 1	42.7
2.	Magnus Olin	S 584	44.7
3.	Guy Liljegren	S 554	46.7
4.	Lennart Gustafsson	S 589	64.0
5.	Lou Nady	US 150	73.0
6.	Alex Welter	BL 5	73.4
7.	Bernt Johnsson	S 521	91.7
8.	Jacques Busquet	F 196	98.7
9.	David Schmidt	KZ 111	99.0
10.	Kent Carlsson	S 509	104.0
11.	G. Ehlers	G 1277	110.0
12.	J.P. Boumans	B 1	114.0
13.	P. Mondéteguy	F 6	133.0
14.	Claudio Biekarck	BL 10	137.0
15.	Jonty Farmer	KZ 149	139.7
16.	Mauro Pelaschier	I 460	150.0
17.	Bernhard Reist	Z 224	156.0
18.	Richard Hart	K 331	157.0
19.	Prenat	F 435	159.0
20.	Thomas Jungblut	G 1335	161.0
21.	Robert Holbrook	K 351	162.0
22.	Mikael Brandt	S 389	165.0
23.	David Howlett	K 341	166.0
24.	Werner Sülberg	G 1169	170.0
25.	Jean Grandchamp	F 700	175.0
26.	Patrice Charee	F 8	182.0
27.	Kees Douze	H 7	182.0
28.	Achim Türklitz	G 1270	184.0
29.	Craig Thomas	US 934	185.0
30.	Tiemen de Vries	H 500	188.7
31.	J.G. Pasturaud	F 675	192.7
32.	Chedeville	F 60	204.0

19. Gold Cup 1974
Long Beach, USA, August 10-17
96 entries from 19 countries

The first Gold Cup in the USA was also won for the first time by a US sailor. After a number of failed attempts Henry Sprague III finally managed to put together a remarkable series. After he finished first with a port start at the pin end in the first race but was disqualified for a PMS, he won three more races twice scored a second and once had a tenth. Although he could not afford another throwout, Henry twice risked again a port start over the entire fleet approaching the pin end at full speed on a screaming port reach and got away with it. But the tension remained up until the last race Since Henry had to count a 10th Ed Bennett too still could have won the Gold Cup. When everybody expected a fascinating duel between the two US sailors, the mob was disappointed. Ed Bennett went inshore in the first beat and ended up 46th, while Henry went out and was 6th. Finally Sprague improved to 2nd to take the trophy with a remarkable 21 points lead, while Ed Bennett improved only to 17th and was finally 4th.

Final Results Gold Cup 1974

1.	Henry Sprague	US 533	22.0
2.	Guy Liljegren	S 554	43.0
3.	Kent Carlsson	S 509	47.7
4.	Ed Bennett	US 403	49.4
5.	Lennart Gustafsson	S 589	67.7
6.	Craig Thomas	US 945	68.4
7.	Dave Howlett	K 341	83.0
8.	Magnus Olin	S 616	85.7
9.	Serge Maury	F 1	87.0
10.	James Hahn	US 692	103.7
11.	Jonty Farmer	KZ 149	105.0
12.	Elias Hatzipavlis	GR 176	110.7
13.	Ron Dougherty	US 919	121.7
14.	Jaques Busquet	F 496	122.7
15.	Claudio Biekarck	BL 69	133.0
16.	Jim Santroch	US 111	141.4
17.	Richard Hart	K 331	166.0
18.	David Schmidt	KZ 111	169.0
19.	Randy MacLaren	US 151	172.0
20.	Lou Nady	US 150	173.0
21.	Tom Jungblut	G 1	173.0
22.	Sanford Riley	KC 143	187.0
23.	Hans van Elst	H 424	188.0
24.	Danny Thompson	US 534	189.0
25.	Lars Ek	S 534	194.0
26.	Brian Todd	KC 1 23	197.0
27.	Tony James	KA 117	199.0
28.	Andreas Von Eicken	G 12	204.0
29.	Jean J. Grandchamp	F 710	213.0
30.	Ulf Arvidsson	S 598	217.0
31.	Peter Conrad	US 951	219.7
32.	Roy Christianson	US 841	220.0
33.	Robbie Butler	KC 89	221.0
34.	Thomas Lundquist	S 532	223.0
35.	Bret de Thier	KZ 163	236.0
36.	Murray Norris	KA 104	241.0
37.	John Eastwood	KC 100	243.0

20. Gold Cup 1975

Malmö, Sweden, June 10-19
141 entries from 27 countries

After three sunny days of measurement this Gold Cup started with a surprise-drum-roll-symphony. The first race on Friday 13th started with a force 6 from from the west, a current of 2 knots to the southwest, the water only 5-8 metres deep and cold, rainy weather. 52 boats retired. There must have been about 400 capsizes that day. After the second race the winner John Bertrand from Australia was disqualified for having 22 kg of wet clothing. The next day a strong current against a light wind caused 8 General Recalls, every time the entire fleet drifting over the line without doing anything. Two races on June 16 were abandoned because of too light a wind. Magnus Olin won the next race and was thus leading overall, but collected a DSQ for an early start the next race By contrast David Howlett enjoyed some water skiing behind the team boat to pass the time while waiting for the wind and could not find his boat when the race finally started. With a throwout Magnus Olin, Jonty Farmer, Baudouin Binkhorst and John Bertrand could still win the Cup after one more race Without another race Serge Maury would have won. Finally a drifter was started. Binkhorst was leading at the last leeward mark, but failed to cover the fleet and lost the Cup. Olin recovered to 21st which was just enough but Maury couldn't come further than 14th which was not.

Final Results Gold Cup 1975

1.	Magnus Olin	S 616	46.0
2.	Baudouin Binkhorst	H 6	49.0
3.	Jonty Farmer	KZ 149	54.7
4.	Serge Maury	F 711	55.4
5.	Kent Carlsson	S 509	61.0
6.	Chris Law	K 321	71.0
7.	Per Sundelin	S 271	80.7
8.	Guy Liljegren	S 554	86.0
9.	Göran Andersson	S 516	94.0
10.	P. Mondéteguy	F 713	100.0
11.	Bernt Johnsson	S 521	101.0
12.	Lennart Gustafsson	S 589	109.0
13.	Kees Douze	H 7	109.0
14.	Jürgen Wolff	DDR 29	116.0
15.	David Howlett	K 341	118.4
16.	Jacques Rogge	B 2	120.7
17.	Robert Butler	KC 89	133.0
18.	Andrzej Zawieja	PZ 321	133.0
19.	Tom Sandberg	S 637	136.0
20.	D. Breitenstein	L 183	144.7
21.	J.-P. Boumans	B 1	150.0
22.	Walter Mai	G 1341	152.0
23.	Claudio Biekarck	BL 69	156.2
24.	Thomas Jungblut	G 1	157.0
25.	Robert A.H. Holbrook	K 351	161.0
26.	Minski Fabris	Y 50	162.0
27.	Jörgen Lindhardtsen	D 126	167.0
28.	Mikael Brandt	S 389	170.0
29.	Ed Bennett	US 403	173.0
30.	Luciano Lievi	I 517	181.0
31.	A. Fravezzi	I 526	183.0
32.	Gerd Hübner	G 1298	183.0
33.	Jacques Busquet	F 496	183.0
34.	Wolfgang Gerz	G 1519	184.0
35.	Romuald Knasiecki	PZ 49	186.0
36.	Werner Sülberg	G 1511	188.0
37.	B.Gros	H 412	189.0
38.	Svante Björkman	S 550	192.0
39.	Egbert Vincke	G 1300	193.0
40.	Gus Miller	US 275	196.0
41.	M. Lidholm	S 583	198.0
42.	Harro Jäger	G 1428	200.0
43.	John Bertrand	KA 151	201.0
44.	Sandy Riley	KC 143	205.0
45.	Thomas Lundquist	S 532	205.0
46.	Richard Grönblom	L 171	206.0
47.	Graeme Woodroffe	KZ 9	209.0

21. Gold Cup 1976

Brisbane, Australia, January 2-10
82 entries from 14 countries

Despite the travelling difficulties but because of the hospitality of the organiser 76 boats from 13 nations finally gathered for the first start. Most of the races were in very strong wind and a short bumpy sea. Chris Law who had been preparing himself for months to beat his Olympic rival David Howlett, showed exceptionally skilful boat handling in these exceptionally rough conditions and went into an early lead overall. In the sixth race the wind shifted and the race committee signalled a change of course for the last beat. In accordance with the sailing instructions this required a rounding of the mark the opposite way. Only Ed Bennett and Jacques Busquet did so. When Ed finished fourth and got the gun, Farmer, Riley, Law and the rest of the fleet recognised their mistake, rushed back to the leeward mark to unwind and reround the mark, careful not to inform those still labouring upwind, that they had rounded incorrectly. After a heated protest hearing the International Jury overruled the Race Committee and threw the race out. In the last race only Farmer could have taken the Cup from Law. But Chris managed a second behind superb John Bertrand in hair-raising survival conditions with Farmer 4th. Law in 1st, Farmer in 2nd and Howlett in 4th sailed the new double-bottom fibreglass hulls by Peter Taylor, which were extremely fast downwind.

Final Results Gold Cup 1976

1.	Chris Law	K 321	11.7
2.	Jonty Farmer	KZ 149	22.0
3.	John Bertrand	KA 151	26.7
4.	David Howlett	K 341	40.0
5.	Lennart Gustafsson	S 589	47.8
6.	J. S. Douglas	KZ 169	63.0
7.	Robert Butler	KC 89	70.4
8.	Sanford Riley	KC 143	73.7
9.	Bret de Thier	KZ 163	78.0
10.	Hans Werner Zachariassen	G 1399	84.7
11.	Kent Carlsson	S 509	86.0
11.	Craig Thomas	US 963	86.0
13.	James Hahn	US 973	87.0
14.	John Ferguson	KA 133	97.0
15.	Nick Oundjian	KC 145	100.0
16.	Bryan Treleaven	KZ 176	107.0
17.	Peter Vollebregt	H 4	110.7
18.	H. G. Ehlers	G 1277	113.0
19.	Barry Thom	KZ 174	120.7
20.	Magnus Olin	S 600	127.0
21.	Gus Miller	US 975	137.0
22.	Tommy Sandberg	S 591	145.0
23.	Ed Bennett	US 403	150.0
24.	David Schmidt	KZ 179	155.0
25.	Richard Grombloom	L 171	157.0
26.	Guy Liljegren	S 554	160.0
27.	Ron Jenyns	KA 132	169.0
28.	Tom Anderson	KA 142	173.0
29.	Neville J. Paul	KZ 181	175.0

22. Finn World Week 1977

Palamos, Spain, October 6-17
129 entries from 26 countries

Because the Spanish Government refused to accept the participation of one competitor from South Africa, the IFA withdrew the Gold Cup from competition in 1977 and renamed the event as Finn World Week. The week was distinguished by feeble breezes and only five of the total of seven planned races could be sailed. 21 year old Joaquin Blanco won two races, was always among the top 10 and finished with 23.3 points ahead of another Spaniard José Doreste. They both used older Roga boats. The leading sails in these, days were Musto and North. A few Boyce Spars were still among the predominant Needlespars.

Final Results World Week 1977

1.	Joaquin Blanco	E 1	19.7
2.	José Luis Doreste	E 109	43.0
3.	Claudio Biekarck	BL 89	43.0
4.	Andrei Balashov	SR 2	47.0
5.	Lennart Heselius	S 589	52.4
6.	Kent Carlsson	S 677	69.0
7.	Magnus Olin	S 644	61.0
8.	Tomasz Rumszewicz	PZ 379	62.0
9.	Mauro Pelaschier	I 509	69.0
10.	David Howlett	K 341	69.0
11.	Guy Liljegren	S 665	69.7
12.	David Buemi	US 965	71.7
13.	Paul Higgins	KC 156	80.0
14.	Hans Werner Zachariassen	G 1559	80.0
15.	Chris Boumans	B 1	81.0
16.	Christopher Law	K 321	86.0
17.	Paul Rudling	KZ 186	95.0
18.	August Miller	US 975	105.0
19.	Werner Sülberg	G 1511	110.0
20.	Peter Vollebregt	H 535	112.0
21.	Graham Deegan	KZ 185	112.7
22.	Jean Grandchamp	F 730	117.7
23.	Zakhorow	SR 3	119.0
24.	Kiepa	SR 8	127.0
25.	Anthony Hermann	US 989	127.7
26.	Douglas	KZ 35	133.0
27.	Minski Fabris	Y 53	134.7
28.	Ryszard Skarbinski	PZ 28	134.7
29.	Derek Breitenstein	L 96	146.0
30.	A. Lochbrunner	G 1478	148.0
31.	Marteau	F 702	149.0
32.	A. Hellbrügge	G 1513	150.0
33.	Theodis	GR 69	155.0
34.	Elias Hatzipavlis	GR 180	164.0

23. Gold Cup 1978

Manzanillo, Mexico, November 16-26
69 entries from 14 countries

There were light to medium winds in the most beautiful setting for a Gold Cup up to now. Most of the sailors had problems coping with the heat in November. Generally the wind was shifty and there was no pattern to follow, so nobody knew what to do. There were also strong currents appearing and disappearing. Consequently, many sailors had erratic results. A few old faces met a large number of young new ones. John Bertrand, up to then an unknown US newcomer from the Laser class, was not granted the chance to beat the well known John Bertrand from Australia but only the rest of the top skippers. In the fourth race there were 5 General Recalls. Therefore the race committee invoked a one-minute rule with a DSQ, but did not notify the boats which were thrown out. 24 boats were disqualified, including Blanco and Law, who in subsequent starts pushed other boats over the line. After the race Law protested the entire race, which would have given him the Cup. The appeal went to the IYRU but was finally refused. For the first time 9 of the top 10 boats were Vanguards.

35.	Hanbrook	B 11	167.0
36.	Gerd Hübner	G 1562	167.0
37.	Martensson	S 655	167.0
38.	Delfs	S 633	171.0

Final Results Gold Cup 1978

1.	John Bertrand	US 1007	46.7
2.	Joaquin Blanco	E 1	59.7
3.	Carl Buchan	US 1015	61.0
4.	Loui Nady	US 150	64.7
5.	Lawrence Lemieux	KC 201	75.0
6.	Buzz Reynolds	KC 996	80.7
7.	August Miller	US 975	84.0
8.	Ed Bennett	US 3	84.0
9.	Minski Fabris	Y 53	89.0
10.	Cam Lewis	US 971	90.0
11.	Chris Law	K 321	91.0
12.	Rick Hewitt	KC 179	92.0
13.	Peter Higgins	KC 156	96.7
14.	Jere White	US 999	98.0
15.	Jesus Turro	E 77	107.7
16.	Sanford Riley	KC 143	112.0
17.	Jim Santroch	US 111	117.0
18.	Kent Carlsson	S 677	122.4
19.	Ed Baird	US 419	125.0
20.	Brian Todd	KC 164	126.7
21.	Craig Healy	US 422	127.0
22.	Tony Herrmann	US 989	141.0
23.	Randy McLaren	US 1013	141.0

Below: lauching in 1978
Below right: John Bertrand (US)
winner 1978
Below left: the fleet in 1977

24. Gold Cup 1979

Weymouth, England, September 5-15
135 entries from 27 nations

After the disaster of Whitstable in 1964 the British had finally recovered from their shock and asked to organise the Gold Cup again. In contrast to the reputation of Weymouth the wind was light and shifty the entire week. The current was frequently the strongest factor for sailing. In the first race it separated three boats at the leeward mark who had just managed to round, when the entire fleet started to drift back to the windward mark. In the second race the current going against the wind collected about 100 boats at the gybe mark packed together like logs. Whoever tried to sail outside, around the pack, had no wind behind the pack and drifted without hope, right into the other boats. This Gold Cup was dominated by a gang of new US ex Laser sailors. John Bertrand, the 1978 winner, lost the Cup in the third race, when he did not make it passed Lester on port tack. John Bertrand, who had dominated the North American and European races of that year previously, was leading overall up to the last beat of the last race, but finally had to relinquish the Gold Cup to his team mate 21 year old Cameron Lewis.

Final Results Gold Cup 1979

1.	Cameron Lewis	US 1027	38.0
2.	John Bertrand	US 1037	41.0
3.	Mark Neeleman	H 555	51.0
4.	Andrew Menkart	US 1028	57.0
5.	Stewart Neff	US 1004	66.0
6.	Carl Buchan	US 1015	78.0
7.	Wolfgang Gerz	G 1573	82.0
8.	Joaquin Blanco	E 1	85.0
9.	Thomas Jungblut	G 1	88.0
10.	Alex Smigelski	US 1002	92.0
11.	Michael Nissen	G 1706	95.0
12.	Serge Khoretski	SR 23	110.0
13.	Minski Fabris	Y 53	122.0
14.	Juan Mägli	GU 1	127.0
15.	Miroslav Rychcik	PZ 75	127.0
16.	Kent Carlsson	S 679	133.0
17.	Jörg Vetter	DDR 12	140.0
18.	Magnus Liljedahl	S 569	140.0
19.	Larry Lemieux	KC 201	150.0
20.	Jorgen Lindhardtsen	D 141	150.0
21.	Paul Rudling	K 452	164.0
22.	Mike McIntyre	K 423	173.0
23.	Erik Braathen	H 111	174.0
24.	Jacques Rogge	B 2	176.0
25.	Geoffrey Davidson	KA 165	182.0
26.	Guy Liljegren	S 675	183.0
27.	Claudio Biekarck	BL 88	183.0
28.	Patrick Spängs	S 666	189.0
29.	Buzz Reynolds	US 936	195.0
30.	Otto Pohlmann	G 1650	201.0
31.	Lue Van Keirsblick	B 24	201.0
32.	Chris Law	K 321	202.0
33.	Willy Hambrouck	B 11	207.0
34.	Rob Woodbury	KC 190	203.0
35.	Frank Butzmann	DDR 19	203.0

25. Gold Cup 1980

Takapuna, New Zealand, February 18-27
66 entries from 14 countries

Picking up where they left off in England in 1979, United States sailors again set the pace and dominated the 1980 Finn Gold Cup, down under in New Zealand. Cameron Lewis continued his private duel with John Bertrand. Going into the last race only 0.9 points separated Lewis and Bertrand. It boiled down to a match race between them. On the last beat in 30 knots wind Bertrand tacked 32 times and Lewis covered 32 times and thus won the Cup. Up to race five, Larry Lemieux was leading overall but finally capsized twice, hit a couple of marks, and was third at the end. Lewis, Bertrand, Lemieux and Menkart had shipped their boats together in one container,

and that 'Container' as the gang was referred to, won 5 of the 7 races and ended up 1/2/3/5 overall. Most of the Europeans came shortly before the event from a cold climate and lacked time in their boats. The 'Container' had practised for weeks before and had adjusted to the climate.

Final Results Gold Cup 1980

1.	Cameron Lewis	US 1027	29.7
2.	John Bertrand	US 1037	34.7
3.	Larry Lemieux	KC 201	58.0
4.	Kent Carlsson	S 655	70 4
5.	Andy Menkart	US 1028	74.0
6.	Chris Law	K 321	74.7
7.	Graham Deegan	KZ 211	82.1
8.	Tom Dodson	KZ 214	85.0
9.	Jorgen Lindhardtsen	D 142	88.7
10.	John Douglas	KZ 3	108.7
11.	Bruce Deegan	KZ 204	108.7
12.	Richard Dodson	KZ 220	108.7
13.	Leith Armit	KZ 177	118.7
14.	L. Breitenstein	L 1	119.7
15.	Michael Nissen	G 1706	123.0
16.	Esko Rechardt	L 185	133.0
17.	John Ferguson	KA 161	139.0
18.	Dave Schmidt	KZ 222	145.0
19.	Mike McIntyre	K 423	151.0
20.	Graeme Woodroffe	KZ 180	152.0
21.	Rob Woodbury	KZ 190	155.0
22.	Geoffrey Davidson	KA 175	158.0

Above: Start line in 1979
Below: Start line in 1980

26. Gold Cup 1981
Grömitz, Federal Rep. Germany, July 5-19
110 entries from 22 countries

After three years of US dominance Europe struck back. As much as John Bertrand had dominated the Finn scene in the previous years and Lewis had won the Gold Cup twice, now a new star had risen. Ex Laser sailor Lasse Hjortnäs from Denmark had won 22 out of 24 important individual races in the previous international top events. Everybody expected Lasse to win the Gold Cup as well. However in Grömitz Hjortnäs had gear problems with Carl Buchan's old Vanguard and dropped back. Instead, Wolfgang Gerz with his fairly old Lanaverre, had tremendous speed and could afford to play it safe. He always started very conservatively but finally had two wins and three 2nds with a 4th as his discard to win the Gold Cup with 9 points, the lowest score since the new Olympic scoring system was used. Wolfgang also was the oldest Gold Cup winner up to now. After the racing Wolfgang consoled Lasse, half as old as himself, that there will be many more Gold Cups to be won, a word Hjortnäs remembered well in 1982, 84 and 85.

Final Results Gold Cup 1981

1.	Wolfgang Gerz	G 1573	9.0
2.	Lasse Hjortnäs	D 143	29.7
3.	Miroslav Rychcik	PZ 75	49.4
4.	Otto Pohlmann	G 1787	53.0
5.	Jorgen Lindhardtsen	D 142	72.7
6.	Martin Palsson	S 684	76.0
7.	Henry Blaszka	PZ 6	90.7
8.	Tim Law	K 467	94.7
9.	Larry Lemieux	KC 204	95.7
10.	Fillip Willems	B 15	100.0
11.	Patrick Spängs	S 685	115.0
12.	Russ Silvestri	US 1059	115.0
13.	Ivor Ganahl	Z 383	127.0
14.	Michael Nissen	G 1796	130.7
15.	Don Norquist	S 690	131.7
16.	Juan Mägli	GU 1	132.0
17.	Martin Van Leeuwen	H 565	139.0
18.	Monty Spindler	US 1059	142.0
19.	Thomas Schmid	G 1749	142.0
20.	Thomas Rudolphi	G 1689	148.0
21.	Alfis Georgiadis	GR 69	150.0
22.	Wolfgang Mayrhofer	OE 199	151.0
23.	Robert Anoll	US 1058	153.0
24.	Andy Pimental	US 1056	153.0
25.	Mike McIntyre	K 423	162.0
26.	Rob. Woodbury	KC 19	162.0
27.	Paolo Semeraro	I 666	171.7
28.	Werner Suelberg	G 1511	179.0
29.	Joaquin Blanco	E 179	161.7
30.	Franciso De Angeles	I 655	189.0
31.	Francois le Castrec	F 741	190.0
32.	T. Schmidt-Grael	BL 9	196.0
33.	Jacek Sobkowiak	PZ 7	203.0
34.	Walter Mai	G 1726	206.0
35.	Craig Healy	US 1041	207.0
36.	Lennart Persson	S 680	207.0

27. Gold Cup 1982
Medemblik, Holland, September 9-19
126 entries from 22 countries

After 1963, Medemblik was the site of the Gold Cup once again in 1982. The Ijsselmeer generally enjoys good wind conditions, but obviously does not like to be used for the Gold Cup and had poor weather conditions as 19 years before. Only five races were sailed in light winds and sometimes heavy fog. There was a full station measurement for all boats. After Lasse Hjortnäs was nosed out the previous year by Wolfgang Gerz in Grömitz, he won the Cup in this shortened series. In the second race, Lasse was disqualified in a severe five minute rule incident together with 12 other boats. So he only could hope for a minimum of 5 races and therefore one discard. Generally Lasse showed an outstanding ability to pick the correct side on the beats. Henryk Blaszka was the most consistent and ended up second by conservative sailing and good speed.

Final Results Gold Cup 1982

1.	Lasse Hjortnäs	D 143	28.0
2.	Henryk Blaszka	PZ 6	42.4
3.	Buzz Reynolds	US 996	51.0
4.	Wolfgang Gerz	G 1573	61.0
5.	Terry Neilson	KC 69	72.7
6.	Joaquin Blanco	E 179	90.0
7.	Martin Van Leeuwen	H 565	91.0
8.	Mark Neeleman	H 555	95.0
9.	Francois le Castrec	F 888	98.0
10.	Per Nilsen	N 120	99.7
11.	Tom Jungell	L 200	101.7
12.	Ivor Ganahl	Z 383	105.0
13.	Peter Eriksson	S 679	111.0
14.	Peter Vollebregt	H 535	111.0
15.	Luc Choley	F 100	113.0
16.	James Hahn	US 1034	115.0
17.	Michael Nissen	G 1828	117.7

18.	Karsten Kaufmann	G 1706	119.0
19.	Andy Pimental	US 1052	120.0
20.	Mats Ehrnrooth	L 201	121.0
21.	Miroslav Rychcik	PZ 75	125.0
22.	Lutz Patrunky	G 1806	128.0
23.	Chris Frijdal	H 586	129.0
24.	Juan Mägli	GU 1	130.0
25.	Kimo Worthington	US 1066	131.0
26.	Martin Palsson	S 684	131.7
27.	Don Nordquist	S 690	133.0
28.	Jacek Sobkowiak	PZ 7	137.7
29.	Mark Lammens	KC 19	138.0
30.	Tim Law	K 488	138.0
31.	Jorgen Lindhardtsen	D 142	142.0
32.	Esko Rechardt	L 203	142.7
33.	Patrick Spängs	S 685	143.0
34.	Tony Nyren	S 686	148.0
35.	Stefan Myralf	D 148	150.0
36.	Nigel Walbank	K 481	157.0
37.	Sjaak Haakman	H 577	162.7
38.	Jörgen Rosengren	S 699	165.0
39.	Han Beverijk	H 558	173.0
40.	Kurt Schimitzek	OE 2	174.0
41.	Thomas Schmid	G 1793	175.0
42.	Josef Oberbauer	G 678	176.0

28. Gold Cup 1983

Milwaukee, USA, August 11-20
94 entries from 25 countries

After all the heck-meck with the station 8/6 in the previous years the Americans decided to teach the Finn world a lesson and staged the 1983 Gold Cup in a pond in the back yard of the Harken brothers in front of the Milwaukee breweries. John Christianson was called back on duty to build the most perfect jig and there was no dispute about what is a Finn or not. Consequently the IFA decided to make the Christianson jig the standard for all future Finn measurement. In the first race the international jury disqualified four potential winners for infringement of rule 60 (Means of Propulsion) setting another standard of highest moral. Most of the races were sailed in light and shifty winds, veering with the sun. Only two races enjoyed fresh air. Without winning a single race Paul van Cleve, from the U.S. Navy, won the Cup in front of Wolfgang Gerz, who had two 1sts but a 25th to count. Terry Neilson also with two victories collected a 33rd in the last race after a DSQ in the first, by going up the wrong side and lost. Mark Neeleman was another potential winner with a 14th as his discard.

Final Results Gold Cup 1983

1.	Paul Van Cleve	US 1023	54.7
2.	Wolfgang Gerz	G 1573	62.0
3.	Mark Neeleman	H 555	67.4
4.	Mike McIntyre	K 491	88.7
5.	Henryk Blaszka	PZ 6	96.7
6.	Terry Neilson	KC 69	99.0
7.	Lasse Hjortnäs	D 143	105.0
8.	Reynolds	US 996	119.1
9.	John Greenwood	K 495	142.0
10.	Larry Lemieux	KC 201	145.0
11.	Nigel Walbank	K 481	151.7
12.	Larry Kleist	KA 181	154.0
13.	Russell Coutts	KZ 226	158.0
14.	Miroslav Rychcik	PZ 75	159.7
15.	Jorge Zarif	BL 99	160.8
16.	Sjaak Haakman	H 577	161.7
17.	Paolo Semeraro	I 6	172.0
18.	Martin Van Leeuwen	H 565	172.0
18.	Kimo Worthington	US 1066	172.0
20.	Andy Pimental	US 1052	177.0
21.	Peter Quigley	US 1040	190.0
22.	Patrick Spängs	S 585	199.0
23.	Tom Dodson	KZ 229	204.0
24.	Juan Mägli	GU 1	207.0
25.	Roddy Bridge	K 493	208.0
26.	Lutz Patrunky	C 1806	209.0
27.	Lou Nady	US 1009	210.0
28.	Tim Law	K 488	212.0
29.	Jorgen Lindhardtsen	D 142	213.7
30.	Lammens	KC 19	217.0
31.	Alex Smigelski	PZ 1002	218.0
32.	Derek Mess	KC 115	222.0

29. Gold Cup 1984

Anzio, Rome, Italy, May 17-27
103 entries from 29 countries

Strong winds up to gale force characterised this world championship. Nice breezes during the measurement days were followed by days of storms, not allowing any race to be sailed. Five days of strong wind allowed 6 races, but on the last day the wind and waves were again too much. Terry Neilson, who was just behind Lasse, would have liked to sail again but Hjortnäs found it to be too dangerous. The old man of the sea Jörgen Lindhardtsen aged 39 was leading overall up to race 4 but later collected 22nd and 20th and was finally third. For his mental son Lasse Hjortnäs, 2/4/11/3/3 was good enough to win the Cup for the second time after 1982, just 0.3 points ahead of Terry Neilson. Larry Lemieux had some water in his double bottom in the beginning, but won two races after he took it out. Buzz Reynolds, who at the time of the Gold Cup thought he was to be the US representative for the Olympics damaged his best mast on the first day in the gale.

Final Results Gold Cup 1984

1.	Lasse Hjortnäs	D 143	39.4
2.	Terry Neilson	KC 69	39.7
3.	Jörgen Lindhardtsen	D 142	55.0
4.	Lawrence Lemieux	KC 201	62.0
5.	Thomas Schmid	G 1793	70.0
6.	Thomas Oljelund	S 700	71.7
7.	Russell Coutts	KZ 1	77.4
8.	Mark Neeleman	H 555	79.7
9.	Patrick Spängs	S 685	83.7
10.	Buzz Reynolds	US 1073	89.0
11.	Ingvar Bengtsson	S 698	99.0
12.	Martin Palsson	S 684	102.7
13.	Peter Vilby	D 146	104.0
14.	Paolo Semeraro	I 6	121.0
15.	Wolfgang Gerz	G 1573	122.7
16.	Antonio Ferrer	E 170	134.0
17.	Larry Kleist	KA 181	135.0
18.	Mark Page	KZ 2	138.0
19.	Bert Zielhuis	H 544	139.0
20.	Roberto Benamati	I 658	143.0
21.	Juan E. Mägli	GU 1	143.7
22.	Luc Choley	F 100	151.0
23.	Henryk Blaszka	PZ 6	155.0
24.	Jacek Sobkowiak	PZ 7	158.0
25.	Miroslav Rychcik	PZ 75	160.0
26.	Lutz Patrunky	G 1806	163.0
27.	Derek Mess	KC 115	164.0
28.	Johan Hedberg	S 697	164.0
29.	Benedetto Allotta	I 9	168.0
30.	Vilhelm Roberts	L 201	182.0
31.	Peter Holmberg	VI 1	184.0
32.	Jorge Zarif	BL 99	184.0
33.	Roy Heiner	OE 229	187.0
34.	Ron van Manen	H 616	189.0
35.	Jaroslaw Macuik	PZ 52	193.0
36.	Othmar Mv Blumencron	G 1835	196.0
37.	Kristian Sjöberg	L 195	197.0
38.	John Hofland	H 622	197.0

30. Gold Cup 1985

Marstrand, Sweden, June 26 - July 6
101 entries from 25 countries

In contrast to all predictions the wind in Marstrand never increased above force 3 during this Gold Cup. The current was fairly strong. However nobody was able to read it, let alone predict it. Those who neglected it and did not worry about it had the best results. Everyday a different sailor was leading overall. Biased start lines required the severe sudden death five minute rule to be frequently applied and a number of favourites were disqualified. The jury was busy to grant a few additional DSQs. There was only one man, who finished six times among the top 6 boats, Khoperski, however one line honour was scored as PMS. The jury also gave a severe warning because of team sailing. At the beginning of the last race, four people still could have won the cup. Sobkowiak eliminated himself with a bold PMS under the five minute, rule. Peter Vilby played it safe for the competition by sailing closer to 100 than to 1st. The Gold Cup 1985 was open between Oleg Khoperski, who gradually fell back from fourth position, and Lasse Hjortnäs, who improved slowly after a poor start. Finally Lasse was only one place behind Oleg, enough to take the Gold Cup for the third time after 1982 and 1984. There was only 0.1 points between him and Khoperski, the closest win ever between Gold and Silver in the history of the Finn World Championship.

Final Results Gold Cup 1985

1.	Lasse Hjortnäs	D 143	74.0
2.	Oleg Khoperski	SR 21	74.1
3.	Ingvar Bengtsson	S 698	83.7
4.	Steve MacLoud	US 1070	83.7
5.	Jacek Sobkowiak	PZ 7	89.7
6.	Lawrence Lemieux	KC 201	92.7
7.	Stig Westergaard	D 155	100.4
8.	Brian Ledbetter	US 1080	111.0
9.	John Cutler	KZ 234	112.0
10.	Joaquin Blanco	E 179	118.0
11.	Thomas Oljelund	S 700	129.7
12.	Frank Butzmann	DDR 16	121.0
13.	Henryk Blaszka	PZ 6	131.7
14.	Heike Birke	DDR 19	139.0
15.	Russ Silvestri	US 1074	140.7
16.	Peter Vilby	D 156	146.0
17.	Arnoud Hummel	H 577	153.0
18.	Peter Peet	H 630	161.0
19.	Jörgen Lindhardtsen	D 142	161.0
20.	K. Gordeiko	SR 32	161.0
21.	Mark Lammens	KC 19	162.0
22.	Jaroslav Maciuk	PZ 52	178.0
23.	John Greenwood	K 495	179.0
24.	Derek Mess	KC 115	180.0
25.	Terry Neilson	KC 69	181.7
26.	Marco Passoni	I 8	203.0
27.	V. Roberts	L 210	204.0
28.	Johan Hedberg	S 697	207.0
29.	Lauri Rechardt	L 185	209.0
30.	Miroslav Rychcik	PZ 75	213.0
31.	Tony Nyren	S 509	228.0
32.	Thomas Schmid	G 1793	235.0
33.	Kristian Sjöberg	L 201	236.0

31. Gold Cup 1986

Palma de Mallorca, Spain, July 5-13
82 entries from 21 countries

The event was clouded by problems. To start with there were measurement problems after a Vanguard with an illegal centreboard was disqualified from the first race. Many sailors were then seen with their boats on their sides working on their centreboards. Then there was the weather conditions which proved very tricky with corridors of stronger wind over the course which favoured those who knew where they were. Then there were protests of team racing in the final deciding race when any of four boats could have won the Gold Cup. Of the five sailors who could have won going into the last race Paolo Semeraro blew his chances by being PMS. Peter Vilby, Frank Butzmann and José Doreste (winner of two races) had a bad race, as did the overall winner Stig Westergaard, who didn't win a single race but was ahead on points after the final count.

Final Results Gold Cup 1986

1.	Stig Westergaard	D 155	90.0
2.	Brian Ledbetter	US 1080	97.0
3.	José Luis Doreste	E 109	101.0
4.	Dirk Löwe	DDR 14	107.0
5.	Johan Hedberg	S 700	111.0
6.	Jali Makila	L 207	112.7
7.	Peter Vilby	D 156	116.0
8.	Paolo Semeraro	I 6	120.0
9.	Frank Butzmann	DDR 16	123.1
10.	Christoph Bergmann	BL 96	129.7
11.	Jacek Sobkowiak	PZ 7	135.0
12.	Heiko Birke	DDR 19	138.0
13.	Joaquin Blanco	E 179	143.0
14.	Stuart Childerley	K 503	146.0
15.	Lauri Rechardt	L 185	148.0
16.	Ralf Kadenbach	G 6	149.7
17.	Lasse Hjortnäs	D 143	151.7
18.	Peter Truslow	US 47	173.0
19.	Gordie Anderson	KC 171	173.0
20.	Thomas Schmid	G 1793	175.0
21.	John Cutler	KZ 234	175.7
22.	Roddy Bridge	K 493	177.0
23.	Lawrence Lemieux	KC 201	184.7
24.	Bart Zielhuis	H 544	185.0
25.	John Hofland	H 622	193.7
26.	Mark Lammens	KC 19	194.0
27.	Miguel Noguer	E 162	194.7
28.	S. Fleckenstein	KC 8	197.0
29.	Derek Mess	KC 115	199.0
30.	Timothy Tavinor	K 504	205.0
31.	Henryk Blaszka	PZ 6	212.0
32.	Kristian Sjöberg	L 201	221.0
33.	Henrik Hammelso	D 158	223.0
34.	Enrico Passoni	I 722	223.7
35.	Anders Lundmark	S 708	225.7
36.	Peter Peet	H 630	229.0
37.	Ch. van Voorhis	US 1052	231.0

32. Gold Cup 1987

Kiel, West Germany, June 26 - July 7
57 entries from 17 countries

Straight after Kiel Week were held the 'Kiel Worlds '87', a joint World Championship for several classes. The Finns shared a course with the 470s, a two hour sail from the beach. Measurement problems again overshadowed the racing, with several boats being found illegal, even after several years of competition, and protests were numerous. In the fifth race, Doreste was already the sure winner of the Gold Cup, finishing second. In the sixth race, Doreste did not have to sail and Lasse Hjortnäs managed a 4th, thus finishing as runner up to Brian Ledbetter.

Final Results Gold Cup 1987

1.	José Luis Doreste	E 109	19.7
2.	Lasse Hjortnäs	D 143	61.0
3.	Brian Ledbetter	US 1080	83.0
4.	Ralf Kadenbach	G 6	95.0
5.	Roy Heiner	H 638	102.0
6.	O M von Blumencron	G 1892	103.0
7.	Mark Neeleman	H 555	115.7
8.	Welf-Bodo Lixenfeld	G 1706	127.7
9.	Hans Spitzauer	OE 218	129.7
10.	Armando Ortolano	GR 211	139.0
11.	Lawrence Lemieux	KC 201	148.0
12.	Emmanuele Vaccari	I 727	154.4
13.	Stuart Childerley	K 503	154.7
14.	Henryk Blaszka	PZ 8	161.7
15.	John Cutler	KZ 234	164.0
16.	John Irvine	KZ 235	167.0
17.	Louis Verloop	US 1066	169.0
18.	Mike Milner	KC 4	172.0
19.	Peter Vilby	D 156	181.0
20.	Lawrence Crispin	K 498	182.0
21.	Gordon Anderson	KC 171	183.7
22.	Mark Littlejohn	K 481	185.0
23.	Lauri Rechardt	L 185	191.0
24.	Kristian Sjoeberg	L 201	192.0
25.	Thomas Schmid	G 1793	197.0
26.	Wolfgang Gerz	G 1573	197.0
27.	Bart Zielhuis	H 544	200.0
28.	Michael Fischer	OE 223	203.0
29.	Nicolai Suchorokov	SR 1	205.0
30.	Rubën Serra	E 106	210.0

33. Gold Cup 1988

Ilha Bela, Brazil, January 31-February 11
48 entries from 11 countries

Almost all the sailors arrived a week early, but unfortunately the boats arrived late because of a queue of ships in Santos harbour. However all boats arrived on time for the Championship. As soon as the Championship began, with measurement and registration, the sun didn't come out any more and it rained every day. The racing was hard and the sailors were faced with all kinds of different situations and wind strengths. The winner, Thomas Schmid, was the best on the water, leading from race 3 onwards and winning race 4. No sailor won more than one race and going into the last race only Roy Heiner could beat Schmid. But Schmid finished 27th to Heiner's 28th and after the prizegiving paid for 300 beers for everyone.

Final Results Gold Cup 1988

1.	Thomas Schmid	G 1903	48.8
2.	Roy Heiner	H 638	58.4
3.	Gordon Anderson	KC 171	78.7
4.	Welf-Bodo Lixenfeld	G 1706	81.0
5.	Lasse Hjortnäs	D 143	85.0
6.	Stuart Childerley	K 503	92.0
7.	Lauri Rechardt	L 185	105.0
8.	Peter Tanscheit	BL 68	106.7
9.	Lawrence Lemieux	KC 201	107.0
10.	Brian Ledbetter	US 1080	110.0
11.	Othmar M v Blumencron	G 1892	110.7
12.	Fred Kennedy	KC 221	116.0
13.	Emanuele Vaccari	I 727	117.0
14.	John Hofland	H 622	121.0
15.	Arnoud Hummel	H 577	122.7
16.	Lawrence Crispin	K 498	126.7
17.	Paolo Semeraro	I 716	128.0
18.	Peter Vilby	D 156	130.0
19.	Peter Shope	US 1000	130.0
20.	Kristian Sjöberg	L 201	134.0

34. Gold Cup 1989

Alassio, Italy, April 6-16
72 entries from 20 countries

Held in the beautiful Alassio Bay, the wind
was the only problem: too much or too little.
Among the favourites were Thomas Schmid,
Stig Westergaard and Oleg Khoperski. After
race 5, Mexican Eric Mergenthaler was leading
overall, winning races 1 and 5. Veteran Danish
sailor Jörgen Lindhardtsen won race 2,
Khoperski won race 3 and Armando Ortolano
won race 4. In race 5 Khoperski broke his
mast and had to count a 38th in his final score.
Still wide open going into the last day, 2 races
were sailed in strong winds. Defending
Champion Schmid scored a 1st and 2nd to
move to 7th overall. Mergenthaler recorded
two mid-teen results to drop to second overall
and with Stig Westergaard winning the final
race, the Gold Cup was his again, after first
winning it in 1986.

35. Gold Cup 1990

Porto Carras, Greece, July 5-15
105 entries from 25 countries

The Canadians almost cleaned up in 1990 with
only Lasse Hjortnäs and Eric Mergenthaler
stopping a 1,2,3 for Canada. After losing the
Gold Cup in the last race of the 1989 event,
Mexican Eric Mergenthaler was out to win.
He moved into the lead after five races and
going into the last race was 19 points clear of
Hank Lammens and 34 points clear of Larry
Lemieux. However he also had a DSQ in race
2 for pumping, so could not afford a bad result
in the final race. As it turned out he was 48th
at the gybe mark, pulled back to 31st after the
second beat and eventually finished 34th. But
it wasn't enough. Lammens finished 13th and
Lemieux 3rd, which dropped Mergenthaler to
3rd overall. It was the first time that a Canadian
had won a Finn Gold Cup and they had three
boats in the top five as well. Anders Lundmark,
who had lead at the first mark four times
during the week finally won the last race and
ended up 7th overall.

Final Results Gold Cup 1990

1.	Hank Lammens	KC 19	75.7
2.	Lawrence Lemieux	KC 201	77.4
3.	Eric Mergenthaler	MX 33	77.7
4.	Lasse Hjortnäs	D 143	87.7
5.	Mike Milner	KC 4	97.7
6.	Kiko Villalonga	E 106	99.7
7.	Anders Lundmark	S 700	107.7
8.	Alex Cutler	US 1044	107.7
9.	Philipp Malte	DDR 25	113.0
10.	Dirk Löwe	DDR 16	140.4
11.	Simon Gorman	KA 175	146.0
12.	Fredrik Lööf	S 684	149.0
13.	Enrico Passoni	I 722	161.0
14.	Joaquin Blanco	E 179	169.0
15.	Jeremy Fanstone	K 498	171.0
16.	Stig Westergaard	D 155	171.0
17.	Gordie Anderson	KC 171	175.0
18.	Toni Poncell	E 12	178.5
19.	Yuri Tokovoi	SR 21	180.7
20.	Hans Spitzauer	OE 218	181.0
21.	Brian Ledbetter	US 1080	182.0
22.	Richard Clarke	KC 11	184.0
23.	Alexander Rinne	G 1912	207.0
24.	Oleg Khoperski	SR 14	209.0
25.	Thomas Schmid	G 1903	211.0
26.	Mats Caap	S 718	218.4
27.	Armando Ortolano	GR 211	221.7
28.	Tim Tavinor	K 521	225.0
29.	Peter Aldag	G 1920	226.8
30.	Maciej Skibski	PZ 75	229.0
31.	Otto Strandvig	D 146	237.0
32.	Nick Jako	KC 13	240.0
33.	David Drappeau	F 758	242.0
34.	Lauri Rechardt	L 185	250.0
35.	Attila Szilvàssy	M 211	250.0
36.	Arif Gürdenli	TK 211	251.0
37.	A Papantoniou	GR 205	264.0
38.	Haluk Babacan	TK 52	264.0
39.	Ville Aalto-Setala	L 198	266.0
40.	Gerd Griegel	G 1711	268.8

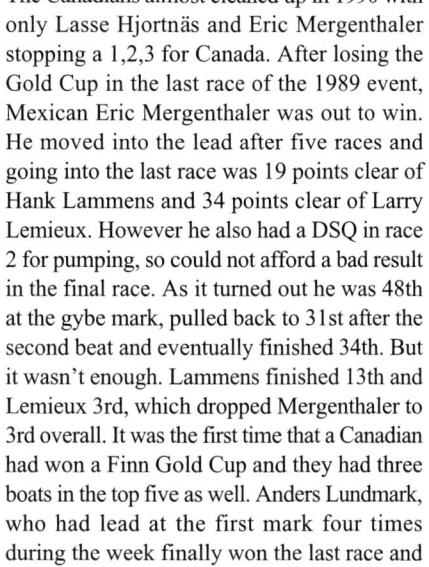

Final Results Gold Cup 1989

1.	Stig Westergaard	D 155	54.4		16.	Anders Lundmark	S 700	129.0
2.	Eric Mergenthaler	MX 33	63.0		17.	Othmar M v Blumencron	Z 418	131.0
3.	Oleg Khoperski	SR 14	63.4		18.	Jali Makila	L 212	139.0
4.	Hans Spitzauer	OE 218	65.7		19.	Bart Zielhuis	H 544	148.0
5.	Dirk Löwe	DDR 16	74.7		20.	Emmanuele Vaccari	I 727	152.0
6.	Yuri Tokovoi	SR 21	81.4		21.	Per Erik Wall	S 713	153.0
7.	Thomas Schmid	G 1903	87.0		22.	John Hofland	H 6	154.0
8.	Armando Ortolano	GR 211	88.7		23.	Welf-Bodo Lixenfeld	G 1706	165.0
9.	Enrico Passoni	I 722	89.7		24.	Alexander Rinne	G 1912	175.0
10.	Lauri Rechardt	L 185	103.4		25.	Peter Aldag	G 1893	176.0
11.	Heiko Birke	DDR 19	107.0		26.	Bo Steffan Andersson	S 714	176.0
12.	Marco Passoni	I 710	107.0		27.	Roger Schulz	G 1984	179.0
13.	Mats Caap	S 718	111.0		28.	Marco Fioretto	I 701	180.0
14.	Lars Bergenzaun	S 698	115.7		29.	Francisco Villalonga	E 106	188.0
15.	Jörgen Lindhardtsen	D 142	121.7		30.	Michael Maier	CZ 304	202.0

36. Gold Cup 1991

Kingston, Canada, August 22-September 2
96 entries from 21 countries

Defending Champion Hank Lammens opened the series with a win and apart from one bad race was always in the leading bunch and took the title by 10.7 points. The weather conditions were very variable and provided some of the windiest conditions of recent Gold Cups. Lammens led until the sixth race, until a string of good results brought Fredrik Lööf into the top spot going in the last day. Any of four boats could have taken the Gold Cup on the last day. Lööf was leading the score sheet, but Lammens, Brian Ledbetter and Oleg Khoperski could also win, but all had already got a bad result, so they couldn't afford another one. Lööf started badly and was out of it from the start. Lammens won the race to be sure of his second consecutive Gold Cup. Ledbetter was third to finish runner up and Khoperski was seventh in the race to take third overall

Final Results Gold Cup 1991

1.	Hank Lammens	KC 19	46.7
2.	Brian Ledbetter	US 1080	57.4
3.	Oleg Khoperski	SR 14	77.7
4.	Fredrik Lööf	S 684	80.7
5.	Stuart Childerley	K 503	96.0
6.	Stig Westergaard	D 165	106.0
7.	Xavier Rohart	F 748	109.0
8.	François le Castrec	F 749	115.0
9.	Lawrence Lemieux	KC 201	118.0
10.	Anders Lundmark	S 700	120.0
11.	Hans Spitzauer	OE 218	120.0
12.	Glenn Bourke	KA 182	123.0
13.	Eric Mergenthaler	MX 33	128.0
14.	Richard Clarke	KC 11	129.0
15.	Dirk Löwe	G 14	129.0
16.	Yuri Tokovoi	SR 21	145.0
17.	Michael Fellmann	G 1916	153.0
18.	Malte Philipp	G 25	161.0
19.	Thomas Schmid	G 93	164.0
20.	Peter Aldag	G 1920	167.0
21.	Mark Herrmann	US 1026	172.0
22.	Kiko Villalonga	E 106	178.0
23.	Craig Monk	KZ 237	181.0
24.	Mats Caap	S 718	182.0
25.	Alec Cutler	US 1044	183.0
26.	Luca Devoti	I 789	186.0
27.	David Himmell	US 1066	186.0
28.	Otto Strandvig	D 146	192.0
29.	Richard Byron	US 1060	197.0
30.	Mike Milner	KC 4	199.0
31.	Richard Lott	K 484	200.0
32.	Philippe Presti	F 762	202.0

37. Gold Cup 1992

Cadiz, Spain, May 7-17
94 entries from 32 countries

The 1998 Gold Cup was held in Cadiz as part of the Mundo Vela '92, a series of sailing events involving Olympic classes and offshore racers to commemorate the discovery of America by Columbus. At the opening ceremony, Vice President (Sailing) Björn Westergaard, reminded everyone that long before Columbus 'discovered' the Americas, a Dane called Eric the Viking had landed there. After two light weather races, the first being won by Oleg Khoperski and the second being won by 57 year old Gus Miller, the wind arrived. Peter Aldag won the third race in strong winds. A day was then lost because the wind was too strong, and then Craig Monk won the windy 4th race. Two races were sailed on the last day. The first went to Xavier Rohart. Craig Monk was leading after five races, but a protest from the jury about his black bands in race 5 affected him so much he dropped out of the last race and applied for average points. In the race Eric Mergenthaler was now the favourite, but his boom broke halfway up the final beat. This meant that either Glenn Bourke or Hans Spitzauer could win if they did well enough - but they didn't and Brian Ledbetter won the race. Monk's protest was disallowed and the jury penalised him with a DND which dropped him to 19th overall. This meant that Eric Mergenthaler had finally won the Finn Gold Cup.

Final Results Gold Cup 1992

1.	Eric Mergenthaler	MX 33	61.7
2.	Glenn Bourke	KA 182	64.7
3.	Hans Spitzauer	OE 218	65.0
4.	Brian Ledbetter	US 1080	74.0
5.	Peter Aldag	G 1920	82.7
6.	Hank Lammens	KC 19	83.7
7.	Xavier Rohart	F 748	92.0
8.	Björn Westergaard	D 165	102.0
9.	Oleg Khoperski	IYRU 14	104.0
10.	Stuart Childerley	K 503	106.0
11.	Christoph Bergmann	BL 87	109.0
12.	Stig Westergaard	D 155	109.7
13.	Armando Ortolano	GR 1	110.0
14.	Lasse Hjortnäs	D 143	114.0
15.	Jali Makila	L 212	114.7
16.	Enrico Passoni	I 722	131.0
17.	Anders Lundmark	S 700	131.7
18.	Fredrik Lööf	S 684	132.0
19.	Craig Monk	KZ 237	135.7
20.	Jeremy Fanstone	K 498	140.0
21.	Michael Fellmann	G 1916	144.0
22.	José van der Ploeg	E 105	144.0
23.	Emanuele Vaccari	I 727	147.7
24.	Alexander Rinne	G 31	148.0
25.	Dirk Löwe	G 14	149.0
26.	Othmar M v Blumencron	Z 418	152.0
27.	Philippe Presti	F 762	152.0
28.	Luca Devoti	I 789	156.7
29.	Bart Zielhuis	H 544	161.7

Left: Gus Miller leading race 2 in 1992
Below: Monk and Merganthaler

38. Gold Cup 1993

Bangor, Northern Ireland, July 9-19
61 entries from 19 countries

No one managed to win more than one race, the overall results saw a different leader after each race and the overall winner Philippe Presti didn't win a single race. The racing was very close and for the first time in many years a variety of hulls filled the top positions (4 different hulls in top 5). In addition, carbon masts were starting to be used (Lööf and Westergaard). After six races Roy Heiner was leading but with only 6.25 points separating the top 5 places it was all down to the last race. Heiner went the wrong way and ended up 12th. Spitzauer dropped out with gear failure, so now it was down to three. At the last mark Presti in the new Devoti hull was 3rd, Lööf 4th and Richard Clarke sailing the new boat from Larry Lemieux was 5th. Lööf passed Presti but needed to pass one more boat to take the title. But it wasn't to be. Lööf finished 3rd, and Presti crossed the line 4th, less than half a meter ahead of Clarke. Philippe Presti had won and again Fredrik Lööf would have to wait another year.

Final Results Gold Cup 1993

1.	Philippe Presti	FRA 762	28.00
2.	Fredrik Lööf	SWE 7	28.75
3.	Richard Clarke	CAN 11	34.00
4.	Roy Heiner	NED 638	34.75
5.	Hans Spitzauer	AUT 1	35.00
6.	Hank Lammens	CAN 19	37.00
7.	Jali Makila	FIN 1	47.75
8.	Othmar Mv Blumencron	SUI 1	49.75
9.	Stig Westergaard	DEN 155	58.75
10.	Mark Herrmann	USA 1026	60.00
11.	Will Martin	USA 1132	66.00
12.	Anders Lundmark	SWE 699	70.00
13.	Craig Monk	NZL 237	71.75
14.	Xavier Rohart	FRA 778	101.00
15.	Michael Fellmann	GER 79	102.00
16.	David Shelton	USA 1109	104.00
17.	Mark Lammens	CAN 9	106.00
18.	Luca Devoti	ITA 789	108.75
19.	Mauro Fioretto	ITA 791	116.00
20.	Ville Aalto-Setala	FIN 2	122.00
21.	Darrell Peck	USA 1081	124.00

Philippe Presti

39. Gold Cup 1994

Pärnu, Estonia, August 12-21
69 entries from 23 countries

After being the first Olympic class to sail its World Championships in Northern Ireland in 1993, the Finns again found an unconventional place to sail the Gold Cup. Just over 100km away from the site of the 1980 Olympic regatta in Tallinn, the Finns found beautiful sailing water with good winds and good racing: one of the best Gold Cups ever was the unanimous verdict. The weather started wet and windy and ended with more moderate conditions. No sailor won more than one race and the racing was tight until the end. Fredrik Lööf had twice lost the Gold Cup on the last day. This time he took the lead after day two, won race four and then taking each day as it came maintained his points lead over Hank Lammens. Half way through the last race, Lammens had the lead with Lööf in 10th, enough for Lammens to win his 3rd Gold Cup. But José Maria van de Ploeg went more to one side and took the lead. Lööf fought back to 7th while Lammens slipped to 3rd. It was enough for Fredrik Lööf to win the Gold Cup for the first time.

Final Results Gold Cup 1994

1.	Fredrik Lööf	SWE 7	21.75
2.	Hank Lammens	CAN 19	24.75
3.	José Maria v d Ploeg	ESP 105	28.75
4.	Hans Spitzauer	AUT 1	30.00
5.	Richard Clarke	CAN 11	32.75
6.	Craig Monk	NZL 237	38.75
7.	Dirk Löwe	GER 14	48.00
8.	Philippe Presti	FRA 762	57.75
9.	Othmar Mv Blumencron	SUI 1	65.00
10.	Xavier Rohart	FRA 778	77.75
11.	Michael Maier	CZE 304	88.00
12.	Lawrence Lemieux	CAN 201	93.00
13.	Mateusz Kusznierewicz	POL 17	101.00
14.	Dominik Zycki	POL 4	102.00
15.	Sebastien Godefroid	BEL 7	107.00
16.	Darrell Peck	USA 1081	120.00
17.	David Shelton	USA 1137	131.00
18.	Michael Fellmann	GER 79	133.00
19.	Jali Makila	FIN 1	134.00
20.	Philippe Rogge	BEL 2	134.00
21.	Mauro Fioretto	ITA 781	136.00
22.	John Driscoll	IRL 1	137.00
23.	Robert Eric Oetgen	USA 1087	142.00
24.	Will Martin	USA 1182	143.00
25.	Kalle Akerson	SWE 700	145.00
26.	Mark Lammens	CAN 9	154.00
27.	Igor Tkachuk	UKR 119	159.00
28.	Paul McKenzie	AUS 165	160.00
29.	James Lyne	GBR 534	164.00
30.	Andre Budzien	GER 70	164.00

40. Gold Cup 1995

Melbourne, Australia, January 9-15
65 entries from 23 countries

The 40th Finn Gold Cup was hosted by Black Rock Yacht Club, an off-the-beach dinghy club on Port Phillip. With the exception of Denmark and the Netherlands every Finn country with medal potential had sent its top sailors. Competition was therefore fierce. After conditions ranged from no wind to 25 knots during the first six races, the championship reached its climax with Hans Spitzauer leading defending champion Fredrik Lööf and Philippe Presti just 2 points further back. With no race possible after 3 pm and no wind at 2:45, everyone was convinced that there would be no race. But the wind kicked in and the start gun was fired at 2:59. With the biased line, the boats at the pin were over and a general recall was fired. So, Hans Spitzauer won the Gold Cup as they couldn't make another start. Spitzauer didn't win a race but his series score of 7, 2, 2, 2, 8, 4 was consistent enough to win by the smallest of margins. Fleet depth was also shown once more by the fact that the top 14 sailors came from 12 different countries.

Final Results Gold Cup 1995

1.	Hans Spitzauer	AUT 1	17.00
2.	Fredrik Lööf	SWE 7	17.75
3.	Philippe Presti	FRA 762	19.75
4.	Richard Clarke	CAN 11	28.75
5.	Xavier Rohart	FRA 778	31.75
6.	Hank Lammens	CAN 19	36.00
7.	Michael Fellmann	GER 79	42.00
8.	Luca Devoti	ITA 789	44.00
9.	José Maria v d Ploeg	ESP 105	62.75
10.	Michael Maier	CZE 304	64.00
11.	Jali Makila	FIN 215	68.00
12.	Dean Barker	NZL 247	71.00
13.	Peter Theurer	SUI 2	72.00
14.	Karlo Kuret	CRO 110	74.00
15.	Leith Armit	NZL 241	85.00
16.	Othmar Mv Blumencron	SUI 1	86.00
17.	Oleg Khoperski	RUS 21	88.0
18.	Paul McKenzie	AUS 208	99.0
19.	Andreas Buchert	GER 6	100.0
20.	Richard Stenhouse	GBR 540	101.0
21.	Larry Lemieux	CAN 201	103.0
22.	Dirk Löwe	GER 14	105.0
23.	Andre Budzien	GER 70	105.75
24.	Emanuele Vaccari	ITA 727	106.0
25.	Philippe Rogge	BEL 2	108.0

41. Gold Cup 1996

La Rochelle, France, May 1-10
71 entries from 27 countries

For the first time ever the Finn Gold Cup was combined with the Finn World Masters to bring together nearly 200 Finns from all over the world. The winds were generally strong and as usual the Gold Cup was decided on the last beat of the last race. Initially it looked as if defending champion Hans Spitzauer was going to have it easy collecting a 2nd and two wins. Philippe Presti then scored a 1st and a 2nd, closing the gap. Day 6 saw two windy races both won by Luca Devoti, an achievement not equalled by any other Finn sailor for many years. Going into the last race Spitzauer was 0.25 points clear of Presti with Jali Makila, Karlo Kuret and Fredrik Lööf not far behind. Initially it looks as if the Gold Cup was going to Makila, but a big shift on the second beat brought Lööf and Presti back to the front. Lööf finally won the race with Presti in 5th and Spitzauer in 6th. Philippe Presti had done enough to win his second Finn Gold Cup.

Final Results Gold Cup 1996

1.	Philippe Presti	FRA 762
2.	Hans Spitzauer	AUT 1
3.	Fredrik Lööf	SWE 7
4.	Karlo Kuret	CRO 11
5.	Jali Makila	FIN 215
6.	Sebastien Godefroid	BEL 7
7.	Roy Heiner	NED
8.	Yuri Tokovoi	UKR 21
9.	Michael Maier	CZE 304
10.	Hank Lammens	CAN 19
11.	Oleg Khoperski	RUS 21
12.	Xavier Rohart	FRA 778
13.	John Driscoll	IRL 1
14.	Luca Devoti	ITA 789
15.	Richard Stenhouse	GBR 540
16.	Mateusz Kusznierewicz	POL 17
17.	Michael Fellmann	GER 79
18.	Thomas Schmid	GER
19.	Richard Clarke	CAN 11
20.	Peter Theurer	SUI 440
21.	Paul McKenzie	AUS 208
22.	Walter Riosa	ITA 55
23.	Ian Ainslie	RSA 1
24.	Dominik Zycki	POL 4

42. Gold Cup 1997

Gdansk, Poland, July 3-13
81 entries from 29 countries

A good number of Finns turned-out for the post Olympic year Gold Cup which was held in the rough and often windy Gdansk Bay. As ever, the racing was close and intense and the depth of the fleet was demonstrated by the fact that the top 15 sailors came from 15 different countries and each race had a different winner. After 5 races Xavier Rohart was in the lead, but then a win by Luca Devoti moved him into the lead ahead of Fredrik Lööf and Rohart. Going into the last race there were only 3 points separating the top 3 boats. Each could win the Gold Cup on the last race, but Fredrik Lööf made sure of his second Gold Cup win by winning the last race to beat Luca Devoti by 3 points.

Final Results Gold Cup 1997

1.	Fredrik Lööf	SWE 7	21
2.	Luca Devoti	ITA 1	24
3.	Xavier Rohart	FRA 778	32
4.	Richard Clarke	CAN 11	45
5.	Sebastien Godefroid	BEL 7	49
6.	Hans Spitzauer	AUT 1	52
7.	Yuri Tokovoi	UKR 21	53
8.	Mateusz Kusznierewicz	POL 17	54
9.	Emilios Papathanasiou	GRE 6	65
10.	Michael Fellmann	GER 79	69
11.	Karlo Kuret	CRO 11	70
12.	Ian Ainslie	RSA 1	70
13.	Richard Stenhouse	GBR 550	72
14.	Rafael Trujillo Villar	ESP 100	75
15.	Oleg Khoperski	RUS 21	77
16.	Andreas Buchert	GER 6	79
17.	Michael Maier	CZE 304	80
18.	Iain Percy	GBR 540	86
19.	Ian Baker	NZL 242	87
20.	Dominik Zycki	POL 4	111
21.	Peter Theurer	SUI 456	120
22.	Philippe Rogge	BEL 2	130
23.	Paul McKenzie	AUS 208	136
24.	Dariusz Migacz	POL 40	148
25.	Darrell Peck	USA 1144	154
26.	John Driscoll	IRL 1	157
27.	Walter Riosa	ITA 55	162
28.	Igor Tkachuk	UKR 1	175
29.	Nenad Viali	CRO 14	183
30.	Michael Apoukhtin	RUS 14	183

43. Gold Cup 1998

Athens, Greece, August 16-23
84 entries from 26 countries

Sailed on the planned site for the 2004 Olympic Regatta in mainly light to moderate winds, this Gold Cup was a superb example of how to run an event. Everything was done to make sure that the competitors enjoyed themselves both on and off the water. Since his Gold Medal in the 1996 Olympics Mateusz Kusznierewicz had not won a title. But he was ready and prepared to do it this time. Having just won Kiel Week by a large margin he was fast and confident. He was only once out of the top ten and a score line of 1-2-3-9-2 was enough to win the Gold Cup. With an unstable wind the final race was cancelled. Runner-up Fredrik Lööf was leading the series in the middle but Mateusz took the lead when he could discard his 24th in race 2. Third placed Xavier Rohart won two races but was not consistent enough in the early part of the regatta to capitalise on it.

Final Results Gold Cup 1998

1.	Mateusz Kusznierewicz	POL 17	16
2.	Fredrik Lööf	SWE 7	20
3.	Xavier Rohart	FRA 778	27
4.	Sebastien Godefroid	BEL 7	28
5.	Emilios Papathanasiou	GRE 6	32
6.	Karlo Kuret	CRO 11	38
7.	Iain Percy	GBR 54	39
8.	Michael Maier	CZE 304	44
9.	Michael Fellmann	GER 79	51
10.	Richard Clarke	CAN 11	70
11.	David Burrows	IRL 8	73
12.	Andreas Buchert	GER 6	84
13.	Ian Ainslie	RSA 1	86
14.	Nenad Viali	ITA 14	86
15.	Dominik Zycki	POL 4	88
16.	Bartul Misura	CRO 118	99
17.	Martijn van Muyden	NED 701	100
18.	Richard Stenhouse	GBR 550	100
19.	Massimo Gherarducci	ITA 71	102
20.	Clifton Webb	NZL 27	107
21.	Anthony Nossiter	AUS 221	108
22.	Yuri Tokovoi	UKR 21	109
23.	Oleg Khoperski	RUS 21	109
24.	Bruno Prada	BRA 1	113
25.	Russ Silvestri	USA 1074	121
26.	Ian Baker	NZL 242	122
27.	Walter Riosa	ITA 55	123
28.	George Kontogouris	GRE 1	123
29.	Jamie Lea	GBR 564	135
30.	Tim Carver	GBR 8	136

44. Gold Cup 1999

Melbourne, Australia, January 6-16
71 entries from 29 countries

The 1999 Gold Cup was part of the 1999 World Sailing Championships which combined 14 different classes World Championships on Port Philip. For the first time ever, the Finns had a modified racing programme, sailing an eleven race series with two discards. Defending Champion Mateusz Kusznierewicz looked set to retain his title from early on in the series, taking the lead after day 3 and holding onto it until the last race. After a inconsistent start, double Finn Gold Cup winner Fredrik Lööf closed the gap in the second half of the regatta. Meanwhile Iain Percy scored three wins but was inconsistent otherwise. Similar was Michael Fellmann who also won three races but also had some high scores to count. Mateusz did not win a single race, Fredrik only one and going into the final race it was between these two only, well clear of the others on points. Iain Percy just needed a good race to hang onto the bronze. However, light winds caused up upset when both Mateusz and Iain failed to finish, leaving Fredrik the winner of the Gold Cup for the third time and Richard Clarke moving up to third overall. The winner of the last race was the Australian, Finn Taylor, who finished 32nd overall.

Final Results Gold Cup 1999

1.	Fredrik Lööf	SWE 7	38
2.	Mateusz Kusznierewicz	POL 17	39
3.	Richard Clarke	CAN 11	63
4.	Iain Percy	GBR 54	69
5.	Karlo Kuret	CRO 11	72
6.	Sebastien Godefroid	BEL 7	72
7.	Michael Fellmann	GER 79	95
8.	Martijn Van Muyden	NED 701	102
9.	Xavier Rohart	FRA 1	110
10.	Michael Maier	CZE 304	110
11.	Ian Ainslie	RSA 1	114
12.	Dave Mellor	GBR 540	117
13.	John Driscoll	IRL 1	132
14.	Andreas Buchert	GER 6	133
15.	Nenad Viali	ITA 14	147
16.	Paul McKenzie	AUS 222	151
17.	Ian Baker	NZL 242	152
18.	Philippe Rogge	BEL 2	171
19.	Peter Theurer	SUI 464	172
20.	Dominik Zycki	POL 4	174
21.	Anthony Nossiter	AUS 221	178
22.	Yuri Tokovoi	UKR 21	179
23.	Jamie Lea	GBR 564	183
24.	Bartul Misura	CRO 1	186
25.	Emilios Papathanasiou	GRE 6	201

1. Junior Gold Cup 1999

In 1999 the first ever Junior Finn Gold Cup took place in conjunction with the senior event. The places were scored directly from the overall results. A 9th place in race one and a 17th place in the final race gave Charlie Cumbley from the UK just enough of a points margin to become the first Junior Finn World Champion, by finishing 38th overall, only in the last race beating runner up George Kontogouris was 39th overall, just 5 points behind. The 3rd place went to the 1998 Junior Finn European Champion, Clifton Webb from New Zealand, who broke his arm before the last race, was some way behind in points and finished 44th overall.

Final Results Junior Gold Cup 1999

1.	Charlie Cumbley	GBR 15	271
2.	George Kontogouris	GRE 1	276
3.	Clifton Webb	NZL 27	341
4.	Daniel Bush	NZL 12	419
5.	Mauricio Bueno	BRA 100	459

18. The 'Perfect' Mast

by Antonio Latini

The relationship between the Finn sailor and his mast is really important and I think there is nothing comparable in the sport of sailing. It's a real love and hate relationship. There's no doubt that the mast, together with the sail, is the most important part of the Finn equipment. It's easy to imagine how much time and energy a Finn sailor dedicates to improving the performance of his rig. Sometimes it becomes an obsession for the Finn sailor. As a consequence every Finn sailor expects a 'magic' mast from the mast maker.

After the introduction of carbon-fibre in Finn masts there has been a real revolution and at first we all tried different solutions to the problems of design, aerodynamics, materials, construction methods and mast bend.

Design and Aerodynamics

The rules of the Finn class allowed us to build an aerodynamic profile that we call the 'wing mast'. Before the 'wing' we built masts with elliptical or round sections. The shape of the mast for a Finn does not have a big impact on its performance, even if it has been demonstrated that a 'wing' mast is aerodynamically more efficient. In practice this advantage is very small. The mast on a Finn does not rotate completely because it's restricted by the boom and this fact means

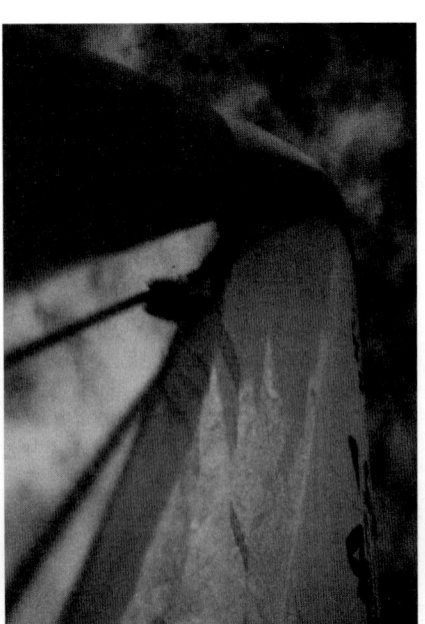

that the 'wing mast' does not reach the ideal angle of incidence to the wind. Another fact is that the Finn is a very slow boat and often the air flow on the sail is not laminar. The combination of the mast and the sail is the most important element of the problem, in spite of the mast shape (round or wing). Anyway, the 'wing' mast is now standard because at the very highest levels of competition, even a small advantage is important and everybody wants the 'best'.

Materials and Construction

There are several types of carbon fibre, and the mechanical characteristics of the fibres are very different from a type to another. We have 2 important specifics: Modulus and K number. The modulus shows the tenacity of the fibre and the K number shows the size of the fibre. Of course the price of the fibre is much higher for the high modulus and the low K carbon. Then we have carbon fibres like woven clothes and unidirectionals. We use both types in order to get the right mast bend, by changing the orientation of the fibres, and making the mast strong enough so that it won't break. This is what makes the Finn mast difficult to build: it's not the only problem to build a light and strong mast, but a light, strong and 'perfect' bending mast . . . !

Carbon fibres can be pre-preg or not. In the first case they are impregnated with epoxy

resin by the factory and they need to be thermo cured at high temperatures (from 60 to 120 °C) during moulding . We have to keep them refrigerated until we use them. In the second case they have to be impregnated by hand or with a machine with an epoxy resin that can be moulded at low temperatures (20-25 °C) and then post-cured at high temperature to reach the best mechanical characteristics. The pre-preg are much more expensive but we have more accurate control of the quantity of

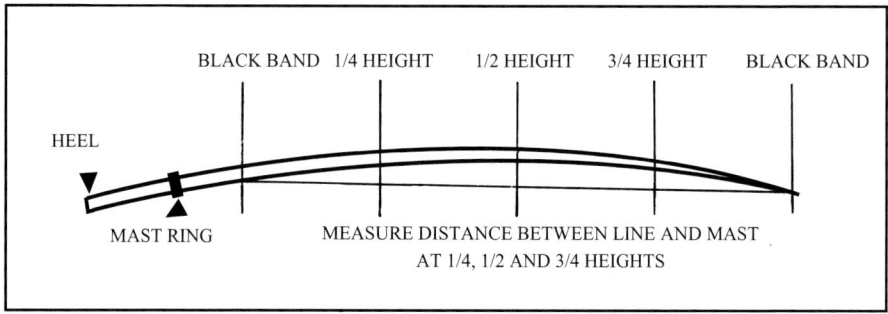

BLACK BAND   1/4 HEIGHT   1/2 HEIGHT   3/4 HEIGHT   BLACK BAND

HEEL

MAST RING   MEASURE DISTANCE BETWEEN LINE AND MAST
                 AT 1/4, 1/2 AND 3/4 HEIGHTS

Example

	Bottom	Middle	Top	Tip deflection
Fore/Aft:	90 (69%)	130	98 (75%)	540
Sideways:	79 (64%)	123	111(90%)	400

resin in the laminate. The dry fibres allow us to use simpler methods and also to keep the price of the mast down. There are different methods for moulding a mast and every mast maker has his own tricks.

Here are 2 different technologies:

Filament winding: using a machine that applies the fibres moving up and down along a male mandrel (best used for round tubes).

Inside inflating bag: using a nylon bag inside the carbon fibres to push them against the walls of a female mould.

With the carbon mast there is also the possibility to add some reinforcements to change the bend of a mast. We can also make it softer by sanding it. This practice was very popular with the round mast at the beginning of the 'carbon era', but it's more dangerous with wing masts because the thickness of the walls of a wing mast is generally thinner than a round mast.

Mast Bend
We use the cantilever test to measure the mast bend. 12 kg is suspended from the tip with the mast bent both fore and aft and sideways. Then we put a line from the measurement band at the gooseneck to the measurement band at the tip and measure the deflection at top quarter, middle and bottom quarter.

Also we measure the tip deflection before and after applying the 12 kg. weight. This test gives a general idea of the bend characteristics. It is also interesting to calculate the percentage between the middle measurement and the measurements at the top and bottom quarters.

These measurements help the sailmaker to determine the luff curve of the sail. It is also important to measure the weight and centre of gravity - they have to be near the minimum. Every sailor has to decide what is the best bend for his weight and preferences. The heavier helmsmen can use a stiffer and more powerful mast. However, it is very important to have an all round mast in order to have good performance in all conditions.

Top sailors are always testing a lot of mast/sail combinations and they spend a lot of time on the water so they often know exactly what they are looking for. It is not the same for the week-end sailors and it's more difficult for them to know exactly what is the best combination to use. In any case the choice of the mast and sail is part of Finn sailing and it's always one of the favourite topics of conversation between Finn sailors.

19. History of IFA Development Clinics and Camps

by Gus Miller

No one ever does something entirely alone, even winning a Finn Regatta wouldn't happen without all the other Finnsters. A Finnster learns to master himself as he learns to master the Finn (which no one ever really does) and he soon learns it is far more important to master yourself than to master others. So it was with the idea for the IFA Development Program.

The IFA Development Program really began long ago as the informal mixed country training sessions that we all enjoy today. As more countries in the 1950s began to take up Finn sailing, they would invite top Finnsters to come give their young sailors training camps. It became formalised as a goal of IFA in 1979 when I was Vice President Sailing. Since then, sailors from some fifty countries have benefited from the program. Some attendees have gone on to win Olympic Medals and World Championships and credit the clinics with really helping their knowledge and development. Funding has come from Olympic Solidarity, many countries Sailing Organisations and Olympic Committees and private individuals. The network of people involved have spread their knowledge throughout the sailing world. That network has also been important in keeping the Finn in the Olympics during the political battles to replace it with other boats. The program itself was an original and became the model for other classes and sports. Samaranch liked it because it produced what it said it would and most of the funds went directly to support and develop athletes and not officials. Over time, the program has spread to include other classes. especially the 470, Europe, Sailboards and Laser. Classic Finn leadership!

In 1967, I went to the pre-Olympic Regatta in Acapulco as an adventure and learned much just watching and listening. I especially remember Paul Elvström walking around his rigged boat, experimenting with the sail controls to learn his rig before he launched it. I was racing big boats and did not bother with our trials in 1972 but in 1973, at the suggestion of friends, I went to the Canadian pre-Olympics, finished fifth, met David Howlett and enjoyed the racing immensely which enticed me into going for my first real Finn campaign. I was also impressed with the openness of the Finnsters with sharing their knowledge with each other. I quickly realised that this quality of character was what made the Finn Class sailors so great. As a chemistry teacher, I already knew that being open paid off because when you answer someone's question, you generally learned more from thinking about the answer than the person you are giving the answer to. Classic Finn thinking!

In the next three years before the 1976 Olympics I sought out and learned a great deal from Finn sailors and coaches outside the US. David Howlett from the UK, Guy Liljegren from Sweden, Sandy Riley from Canada, John Bertrand from Australia, Andy Zawieja from Poland and Andrei Balashov from Russia were six that I trained with and shared especially good insights into racing a Finn. Jacques Rogge, Gilbert Lamboley, Oleg Shilov and many others were fun to get to know besides picking their brains about Finns. After improving to being third in the Europeans, I came second in our trials (I hadn't learned that I could win yet but that fall I finally won the North Americans) and went to the Sailing Olympics in Kingston as a tune up partner. Classic Finn story!

The Kingston experience changed my view and understanding of the Olympics. It was quite interesting to see and be a small part of that event. Besides training with the American, I had the chance to go sailing with all my worldwide Finnster friends again. I even had Prince Philip come up at one point and ask how the day was going. Then Jessie Villarreal from the Philippines and some of the other coaches asked me to work with a Philippines sailor who had never sailed a Finn before. After my duties with the US Team were over I defected to become the Philippines Finn boat

**Gus on his way to winning
Race 2 of the 1992 Gold Cup**

boy. My sights changed from going for an Olympic berth and Medal to making sure that a newcomer got around the course safely and was actually racing. Classic Finn evolution!

I now saw the Olympics as a great international carnival with a focus on excellence in sport where most had no chance at a medal but were participating in a fabulous tradition. That ideal of shared excellence, which is carried into the world, is a wonderfully powerful force. Especially so in the face of the self interested corruption that now soils the Olympics. Classic Finn ideals!

In 1977 Pat Healy was secretary of the USA Finn Association and organised a Finn clinic in Annapolis. He had left Pewaukee, Wisconsin which was then an important centre of the Finn world and was coaching the Naval Academy dinghy racing team. I was the Finn representative on the US Olympic Yachting Committee and pushed to get as many Americans as possible to sail with the rest of the world. Classic Finn subversion!

In 1978 Ontario Sailing Association put on a week long Finn clinic for Canadians and asked Paul Elvström and me to be the coaches. Their ambassador to Denmark asked the Danish Government to arrange Paul's trip as a favour to Canada. I think there were as many reporters paying their own way to attend than sailors. Classic reaction to Finn sailors!

In 1979 I became IFA VP Sailing in Weymouth which the Americans dominated. At the Tallinn pre-Olympics, where I was third, and in Helsinki I was asked for coaching help by many, especially the Estonians who asked for me to come back for a training camp. At that time we began to organise a camp in Helsinki before the 1980 Regatta in Tallinn.

In 1980 President Carter's mistaken boycott changed everything, including my Finn sailing focus. I still enjoyed racing hard, but coaching and sharing the personal development of Finn sailors became the biggest interest. I was as interested in and enjoyed the guys at the back of the fleet who were suffering and working hard as I was those in the front of the fleet (where I still would make occasional appearances). I also had a great pride that the

Finn had the hardest and best level of racing in the world. Other classes had their moments but nothing I saw in them ever matched what I saw in the Finn. Classic Finn racing!

In 1983 in Milwaukee, after a couple of years out of the Finn because of knee surgery to repair a stupid weight lifting mistake, we again began to do clinics before Finn Gold Cups.

In 1984 we were looking for a US host for a pre-Olympic training camp in Los Angeles but no clubs were willing, they were all too involved with getting ready to put the Games on. Pat Healy had become the Canadian National Coach and was a landed immigrant in Canada. He got support from the Ontario Sailing Association and CYA. Gerardo got Samarach's personal help and found out about unused Olympic Solidarity funds available for ISAF. Andy Zawieja and I joined forces with Pat and sixteen countries sent Olympic bound sailors for training. Andy and I followed them to Los Angeles where we measured 80 masts to get the best rig for each of our sailors. A local fitness club gave free access to Olympic sailors and we watched Russell Coutts get huge; he is a shadow of his former self now. My van became a bus for Finn sailors but one night with Andy, the cooling system failed in downtown Los Angeles. The Japanese sailor who won the Training Regatta in Canada wasn't allowed in the Olympics because his coaches in their ignorance didn't think he was good enough. The Taiwan Chinese translated for the Mainland Chinese. A Pakistani and an Indian trained together happily and an Egyptian fought hard with a Fijian to stay out of the back of the fleet. I most remember the day when Trini almost won a race and the entire fleet was on the beach congratulating him when his delegation arrived to see what he was up to. Classic Finnster training and luck!

In the summer of 1986 Craig Monk appeared on my back porch, said he wanted to do a Finn campaign and asked if I would be willing to help him. That was the beginning of a long friendship all over the world and was a step towards Craig's Bronze in Barcelona.

It was a wonderful moment when he came back to that back door after Barcelona to say thank you and show me his scrap books and the medal. The medal was a replacement the Spanish had given him because the original had become badly abused during Craig's celebration after the award ceremony. When the taxi bringing him home dropped him off at the village, he sat on the curb for a little rest before he climbed the stairs to his bed. About 45 minutes later, another taxi load of Kiwis were dropped off when they saw a body in the street gutter. They said, "Oh, look at the dirty body in the gutter...oh, it's Craig! We better get him to his bed." Craig's beautiful

white presentation uniform of the medal ceremony was now black and smelly. Classic Finn sailor!

1988 was an adventure. There were five clinics around the world. Andy Zawieja put on one in Palma de Majorca, Mike Fletcher and John Bertrand joined forces for one in Brisbane, we had one in Miami and I went to Tallinn to do one in the Soviet Union with the help of Heino Lind and Juri Saraskin.

The 1988 Miami clinic almost didn't happen because two containers of Finns for the clinic were on a freighter coming back from the Gold Cup in Brazil when the ship's itinerary was redirected from Miami to Norfolk. It was a mess because there were sailors from fifteen countries already in the air on their way to Miami. It took two days to undo the mess. The Shipping line had to allow their ship to be unloaded to get the containers off the bottom of the stacks. The Freight Terminal had to allow their equipment to be used on a holiday for free. The Longshoremen had to allow their workers to work for nothing on a holiday. The Teamsters Union had to make arrangements for truck the container overnight 1000 miles from Norfolk to Miami. Thanks to the generosity of many, it all came together and the sailors unloaded the containers the night before the clinic was scheduled to begin. Peter Holmberg was an attendee at that clinic and spent as much time in the coach boat watching and coaching as he did in the Finn practising. Classic Finn sailor!

During the '88 clinic in Tallinn, I worked with a young North Korean and invited him to the clinic I was going to give in Pusan before the Olympics. This was important to me because the North Koreans had been an opponent for a year when I was a young Marine, and I needed to make an effort to change that relationship. When I notified the 65 nations in IFA about the Pusan Clinic, I mentioned that the young North Korean was going to come because at that point, the North was scheduled to send a Team. Well, the South Korean Government didn't like this idea and complained to the US State Department who asked US Sailing what was going on. The State Department accepted my explanation but the South Koreans sent me a Telex telling me not to come. I threw the Telex in the trash and went, knowing it would be an effort to make the clinic happen. In the end it was a great success. I had a Korean Marine commando boat driven by two Korean Marine as a coach boat and received a salute every time I passed a guard at a door or passed the harbour entrance. Classic Finn attitude!

16 Estonian Finn and 470 sailors joined a 1989 IFA clinic in Miami that the US Olympic Committee gave $10,000 to fund. In 1990 we

had a memorable training in Greece that IFA organised with a number of coaches giving training.

In 1991 we had an IFA training camp before the Kingston Gold Cup based in my Rhode Island home that Luca Devoti came to. I had him practice meditation every morning for 45 minutes to train his mind to calm down and concentrate. My message to him before each race was to either finish the race or commit suicide because if he didn't finish, I was going to kill him. I nearly killed him when he black flagged a Gold Cup race and his excuse was, "But Hansie sheeted in first." That training camp is where I learned that when Valentin Mankin complained to Oleg Shilov when Oleg broke Valentin's best mast, Oleg responded, "What could I do, you are so fast." Classic Finn trick!

The 1992 clinics again involved a number of coaches. The Olympics were interesting because all the Finn coaches were on one boat and not much happened on the course that wasn't closely observed and talked about. It was an effective coaching clinic. One time when Craig started deep the wrong way, John Cutler said in his quiet way, "I wouldn't have done that." Classic Finn coach!

In 1994 the New Zealand Yachting Federation, at Craig's suggestion, asked me to do a clinic for all their Olympic Classes. The lecture notes I gave there appear elsewhere in this book [p.164]. While there I learned about the WaterWise program for school children. It is the best, most effective program of its kind that I have seen in the world and is what I am trying to take to the world after the Finn. I always thought that if the IFA had the funds devoted to one America's Cup campaign, it could transform dinghy racing in the world. Using IFA's position as a leading Class to disperse WaterWise can also have such a powerful effect on sailing around the world. Classic Finn influence!

1995 saw a clinic before the Gold Cup in Melbourne that directly led to the 1999 World Sailing Championships. 1996 saw the IFA training more focused on the back of the fleet because more competitors had private coaches.

The IFA is world famous for its coaching and development with a solid program and many people committed to Finn excellence. Classic Finn Tradition!

Gus Miller

20. From the Experts

by Pat Healy   Reprinted from Yacht Racing/Cruising Magazine 1980

In 1980, the U.S. was in the enviable position of having more high calibre Finn sailors than any other country, with Americans totally dominating the previous three Gold Cup events. So powerful was the U.S. contingent that, prior to the announced boycott of the 1980 Moscow Games, speculation in foreign sailing circles revolved not around which country would win a Gold Medal in Finns, but rather, which American would win a Gold Medal in Finns. With such tremendous talent at hand, YR/C Contributing Editor/Finn sailor Pat Healy, who also coached the Naval Academy Sailing Team and, when travelling abroad, the U.S. Finn representatives, assembled the ideas and comments of five highly regarded American Finn sailors to create this "From the Experts". Included were:

John Bertrand 6'1", 185 lbs.
Finn Gold Cup 1st (1978), 2nd (1979), 2nd (1980); Finn Europeans 1st (1979), 2nd (1980); US Trials 1st (1980)

Andrew Menkart, 6'1",185 lbs.
Finn Gold Cup 4th (1979), 5th (1980); US Trials 2nd (1980)

Cam Lewis, 6'1", 190 lbs.
Finn Gold Cup 1st (1979), 1st (1980); US Nationals 1st (1979)

Carl Buchan, 6'5", 195 lbs.
Finn Gold Cup 3rd (1978), 6th (1979)

Stewart Neff, 6'1", 210 lbs.
Finn Gold Cup 5th (1979); Nordics 1st (1979); US Trials 5th (1980)

Over the years, Finn sailors have been stereotyped as fair-haired endomorphs that could take on an entire football team in a street brawl and win. In a way, this may be possible, since the majority of top Finn sailors are over six feet tall and approach 200 pounds. But there's more to the Finn class than simply raw beef. A close inspection of the resumes of present and past championships in a number of other classes reveals a common thread - the Finn. George O'Day, Bruce Goldsmith, Charles Ulmer, Robbie Doyle, Peter Barrett, Gordy Bowers, Dick Tillman, Bill Cox, Tom Allen, Glen Foster, Andy Kostanecki, Harry Anderson - all have been indoctrinated to the finesse and toughness of sailboat racing via the Finn.

What makes the Finn so demanding is not only the intense calibre of competitor it attracts, but also its sheer size. Designed in 1949, the

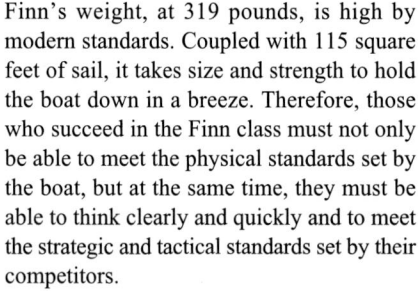

Finn's weight, at 319 pounds, is high by modern standards. Coupled with 115 square feet of sail, it takes size and strength to hold the boat down in a breeze. Therefore, those who succeed in the Finn class must not only be able to meet the physical standards set by the boat, but at the same time, they must be able to think clearly and quickly and to meet the strategic and tactical standards set by their competitors.

Hulls

The major North American Finn manufacturer, Vanguard, has all but cornered the world market in Finns, with half of their 1980 production scheduled to be shipped outside the U.S. Used by all five of these Finn sailors, the current Vanguard hull has been optimised to the point where what has evolved is a shape that is fairly narrow and as straight as possible on the waterline, but as wide as possible in the transom area, all within the limits of the class rules. "The bigger transom makes Vanguards a little quicker to plane," says Buchan, "and the narrowness makes them a little faster upwind, particularly in light air. It does make them a little tippier, though."

With wide acceptance of the Vanguard hull shape, the most recent concerns have focused on weight in the ends and the centre of gravity, both of which have to do with pitching moment. To determine the location of the centre of gravity and the amount of weight in the ends, making sure both are within class rules, moment-of-inertia tests are made on each hull at some major Finn events. Most

Finns come out of the mould on the light side and are brought up to weight by adding lead corrector weights, the placement of which can affect the moment-of-inertia tests. "If you've got to add much lead," says Lewis, "be sure you don't put in separate pieces of lead in different parts of the boat. For example, don't put some lead up by the mast step and some back by the centreboard. Keep the lead together and generally try to keep it as far aft as possible. In that way, the weight is over the wider, flatter stern section, which is the most buoyant part of the boat."

Most modifications made by Bertrand, Buchan, Lewis, Menkart and Neff fall into two categories - the relatively easy, straight forward work and the major structural projects. Some of the more easily made modifications include:

1. To help stiffen the thwart and reduce sideways centreboard movement, all five have glassed in wood support pieces under the centreboard cap and traveller.

2. The forward hiking strap base location has been adjusted to accommodate individual leg length. The longer one's legs, the further inboard the base is mounted. Some, such as Menkart, have mounted the bases on short lengths of track, allowing them to be slid inboard or outboard as conditions change.

3. Each of the five uses a compass, but there are different ideas about how many to use, where to mount them and when to use them. Bertrand has been known not to use a compass at all, relying instead on angles of surrounding boats to give him an idea of whether he's being headed or lifted. However, for the 1980 U.S. Trials, he did add a center-mounted compass, carried on a small base off to one side of the centreboard trunk, by the thwart. Buchan also carries his compass there, but admits to only occasionally using it. "Probably the only time I use my compass," says Buchan, "is when rounding the leeward mark. It gives me a quick reference as to what the wind is doing." Menkart and Neff also carry center-mounted compasses. "I like the single compass because it's difficult to get side compasses to read the same," says Menkart, "and it helps keep weight down a little." Lewis is the only one who carries dual side compasses. "I don't want to have to look in the middle of the boat

to read the compass," says Lewis. "My compasses are mounted so that, when I'm in a hiked position, they are right in line with my eyes and the front of the boat. In that way, I never have to look very far away from where the boat's heading."

4. Each has customised the side tank pads to one degree or another. In general, the longer your legs, the more padding you need to increase the distance between your calf and thigh and help keep your derriere out of the water when hiking. Since all five are relatively tall, each uses two or more thicknesses of padding on each side of the boat. Menkart has taken pad modification a step further by shortening them, fore and aft. "I made them just wide enough to hike on," says Menkart, "so that the boom will not hit the pads when sheeted in tight. That allows the boom to be carried a little closer to the deck." (Because the mast is so far forward, the boom is never carried further inboard than the leeward side tank.)

The major construction questions revolve around double bottoms and whether or not to utilise Menkart's 'Laser' deck layout. At the 1979 U.S. Pre-Trials, only Bertrand and Buchan carried a double bottom, which is basically plywood glassed over the aft half of the cockpit to create a watertight compartment. "The problem," says Buchan, "is that Vanguard hulls have a lot of stringers in them, along which water tends to collect. The double bottoms cover those, allowing the boat to stay a lot drier." At this year's Olympic Trials, practically everyone had a double bottom of one form or another. Bertrand, Buchan and Neff carried the idea one step further by extending the double bottom up toward the forward bulkhead, along each side tank, which provides a small 'canal' along the centreboard trunk where water can be funnelled aft to the bailers, "The dryness is really important when

going into that first reach," says Buchan. "If your boat is dry as you start that reach and others have water sloshing around, you're going to be a lot faster."

For deck layouts, one of the problems with having all major control lines passing through the deck around the mast area, as traditionally done, is that water passes through there as well, adding weight to a weight-sensitive section of the boat. Menkart overcame much of this problem by deck-mounting all of his control lines. By so doing, he sealed off the front of the boat. To prevent water from entering where the spar passes through the deck, he globs grease on the mast collar, which, even on a heavy-air day, prevents all but a couple of spongefulls of water from entering. According to Menkart, "There is a bit more windage with the control lines in the open, but there's already a lot of turbulence around the gooseneck and splash rail anyway. And a little turbulence is better than having water rush up to the bow and sink the boat."

The other four sailors stuck with the standard layout or some variation thereof. Neff has worked out a fairly simple valve system.- "I have a bulkhead up there," says Neff, "that has a small, neoprene flap, on each side of the centreboard trunk. Water can run aft through the flaps, but not forward." Lewis simply built the bilge area up around the mast step with micro balloons, thus creating a small 'ramp' which helps funnel any water aft.

One other major modification deals with the centreboard. Standard Vanguard Finns come with five-sixteenth-inch wide boards. However, the Vanguard centreboard trunk will accommodate up to a three-eighth-inch board. Consequently, Lewis, along with several others, has switched to the thicker board. "According to engineers, the wider board is considerably stiffer," says Lewis. "It is,

however, eight pounds heavier than the standard boards, but because the weight is centralised and down low, I don't think that the added poundage outweighs the advantages gained by the extra stiffness." Menkart solved the extra weight problem by cutting out a section in the top of the board.

Masts

Since the 1972 German Olympics, all of the top sailors in the class have been using metal Needlespar 3M masts. All of the 3Ms are quite similar, but since the Finn mast is unstayed, slight manufacturing variances can significantly change bending characteristics. Finding a 'fast' mast is the quest that most Finn sailors' dreams are made of. Most have experimented with more than one mast. Bertrand has owned nine; Lewis has owned five. Says Bertrand, "I don't measure bend characteristics like some people. I have to see it on the boat to tell you if I like it or not." Lewis agrees: "I'm not a parking lot sailor."

How does one determine what looks good under sail and what doesn't? According to Bertrand, "The mast should work sideways when you are sailing upwind. It is this 'fanning' or pumping of the top of the sail that is really fast." Neff adds, "The mast should have good 'elasticity'. allowing it to spring right back when bent to leeward." Neff also mentioned that the heavier you are, the stiffer the spar should be sideways.

For fore-and-aft bend, Bertrand says, "I look for an even bend, one which matches the luff curve on my sail. The front of the sail should be flat, while the leech is open and allowed to work."

Lewis also looks for a nice, even mast curve and suggests checking to be sure the track is on straight. If not, it can often affect bend. For Neff, the best spar is one which has an even curve in the top and bottom third, with the centre third smoothly connecting those two.

Regardless of personal preferences, all stress the importance of finding a spar that matches the luff curve of the sail.

One necessary mast-related change is the replacement of the aluminium mast collar with one made of Delrin or HMW plastic. Although fairly expensive, it does considerably reduce friction and provide a much tighter fit. Some, such as Menkart, add a Teflon ring outside the Delrin collar. "The Teflon," says Menkart, "is attached to the hull, while the Delrin rides snugly around the mast. In that way, the only friction is between the Delrin and the Teflon, and that isn't much." Menkart also suggests moving the mast as far forward as is possible at deck level (on Vanguards it's usually only a centimetre or so) to provide a better helm in a breeze. "I generally move the spar forward by cutting a little out at the front end of the mast hole and making the Teflon a little wider at the aft end says Menkart.

Mast rake is measured with a tape from the hoisted halyard shackle to the transom, and there is some disagreement among the five as to how to adjust rake as conditions change. Bertrand and Menkart begin easing their masts aft as the winds pick up, contending that it helps soften the leach, allowing air to spill out of the sail easier. Neff and Lewis pull their masts forward as the wind increases. According to Lewis, this gives them a flatter sail and actually makes the sail a bit smaller by shortening the roach, taking a little more cloth out of the back of the sail. Buchan leaves his set in the same place all the time, contending that his speed in all conditions is 'just fine'.

Sails

Like hulls and spars, there is one sail that almost everyone agrees on - the North T3+B design, made from 3.8 ounce cloth. Designed by the Australian John Bertrand (hence the '+B') for the 1976 Olympics, the sail has yet to be really improved on. With its optimum conditions appearing in light to moderate

winds, only Lewis uses another sail when the wind picks up beyond that: "Once whitecaps begin to appear, I usually switch over to a standard 3.8 ounce Deegan sail, made by a New Zealander who owns a loft in Cowes, England. The Deegan cloth feels firmer than the North,"

Controls

With five sail-shape controls, plus the centreboard pennant, all led aft to the skipper, the Finn is an easy boat to adjust.

Outhaul - The outhaul controls the top third of the leech, opening and closing it as the outhaul is tightened and loosened. All five frequently adjust the outhaul on upwind legs, pulling the clew close to the black band to depower the sail in heavy air and easing it away from the band when more power is needed, such as in light air and/or chop. Care must be taken when easing the outhaul, since a tight upper leech is very sensitive to wind direction and stalls easily.

Cunningham - The cunningham works similarly to the outhaul, but controls the middle third of the leech. Generally, no one touches the cunningham, even if there are wrinkles along the luff, until they begin to get overpowered, Then, the cunningham is tightened, along with easing the traveller.

Inhaul - The inhaul controls the bottom third of the leech. On beats, the inhaul is usually set and left alone unless there are major changes in conditions. At starts, however, to decrease the angle of attack and allow better pointing, the inhaul is usually eased away from the mast.

Mainsheet - Unlike boats with sidestays and forestays, easing the mainsheet reduces leech tension and creates twist. As the boom comes off the deck the mast goes forward and straightens out. According to Menkart, "the luff curve is built for a bent mast, which means the sail becomes fuller and the draft moves forward as the mainsheet is eased."

Usually, it is important to have a sail with the draft aft rather than right next to the mast. For this reason, the mainsheet is rarely eased to the point where the boom is much more than a foot above deck level.

Vang - Upwind, the vang is set so that you can just fit under the boom when tacking. This allows the sail to stay close to the optimum shape during the tack. There is even a slight amount of vang used in zero to five knots, mainly to keep the mast bent slightly.

Centreboard - Unlike boats with more efficient centreboards (such as Lasers), the Finn's flat-plate board is generally kept all the way down upwind, regardless of conditions. And unlike Lasers, Finns will steer with practically no board down at all, so offwind, the board is usually raised, although for stability, most only raise it part way. Says Buchan, "Downwind, you should pull the board up as much as you dare." In really heavy winds, the boat may start oscillating, and once it starts, a death roll or roundup to windward is usually imminent, unless you get the board back down. On reaches, the board is lowered only enough to keep the boat from sideslipping.

Boat handling, Steering and Sheeting

Bertrand, Buchan, Lewis, Menkart and Neff all have spent so much time in Finns that boat handling, steering and sheeting are instinctive. Consequently, obtaining specifics about certain techniques is difficult, as most of the time these five are simply into the rhythm of the race rather than specifically thinking about technique. However, a few points do stand out. Upwind, Bertrand tries not to steer too much, because he feels the flat, thin centreboard stalls out easily. For Menkart, upwind sailing speed, particularly in gusty conditions, hinges on his ability to effectively depower. "Since the cunningham has such a drastic effect on leech tension, I use it to depower the sail. A lot of people sail Lasers without side cleats, but there's no way you can sail a Finn that way. The sail pulls too hard, and you just have to leave it cleated, especially in a breeze. However, I do play the main in light and medium winds, easing it for power, such as when going through waves, and tightening it for speed."

Offwind, Buchan mentions that when he has been out of the Finn for some time, he has trouble regaining the 'near-disaster' groove necessary to attain top speed. "When running," he says, "it seems the closer you are to rolling to weather, the faster you go." For Neff, a major factor in offwind speed is vang tension, and he sees a close relationship between it and the ability to catch waves. "Generally," says Neff, "I carry the vang looser on a reach than on a run, and when I miss a wave I think I should have caught, I ease the vang some more."

Lewis is the most outspoken about the absolute necessity of making every move second nature by simply getting out and sailing a lot. Once the moves are down, the next step, according to Lewis, is to learn as much as you can about where you're going to be sailing, or better yet, spend some time sailing there.

All agreed that Finn sailors must be strong and have a lot of stamina. Says Menkart, "Offwind in a lot of breeze, it is much faster to take the main 1:1 from the boom, but that's tough. And when you jibe, it gets even tougher. Once the boom crosses and the sail fills, it tugs so hard that it feels like it's going to pull you right out of the boat."

Similarly, body movement is very important in the class. Since all five sailors have strong Laser backgrounds, many movements and big-fleet tactics from that class have filtered into the Finn. But with the Finn weighing 319 pounds, compared to the Laser's 130, and the Finn's sail area totalling 115 square feet to the Laser's 75, some Laser movements are simply not as effective in the Finn. But they do provide enough of an edge to enable these five sailors to continually finish in the forefront of international Finn competition.

Finn Philosophy

Bertrand: "Often, someone is very fast during the first five minutes of sail testing or during the first third of the windward leg. But when it takes something extra to withstand the pain and still be aggressive, people often begin to fade. One thing you learn when sailing Finns is that you have to develop the ability to be scrapping all the time."

Buchan: "A lot of people need to work harder at having good speed right at the start. At the start, I'm often sailing hard and well into the race while others are still making adjustments. I try to get all my testing done before the race. That gives me confidence that, after a good start, I can stay in clear wind."

Lewis: "The only things that help win sailboat races are sailing smart, time on the water and time around the buoys."

Neff: "I'm afraid a Finn sail is only at its peak from the second to the seventh or eighth regatta, After that, it gets slower. Many people I'm sailing against would go better if they simply bit the bullet and bought a new sail more frequently."

Menkart: "Too many have a fear of basic Finn manoeuvres, such as jibing. I did, too, when I first started. But it's really not that hard, especially if you remember to ease the vang. However, a survival jibe - that is, just staying upright through the manoeuvre - is easy. A good jibe is tough and simply takes a lot of practice time."

And by the same token, good Finn sailing is tough, for the fraternity of Finn sailors are in a league by themselves as far as ability and physical endurance are concerned. But like all other things, you only get out of Finn sailing what you put into it.

21. History of the Finn in the Olympic Games

by David Leach, Richard Creagh-Osborne, Georg Siebeck and Robert Deaves Reprinted from FINNLOG

In the ancient Olympic Games from the 8th century B.C. until the 4th century A.D. there were no sailing events.

The Start of Olympic Yachting

At first of the modern Olympics at **Athens**, Greece in **1896**, the organisers decided to have an exhibition regatta in connection with the Games. However, on the days when the series was to be sailed, storms prevented any racing and it was cancelled.

The organisers of the **1900** Olympic Games in **Paris** decided that they should have some yachting events and got some internationally scheduled events to be sailed at Le Havre, France. 4 large meter formula classes were scheduled and 10 boats from four nations competed. The yachting events were treated as a sideshow and the entries were all large yachts from European nations sailed by rich people with paid crews.

St. Louis, Missouri was the site of the Olympics in **1904** and since there was no suitable place to race the deep keel boats, no yachting events were scheduled. In **1906**, **Athens** decided to hold an Olympics on their own but no yachting events were scheduled, and this was not considered an official Olympics. However, the British, French, and Germans agreed on a set of international racing rules in 1904 and this was the start of the improvement in yacht racing.

The first full-fledged Olympic yachting events were held at the **1908** Olympics in **London**, England. The British had 4 classes of formula boats with entries from 5 European nations. A nation could enter more than one boat in an event at this time. 13 boats participated.

In **1912**, **Stockholm** held the Games with the yacht racing nearby at Nynas. There were to be two races for each of the 6, 8, 10 and 12-Metre classes and the points system was revised to 7-3-1 for each race - the first time that a biased system was used. 24 boats participated and even Russia sent an entry for this Olympics. The yachting events drew much more attention at these games than they had before. However, it was 8 years before another Olympics was held as World War I prevented the 1916 Olympics.

The **1920** Olympic yachting events were held at **Ostend**, Belgium in very heavy seas and marked the end of an era in Olympic sailing. The Belgians were going to have the usual 6, 8, 10 and 12-Meter classes with their big boats and paid crews and the six major European yachting nations sent entries. The international rules had been changed in 1919 and 1920 so they had to run separate events for the boats that qualified under these classes in both the old and the new rules. They also tried to attract four other meter classes up to the mammoth 40 meter class and only got one or two boats in each class. And to please everyone, they had an 18' centreboard class but Holland sent the only entry.

Of interest for our history of the Finn in the Olympic Games is that they also scheduled a single-handed or Monotype class but the only entries were two sailors from Holland. However, despite all the confusion and the multitude of classes, the Olympic yachting events were not restricted to the big formula classes with their professional crews.

The Reformation

The Olympic Yachting events had been treated as a 'sideshow' for the wealthy Europeans and controlled primarily by the host country. The increasing interest and the confusion at the 1920 Olympics resulted in the International Olympic Congress placing the control of all future Olympic yachting events in the hands of the International Yachting Federation (later called the International Yacht Racing Union, now called the International Sailing Federation), which immediately set about to reform the Olympics. The following changes were made by the IYRU:

There would be only three events. They would be as follows: 1 - 8-Meter Class with a crew of five; 2 - 6-Meter Class with a crew of three; 3 - Less than 5 meter (16 feet) with a crew of one. All crew members had to be from the country represented. There could be only one entry from each nation. The host country would designate and furnish the singlehander so that even the poor nations could compete in the yachting events of the Olympics.

The **1924** Games of **Paris** was the first occasion in which the yachting was organised in anything like the modern manner. There were three classes. The 8-Meters and 6-Meters raced at Le Havre whilst the Monotypes, which drew seventeen entries, raced on the Seine at Meulan. Besides the winner, Norway and the usual European nations, Spain, Argentina, Cuba, South Africa and Canada sent entries to the new Monotype event. A special fleet of boats, truly strange to modern eyes. was built for the single-handed class. They were 5-Meter gaff-sloops. Spinnakers were also supplied but it is doubtful if they were actually used. Boats were drawn for eight days in advance and heats were run. In the finals L. Huybrechts of Belgium scored two wins and took the Gold with H. Robert of Norway 2nd and H. Dittmar of Finland 3rd. The Monotypes started from a fixed transit line on the C.V.P. club house and merely sailed up and down the river. Another interesting tit-bit of information gleaned from the records was that Mlle. Ella Maillart, aged twenty-one of Switzerland, sailed in the Monotype Class but just failed to reach the finals. She earned a special mention.

In **1928** in **Amsterdam** the classes were 5-Meters, 6-Meters and the International 12 ft. dinghy. The Dutch furnished the 12 ft dinghies for the Monotype and 10 boats started. Manfred Curry, who later gained fame for his books on yachting and aerodynamics, participated in the Monotype and ended up in the middle of the fleet. The races were sailed in heats and a peculiar points system was used which combined and averaged the results. The dinghies raced at Durgerdam in the south-west corner of the Zuider Zee, whilst the keelboats had a course between Muiden and Marken, just offshore.

The 10th modern Olympics was hosted by **Los Angeles**, California in **1932**. As one-design yachting was catching on throughout the world, the United States convinced the IYRU that the one-design Star would make an excellent Olympic event. So there were four events in 1932: a one man boat; a two man boat - the Star; a five man formula boat; and the 6-Meter. The United States nominated the Snowbird for the Monotype. The races were held in Los Angeles Harbour. The number of entries was held down by the tremendous cost to ship boats from Europe.

This was the first time that the Olympics had been held outside of Europe since 1904, when there were no yachting events. The Snowbirds were heavy hard chine boats about 13 ft. long with nearly flat bottoms and with a single sail set on a mast only stayed with a forestay. They were to have been raced in the mornings but there was never any wind then, so they raced after mid-day often in very fresh conditions. It was noted that there were no capsizes and it also appears that running starts were frequently given.

We now move on to the famous Games of **Berlin** in **1936**. The sailing was held on the beautiful Kiel fjord in 8-Meters, 6-Meters, Stars, and a new Olympic Monotype, usually called the O-Jolle, which was designed by that famous and delightful helmsman Helmut Stauch. Helmut represented South Africa in the Finn in 1952. There were twenty-five entries in the Monotype Class and the Dutchman D. Kagchelland won from the German W. Krogmann, with Peter Scott of Britain 3rd. Except for the first race it was mainly light weather.

Post World War II
World War II prevented any Olympic competition until **1948** when the XIV Olympics were scheduled for England, with the sailing taking place in **Torbay**. The IYRU decided that the 8-Meters were too expensive and dropped them in favour of a three man keel boat that was popular in Europe, the Dragon. They kept the 6-Meter boat and the two man Star boat and added the Swallow. For the Monotype, the British furnished a newly-designed British boat called the Firefly. This dinghy is normally sailed by two persons and the skippers in the Monotype class had their hands full trying to handle the mainsheet, the jib, the tiller, the centreboard, and bail at the same time. Trying to sail it was a real challenge to the 21 representatives. Ralph Evans Jr., the U.S. entry, was leading the series until the last race when a young upstart named Paul Elvström from Denmark nosed him out and won the Gold Medal. Rickard Sarby from

Sweden did not do so well in the Firefly but gained much valuable experience by capsizing during the racing. Elvström had a remarkable sheeting system on his Firefly. He had a bar across his tiller with a swivel cleat for the mainsheet. His technique on tacking was to free the main a few inches and re-cleat it. Then free the jib and tack. Finally the jib would be cleated and then the main tightened. A very dangerous operation unless done with split second timing

Enter the Finn
The Olympics for **1952** were assigned to **Helsinki**, Finland and the IYRU decided to keep the formula boat, the 6-Meter, for the last time. The 6-Meter had been in every Olympic games since they had started. The two-man keel boat, the Star was kept and the other one-design boat was the Dragon. The Swallow was replaced by the 5.5 meter which was a formula boat which required that it have a rating of 5.5 meters. The designers had a field day after the IYRU approved the new class in 1949 trying to design a boat to this rating that would be fast. The boats usually ended up about 32 feet long with a keel and a crew of three. The Firefly and the Olympia-Jolle had been so unsatisfactory and there was no Scandinavian dinghy worthy of being used as the Monotype for the Olympics. So, the Finish Yachting Association, who had been assigned the job of selecting the class for the Monotype, set about to run a contest for a new boat designed specifically for the Olympics which could also be used for sailing competitions in Scandinavia. This was the birth of the Finn about which Rickard Sarby has given a candid record. Finally the Finn became selected for the monotype for the 1952 Olympics. As everyone now knows, put Elvström in anything and he will win. And so he did in the Finn at the 1952 Olympics.

Elvström this time swept the board and was nearly 3,000 points ahead of Charles Currey of Great Britain at the end. He won four of the seven races in a fleet of 28 boats and set a standard which has never been equalled. The

The fleet at the 1952 Olympics

1920 Antwerp, Belgium
2 entries, 1 country, Dutch 12 Ft. Dinghy
1. Johannes Hin, Holland
2. A. van der Beisen, Holland

1924 Paris, France
17 entries, 17 countries, 5 Meter Dinghy
1. L. Huybrechts, Belgium
2. Henrik Robert, Norway
3. Hans Dittmar, Finland
4. Santl. Cansino, Spain
5. Johannes Hin, Holland
6. Clar. Hammag, Sweden
7. G. Fowler, Great Britain
8. F. Gull-Burnay, Portugal

1928 Amsterdam, Holland
23 entries, 20 countries, Dutch 12 Ft. Dinghy
1. Sven Thorell, Sweden
2. Henrik Robert, Norway
3. Berth Broman, Finland
4. Wm. de Vries, Holland
5. Egon Beyn, Germany
6. Tito Nordio, Italy
7. J. J. Andersen, Denmark
8. H. R. Gaydon, Great Britain

1932 Los Angeles, California, U.S.A.
11 entries, 11 countries, Snowbird
1. Jaques Lebrun, France   87
2. Adriaan Maas, Holland   85
3. Santl. Cansino, Spain   76
4. Edgar Behr, Germany   74
5. Reginald Dixon, Canada   72
6. Colin Ratsey, Great Britain 69

1936 Kiel, Germany
25 entries, Olympia Jolle
1. D. Kagchelland, Holland   163
2. W. Krogmann, Germany   150
3. Peter Scott, Great Britain   131
4. Wirchmann-Harbeck, Chile   130
5. Guiseppe Fago, Italy   115
6. Jaques Lebrun, France   109
7. von Heinrich, Hungary   102
8. W. Pieper, Switzerland   99
9. Jewett, United States   97
10. equal Thorwaldsen, Norway
    Nyman, Finland   93
12. equal Christensen, Denmark
    Eriksson, Sweden   92

1948 London, England
21 entries, 21 countries, Firefly
1. Paul Elvström, Denmark   5543
2. R. Evans, United States   5408
3. Koos de Jongh, Holland   5204
4. Rickard Sarby, Sweden   4603
5. Paul McLaughlin, Canada   4535
6. F. S. Castellanos, Uruguay   4079
7. J. Herbulot, France   4068
8. P. von der Haeghen, Belgium 3660
9. A. McDonald, Great Britain   3456
10. A. Oswald, Switzerland   2915

Prizegiving in 1952
Gold: Paul Elvström, Silver: Charles
Currey, Bronze: Rickard Sarby

Finn's designer, Sarby just managed to turn the tables on De Jongh this time, in spite of badly injuring his hand before the sixth race, but the Americans dropped from 2nd at Torbay to last at Helsinki. Note Jaques Lebrun still competing in the Monotype Class after twenty years, whilst Helmut Stauch appears in the new boat which is superficially similar to his 1936 Monotype design. Paul Elvström won because of his hiking technique, which he had developed practising in his own boat. Most of his competitors were rather sitting on the sidedeck instead of hiking on the sheer guard, as everybody does now-a-days. In addition Paul attached a sort of traveller to his boat, which was not supplied by the organiser. Most competitors considered this alteration to be illegal but the Dane got away with it. However after the fifth race, when it was already for sure, that he had won the Gold medal, Elvström removed the device again, in order to calm the grumbling feelings. A second incidence caused the protest of 16 participants. The British and the South African sailor had their sails altered after the fifth race. In those days the cotton sails were extremely sensitive and changed considerably during the regatta. Between the races most of the competitors had their sails up on the masts in order to shape the mains ashore. During the races the sails got wet in addition to being under stress and the shape deteriorated. Having the sails repaired by a professional sailmaker gave the two competitors an advantage. However the jury dismissed the protest and thus Charles Currey won the silver medal.

In **1956** Olympics were assigned to **Melbourne**, Australia. The IYRU decided that the 6-Meter class had become too expensive for many countries to afford and so authorised a new formula class of 5.5 meters

for the Olympics. The old 8-Meter class was completely eliminated and a 'Sharpie' class, a 12 m2 formula boat was used. The Dragon, Star and Monotype were the other events. The Finn had proved to be such a great competitive boat in the 1952 Olympics that it was retained as the Monotype for the 1956 Olympics. The Finns mustered twenty-two entries and again Elvström slaughtered the opposition, this time with five wins in his score - a fantastic feat! Going into the last race it looked as though the American John Marvin, who had never raced a Finn before, might topple the clever and the outstanding Belgian Andre Nelis since they were level on points at 2nd. But Nelis pulled out all the stops and kept Marvin covered whilst notching up a second place himself.

At the other end of the scale the battle between the enormous and perpetually grinning Burmese weight-lifter Maung Maung Lwin and the equally enormous Fijian reserve helmsman to keep off bottom place kept everyone just as much on tenterhooks. The first question the shore party asked was always "Who won?" but they did not mean Elvström! For the record - Burma triumphed. The weather was comparatively kind with the exception of the first race, in winds up to Force 7 gusts, and the fourth when the wind reached 55 m.p.h. The Finns fortunately did not have to face this latter test since they started last and were postponed. The other classes were under way before the wind really got going.

Major Changes
In 1956 the International Finn Association was organised to administer the rapidly growing class under the cognizance of the IYRU and to assist with the Olympic games. For the **1960** Olympics in **Rome** with the yachting events in Naples the Sharpie was dropped from the Olympics and the two man centreboarder, the Flying Dutchman was added. This left only the 5.5 Meter as a formula boat for designers to play with. The winds were light but rather variable in direction and the sun shone out of a hot sky. Who could blame the people of Italy for ignoring the greatest sporting festival of our time? There was sunbathing to be done and important activities like underwater swimming and drinking good wine to be got through at some time during the long day.

The competitors even were sometimes tempted to forget that the object of their visit was to persuade a painfully slow floating object to travel by a vaguely defined route a shade less slowly than a few others. It really was altogether too nice a place to hold Olympic yachting. But the competitors rose to the challenge in the end and a very good if somewhat uninspiring series resulted.

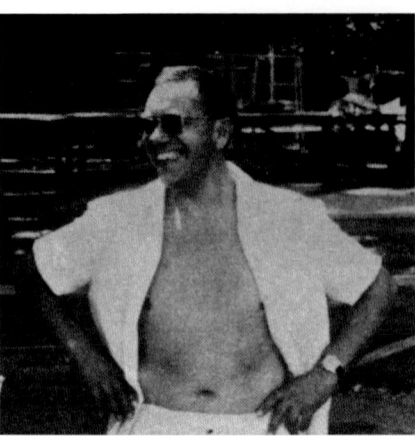

4 times Gold - Paul Elvström

There was a great increase to thirty-five Finns and Elvström did it again! This time he only won three races and had to withdraw from the last through illness, but he was never lower than 5th in conditions which did not enable him to gain by his fantastic strength and endurance. This was the year that Russia arrived as a top sailing nation and in the Finns the Silver Medal was won by Chuchelov. Nelis of Belgium was thus displaced to 3rd. A glance at the list of competitors shows that only a few previous Olympic entrants appear again. Our Burmese weightlifter is here again and moves up marginally, The only other 'old' names are Kenneth Albury, the Bahamian who was at Helsinki and Melbourne, where he was one of a total national Olympic team of three men, and the Belgian Andre Nelis. Albury surprised everyone including himself by winning one of the races and finished 8th on points, whilst Nelis moved down one to 3rd.

The **1964** Olympics was assigned to **Tokyo**, Japan. The IYRU decided to keep the same classes for this Olympics. The problem of the choice of the Monotype had been solved with the Finn. Here was a class that required training and conditioning like other Olympic events, required skills and dexterity to sail competitively, and was being sailed throughout the world by competitive athletic sailors. The changing of the Monotype competition each Olympics to some local dinghy that other countries had not seen or been able to practice

The fleet at the 1960 Olympics

Gold Medal Winner 1964 Willy Kuhweide

with, was finally gone. However, for the 1964 Olympics, the hull of the boats to be furnished by the Japanese would be fibreglass instead of wood. The Finn event in the Olympics was actually sailed at Enoshima in Tokyo Bay. Paul Elvström did not enter the Finn class but Henning Wind of Denmark took 3rd in a 33 boat field.

In 1964 Germany was the leading nation in the Finn. The Federal Republic of Germany and the German Democratic Republic had agreed to send one team and therefore only one competitor in the Finn event. The internal trials in Germany ended up with team sailing and endless protests. So both top representatives Willy Kuhweide and Bernd Dehmel went to Tokyo, where the Japanese were kind enough to organise the final trials between the two competitors only, with no possibility of further team sailing. When Dehmel did not appear on the water Kuhweide was assigned to represent Germany. Willy had the mental strength to stay on top of the Finn fleet in actual Olympic racing as well, despite a severe infection of the middle ear. Before the last race Kuhweide had 6018 points, Peter Barrett scored 5599, and Henning Wind 5570. However in that race the American and the Dane watched each other and finished 7th and 10th, allowing the German once again line honours and Gold.

The **1968** Games were in **Mexico** with the yachting events being sailed at Acapulco. The classes remained the same for the third consecutive Olympics: 5.5 Meter formula boat, Dragon, Star, Flying Dutchman and Finn. However, there was movement on the part of the IYRU to develop new classes for the Olympics. Some picked Henning Wind, the

Danish Finn sailor who had won the Gold Cup and was second in the Europeans this Olympic year. Others favoured Willy Kuhweide, the 1964 Olympic Gold Medalist, or Jörg Bruder, the Brazilian who had won the Pan American Games last summer. Few felt that Valentin Mankin, the veteran Russian Finn sailor and an excellent heavy weather helmsman, had much of a chance for the Gold Medal in the light weather so typical of Acapulco.

**Gold Medal Winner 1968
Valentin Mankin**

But the wind disobeyed the weathermen, and Mankin surprised everyone with a week of almost flawless tactical racing. Never below seventh at any turning mark, the Russian compiled a record of three firsts, two seconds and a third in the seven races to beat Hubert Raudaschl of Austria by almost 42 points. Fabio Albarelli of Italy won the Bronze Medal, finishing only 1.7 points behind Raudaschl. The winds were basically sea-breezes. Off Acapulco the sea-breeze (mainly S.S.W.) would tend to back in the morning and veer in the afternoon. The Acapulco sea-breeze shifts continuously by anything up to 30 deg. at a time. One never knew whether a shift was temporary or part of an overall back or veer. The swell was most difficult with tremendous

The fleet at the 1968 Olympics

1952 Helsinki, Finland
(28 entries)

1.	Paul Elvström	D	8209
2.	Charles Currey	K	5449
3.	Rickard Sarby	S	5051
4.	Koos de Jongh	H	5033
5.	Wolff Erndl	OE	4373
6.	M. Skaugen	N	4073
7.	Adelchi Pelaschier	I	4068
8.	Paul McLaughlin	KC	4033
9.	A. F. Bercht	BL	3711
10.	R. Balcells	E	3644
11.	Jaques Lebrun	F	
12.	P. Gorelikov	SR	
13.	Willy Pieper	Z	
14.	Kenneth Albury	BA	

1956 Melbourne, Australia (20 entries)

1.	Paul Elvström	D	7509
2.	Andre Nelis	B	6254
3.	John Marvin	US	5953
4.	Jürgen Vogler	DDR	4199
5.	Rickard Sarby	S	3990
6.	Eric Bongers	SA	3912
7.	Adelchi Pelaschier	I	3409
8.	Bruce Kirby	KC	3213
9.	Kenneth Albury	BA	3182
10.	Colin Ryrie	KA	2965

1960 Naples, Italy (35 entries)

1.	Paul Elvström	D	8171
2.	A. Chuchelov	SR	6520
3.	Andre Nelis	B	5934
4.	Ron Jenyns	KA	5758
5.	Reinaldo Conrad	BL	5176
6.	R. Roberts	KZ	5140
7.	Ian Bruce	KC	5123
8.	Kenneth Albury	BA	5092
9.	Yves Louis Pinaud	F	4604
10.	Tonko Pivecevic	Y	4358
11.	Peter Barrett	US	3976
12.	Vernon Stratton	K	3871
13.	Per Jordebakke	N	3822
14.	Bruno Trani	I	3553
15.	H. de Oliviera	P	3488
16.	Jouko Valli	L	
17.	Peter Fürst	OE	
18.	J. Somers Payne	IR	

1964 Enoshima, Japan (33 entries)

1.	Willy Kuhweide	G	7638
2.	Peter Barrett	US	6373
3.	Henning Wind	D	6190
4.	P. Mander	KZ	5684
5.	Hubert Raudaschl	OE	5405
6.	Colin Ryrie	KA	5273
7.	Jörg Bruder	BL	4956
8.	P. Kouligas	GR	4546
9.	G. Devillard	F	4528
10.	Andre Nelis	B	4210
11.	Bruce Kirby	KC	4178
12.	Alexander Chuchelov	SR	3774
13.	György Finaczy	M	3771
14.	Boris Jacobson	S	3692
14.	Per Jordbakke	N	3687
16.	Willems	H	3281

differences in wind strength between crest and trough. The great danger was that the boat would stall on the crests, leaving you wallowing and fighting to get back into the boat in the trough. The currents were wind driven from 1/2 to 11/2 kts, but only the top few feet of water was affected, sliding over the colder, more dense water underneath. The inertia of such a mass of moving water is enormous and once a current was set in motion it would take up to 48 hours for a wind in the opposite direction to reverse the flow.

The **1972**, the Olympic yachting events were scheduled for the same location as the 1936 Olympics - **Kiel**, Germany. The IYRU had conducted a design competition for new Olympic classes. The Australian-designed Contender, a singlehander slightly longer than the Finn with stays and a trapeze, won the monotype competition. The theory was that the trapeze would minimise the weight competition which was a factor in heavy weather Finn sailing. However, it turned out that it takes longer to tack a Contender and consequently the competition and tactics in a race tend to be reduced. Since the factors which were being minimised (strength, endurance, agility, etc.) are factors which most Olympic events are designed to test, the IYRU decided that the Finn was still the best Olympic Monotype boat. However, the IYRU did permit the Finn Class to be modernised by having the host country provide aluminium masts instead of wooden ones for the 1972 Olympic Games.

For the 1972 Olympics, IYRU decided to drop the 5.5 Meter, which was the last formula boat in the Olympics where design was a factor. Besides the Finn and Flying Dutchman, they retained the 3 man keel boat, the Dragon and the two-man keel boat, the Star. The

Gold Medal Winner 1972 - Serge Maury

replacements for them were also approved for the Kiel games, a new type three-man keel boat, the Soling, and a two-man keel boat, the Tempest. This increased the number of Olympic events from five to six. Kieler Fiord is often thought of as synonymous with strong winds and heavy weather sailing, but the wise will tell you "anything can happen at Kiel". But even few of the wise would have been

The fleet at the 1972 Olympics

prepared to forecast two weeks of mild weather and light winds for the sailing events of the XX Olympiad. Thus the 35 helmsmen who competed in the Finn Class at the 1972 Games found their long hours in the gym of little use to them and had instead to call on all their resources of skill, light weather tactics, strategy and patience to finish well - or sometimes just to finish.

Before the Olympics there had been a severe controversy about the masts to be supplied by the organiser. Most of the competitors favoured the old wooden masts, which they were used to, and had qualified with in their national trials. Only a few skippers had gained experience with the new aluminium masts they were forced to use in the Games. The Finn competition in Kiel ended with some big names quite down on the scoreboard! In surprising light air, Serge Maury of France won the Olympic Gold Medal while Elias Hatzipavlis from Greece got 2nd and Victor Potapov from Russia 3rd. The decisive race was the fifth, when only three boats were able to finish within the time limit.

Montreal, Canada was scheduled to host the Summer Olympic Games **1976** with Kingston, Ontario on the Great Lakes to be the scene of the yachting events. By a unanimous vote, the Finns were determined to be the best monotype for the 1976 Olympics. At the request of the International Finn Association, the IYRU did modify the regulations concerning the Finn. Canada would furnish the hulls, however if the contestants so desired, they could bring their own sails and masts and did not have to use those furnished by Canada provided the choice was made in advance. This would eliminate the practice at other Olympics where the contestants spent innumerable hours shaping and tuning the rigs furnished by the host.

Not until the weather mark of the last race was it clear how the medals would be distributed in the Finns. First around was Jochen Schümann from the German Democratic Republic with a tenacious cover on Andrei Balashov of the Soviet Union. Australian John Bertrand, the other contender

**Gold Medal Winner 1976
Jochen Schümann**

for the gold was a distant 12th. Although later passed by two boats, Schümann finished comfortably ahead of the Russian and the Australian to assure his win. As striking as Schümann's excellent performance was the poor showing of the pre-race favourites, David Howlett of England and Serge Maury of France. The fact that they had to use hulls provided by the organiser, had upset many of the top helmsmen, who had done superbly well in their own Finns between the Kiel and the Kingston Olympics. Those who usually had the boat speed to pull them out of a hole were now in a position in which they had to

**Gold Medal Winner 1980
Esko Rechardt**

The Olympic fleet in 1984

rely on their tactical prowess, and they had very little practice at pulling up through the pack with a boat of only average speed.

With the Star and Dragon eliminated, the Tempest and Soling classes were scheduled again. To fill out the schedule, a two-man catamaran, the Tornado was chosen in recognition of the growing popularity of this type of sailing. The Flying Dutchman two man centreboard class was rescheduled but the IYRU was so impressed with the new 470 class, another two-man centreboard class, they scheduled it also, thus keeping six yachting events in the Olympics for 1976.

For the **1980** Olympics in **Moscow**, with the yachting events in Tallinn the IYRU decided to bring back the Star into the Olympic programme and to eliminate the Tempest again. The event suffered severely from the boycott which was initiated by the United States. A number of potential winners were excluded from the start. Some of those who came, felt uncomfortable within the narrow limits of the strict organisation and performed poorly. The favourites: Jochen Schümann, Mark Neeleman, Lasse Hjortnäs, and Minski Fabris failed to collect the medals. Outsiders like Esko Rechardt (Gold) and Wolfgang Mayrhofer (Silver) took the honours in front of the only successful favourite Andrei Balashov who won Bronze. Another favourite José Luis Doreste was disqualified twice for pumping in the first and second race and was totally demoralised. Wind conditions were better than expected based upon the experiences from the Pre-Olympics, varying between 3-5 Beaufort.

For the **1984** Olympics in **Los Angeles** with the yachting events in Long Beach the IYRU kept the six classes from Tallinn: Finn, FD, Star, Soling, 470, Tornado and added a board, the Windglider. The Games suffered once again from a boycott, this time initiated by the USSR as a revenge for 1980. So in Long Beach the favourites from the DDR, Poland and the USSR were excluded. In the Finn class the actual Olympic sailing was preceded by an undignified controversy after the US trials. John Bertrand was declared the representative only 24 hours before the first start. In that race he had a collision with the later Gold medal winner Russell Coutts from New Zealand and was disqualified. Disregarding the mental strain of the qualification battle and the

Gold Medal Winner 1984 - Russell Coutts

disqualification in the first race, Bertrand was leading after the fifth and sixth race. In the last race however, he lost the Gold to Coutts, and Terry Neilson from Canada won the Bronze medal.

The **1988** Olympics were staged at **Seoul**, Korea with the regatta being held in the Bay of Pusan. The classes were the same as at Long Beach except now there were men's and women's divisions in the 470 class and the windsurfer. The final winner, José Luis Doreste, who had competed in both the 1976 and 1980 Olympics was disqualified in race 4 for a collision. The silver medalist Peter Holmberg was PMS in race 4 and one of the favourites Lasse Hjortnäs broke his mast in race two after winning the first race. These events opened up the racing as one further bad result would drop these sailors down the scoreboard. Eventually John Cutler won the last two races to take the bronze. Five men had a chance of winning going into the final race, but the final three medal winners finished

Gold Medal Winner 1988 - José Doreste

1968 Acapulco, Mexico (36 entries)

1.	Valentin Mankin	SR	11.7
2.	Hubert Raudaschl	OE	53.4
3.	Fabio Albarelli	I	55.1
4.	Ron Jenyns	KA	67.0
5.	P. Kouligas	GR	71.0
6.	J. Winquist	L	72.0
7.	Arne Akerson	S	77.0
8.	Philippe Soria	F	80.0
9.	Jörg Bruder	BL	90.0
10.	Hyt	KR	91.7
11.	Jonty Farmer	KZ	90.7
12.	Andy Zawieja	PZ	115.7
13.	Jürgen Mier	DDR	117.7
13.	Carl Van Duyne	US	117.7
15.	Willy Kuhweide	G	120.0
16.	A. Bally	Z	124.7
17.	Obarrio	A	125.0
17.	Henning Wind	D	125.0

1972 Kiel, Federal Republic of Germany (35 entries)

1.	Serge Maury	F	58.0
2.	Elias Hatzipavlis	GR	71.0
3.	Victor Potapov	SR	74.7
4.	John Bertrand	KA	76.7
5.	Thomas Lundquist	S	81.0
6.	Kim Weber	L	85.7
7.	Christian Schröder	DDR	91.0
8.	György Finaczy	M	94.0
9.	Claudio Biekarck	BL	105.7
10.	Bret de Thier	KZ	109.7
11.	Jose Manuel Quina	P	109.7
12.	Walter Mai	G	111.7
13.	Mauro Pelaschier	I	114.7
14.	Jacques Rogge	B	117.7
15.	Paul Hiles	KB	119.0
16.	Miroslav Vejvoda	CZ	123.0
17.	Walter Bachmann	Z	132.7
18.	Patrick Pym	K	133.7

1976 Kingston, Canada (28 entries)

1.	Jochen Schümann	DDR	35.4
2.	Andrei Balashov	SR	39.7
3.	John Bertrand	KA	46.4
4.	Claudio Biekarck	BL	54.7
5.	Kent Carlsson	S	66.4
6.	Anastas Boudouris	GR	77.0
7.	David Howlett	K	77.7
8.	Sanford Riley	KC	83.0
9.	Mauro Pelaschier	I	87.7
10.	Serge Maury	F	88.0
11.	Peter Commette	US	95.7
12.	José Luis Doreste	E	98.7
13.	Minski Fabris	Y	103.0
14.	Jörgen Lindhardtsen	D	106.0

1980 Tallinn, USSR (21 entries)

1.	Esko Rechardt	L	36.7
2.	Wolfgang Mayrhofer	OE	46.7
3.	Andrei Balashov	SR	47.4
4.	Claudio Biekarck	BL	53.0
5.	Jochen Schümann	DDR	54.4
6.	Kent Carlsson	S	71.1
7.	Ryszard Skarbinski	PZ	71.7
8.	Mark Neeleman	H	76.0
9.	Istvan Rujak	M	83.4
10.	Elias Hatzipavlis	GR	89.0
11.	Minski Fabris	Y	91.7

**Gold Medal Winner 1992
José Maria van der Ploeg**

in the reverse of that order with another favourite, Stuart Childerley (who had his best masts broken in transit), finishing sixth in the race and fourth overall. Another Finn sailor to get a medal was Larry Lemieux who gave up a good position in the fifth race to rescue a Singapore 470 sailor from the water after he had lost contact with his boat. He was awarded a silver medal for this feat. Once again the sailors had to use boats that were provided by the organisers, and although they were similar to each other they were not as quick as the sailors own boats.

The **1992** Olympic Regatta was held in **Barcelona**, Spain in generally light to moderate conditions. The only change to the classes was the introduction of the Europe class as the women's singlehander. The Finn fleet was the deepest ever and it was generally agreed that anyone in the first 15 could win the Gold Medal and anyone of the first 22 could win a race. The boats were provided by Vanguard of the USA and although the boats were excellent and more importantly equal, everyone of course could detect differences from their personal boats. The final winner José Maria van der Ploeg never scored worse than sixth and didn't have to sail the final race. The two favourites, current World Champion Eric Mergenthaler and three times Laser World Champion Glenn Bourke performed poorly and finished 18th and 20th. Double world Champion Hank Lammens blew his chances with a DSQ in race two for not having the required life jacket on board and a PMS in race three. Brian Ledbetter was one of the few consistent sailors and won the Silver medal. In the manner of John Cutler four years earlier, Craig Monk, also from New Zealand, won the last race the snatch the bronze away from

The Olympic fleet in 1992

Stuart Childerley again. Prior to the regatta, the IFA conducted a two week training clinic for those countries desiring assistance.

Whilst some people inside and outside of the Finn class saw the Laser as a possible threat to its Olympic status, many also saw the benefits of this popular class in acting as a feeder to the Finn class. In fact the majority of Finn Champions in recent years had sailed the Laser at some point, most of them successfully and had regarded the Finn as the next logical step in singlehanded sailing, the Finn being regarded as the supreme singlehanded challenge. Therefore when the numerically stronger Laser was bidding for Olympic status many thought that it would replace the Finn as the Olympic singlehander for men. However this was not to be as the Flying Dutchman was dropped instead and the Olympics in 1996 were to have two singlehanded dinghies. This worked well, as it meant that there was effectively two boats for two different weight categories: Lasers for the lightweight helms and the Finn for the heavier helm. At present it was considered impossible to have a singlehander that would suit all weights of sailor, and two singlehanders provided the best solution for this problem as well as allowing more countries to be represented at the Games at less cost. Without the Finn, the heavyweight helm had no chance of sailing a dinghy at the Olympic Games.

In the **1996** Atlanta Olympics, the Laser replaced the Flying Dutchman and all other classes remained the same: Finn, 470 (M&W), Europe (W), Windsurfer (M&W), Soling, Star, Tornado. The advance weather reports for **Savannah**, USA, suggested a light wind regatta. However, this was not to be and thunderstorm activity resulted in some spectacular weather and strong winds. Poland's first ever sailing medal was won by Mateusz Kusznierewicz with a race to spare, and this in spite of losing his watch early on in the series and using the clock on the starting boat instead. After an inconsistent start, a 1, 2, 1,

**Gold Medal Winner 1996
Mateusz Kusznierewicz**

1 in the latter half of the series sealed the Gold Medal. Sebastien Godefroid from Belgium took the Silver with only one result to count outside the top 7, whilst relative Olympic veteran Roy Heiner took the Bronze on the last race with a second place, to relegate Hans Spitzauer to fourth. The current world champion Philippe Presti only had a few good results and never found the form that won him his second Gold Cup a few months before. Defending champion and current European champion José Maria van der Ploeg started well by winning the first race and then remained inconsistent to the end of the series.

At the end of 1996, the classes for 2000, in Sydney, Australia were chosen by ISAF. Again it was decided to have three singlehanded dinghies in the Olympics: Finn, Laser and Europe. The singlehanded dinghy provides the best possible realisation of the Olympic ideal, athletes at the top of their sport battling out a competition one-on-one, so it is only natural that every sailor has the chance to sail a singlehanded dinghy at the Olympic Games. Many classes went into overdrive to ensure

The Fleet at the Olympics in 1996

the Olympic survival of their class and in a bizarre twist, the Star was dropped for the second time in its Olympic history to be replaced by the skiff-type boat, the 49'er. However by 1998, the Star was reinstated in its Olympic slot when the IOC gave the sailing events for 2000 another set of medals.

Conclusion

The Olympics were established as an international festival of athletes who have accepted the challenge of measuring themselves against one another to determine the best. Dedication, perseverance, imagination and creativity, stamina, self-discipline, self-reliance, working with others, and sacrifice are the attributes required to be a winning Olympic participant.

Unfortunately, in the beginning, the Olympic yachting events were strictly for the wealthy with large boats and paid crews, who raced with their pocketbooks by trying to have the fastest designed boat. We have progressed a long way since those days. There is continuing pressure placed on the ISAF to add classes to the Olympic events and they have increased from three in 1924 to the present 11 events (9 classes). Due to the mounting costs further increases are impractical and would only serve to dilute interest in the other events. So then there is pressure on the ISAF to change the classes. The ISAF must remember the purpose of the Olympics when deciding the events for future Olympics.

The Monotype event was added to the Olympics in 1920 so that one yachting event would be available to all nations as the host country would provide the boat and that only pure sail-boat racing skill would be exhibited and design and special equipment would not be a factor.

A problem in these events up to 1948 was, that the type of boat was changed for each Olympic Game. Participants had difficulty learning the characteristics of the new class and to practice and develop their skills. With

the introduction of the Finn in 1952 this problem was solved. The Finn was designed as an Olympic singlehander that could be sailed worldwide and aspiring Olympic candidates could practice and develop the required skills prior to the games. In the world today, there are a group of highly dedicated and determined athletes constantly practising in the Finn.

The changes in the Olympic classes throughout the years have been to eliminate the money and design influence on the games and to make the yachting events reflect the spirit and purpose of the Olympics. The Finn class, having been born with this in mind, has established strict class rules and regulations to reflect this. Because of this the Finn has proven to be a true Olympic class reflecting the Olympic spirit. Attempts to find another class that adequately tests the true meaning of Olympic competition have failed.

The ISAF must keep class changes to a minimum as such changes are unfair to the true Olympic competitor as it requires him to redevelop his skills and dedication. It also puts financial burdens on the class itself to promote and maintain its Olympic status and also on the many countries and sailors around the world who have invested time, training and gear in these classes. Unless another type of boat is proven to be superior in demonstrating the skills, stamina, dedication and perseverance of a true Olympic athlete, the classes should not be changed. The intense devotion to the Finn competition by many fine sailors throughout the world and a large number of former Finn sailors in other classes in the Olympics who learned their Olympic competitive spirit in the Finn class, demonstrates that the Finn class is a true Olympic Class and will be retained until a better class can prove superiority to the true Olympics spirit. Therefore it would be quite logical, that the ISAF selects the Finn again as the singlehander for future Olympics.

1984 Long Beach, USA (28 entries)

1.	Russell Coutts	KZ	34.7
2.	John Bertrand	US	37.0
3.	Terry Neilson	KC	37.7
4.	Joaquin Blanco	E	60.7
5.	Wolfgang Gerz	G	66.1
6.	Chris Pratt	KA	68.0
7.	Michael McIntyre	K	70.7
8.	Jorge Zarif Neto	BL	78.7
9.	Mark Neeleman	H	81.7
10.	Ingvar Bengtsson	S	84.0
11.	Peter Holmberg	VI	86.0
12.	Lasse Hjortnäs	D	93.7
13.	William O'Hara	IR	96.0
14.	Esko Rechardt	L	105.7

1988 Pusan, Korea (33 entries)

1.	José Luis Doreste	E	38.1
2.	Peter Holmberg	VI	40.4
3.	John Cutler	KZ	45.0
4.	Stuart Childerley	K	50.7
5.	Lasse Hjortnäs	D	51.0
6.	Thomas Schmid	G	72.1
7.	Roy Heiner	H	78.4
8.	Oleg Khoperski	SR	81.0
9.	Lauri Rechardt	L	88.8
10.	Brian Ledbetter	US	91.0

1992 Barcelona, Spain (28 entries)

1.	José Maria van der Ploeg	ESP	33.4
2.	Brian Ledbetter	USA	54.7
3.	Craig Monk	NZL	64.7
4.	Stuart Childerley	GBR	68.1
5.	Fredrik Lööf	SWE	68.7
6.	Othmar Müller v Blumencron	SUI	70.0
7.	Xavier Rohart	FRA	75.0
8.	Hans Spitzauer	AUT	79.4
9.	Armando Ortolano	GRE	81.7
10.	Christoph Bergmann	BRA	84.0
11.	Arif Gürdenli	TUR	94.7
12.	Stig Westergaard	DEN	97.7
13.	Hank Lammens	CAN	102.0
14.	Emanuele Vaccari	ITA	103.0
15.	Peter Aldag	GER	108.0
16.	Oleg Khoperski	EUN	108.0

1996 Savannah, USA (31 entries)

1.	Mateusz Kusznierewicz	POL	32
2.	Sebastien Godefroid	BEL	45
3.	Roy Heiner	NED	50
4.	Hans Spitzauer	AUT	54
5.	Fredrik Lööf	SWE	57
6.	Paul McKenzie	AUS	67
7.	José Maria van der Ploeg	ESP	69
8.	Ian Ainslie	RSA	72
9.	Richard Clarke	CAN	75
10.	Christoph Bergmann	BRA	79
11.	Jali Makila	FIN	82
12.	Richard Stenhouse	GBR	83
13.	Craig Monk	NZL	86
14.	Michael Maier	CZE	86
15.	Philippe Presti	FRA	87
16.	Luca Devoti	ITA	90
17.	Yuri Tokovoi	UKR	91
18.	Oleg Khoperski	RUS	107
19.	Karlo Kuret	CRO	109

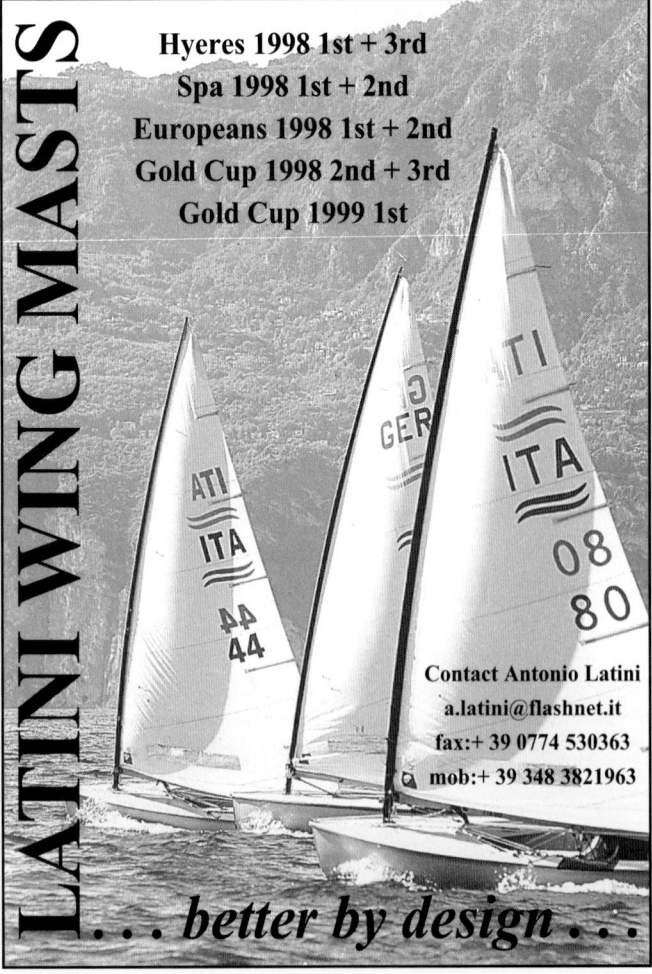

Finn, the ultimate challenge . . .

Sometimes man is presented with opportunities in life to excel, to push himself all the way and beyond, to reach levels he thought unattainable.

This is the essence of Olympic competition embodied in the motto:

Citius, Altius, Fortius . . .

The nature of the competition must provide the ultimate challenge to be a true test.

In the sport of yachting the Finn is such a challenge.

The Finn challenges the sailor in all aspects of yachting.

It rewards those athletes who discipline themselves to drive this powerful boat full out, while managing the strategic, tactical and psychological aspects of the race.

To succeed, however, the Finn sailor must at the same time master the art of adapting the mast, sail and boat to his physique and sailing style.

The Finn's challenge is timeless . . .

Behind the elegant simplicity of the flexible unstayed rig and graceful hull, the Finn is in continuous evolution.

The class incorporates the latest developments in materials and techniques, thus ensuring that the Finn continues to be the most affordable, durable, accessible and rewarding boat to sail.

Thanks to these qualities the Finn has developed a tremendous following of people who know that year after year they will continue to find new challenges and old friendships . . .

The Art of Sailing

Finn racing in the UK in the sixties

Igor Tkachuk (Ukraine), Xavier Rohart (France) and Richard Stenhouse (Great Britain)

The Journey is the Reward

The Finn experience is an exhilarating personal journey shared by all sailors in the class.

It offers each individual sailor the opportunity to develop from a good national competitor into a true member of the international yacht racing family.

Along the way Finn sailors develop friendships and learn to manage the ordeals of international competition and travel. They develop the mental and emotional control necessary for success and the tenacity and determination to set and achieve goals.

The fruits of such a journey cannot be bought ...

they can only be earned through long hours of hard work, courage, perseverance and the realisation that the reward is not in the winning but in performing at the best of one's ability.

These are the values that stay with the athlete for the rest of his life.

Massimo Gherarducci (Italy), Sebastien Godefroid (Belgium), Paul McKenzie (Australia) and Anthony Nossiter (Australia)

Three times World Champion Fredrik Lööf (Sweden)

Andreas Buchert (Germany)

Take a ride on the Finn Side . . .

Karlo Kuret (Croatia)

Hong Quan Li (China)

The challenge is yours.

All you need is time, the boat and a lot of effort.

You can expect a warm welcome from a group of international sailors of all ages who know how to have fun while they push themselves to the limit - the group of sailors who choose the test themselves in the tradition of Paul Elvström and John Bertrand.

Campaigning a Finn is the ultimate challenge: faster, higher, stronger - a truly Olympic experience.

22. FINNFARE - History of a Magazine

by Robert Deaves

FINNFARE is the official publication of the International Finn Association - the magazine that brings the news and events of the Finn world to the sailors and the sailing world. FINNFARE started life in the spring of 1961, initiated by Fred H Miller as the magazine of the USA Finn Association, but with International aspirations.

Fred Miller published 8 issues of FINNFARE from the USA, but the magazine was costing too much money. For the Spring 1962 issue Vernon Stratton, then IFA secretary, was also listed as European Editor alongside Fred Miller who was Publisher and Editor-in-Chief. In his later issues, although the editorial was done in America, the printing and distribution was done from Europe to cut costs.

In 1963 Jack Knights took over as Editor until 1965 and published 5 issues (9-13). The printing of FINNFARE moved to Switzerland where the IFA Secretary Fred Auer lived. Manfred Schiller was the next Editor publishing issues 14-17 from 1965 to 1966. The issues that were printed in Switzerland were of a smaller page size (170 x 243 mm) than usual, but when Vernon Stratton took over as Editor in 1967 the page size returned to the usual 210 x 279 mm. Over the next 4 years until 1971, Vernon Stratton published 10 issues of FINNFARE (18-27), producing some of the best and the biggest issues so far.

During this time Iain Macdonald-Smith also did much of the work of editing FINNFARE.

In December 1970 Vernon Stratton produced the largest issue of FINNFARE to date at 52 pages with reports and results from the 1970 Gold Cup. After Vernon Stratton's retirement from the IFA in 1971, Jan-Jaap Van Elst from Holland became the new Editor. During the next 4 years he published issues 28-32.

The next Editor was Georg Siebeck from Germany, who took over in 1975. Georg gave FINNFARE a professional touch and produced 7 very good looking FINNFAREs (nos 33-39) over the next 2 years.

When Georg Siebeck had to take over his father's publishing house in June 1977, work on FINNFARE was reduced and in August 1977 he brought out a 'Short FINNFARE' with apologies for his inaction. As a compensation Georg Siebeck published the most interesting and most beautiful FINNFARE up to now in December 1977. It had a coloured cover (FINNFARE's first), 52 pages, with lots of pictures, race results, technical details and drawings. Unfortunately Georg never produced another issue. The December 1977 issue was to remain his swan-song. For two more years he had the best of intentions, but never burst into print again.

1: Spring 1961
2: Summer 1961
3: Winter 1961

The first three issues of FINNFARE published by Fred Miller

In 1979 Dr. Jacques Rogge took over the presidency of the IFA from Marino Barendson. He refloated FINNFARE by transferring the editorship back across the Atlantic to San Francisco and entrusting Shimon Craig Van Collie with the task.

Over the next year and a half Shimon Craig Van Collie produced 5 16-page issues (40-44), but resigned from the post when Jacques Rogge retired as IFA President. Then he shipped all the material he had received from Georg Siebeck two years earlier back across the ocean to Vienna and to Peter Mohilla.

Fred Miller
Founder and first editor 1961-1963

Jack Knights
Editor 1963-1965

Vernon Stratton
Editor 1967-1971

 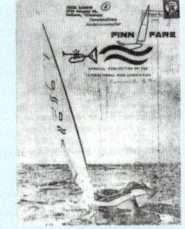     

4: Spring 1962   5: Summer 1962   6: November 1962   7: January 1963   8: April 1963   9: Autumn 1963   10: New Year 1964

11: Spring 1964   12: Summer 1964   13: January 1965   14: Autumn 1965   15: Spring 1966   16: Summer 1966   17: Winter 1966/67

18: Summer 1967   19: December 1967   20: Summer 1968   21: February 1969   22: June 1969   23: October 1969   24: February 1970

25: April 1970   26: December 1970   27: Summer 1971   28: Spring 1972   29: Spring 1973   30: November 1973   31: June 1974

32: June 1975   33: October 1975   34: March 1976   35: July 1976   36: November 1976   37: April 1977   38: August 1977

  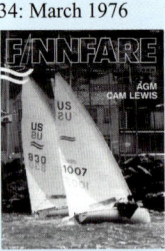    

39: December 1977   40: April 1980   41: July 1980   42: November 1980   43: May 1981   44: October 1981   45: Spring 1982

46: Summer 1982   47: Fall 1982   48: Winter 1982/83   49: Spring 1983   50: Summer 1983   51: Fall 1983   52: Winter 1983/84

53: Spring 1984 54: Summer 1984 55: Fall 1984 56: Winter 1984/85 57: Spring 1985 58: Summer 1985 59: Fall 1985

60: Winter 1985/86 61: Spring 1986 62: Summer 1986 63: Fall 1986 64: Winter 1986/87 65: Summer 1987 66: Fall 1987

67: Printems 1988 68: Summer 1988 69: Fall 1988 70: Winter 1989 71:Spring 1989 72: Fall 1989 73: Winter 1989/90

74:Spring 1990 75: Summer 1990 76: Winter 1990/91 77: Spring 1991 78: Summer 1991 79: Autumn 1991 80: Winter 1991/92

     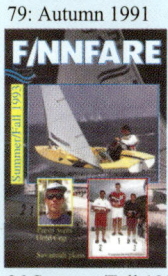 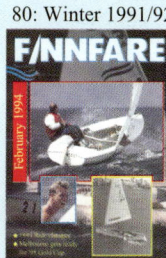

81: Spring 1992 82: Summer 1992 83: Autumn 1992 84: Winter 1992/93 85: Spring 1993 86:Summer/Fall 1993 87: February 1994

     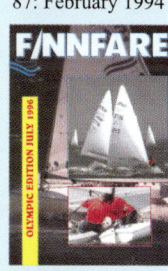

88: June 1994 89: October 1994 90: March 1995 91: July 1995 92: October 1995 93: Gold Cup 1996 94: July 1996

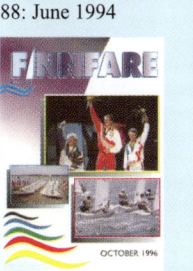    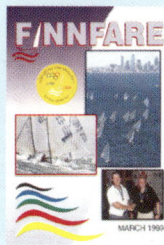

95: October 1996 96: March 1997 97: October 1997 98: March 1998 99: July 1998 100: November 1998 101: March 1999

109

Georg Siebeck
Editor 1975-1977

Shimon Craig van Colllie
Editor 1980-1981

Peter Mohilla
Editor 1982-1987

Peter Mohilla's contribution to FINNFARE history is inestimable. Up to that time no previous editor had managed to sustain both regularity of production or lasted long in the position. Peter Mohilla managed both, producing four issues a year, every year, for five years. He started as he wanted to go on with a 56 page bumper issue with a colour cover and a 27 page section entitled 'Report from the Countries' - a country by country report of Finn sailing in 41 different countries. Peter Mohilla obviously took great delight and care in Finn affairs around the world and even wrote remarks about some countries in the language of that country, notably Korean, Russian and Chinese. The response to his first issue was extremely favourable, although he had to reduce the expense of future issues by cutting pages and the colour cover.

Peter Mohilla was also an enthusiastic writer of articles for his FINNFAREs, many of which appeared in FINNLOG when it was published in 1986. He appeared to take great delight in explaining the intricacies of gybing and tacking Finns, sailing in light and windy conditions, sailing upwind and downwind. and even Finn survival techniques.

Peter Mohilla edited his last FINNFARE in 1986. Over the five years of his editorship, he had produced 20 outstanding issues (45-64). In 1987, the IFA was looking for another editor. Andreas Müller produced a single issue of FINNFARE (65) in the Summer of 1987 before a new Editor was found.

During the Kiel Gold Cup in 1987, Inés Sagué was appointed as the new editor of FINNFARE. Inés was the first editor of FINNFARE who was not an active Finn sailor, although she did sail and had much experience in yachting reporting and was also an accomplished photographer. Between 1987 and 1990 she produced issues 66-74 of FINNFARE from Spain, after which Josje Dominicus from Holland became Editor.

Josje Dominicus introduced a very professional image to FINNFARE, produced more issues than any other FINNFARE editor so far and also held the position longer than any other previous editor. The modern technological era of desktop publishing meant that FINNFARE was easier to prepare that previously and over the next 7 years Josje produced 22 issues (75-96). In 1991 Josje was also appointed as the first Executive Director of the IFA, taking care of all day-to-day affairs of the class, as well as editing FINNFARE.

Josje Dominicus was the first FINNFARE editor who regularly used colour on the covers. Both Georg Siebeck and Inés Sagué had used a spot colour to add a bit of life to the cover and Josje had also done this so far, but for the Olympic Edition in the Summer of 1992, FINNFARE sported a colour cover. Since then FINNFARE has always had a colour cover.

FINNFARE moved back to England for the third time in the Autumn of 1997, with Robert Deaves becoming the 11th Editor of FINNFARE. In November 1998, FINNFARE celebrated its 100th issue, with a special issue devoted to the history of a magazine that has documented the story of the Finn class since its early beginnings.

Inés Sagué   Editor 1987-1990   **Josje Dominicus   Editor 1990-1997**   **Robert Deaves   Editor since 1997**

Philippe Rogge (Belgium)

Previous Page: Mateusz Kusznierewicz (Poland)

John Driscoll (Ireland)

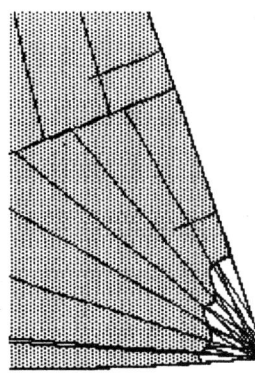

Faster Finn Sails

North Sails New Zealand is currently making two types of Finn sails, both developed to make a consistently faster original sail.

1. **Vectran / Kevlar sail "NZL 32"**
   Full radial sail using the latest full Kevlar Vectran mix . Different designs to customize mast and crew weight. Continuously updated.

2. **The Mylar / Polyester Sail "NZL 38"**
   Specialist light air sail design using Polyester Mylar. Less all up weight than the NZL 32. Radial sail. Continuously updated.

North Sails New Zealand Ltd.

P.O. Box 37419, Parnell
Pakenham Street
Viaduct Basin, Auckland, N.Z.
Phone: 64-9-359 5999
Fax: 64-9-359 5995
Private: 64-9-815 2464
Email: 100405.3551@compuserve.com
Email: mickey@nz.northsails.com
Webpage: www.nz.northsails.com

23. History of the Finn Rules

by Peter Mohilla and Richard Hart   Reprinted from FINNLOG

The objective of this chapter is to document the history of the written rules governing the design of the Finn up to the present standard.

1949

In contrast to the other participants of the design competition in 1949, Rickard Sarby took a different approach. The other contestants designed a boat on paper and wrote a description. Sarby built a boat with very little design work on paper. Of this three dimensional model he made a survey and traced his ideas backward to produce the plans. And finally the concept of the dinghy was expressed in addition in words. Plans and a description were produced to fulfil the requirements of the competition. Thus the oldest remaining written statement about the Finn is the description of the 'FIN' from 1949 which Rickard Sarby handed over to the Finnish Yachting Association as part of his entry to the design competition.

This document lists verbally the material and the dimensions of each part of the boat S 1, which the Sarby brothers had actually built already. It can not be called a set of rules, but it was the beginning of the Finn Rules which control the boat up to the present time. The only restrictive information regarded the weight. The hull had to have 100 kg, fully rigged the boat was supposed to weight 150 kg. The mast had to be 9 kg. Despite the fact, that Sarby's 'FIN' was not at all successful in the competition, had only limited success in the trial races of 1949, and that Rickard was

The building of the first Finn in 1949. Rickard Sarby in centre behind the boat.

very skeptical that 'FIN' would become the Olympic monotype, a large number of Swedish amateurs showed keen interest to build such a dinghy in the winter 1949/50. For their information Sarby handed out the plans and the description of the 'FIN' to them. Thus the material served as an instrument of guidance rather than of control. About 25 boats were built in Sweden in that winter 1949/50. The 'FIN' description of 1949 includes detailed instructions for the diagonal double carvel planking only. No alternative building method is considered.

1950

An improved version of this description exists from early 1950 for the dinghy under the new name of 'FINT'. After the successful trial races in May 1950 the Finnish Yachting Association decided to adopt 'FINT' as the Olympic monotype for 1952, and to change the name to 'FINN'. Rickard Sarby handed over all rights of the Finn to the Finnish Yachting Association who in turn passed them on to the Scandinavian Yachting Union. As early as September 1950 this authority published the first formal collection of written rules in Swedish.

This document is of a mixed nature. It states that the dinghy is to be built in accordance with the drawings and the written specifications. These specifications generally include possible materials and dimensions, sometimes adding optional alternatives and including only a few restrictive statements. The document does not always clearly specify whether the dimensions are minimum or maximum, and whether the boat remains within the class or not, if certain dimensions are changed, if components are omitted or added, or if different construction methods are used. Some items were left to the discretion of the National Authorities to decide, so the rules did not even attempt to be international.

This first set of rules from September 1950 included rules for carvel planking only. No alternative building method is mentioned. It is left open whether any other method would be legal. A special section lists a few measurements to which the dinghy must adhere to in order to qualify as a Finn. Measuring of a Finn in those days required the control of only 20 dimensions and three weights. The hull was controlled at station 0/2/4/6 only and not at station 8. Each builder or measurer could produce for himself the templates for

A Finn in 1951.

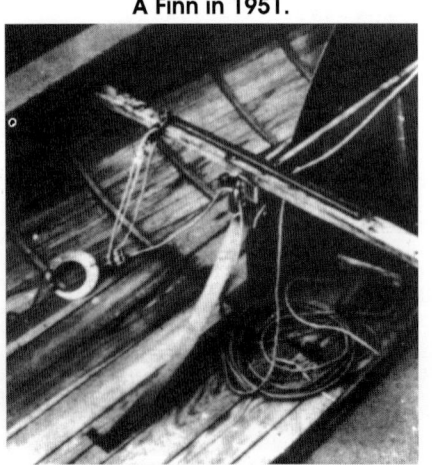

One of the early plastic Finns

station control and these were derived from a table of offsets which accompanied the drawings. The mast was measured not from the keel outside of the boat, but from the deck with the mast in its normal position in the boat. The mast rake was required to be 50/1000. A special arrangement to prevent the mast leaving the step was optional. To require this was left to the discretion of the National Authorities. There was no requirement for any buoyancy. Sailors were even penalised for this item, since any buoyancy bags had to be taken out for weight control and tanks were not allowed. Windows in the sails were not allowed. It might be of further interest, that the position of the mast hole and the centreboard pivot bolt were not specifically controlled by a measurement, and neither was the projection of the centreboard.

1951

In 1951 the Scandinavian Yachting Union printed these rules with a few additions. This set of regulations specified that the dinghy was to be built in accordance with 5 drawings and 23 written specifications. It was not yet quite clear, whether a boat qualified as a Finn

Andre Nelis' Finn in 1957

if some of the items were changed in size, omitted or other parts not mentioned added. There were 5 special regulations for racing the dinghy (one person, arrangements extending outboard and loose ballast prohibited, paddle, bailer and 2 painters on board, four holds optional). The incisive regulations in addition to the more informative 23 specifications mentioned above remained unchanged from the 1950 version.

The most important change in this printed version of 1951, against the set of typewritten rules of 1950, was that two different methods of constructing the hull were allowed. In case of the conventional single carvel planking the number of frames had to be in conformity with the drawings. If the planking was of glued double diagonal carvel (as Rickard Sarby had built his first prototype S 1) or ribboned carvel glued, or if the planking was made of thin stripes of plywood glued together, every second timber could be left out. This printed version of 1951 was made available to interested National Authorities together with a set of plans, in order to construct some Finn Dinghies for the preparation of sailors for the 1952 Olympic Games.

1952

In 1952 the organiser of the Olympic Regatta issued a few more rules, which may or may not be considered as binding for the class in the following years. These rules banned mechanical devices as bailers, which nowadays every Finn has. To adjust the angle between mast and boom only pieces of wood or paper in the boom slot of the mast were allowed, but no vangs.

Loose footed main sails were prohibited, which appeared once again more than 20 years later - to be banned again. It was specifically mentioned, that the head of the paddle may be cut off, so that the paddle can serve as emergency tiller. During the Olympic Races Paul Elvström asked for permission to introduce a relatively small device to serve the function of the present traveller. The original boats had both blocks firmly attached in the centre of the dinghy. The Committee granted Paul to use a wire, which allowed the front block to move about 20 cm to the lee, which many other competitors considered to have been an unfair advantage for the Gold Medal winner.

This was the first incidence of a sailors finding a hole in the rules in order to be faster than his competitors. In the case of the traveller it took 28 years before a rule was approved limiting the movement of the mainsheet block at 550 mm from the centreline and not more than 150 mm in front of station 4.

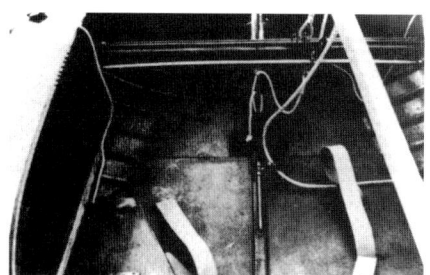

Paul Elvström's Finn in 1957

1953

There was rather limited interest in the further development of the Finn in 1953 and no rule changes are known from this year.

1954

However by 1954 it became obvious to the Scandinavian Yachting Union that a number of new constructions of questionable legality had come up. So a first Technical Committee of experienced Finn sailors was formed, consisting of Elvström from Denmark, Skaugen from Norway, Finell from Finland, and Sarby from Sweden. However the honourable members of the Scandinavian Yachting Union - people who never had sailed a Finn did not trust these young hotshots and changed some of their decisions after the committee had published its findings, creating quite a confusion among the active Finn sailors and the organisers of the 1956 Olympic regattas in Australia.

The Elvström - Sarby Committee suggested to change the measurement of the mast (formerly from the deck) quite logically from the keel (as it is now the rule). But the SYU Committee decided to take all measures from the plane of the gunwale (sheer height) which was very difficult to measure and no improvement over measuring from the deck. Because of improved technology the Australians wanted to construct the 1956 Olympic Finns in hot moulded plywood, which was not allowed before but approved by the Scandinavian Yachting Union in 1954. This allowed the exclusion of the frames completely. The rules were amended accordingly.

1955

By 1955 pressure from outside the Scandinavian countries increased, especially from Belgium and France, to hand over the administration of the Finn and the measurement rules to the IYRU and to form an International Finn Association. After some resistance the Scandinavian Yachting Union cooperated and handed over a set of rules to the IYRU at the end of 1955. This set stated in the beginning, that "the aim of the class rules is to create a real One Design Class and they should be interpreted in that spirit". For clarification it was expressed for the first time, that "the dimensions of the materials are nominal but not binding, unless expressly pointed out".

The amendments in accordance with the Australian Olympic Finns are included in this version of 1955. Of interest might be, that suction bailers were allowed and buoyancy bags were strongly recommended but not yet required. However any buoyancy had to be removed for the control of the hull (105 kg) and the overall (145 kg) weight. Thus sailors using any safety equipment were penalised. In this 1955 version the hull shape had to be controlled also at station 8 for the first time. From that time on, the mast was measured outside of the boat from the keel. There was no regulation controlling the centre of gravity in 1955. The only requirement in this sense was that half of any necessary additional lead was to be fastened to the underside of the deck in front of station 8 and half astern of station 1.

By 1955 a special set of rules had been developed in the United Kingdom. They generally followed the 1955 version of the Scandinavian Yachting Union. The most significant difference is the requirement to have buoyancy bags. Two units of 45 kg buoyancy were necessary. A few more changes were included in response to the rough sailing conditions in England with sometimes strong wind, high and consequently low tides.

In a letter dated September 1955 Richard Murray, Chairman of the British Finn Association, found, that the rules of the Scandinavian Yachting Union were not precise enough. He felt that the form giving dimensions should be changed to either minimum or maximum. Murray remarked, that some of the British Finns have hollow waterlines at station 8, because that section was not controlled at the time.

1956

In 1956 the international Finn Association IFA was formed and acknowledged by the International Yacht Racing Union (IYRU). The rules of 1955 by the Scandinavian Yachting Union mentioned above were reissued without any substantial changes by the International Finn Association in 1956. The only alteration was that disputes regarding the interpretation of these rules had to be referred to the IFA and not any longer to the Scandinavian Yachting Union. From that time on the official language of the Finn Class was not Swedish but English. The first AGM of the IFA in 1956 also elected the first Technical Committee of the IFA, consisting of Rickard Sarby as the chairman and Richard Murray and B. Dotsch as members.

1957

At its AGM in 1957, the newly founded IFA decided upon a number of rule changes and gained its first sobering experiences when the IYRU refused to confirm most of them. The most significant concerned the limitation of the fully lowered centreboard to 700 mm to the keel band. In 1957 the Finn Class was already discussing the possibility of introducing Dacron Sails and Fibreglass Hulls, but did not yet propose this to the IYRU.

1958

By 1958 the IFA had gained some experience in the way to treat the IYRU and got most of the proposals approved. The rule about the fully lowered centreboard was approved with 700 mm from the bottom of the hull and not to the keel bands. The rules about the mast were rephrased. A rake of 50/1000 was recommended, but the rake was not to be adjusted. The mast had to be made of spruce upward from a point maximum 1500 mm above the top of the keel.

The most important change concerned the material of the sail. The limitation to cotton was abandoned and replaced by the requirement to use woven cloth of even thickness. To improve the visibility one transparent panel not exceeding 0.279 m² was permitted. There the IYRU, headquartered in London, managed to introduce a non-metric measurement into the Finn rules, because the odd 0.279 m² is 3 sq feet. Finally a new buoyancy rule was introduced, requiring 200 kg of buoyancy. Tanks were allowed and bags could be included in the weight measurement.

Most important for 1958 was, that the IYRU approved in principle the suggestion of the IFA to allow plastic construction for the hull. For the final approval the IYRU requested a major revision of the rules. In Switzerland and Germany some experiments with Finns in plastic construction had been initiated by enterprising boat builders in 1958, in order to keep the Finn Dinghy up to date. Within the IFA as well, strong forces attempted to avoid that the Class be outmoded by new boats built to more modern construction methods. However the President Henri Leten, the Secretary Richard Murray and Rickard Sarby as the leading forces of the Technical Committee had to consider the existing wooden boats and had to take care that they remain competitive. Murray asked for suggestions for a new set of rules, in which the important regulations which make the boat what it is remain unchanged, while the details of the wooden construction became optional. Murray in addition attempted to draft a special brochure 'Instructions to Measurers', however it took several years before these were published.

Vernon Stratton's Finn in 1961

1959

By March 1959 Richard Murray sent out a new set of suggested rules to the National Finn Associations and the members of the Technical Committee. At the AGM in August 1959 at Copenhagen these rules were discussed in detail. A revised version was handed in to the IYRU in time and generally approved at the November 1959 IYRU meeting. The driving force behind this process was the Secretary of the IFA, Richard Murray from the UK. In order to keep the deadlines he partly exceeded his authority but got away with it. Sometimes you have to ignore the rules of democracy and fall back upon authoritarianism in order to get things done. Murray was aware of this and apologised after the fact, but the final approval of the new rules by the IYRU justified his excess of competence.

The new rules of 1959 had 4 Sections. Section I stated the objective of the rules as the establishment of a One-Design-Class in all matters which affect the speed of the boat, but in which the material and details of construction are left optional. The rules of Section II were obligatory and are the hard core of the new edition. Section III referred to the conventional method of carvel construction and did not need to be followed. Section III became rather short and was intended to serve as a guide for amateur builders who wanted to play it safe and build a conventional boat without the danger of not passing measurement. Section IV concerned the measurement and certificates.

Aside of a complete rearrangement of the rules in four sections, the 1959 edition also included a number of substantial changes. The keel line was defined by distance from a theoretical base line. The measures differed slightly from those presently in force and the method of taking these measures had to be redefined some years later. The stem profile had to be controlled by a template. The appearance of the Finn was changed by the new rule to allow the side decks to be rounded in. This made the boat more comfortable, more modern looking, and allowed for a better construction of buoyancy tanks both in wood and in plastic. Most important was that the material of the hull was optional, thus plastic or any other method was allowed. This regulation was restricted again in the following years excluding sandwich and similar methods.

In order to keep the One-Design character of the Finn for all methods of construction a very important rule about the Centre of Gravity was introduced. When balanced on one gunwale, the hull had to lean with the upper gunwale against a vertical surface maximum 500 mm from the resting point. The position of the mast hole was controlled by measuring from the front of the stemband to the forward side of the mast hole. This was easy to control but gave a tolerance of 30 mm to the position of the mast.

1960

By January 1960 these rules as approved by the IYRU in November 1959 became effective and were printed together with a short history and description of the Finn, the Association Rules of the International Finn Association, the Rules for the Finn Gold Cup and a clean drawing of the new regulations. On the basis of these new printed rules some countries developed Measurement Forms in their local language, listing the correct measurement and empty spaces for the actual measurement and possible remarks.

At about that time the first doubts about the reliability of the template measurement to control the shape of the hull cropped up. Some boats measured once and did not measure the next time. Templates were made locally from a table of offsets and the definition of the stations was rather vague. At the end of 1960 for the first time it was made clear, that the floorboards must not form the top of a double bottom. The height of the floorboards was limited by minimum distances to the sheer line.

1961

In 1961 the sheer height control was included in the template measurement of the stations. The floorboards in front of station 4 were omitted, but between station 2 and station 4 defined in width and height as they are now. The buoyancy rules for plastic boats were tightened, requiring four separate units or foam plastic in such a way, that the boat can support 75 kg if two units are damaged. The maximum height of the thwart below the sheer was increased from 80 to 130 mm. This was an important change, because it allowed a traveller to be placed on the thwart while still being able to pull the boom as far down as before.

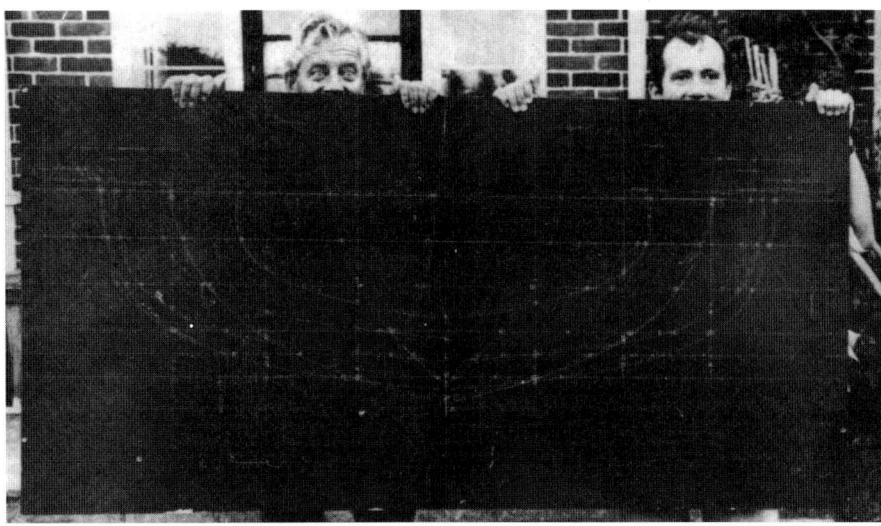

Charles Currey and Gilbert Lamboley with the lines of the Finn on a sheet of aluminium defined by Fairey Marine in 1963

Because of difficulties in template measurements of stations 2/4/6 the table of offsets was found to differ from the original design by as much as 4 mm in some points and had to be changed. This increased the already existing doubts in the method of controlling the hull shape. A proposal of the IFA to the IYRU to allow the mast to be made of any material was refused at that time. The IYRU required to collect more information on the experimental use of aluminium and fibreglass masts before they can be approved.

However there were bigger problems casting their shadows over the Finn Class in 1961. At the Gold Cup in Travemünde the first three boats were made of GRP Glass-Reinforced Plastic. About 2000 owners of older wooden boats were afraid that the rule changes of 1959/60 had outmoded their dinghies. Even more disquieting than the victory of the old champion Andre Nelis was the third position of an unknown sailor from the United States, Fred H. Miller Jr., who finished third. After the Gold Cup Fred Miller sold his magic boat, about which he had told many fantastic stories, to Arne Akerson of Sweden.

1962

At the measurement for the Gold Cup 1962 in Tonsberg, Norway, some hidden lead was found in the bottom of that magic boat, which was against the rules. The Finn Class was in danger of falling apart. The new rules had turned out to be too weak to ensure the One-Design character of the Finn Class. The IYRU threatened to withdraw the international and the Olympic status. Many of the owners of wooden boats were disillusioned, and those of plastic boats considering to hide some lead themselves, only did not know how much and where. Builders outside of Europe were especially confused and did not know how to build a fast boat that was also legal. Therefore a new Technical Committee was elected at

the AGM in Tonsberg to redraft the rules and plans for submission to the IYRU in November 1963. For the time being a few changes were proposed to the IYRU November 1962 meeting in order to solve the most pressing problems.

Most important in the rule changes of 1962 was the requirement to keep the distribution of weight in the hull as near as possible to that of a normal carvel planked boat. In reinforced plastic boats the structural panels had to be made of single skin plastic material with normal reinforcement of glass. Sandwich constructions or trapped air-cells were not allowed. In addition to the older control of the centre of gravity athwart a second control was introduced longitudinally. Supported at station 3 the boat had to have a bow-weight of 21 kg mm.

For an improvement of the unsatisfactory situation with the hull measurement, it was decided to define the stations by measuring along the keel and the rubbing strake from the transom. Later this method proved to be wrong by 9 mm with perfectly legal boats compared with a theoretical definition of the plane of station 8 and was abandoned again. The definition of the keel line was slightly changed to be measured to the flat under the keel band and not to the theoretical point, where the sections meet.

The driving force in the newly elected Technical Committee was Richard Creagh-Osborne from the UK as the Chairman, with Rickard Sarby from Sweden and Ole With from Norway as members.

1963

All through 1962 and 1963 the new Technical Committee worked hard to submit the following for ratification in November 1963 to the IYRU: a set of rules, a standard

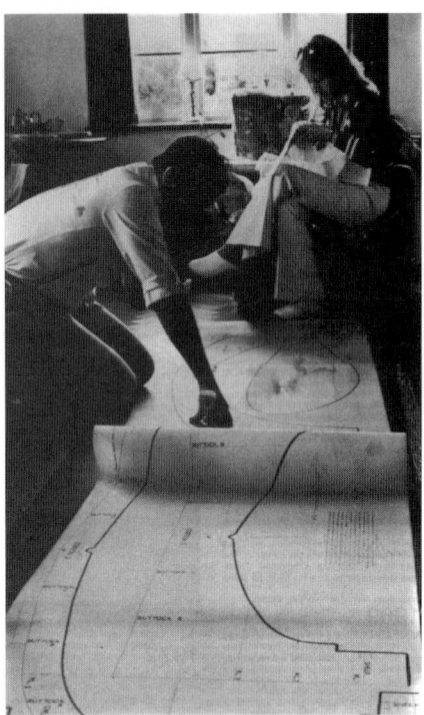

Gilbert Lamboley studying the full size drawing of the templates

measurement form, a set of instructions to measurers, modified plans to assist builders in plastic materials, and a statement of which rules are to apply retrospectively and which are only for new boats. For the information of builders, measurers and boat owners a revised version of the rules as approved in November 1962 by the IYRU was published by the IFA early 1963. Compared with the printed version of 1960, most significant is the statement in Section 1 that builders are not to attempt to get round the spirit or the letter of the rules, to produce boats which are intended to be basically faster than those originally built of conventional carvel timber construction. Furthermore, the rules read that it is the sole responsibility of the owner of the boat that it complies with the plans and rules of the Class at any time.

In 1963 Fred H. Miller jr. again created confusion at the Gold Cup. He distributed a leaflet about his new Wesco Finn, advertising, that his product was built intentionally to be faster than any Finn up to now. Miller thus gave it in writing that he intended to break the basic rule stated above. The boat was not allowed to sail in the Gold Cup, after some obvious cases of inconsistency with the rules were recorded. This incident further undermined the confidence of many sailors in the ability of the Technical Committee to assure the One-Design characteristic of the Finn Class. Working on the plans Richard Creagh-Osborne discovered discrepancies between the drawings and the table of offsets, issued up to then to control the shape of the hull. Templates sent to Japan for the control of the Olympic Finns turned out to be wrong.

With the help of Fairey Marine Ltd., a factory for airplanes and boats, the lines of the Finn were redefined in a full size drawing on a sheet of aluminium. From this master drawing two different reproductions were made on a transparent plastic material which was said not to stretch or shrink. The first was a full size drawing of all the templates and the second of a body plan with all the sections and the stem.

1964

In November 1963 the IYRU discussed the proposals of the IFA Technical Committee in great detail and approved most of them to become effective from May 1 October 1964. There were not many substantial changes, but the lay-out was completely new, clearer and more rational. The rules gave exact instructions to boat owners, builders and measurers. The new set put greater responsibility on the owner to see that his boat was measured correctly and remained in class thereafter. The most important substantial change was the deletion of the former table of offsets from the rules, to be replaced by a new set of official templates. Such templates could be obtained from Fairey Marine through the IFA or produced locally from a set of drawings issued by Fairey Marine on a supposedly stable plastic material.

The side decks were redefined and cut-outs for the traveller prohibited. The traveller must not extend beyond the cockpit edge. Fifteen years later the same problem came up again and was solved in principle in the same way in detail in a slightly different manner. The shape of the centreboard was defined by the large and the small radius and the chord length. The lower mast bearing was allowed to be adjustable but any movable part had to be forward of station 7. The weight of the hull without floorboards, toestraps, centreboard and all other loose gear had to be above 105 kg. In the same condition the location of the centre of gravity was controlled longitudinally and athwartships. The total weight of all hull correctors had to be less than 10 kg. The building in of high or low density material in the hull was prohibited.

In this version of 1964 the mast hole was still to be measured from the stem and not from the transom, which was easier to measure, but inconsistent with all other hull measurements

Wetting down Finns at a Gold Cup

and contradicting the wording of other stipulations, that all measurements are taken from the transom. This new set of rules was complemented by a new measurement certificate, listing all the rules in a table with blank spaces to be filled in with the findings of the measurers, and - for the first time, fulfilling the suggestion of Richard Murray from 1958 - by 'Official Instructions to Measurers'. In these instructions to measurers it was pointed out that plastic boats can shrink. If new moulds were made from existing plastic boats (measuring correctly), the final outcome might turn out to be too small. In this version of 1964 it was still recommended that measurers locate the stations for template control by measuring along the keel, but not along the gunwhale. It was recommended to determine the position of the stations at the sheer by measuring directly from the transom to points on the deck. In addition to the 'Official Instructions to Measurers' a special leaflet 'Measurement Procedure for International Finn Class Boats' was produced.

After the first publication of the decisions of the IYRU from November 1963, the Technical Committee continued to work on the rules. Before the changes even became effective, some more discrepancies were discovered during 1964 and included in the further publications of the new rules. Most important was the definition of the overall length to be 4495 ±15 mm, and the regulation, that the fore side of the mast hole had to 3830 ±5 mm, a few months later changed to 3825 ±10 mm, from the transom.

In 1964 the Technical Committee was enlarged by the adoption of the measurer of the 1964 Gold Cup in Torquay, Vernon Forster. In the years to come, Vernon Forster became the Chief Measurer of the IFA and the terror-horror of builders and top competitors at major events. Forster did not develop new rules, but declared himself as the only authority in the interpretation of the established rules without any possibility of appeal. Meanwhile the new rules as approved by the IYRU in November 1963 were sent to National Authorities and translated into other languages.

The application of the new rules brought unexpected problems to builders, measurers and owners. The Technical Committee, mainly Richard Creagh-Osborne, personally considered every point with admirable patience, and handed in a further list of proposals for rule changes to the IYRU in November 1964. In November 1964 the IYRU approved a number of minor changes in the wording of the rules. Substantial alterations were the prohibition of centreboard slot sealing strips, the change in the measurement of the mast hole position (not any longer from the stem but from the transom), and the exclusion of hollow rudder blades or blades filled with lower specific gravity material.

1965

This revised version became effective January 1, 1965. A new 'Measurement Procedure for International Finn Class Boats' was issued along with the rule changes. The IFA and the IYRU recommended to call upon the newly created Class Measurer (Vernon Forster) in case a larger number of boats was to be measured or if specific problems had come up. In the version of 1965 the suggestion to determine the station points by measuring along the keel was finally abandoned. From now on the rules and the measurement instructions require both for the sheer and the keel points to measure parallel to the base line from the theoretical plane of station 0, in order to determine the position of other stations.

The revised set of rules was properly published, translated into several languages and put to work. At the 1965 Gold Cup in Gdynia, Poland, representative boats of several builders were completely measured. Several discrepancies were observed, mainly regarding the hull shape. Builders were warned, that the following year these boats will not be allowed to race in any major events. With the publication of the new rules in 1964/65 a significant process had taken one further step. In the beginning of the development of the Finn rules with the description of the 'FIN' by Rickard Sarby in 1949, there was a collection of descriptive information about the boat and only the passage about the weight of the dinghy was phrased as a restrictive minimum. By 1965 the rules were about three times as long as in 1949, but contained almost exclusively restrictive regulations and included

only a few options. The objective of the rules had changed from an informative support for an interested amateur home builder to an incisive control system for semi-professional measurer to curb excesses of profit greedy shipyards. While the rules of 1951 to 1958 had a long section with suggested materials and dimensions in front of a brief section with limiting regulation, the rules of 1959 to 1963 consisted of a long restrictive section in front of a brief list of suggestions. After 1964 only a few options were mentioned on some of the rules. The home builder in good faith was left in the wilderness without guidance. In order to remedy this deficiency Richard Murray, IFA secretary up to 1961, and driving force of the rule changes in 1959/60, and Richard Creagh-Osborne published 'Hints for Home Constructors' in 1965.

1966

In 1966 the new rules were published in a neat booklet, which included all the material agreed upon in the previous year. While the older boats remained genuine Finns in national and club races, the new measurement rules were enforced at the Gold Cup and the European Championship irrespective of the year the boat was claimed to have been built. At the AGM 1966 the delegates felt, that the new rules were too long and too complicated and therefore should be shortened and simplified. In addition strong forces called for more modern methods of construction like sandwich and double-bottoms. The main problems concerned the centre of gravity and the thickness of the hull.

1967

The simplification of the rules as proposed by the US was refused at the AGM 1967. However some smaller changes were adopted

A wood Taylor from the early seventies

and later that year approved by the IYRU. The most important was the introduction of an additional control of the keel profile at station 1 with a tolerance of only ±5 mm in order to cope with hollow sections in the aft portion of Raudaschl hulls. Furthermore it was decided at the 1967 AGM to ask the IYRU for permission to use alloy and reinforced plastic as a spar building material. The IYRU agreed in principle and asked for further experiments. Furthermore the IYRU asked the Finn Class to work on a method of controlling the distribution of structural weight in the hull.

1968

In 1965 several spars made of reinforced plastic or aluminium were produced and tested. The IYRU approved to allow these materials in 1969. The AGM 1968 decided to introduce 'Case Laws' as authentic interpretations of the rules by the Technical Committee. These case laws do not require approval of the IYRU.

1969

At the AGM 1969 the representatives asked again for a revision of the rules governing the hull construction. Electronic and electrical aids other than a watch and compasses were banned.

1970

At the 1970 AGM in Cascais, Gilbert Lamboley was elected as the new Chairman of the Technical Committee, because Richard Creagh-Osborne was not able to continue. A decision of that AGM to free the boom to fit through a 85 mm circle and to increase the thickness of the rudder to 28 mm was later refused by the IYRU. The Technical Committee was asked to discuss ways to modernise the Finn and to report back the following year.

Chief Measurers of the Finn Class: Vernon Forster, Peter Mohilla, Robert Laban, Jüri Saraskin

1971

At that time the Technical Committee of the IFA was paralysed by the fight between Vernon Stratton and the Auers about the question of whether wooden or aluminium spars should be used at the 1872 Olympic Games in Kiel. Gilbert Lamboley, the newly elected Chairman of the Technical Committee was working hard on a new method to control the distribution of weight in a dinghy.

1972

In 1972 it was decided to introduce the pendulum test of Gilbert Lamboley for an experimental period. If it turned out to be satisfactory it was intended to delete the existing rules to control the centre of gravity. For years people had been talking about the effect of the distribution of weight upon the performance of a dinghy. The Lamboley test offered a method to measure and limit these factors. The 1964 rules attempted to control the weight distribution by extremely strict controls on the scantings. The introduction of the Lamboley test would allow the relaxation the scanting rules, to free the construction method (including sandwich), to allow double bottoms, and to make measurement easier and faster. In November 1972 the IYRU approved to introduce the Lamboley test in the Finn rules, and expressed its hope that the experiences in the Finn Class in 1973 will pave the way for the introduction of the same method for other classes.

The Finn that Vernon Stratton had built with the first ever double bottom

1973

The pendulum test was made effective for the Finn Class in March 1973. Consequently it was possible to abandon the rules controlling the centre of gravity up to now by measuring the bow weight and tilting the hull on one gunwale. After the pendulum test was successfully introduced and tested, it was then possible to free the construction method of the hull and to allow double bottoms. On the basis of these changes Gilbert Lamboley developed a new measurement book, which had the rules on the right-hand pages and the remarks and instructions to the measurers on the left. The weight of the rudder including tiller was fixed at 3.2 kg, three years later to be raised to 4.0 kg. Without much saying Gilbert changed the size of the sail-window from the odd 0.279 m^2 (3 sq. feet) of 1958 to 0.3 m^2.

1974

At the Gold Cups in 1973 at Brest and in 1974 at Long Beach there were again problems with the templates. Lamboley discovered, that the templates produced by Fairey Marine in the previous years had varied in shape and that the drawings of the body lines and the templates on supposedly stable material were not stable either. Gilbert Lamboley develop a new method for the production of templates from 3 mm tensile aluminium with a computer guided milling cutter on the basis of the full size drawing of the Finn body lines on an aluminium sheet, produced by Fairey Marine under guidance of Richard Creagh-Osborne in 1963. In 1974 it was ruled and approved by the IYRU, that masts had to be watertight. However only three years later this rule was abandoned again. It turned out that this rule rather caused water to be trapped inside the mast rather than keeping it out.

1975

There were problems with the pendulum test. It induced builders of plastic boats to use more expensive building methods. Therefore the IFA asked to increase the minimum radius of

gyration from 1100 mm to 1150 mm. The IYRU approved 1140 mm. Attempts to find satisfactory rules for the control of hull stiffness and of pumping failed. The new templates developed by Gilbert Lamboley found full approval. It was decided that only the IFA Technical Committee would have the ability to issue these templates. The drawings of templates and of the body lines will lose their authoritative status and are of informative value only.

1976

The rule books of 1974 had been all sold and a new 1976 edition had to be printed. The following proposals of the Technical Committee of the IFA found approval of the IYRU in November 1976: The weight of the rudder together with the tiller was raised to 4.0 kg. The radius of gyration was reaffirmed at 1140 mm. Loose footed sails were once again ruled out. The IYRU discretely expressed their indignation, that the IFA frequently asked for rule changes on identical matters within a few years. The Technical Committee of the IFA was asked to discuss matters and conduct proper experiments before handing in rule changes for approval. In 1976 most of the energies of the Technical Committee were absorbed by the internal fight within the IFA, whether the weight of the boat should be reduced or not. The President, Marino Barendson, strongly favoured the reduction of the weight and had the means to travel all around the world in order to find approval. Gilbert Lamboley was sick and had difficulties with his business and could only fight back by writing letters. There was not much productive work performed in regard with the Finn rules

1977

The 1977 AGM decided to delete again the rule about the floatability of the mast, adopted only in 1974. Gilbert Lamboley had attempted to become president of the IFA without success. He was discouraged and did not do much for the Technical Committee of the IFA.

| Rickard Sarby | Richard Creagh-Osborne | Gilbert Lamboley |
| 1956-1962 | 1962-1970 | 1970-1980 |

Chairmen of the Technical Committee since 1956

| David Howlett | Andrzej Ostrowski | Richard Hart |
| 1980-1982 | 1982-1989 | Since 1989 |

1978

A number of new technical developments caused the concern of the Technical Committee. Roga built a Finn with a sidedeck shape not in accordance with an interpretation of the class rules. In the execution of that matter some internal and external problems came up, in regard with the competence of the Chairman of the Technical Committee, the Executive Committee, the Council and individual members to write letters to the IYRU, to boat builders or regatta organisers. A number of rule changes and also changes of the constitution in regard with the Technical Committee were discussed, to be agreed upon and effective in 1979/1980. Some boats were found to be out of shape at station 8.

1979

For the 1979 AGM in Weymouth Gilbert Lamboley had prepared a long list of pending problems, but could not attend himself. Important matters which were discussed, handed in to the IYRU and finally approved included the following. The travel of the mainsheet block was limited by 550 mm from the centreline and not by the edge of the side decks. The pendulum test had to be executed with the centreboard and the control lines in the boat. Hiking fittings made of soft material were allowed but an alteration of the side-deck-shape was prohibited. Steel was included in the list of possible materials for the mast. In 1979 the emphasis in regard with hulls not measuring at station 8 shifted from Taylor to Vanguard. The need for an improvement of the measurement procedure in regard with the definition of the stations became more and more evident.

1980

The tension between the Chairman of the Technical Committee Gilbert Lamboley and the Executive Committee, mainly the President Jacques Rogge, increased in 1980. The official AGM in Takapuna, Auckland, New Zealand in February 1980 expressed its concern with the negative attitude of Gilbert Lamboley and decided upon a change in the constitution, limiting the power of the Technical Committee. Gilbert was granted a time-limit up until a second General Meeting in Helsinki in June 1980 on the occasion of the European Senior Championship, to conform with the desires of the Council. Consequently Lamboley resigned and David Howlett was elected as Chairman of the Technical Committee.

1981

After the AGM 1961 all the rule changes between 1976 and 1981 were printed together as a loose supplement to Finnfare, allowing each owner to bring his rule book up to date. This included the change of the constitution, the procedure for any rule changes, the redefinition of the maximum horizontal play of the mast at the deck and the heel, the materials allowed to make the mast, facilities to drain the mast, the halyard, the travel of the mainsheet block, the redefinition of the pendulum test, the possibility to use any one thickness of material for the sail, and the limitation of weight jackets to 20 kg.

1982

The AGM in Medemblik in 1982 decided to request that lead correctors have to be visible. The IYRU approved two years later. Case laws about the height of the deck ring, the strength of the paddle and of the bailer and the elimination of wedges in measuring the gaps between templates and the hull were agreed upon. Further progress was made in the development of jigs for the definition of the stations at majors regattas. Andrzej Ostrowski was elected as the new Chairman of the Technical Committee.

1983

The discussions of the Technical Committee, the decisions of the AGM and the approval of the IYRU in 1983 covered one rule change and a number of case laws. Masts made of any material were allowed for one year after the 1984 Olympics in order to gain more experience on new techniques. John Christianson had built a jig for the measurement at the 1983 Gold Cup, which was declared the prototype to be required at future major IFA events for the definition of stations for the hull shape measurement. This ended the controversy of the previous years about station 8.

1984

In order to allow for further technical development, the rule about the materials for the sail was amended in 1984. Any combination of flexible materials was allowed.

1985

The 1985 AGM decided to prepare a new edition of the Rule Book to become effective after the Olympic Games 1988. The Technical Committee Chairman requested and the IYRU agreed that the experimental period for masts be extended until the end of the 1986 Gold Cup. Peter Quigley from the US made a prototype mast made of a braided composite material consisting of carbon-fibre and s-glass in an epoxy matrix. This mast appeared to be successful in racing in the US.

1986

The class had authorised experimentation with Carbon Fibre masts, and some were brought by the USA team to the Gold Cup. They were not used in the regatta, but the Technical Committee recommended that the IYRU should allow use of the material after the 1988 Olympic Games. After inspecting these masts, the Technical Committee produced guidelines: the masts should be of similar diameter to Needlespar aluminium masts, which should

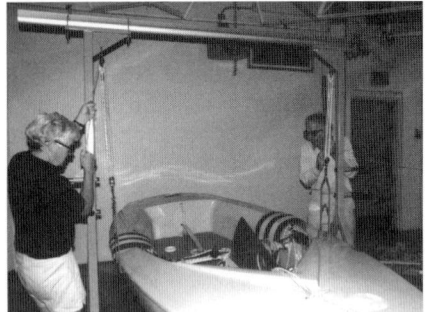

Conducting a Lamboley swing test.

not be made obsolete. There was no suggestion about reducing the minimum weight, even though the experimental masts weighed as little as 6 kilos. At the Gold Cup there was concern over centreplates which were sharper than the permitted half round on the leading edge. Work commenced on a major redrafting of the rules, intended to make them more user friendly. Other matters receiving attention were the limitation of clothing weight and refinement of a class rule governing pumping.

1987

Great effort was going into the redrafting of the Rules for 1989 onwards. The IYRU Centreboard Boat Committee considered a draft in November and made many editorial proposals.

Actual rule changes were limited to alterations governing the introduction of advertising on boats, and minor definitions on sandwich construction (not allowed at that time) and on the definition of 'horizontal' for floorboards.

1988

The new package of rules had been discussed for several years and was adopted by the IYRU.

Peter Mohilla conducting some experiments

1989

By 1989 the class had become very standardised. The best sailors were almost all using Vanguard boats built nearly ten years before, the Needlespar aluminium masts and the Dacron sails had hardly changed in a dozen years. This was starting to cause concern that the class would be seen as stagnant and would fail to achieve selection for the Olympic Games.

Andrzej Ostrowski stepped down after seven years of steady leadership in the Technical Committee, culminating in the editing of a newly revised Rule Book. Richard Hart, an old Finn sailor, was asked to take over. The Technical Committee's brief was defined by Council "to make the Finn cheaper, easier to measure at championships, and suitable for a wider range of helmsman's weights".

1990

There was a marathon Technical Committee meeting at the Gold Cup in Thessaloniki, after which the IFA Council agreed and directed that the rules should be altered to encourage development of Fibre-reinforced plastic masts, with as few artificial constraints as possible. One comment was that "the new masts should not be a bad copy of the aluminium masts, which were themselves a bad copy of the old wooden masts."

This decision was enormously important. It demonstrated the change of attitude in the IFA Council to one which was more responsive to change in the class. For more than twenty five years it had been obvious that the mast should be as far forward as allowed in the boat, and there were always problems at measurement. As part of the 'mast' alterations, the Council agreed that the deck bearing position might be freed.

1991

The class mourned the death of Peter Mohilla, who as Chief Measurer had been a staunch guardian of the rules. He was replaced by another long time Finn sailor, Robert Laban, but during the following year Robert also died.

Rule changes made it easier to mould the stemband shape in plastic boats, and the class started to develop significant rule alterations to follow the 1992 Olympics.

A new Finn builder appeared: Pata from Hungary, who was associated with long-time Finn sailor Laszlo Zsindely.

1992

A rewritten sail measurement rule came into force, basically in accordance with the new IYRU Sail Measurement Instructions, but with one major difference: the half and three quarter height positions on the leech were to be measured from the Head Point, not by folding the leech. The difference allowed sails to be measured without folding and unfolding.

The class appointed Jüri Saraskin as Chief Measurer.

1993

A number of major rule changes, the culmination of several years of discussion in the class, came into effect. Some changes simplified measurement and removed old problem areas: a requirement that the leading edge of the Centreplate be half round was deleted, some floorboard (inner bottom) rules were simplified, and the hulls were to be weighed without the mast, boom and rudder. Another series of changes facilitated the development of reinforced plastic masts. Minimum widths were specified for masts, but the fore and aft maximum dimensions were left large enough to accommodate older masts. Lead correctors were allowed up to 4 kilos, with a statement that the corrected minimum weight of 10 kilos would be reviewed after two years.

Adequate buoyancy in the bow section is very important

The mast hole position in the boat was freed. This simplified the new mast rule and enabled the rig to be moved. In the words of the official submission to the IYRU, henceforth "the boats would feel nicer in the waves".

New boats were starting to appear, such as the Devoti Finn (built in the UK and marketed from Italy) and the Lemieux Finn (built and marketed from Canada). Both boats were associated with leading Finn sailors. New plastic masts were used by several leading Finn sailors, coming second in the Finn Gold Cup and first in the Europeans. The new masts generally weighed about 7 or 8 kg, and the sailors complained bitterly about the big lead correctors to reach the 10 kg still required.

1994

For 1994, there were minor changes to the mast rule. Because the freeing of the mast position made the centreplate pin position less critical, the measurement of this position was simplified.

At the Gold Cup, there were a considerable number of plastic masts, and a prototype sails made from unwoven (reinforced film) material. At the AGM, there was concern about the price of the new plastic masts.

1995

The minimum mast weight was reduced to 8 kilos. Plastic masts were becoming standard on the international circuit.

1996

At the Gold Cup, a 'ginger group' including several veterans (renamed masters) proposed a weight reduction for the hulls. By this time almost all boats built since 1980 were carrying between 5 and 10 kilos of lead correctors in the hull, and it was agreed that the hull weight should be reduced by 5 kilos. At the same time the Council instructed the Technical Committee to submit a rule change deleting the requirement for keel bands except forward of the centreplate slot.

There was considerable disquiet about the cost of some of the new plastic masts, in particular because they exploited the fore and aft tolerance to produce a partial wing section. The possibilities of building the masts over a standard mould (mandrel) and of tightening the fore and aft restrictions were discussed: the second was talked into oblivion at a long meeting of the full Council. In the end it was agreed that market forces would provide the only practicable control on the cost. There was also concern that new one piece sails might be introduced and would be excessively costly, so a rule was introduced requiring that the sails be made from panels of material not more than 1 metre wide.

The efforts of the class were concentrated upon selection for the 2000 Olympic Games.

1997

The rule changes discussed in 1996 came into effect. Keelbands were no longer required except forward of the centreplate slot, and the hull minimum weight was reduced by 5 kilos. At the same time the centreplate was required to conform to what had become standard: 8 mm anodised Aluminium. The minimum boom weight was increased by 0.5 kilo. A number of sails made from reinforced plastic film were in use at the Gold Cup. They went well, but did not outclass the latest Dacron sails.

1998

Since at the 2000 Olympics sailors could use their own boats, it was recognised that there would be increased pressure on the rules. For the first time, a rule appeared that there must be sheerguards! At the Gold Cup there were only about five woven sails in regular use. Many sails were made from reinforced plastic film, others from monofilm (without integral reinforcement). Prices and durability seemed to be satisfactory. There was concern that many masts and sails racing at intermediate level regattas had not been measured, and that these masts in particular were underweight.

1999

New rules required the measurement of masts and sails before they left the manufacturer. At the Gold Cup in January there were some sails made of ultra thin lightweight material, and the AGM instructed the Technical Committee to devise a rule to control the resulting expense.

Summary

The history of the Finn rules reflects the fascinating interplay between the Technical Committee (representing the International Finn Association and the majority of the anonymous Finn sailors) and keen competitors respectively builders, striving for higher performance. It is the story of a battle between those, who wanted the Finn to remain a modern boat and those who were afraid that existing boats could be outmoded by new developments. It reflects a dramatic change between a document, meant to be a guide for the construction of the Finn Dinghy by home builders, to a sophisticated system of control of professional shipyards. It reflects the endeavour to find the proper pace of necessary changes over time, to go ahead with new ideas, without breaking the Finn Class apart. The problem was to allow the strongest and most ambitious to advance only at such a speed, that at least the majority of the ordinary sailors were able to keep pace. Up to the present time, the Finn Class has managed to stay on top of international dinghy development and to remain an Olympic Class for 50 years. Hopefully the Finn rules will continue to guide the Class in that manner far into the future.

Conclusion
by Richard Hart

As Peter Mohilla showed so well, the original rules were designed to show an amateur builder what to build, and in particular how to do it. The inevitable pressure on an Olympic Class made the original rules insufficient, and it was agreed that the rules should ensure that new hull should be basically the same in matters affecting speed as the original design. The rules were refined to define the shape, weight distribution and tolerances more strictly and accurately. This phase of development made a difficulty for the class in that until the middle 1960s, an ordinary Finn sailor might find that a new rule had just put his boat out of class, so far as the Finn Gold Cup was concerned.

Another aspect of the rules lies in the difficulty of application. As the rules started to develop, they ceased to be a guide to an amateur builder and became a set of constraints on a professional builder. The 1964 and 1966 Rule Books started to address the task of measurement by arranging the limiting measurements in groups to be applied 'with the hull upside down' and 'with the hull right way up'. However the rules were really intended and set out to suit the initial measurement of a new boat.

The problems of weight distribution were solved in the 1970s with the Lamboley test. This removed nearly all the 'magic' from the idea of a fast Finn: the hull could be measured and so could the distribution of mass. Sailors could concentrate on the rig.

Even though the Lamboley test made scantling rules redundant, and double bottoms were permitted, the class remained adamant that no alteration should be permitted from the original (supposed) shape of the Finn. It was agreed

A purpose made jig to test hull shape against a set of certified templates

Charles Currey, Richard Creagh-Osborne and Vernon Forster working on the lines of the Finn Plans in the sixties.

maker. A natural sequel to this requirement is to measure hulls, masts and booms to standard bearing and connection dimensions, so that in the future any mast will go into any hull with any boom.

The measurement rules themselves are only half the story. It was found that a dedicated Chief Measurer was essential to the fair application of the rules. Ensuring that all items such as masts, booms and rudders have been measured has been a cause of difficulty: in the early days boats had only one of each!

Another problem in the early days was that different measurers sometimes made different decisions about various details. This was addressed by requiring that doubtful matters be referred to the Technical Committee. If necessary the TC conclusions were promulgated as 'Case Law' until the class submissions could be ratified by the IYRU/ISAF. Nowadays the use of 'Case Law' is diminishing because many of the doubtful points have already been incorporated into the rules.

that the weight should not be reduced, the mast deck ring position remained fixed, and when aluminium masts replaced wood they were made to conform to complex rules designed to ensure that 'the rig was no further forward in the boat.' However, the 1970s was a period when the rules were effective and the class prospered because of their stability.

Such strict rules would never have allowed many of the developments that made the Finn what she is, such as bendy masts, mainsheets near the thwart, suction bailers, and so on. During the 1980s development was tending to stagnate. The Vanguard boats built in 1980-81 were still the preferred equipment of top sailors ten years later, and not a lot had happened to Needlespar masts and the sails. Regatta measurement remained a hated ordeal.

For the 1990s, the class developed a change of attitude. The Technical Committee were instructed to change the rules so as to facilitate the introduction of plastic masts. At the same

time efforts were made to simplify regatta measurement.

New simpler mast rules were introduced, the position of the deck bearing was freed, and after a period of experimentation the mast weight limit was reduced. A tight restriction (half round) on the leading edge of the centreplate was removed.

These changes were seen as beneficial and the class became receptive to other developments. By this time most boats less than 15 years old were carrying nearly 10 kg of lead correctors. The weight limit was reduced without great grief.

In the late 1990s efforts continue to make the rules more workable and to make measurement more easy and practicable, especially at regattas. To reduce the use of unmeasured equipment at local and regional regattas, requirements have been introduced for measurement before the equipment leaves the

The Roles of the Technical Committee
The Technical Committee has two main duties.

Firstly it should ensure that a satisfactory standard of measurement rule observance is maintained. The instruments of this process are all those who check and measure boats, including the Chief Measurer at major regattas. The Technical Committee should see itself sometimes as a police group, but also as an independent referee to resolve possible differences between measurers and sailors.

A second main duty is to influence the development of the class by making recommendations to the class, especially at the Class Council meetings held each year. The Technical Committee then implements the requirements of the Council by drafting rule changes and submitting these for decision by our governing body, the Centreboard Boat Committee of the ISAF.

24. Tacking The Finn

by Robert Deaves

During any single race, many tacks are performed. Therefore the difference between good and bad tacking or even between very good and just acceptable tacking can lead to big differences in apparent boat speed. If a boat loses (or gains) one boat length on each tack during a race, it is not hard to see how much distance can be lost (or gained) by perfecting your tacking technique. Improving your tacking is easy to do, it can be practised at any time, by yourself or in a group. Before you go out on the water though, run through in your mind what you are trying to do; where your boat and where you should be at any point during the tack. Practice the tack mentally in several steps, then practice it out on the water, gradually building it up into one fluent motion.

The tack should be initiated when the boat is moving at the best possible speed, or on a wave crest. If the boat is stalled or not balanced or about to crash into the next wave, then the boat will lose all speed out of the tack and you will be left wallowing and have to build up speed again. Knowing when to tack, especially at sea, (ignoring windshifts, just thinking about the right time and place to tack) is just as important as the manoeuvre itself.

A tack can be broken down into several steps:

1 Make sure that the boat is travelling at maximum possible speed for the conditions. Tacking when the boat is moving slowly will lead to a loss of speed out of the tack. Therefore choosing your moment to tack is as important as the execution of the tack itself.

2 Begin to roll the boat to windward and push the tiller away from you (make sure that end of the tiller is angled down and cannot hit the boom). Slight leeward heel prior to this roll can sometimes aid steering. Keep rudder movements to the minimum and don't oversteer, as any excess rudder movement will slow the boat - try to use sail trim and your body weight to coax the boat round. Only release the sheet at the last moment. (Also, sheeting in as you roll the boat can help to improve the tack.)

3 As the boat turns through the wind, ease the sheet by moving your sheet-hand down to the bottom block on the floor. Duck under the boom, whilst still keeping rudder movements to the minimum.

4 As soon as the boom has passed overhead, stand up in the boat, thereby sheeting in as you do so by bringing your sheet-hand up with you. Move your aft foot across boat and lock it under the toestrap. Start to roll the boat flat.

5 Sit down on the sidedeck and adjust your course. The tiller should now be held in your forehand, behind your back. The sheet should be held in your aft hand, in front of you. This allows you to automatically cleat the sheet across the front of your body, and then move your forehand aft to pick up the tiller

6 Adjust your position if necessary, adjust sheet if necessary and off you go.

7 A refinement is to 'shoot the wind' as you come out of the tack. As you sheet in on the new tack, head up slightly, then roll the boat flat. Doing this will lift the boat slightly to windward and gain you a few metres.

What you are trying to achieve is a fluent tack that does not slow the boat down. Avoid excess rudder and sail movement as this can be detrimental and always choose the right moment to tack. You will know when you have executed a good tack as boat speed will be maintained out of the tack (watch your wake) and your movements will have been smooth and controlled.

Finally remember to watch where you are going - don't tack so that when you turn through the wind you smash into the next oncoming wave and stop dead in your tracks. Watch the waves and tack when you can do it smoothly.

25. Hiking, Steering and Rig Control

By Ian Ainslie   Reprinted from FINNFARE March and October 1997

The Finn may not be your modern 'crash and burn' speedster, but technically, tactically or physically it is still the most demanding boat to sail well. The hull is heavy by modern standards and this requires a special 'oneness' with the boat. 'Bouncing' around, like you would in a Laser is not as efficient as moving in harmony with the natural frequencies of the boat. This may explain why anyone who has sailed a Finn for some time will always have a very soft spot for the boat.

Hiking

After 8 years of sailing Finns (and trying to fool myself) I am now in a position to offer advice for 99% of speed problems in over 10 knots of wind. My advice is this: 'hike like a beast'. Dave Hibberd and I have our standard joke when it's breezy, about 'proving our beasthood' or 'flaunting our beasthood'. Dinghy sailors have been very slow in realising the huge benefits of physical fitness and strength.

I followed a program of strength building and stretching when I wasn't sailing, but I found that the best strength training for Finn sailing, and the most fun, was Finn sailing. It is, however, important to warm up and stretch before you sail to prevent stiffness and injury. In addition to stretching, a massage of thighs, lower back and shoulders can also be tremendously beneficial in relieving stiffness before a race.

Hiking Equipment

A lot of Finn sailors think that pain is an integral part of hiking. This is not so. You have to arrange your hiking pads, pad your

toestraps etc., so that loads are evenly distributed and circulation is not cut off. My wetsuits have hiking battens built into the back of the leg. These are absolutely essential for hiking comfort. You are only going to improve your hiking if you are able to extend your muscles to exhaustion and not having to ease off because of pain due to improper equipment.

Hiking Techniques

There are several different ways to hike on a Finn from straight-legged to drooped. Because the boat has a relatively high freeboard, the actual style is not as important as getting as much of your body away from the boat as possible. I prefer to hike straight-legged because I feel that I am taller and lighter than average, and this gives me the best leverage to move the boat around with my upper body. There are disadvantages associated with having very loose toestraps, like having your mainsheet running over the top of them. The most popular hiking stance of the fast sailors is in between the two extremes: knees bent at about 120 degrees but not having the butt slumped too far under the boat.

Body Movements

You will have to develop some very controlled and subtle body movements to get the boat moving over a chop well. To get the boat to head up, allow a slight heel and let the tiller ease down on its own to bring the bow into the wind. This is also achieved by rotating the boat with your body. When I am hiking, I like to imagine the boat as being part of the back of my knees (which are on the side-deck). To get the boat to head up, I swivel the boat around the fulcrum of my legs by swinging my shoulders back. This puts pressure on the front of my toestrap and also pulls the bow up. To bear off, I swing forward again to push the bow away from the wind while pulling the stern to weather with my back foot in the toestrap. This coincides with the need to lift the bow on the face of an approaching chop and getting it back into the water on the top of the wave (before it can pound down).

The Rudder is a Brake!

My favourite conditions are offwind in a big swell. Styles vary but compared with most of my competitors I find that I tend to move around a lot more but tend not to pump as

much. I also tend to make much bigger course alterations. Sometimes I am able to make dramatic gains by doing this. On other occasions, I have noticed that the sailors who don't steer around that much but just pump hard on each wave to catch a short surf end up sailing a much shorter distance. The difference seems to be determined by whether I am able to plane as well as surf.

Once I am moving fast, I can use the pressure to ride the wave way below the rhumb line. Before I lose the wave, I bring the boat up again so that there is a lot of pressure in the rig. As the next wave approaches, you are not 'low and slow', so you can hook on to it and catch the next ride.

The reason why my movements in the boat are more extreme is that, in order to change course so much, you have to steer with your body. You have to let the tiller follow the boat around and not be resisting you at all. As important as the sideways movement is balancing the boat fore and aft to get the bow the right height out of the water. Encourage the stern to lift as the wave approaches and then shoot back to stop the bow from pushing water as you hook on to the wave. All these movements have got to be controlled, fluid and instinctive.

Playing the Mainsheet

It is better to play the sheet directly off the boom, without purchase, because this allows your arm movements to be smaller, and the control to be more direct. Of course, you have to be strong enough, otherwise you will not be able to move the sail all the time with each variation in speed pressure and course.

My shoulders are angled forward with the tiller extension held out in front of my body so that it doesn't get in the way of the rapid movements. My forward leg is under the toestrap, angled forward, positioned to shoot my body back by pushing against the ratchet block on the cockpit floor. My back leg is mostly bent, so that my heel is able to push against the side of the cockpit, so that I am ready to quickly move my weight inboard.

The only way to get all these movements right is to go out and play in the waves!

Simple Rig Principles

The modern Finn is so adjustable that a very wide variety of body weights and sailing styles are able to go fast over a range of conditions. The carbon fibre masts are extremely powerful in moderate conditions yet tend to whip around more in a big breeze and chop. It is a challenge to master the awesome rig. It almost always generates too much power and incorrect set-up can have you hating life. It is a matter of understanding a few simple principles and exploring the effects of the various sail controls.

Sail Controls

Mainsheet: This is the control that you will adjust the most in light/moderate conditions. As you sheet in, the mast bends and this will affect the overall fullness of the sail as well as the leech tension. Generally you sheet the boom onto the deck as soon as you are completely overpowered.

Traveller: A general guide to the traveller position is that the back end of your boom should be in line with the side of the boat. The traveller will be further eased as you become overpowered. I tend to adjust my traveller more often than most. In strong winds and big chop I will play the control all the time. Most sailors prefer to leave the traveller more static and allow the mast to alter the boat's power.

Tack in-haul: Easing the tack will have the effect of flattening the entry of the sail low down (especially if you tension the outhaul simultaneously) and tightening the lower leech. This is a prerequisite for pointing high, while tensioning the tack control will depower the sail, especially by opening the lower leech. (You will notice that the angle of the lower batten will change). The exact position of the tack is dependent on how much the sailmaker has cut the tack away.

Cunningham: Tensioning the Cunningham depowers the sail by moving cloth from the middle of the sail towards the luff and thereby opening the leech. Because the chord is shortest at the top of the sail, the biggest effect is seen high up. The Cunningham becomes an important control when you are constantly shifting between the pinching mode and the footing or 'scooting' mode. As soon as you want to go fast, albeit lower, pulling on the Cunningham eases pressure on the helm, gets the leech to twist and allows you to sail lower but much faster.

Outhaul: This controls the overall fullness of the sail, especially in the lower third.

Vang: The vang is very seldom used upwind. Occasionally I use it to bend the mast in light and lumpy conditions. I can then really change the angle of the boom a lot by using the mainsheet, without allowing the sail to become too full. For offwind I will tension the vang just enough to get a powerful leech without starting to bend the mast - a bit less in light airs and a bit more in a breeze. If you ever find yourself close reaching in a big breeze, you'll have to ease the vang to depower and prevent the boom from hitting the water.

Luff Curve

Once you fully understand the effects of all the sail controls, you have to work with a sailmaker in order to match your sail luff curve to your mast's bend. By studying other people's rigs and really getting to know yours well, you will develop an eye for what you are looking for.

You will be able to know whether the sail/mast combination is in the ball park by going for a brief sail. Too little luff curve at some point on the sail will show up easily enough. You'll see wrinkles running from that spot on the luff to the clew. Too much luff curve is harder to spot but is more serious, especially in the lower half of the sail. Excess cloth near the mast makes it hard to open your leech, which

measurement will vary from rig to rig but around 6.80 m measured between top black band and transom will get you in the ball park. When I was using a Hall spar, I was up at 6.86 m in a breeze because it was relatively soft down low whereas the mast I use now, is very stiff below the deck and I can't get up more than 6.80 in a breeze and 6.76 in lighter winds. On my boat, I have a track with a slide to adjust the rake at deck level. I use just two holes on the plunger - back for light winds, upright for medium to strong winds and then back again in extremely strong winds.

will over-power you in a breeze and the roundness in the front will make it difficult to point in moderate winds.

The best way to check your mast/sail match is to get someone to swap boats with you in about 10-12 knots. Position yourself behind and to leeward of your boat so that you just able to sight down the leeward side of the mast's sail track. The sail track will be obscured in places where there is relatively too much luff curve.

Mast Bend Characteristics.
There are about as many theories on masts as there are Finn sailors. When it comes to masts, most sailors are fashion conscious. I think that you should understand the basics and not get over technical. You only have to see the massive differences in boatspeed in the Laser class to realise that sailing technique makes the biggest difference to speed.

Sideways Mast Bend
The sideways stiffness is going to affect the sail's twist and the rig's power. A soft mast will make the boat easy to sail upwind in a breeze but you will not point well and you will also lack power as the breeze lightens up. Remember, the harder you hike, the greater the sideways force will be on the rig and the more the mast will bend off. So, before you convince yourself that there is too much power in the rig, make sure that you are hiking hard enough.

As far as the sideways profile goes, I prefer a mast that comes out of the deck straightish and only starts falling away above the half height, progressively bending more to the tip. The bend should be smooth (no 'hinge' points), with the tip working the most in puffs and waves.

Fore & Aft Mast Bend
Without the need for all the sleeves found on the old aluminium masts, the carbon masts have a much more even bend. In general, you can either have a mast which is bendy in the ends or one which is bendy in the middle. The former is normally easier to use and is superior in lighter winds because it allows the leech to open more easily. The latter gives you better control over leech tension in a breeze and, when combined with a flattish sail, is faster upwind in these conditions. However, you are normally raked further back so it is not as quick offwind.

Mast Rake
Adjusting the rake affects the amount of leech tension you have once you have sheeted the boom on to the deck. If your mast is too upright, this will cause too much leech tension and the boat will be staggering around in the puffs and chop. Too little leech tension and you will not be able to point. The exact

26. Regatta Preparation

by Sebastien Godefroid

About sunscreen and some other stuff you have to do...

Finn sailors of today, wear sunscreen. If I could offer you only one tip for the future, sunscreen would be it. A long term benefit of sunscreen has been proved by scientists, whereas the rest of my advice has no basis more reliable than my own meandering experience. I will dispense this advice now.

Peaking
It is almost impossible to be at your best all the time. Therefore it is important to choose some important regattas during the year and peak at those highlights. Remember, sailing is a very complete and therefore complicated sport, so even though you prepared everything perfectly, things can still go wrong, so don't over focus on just one regatta. I think (and I'm quite sure many other good sailors do so), the most important thing is to keep on having fun, no matter how important the results get.

Fitness
In the long term it's very important to feel fit. You can be lucky, and it can be light winds all the time, or there can be a day with no sailing just in time, but mostly this is not the case. You are better off being prepared for the

difficult conditions. This will also make you mentally at ease. Before anything your endurance should be good. Cycling, rowing, blading, running... All kinds of long term exercises with a continuous strain are good to work on your endurance. You must do about 3 months of exercise, about 3 to 4 times a week to get this like it should be. This is if

you were in reasonable condition before. Try to change the exercise now and then, and don't run all the time. The average Finn-sailor does not have the ideal running-body. So be gentle on your knees. You might miss them when they're gone... Anyway, when for one reason or another you do nothing (physical) for two days, and you kind of feel strange, a bit like a junky, then you know you're getting there.

Power
The other very important part is the power. Most of us have enough power to sail pretty well for one or two days, but when you are going to sail more often, you need to be stronger, (especially if you wanna sail like Freddy), first to be able to keep on sailing, but even more important to stay free of injuries. When you are doing power training, try to get someone who knows a lot about it to help you with the program. Normally you start with a quite general program. The closer you get to your goal, the more specific you can work. But what is very important is to keep the balance in your muscles: if you do your quadriceps, also do your hamstrings, and this counts for all the muscles. This again is to be sure that your muscles grow in balance, and you keep on having a 'natural' posture. If you increase your power, you also have to increase your flexibility. So stretch!!!

Diet

Another important feature of being an athlete is your food-intake. If you wanna perform like an athlete, you have to eat like one, and that's pretty hard sometimes. As most of us have a lot of problems keeping the weight up, an often and regular intake of carbohydrates is necessary. Next to that you need to eat enough proteins after the gym. It's really worth looking at a book and studying this part a bit, or again ask a specialist to help you with it. If you don't get this part right, you will be making a whole lot of effort without getting anywhere. I know how it feels, idiot I am.

Training

Once you've got these four basic 'body-things', there's the sailing itself. I won't go into the mast-sail combination stuff, because that's a topic in itself and you'd better ask someone who knows more about it. What I will do is pick some topics and talk a little about them, just not to stay too general. That's also very important when you train: don't just go sailing. You need a plan every time you go training. If you just go sailing, without having anything particular in mind, you will spend a lot of time without improving very fast. Also try to find someone you like to train with and work together. There's nobody who can get to the top alone, we all need partners to train with.

Boat Handling

OK, I'll have a topic as an example. Let's start with manoeuvres. It is very good to start your training with a warm up. Let your body feel that it has to work a bit. For this you can start your training with some tacking and gybing. Also try to find somebody to film it. Sometimes you're surprised how many mistakes you see yourself make. Some ways to make it more interesting and more complete would be to do

some match racing or put out a very small course and include mark roundings. That's also an important topic, getting up to speed after the mark rounding as fast as possible. When you observe some of the good guys at the upwind mark when they dropped back into the fleet, most of the time you see how they win 3-4 places in the first 30 meters after the mark, just because they are on the right track straight away. You are able to do this too, but you have to work on it.

Speed

After that you could do some speed testing. I think there are different kinds of speed. First of all there's the basic speed. This is when you sail, without really concentrating on your speed, but just by feeling. You take time to look around or in training you sail blindfolded. This is very important. You have to be able to have a decent speed, while you're concentrating on something else. Most of the time this is what you're doing in a race too.

Another branch of speed is the acceleration at the start. It is very important to be able to lay still, close to other boats, and at a certain time take off as fast as you can and kill the boats around you. You can train to do this with two boats or more. Finally there's the speed that most of the time is tested before the regattas Just line up, try not to disturb each other, don't worry about the windshifts and just concentrate on your sail and the boat to go as fast as you can. This is done very often, but it almost never occurs during a regatta.

A very important thing when you're testing is not to blame your equipment for your 'slowlyness'. Try again, see what the other is doing different, talk about it, swap boats… When you're training with a partner it's up to the fast one to help the slow one to be as fast as him. I know that sounds like giving your

secrets away, but if you wanna get help when you're in trouble, you had better help the other when he's in trouble - that's teamwork. And if you happen to be number one and two in the world, then there's still enough time to start having (little) secrets for each other.

Training Tips

At the end of a training session I always like to have a race, to put into practice what you've been working on. Very often you will see that the one who was slow during the speed testing, beats the other in a race, just because he's looking around better, or his manoeuvres are better…

After a day of training discuss what happened that day, what the problems are and what you have learned, perhaps while stretching or doing a little run. Also make notes, so you can fall back on them later when you're a little stressed because your regatta goes totally wrong and you don't know what to do anymore. Also make plans again for the next day, while you still know what went right and wrong.

Another tip for training. I'm convinced that training for example in blocks of 7 days helps much more than training 1 day at the time. You're more likely to remember what you did the day before in the same conditions when you trained 7 days in a row than when you trained 1 day and the last time you did this was a week ago. I think the best thing is to plan a weeks training with somebody on a certain theme, and work it out completely. It's of no use to do half work.

All this training should be done way before the regatta you are aiming for. When you go to a regatta you have to be sure that all you could do was done, so you don't have to blame yourself. You did it in the training, so you will be able to do it again during the regatta.

At the Regatta

Just before the major regatta you have to try to get some factors to an optimum. First of all I think it's important to feel at home. Try to be there in time (that's about a week before) and find yourself a nice place to sleep, find yourself the shops you will need, see where you can relax and have some 'quality time'… I think this all helps a lot to be confident and get in your normal training rhythm. You don't want surprises once the regatta starts - most of the time you get enough surprises on the water.

The next thing to prepare is to learn the conditions that prevail there. Get to know the local wind patterns, get to know the current, follow the pressure systems in the paper, talk to locals. Fisherman - most of the time - are a very big help. Try every day to predict what is gonna happen, write down what happened and at what time. Quite often there's a pattern that comes back every day, especially in warm places. All this sounds a lot, but once it gets a habit, it's not hard at all.

Try to get enough rest. It's not those few hours more on the water just before the race that are going to make the difference. You prepared yourself well, now it's time to relax and get fully motivated and with a hunger for sailing. I always like to sail a maximum of two hours the last two days before the race.

Be Positive

Some people like to go to a race with some goals in mind. I rather prefer to go there, just do my best and see what happens. If you want to have some goals anyway, try to make them positive. This means, don't say: I don't want to capsize, but say: I want to stay upright. It is a bit the same as when you say to a room full of prisoners: Don't think about naked women, and you can imagine what they will be thinking about, just by using the words naked women, although there's a 'don't' in

front. Also try not to relate your goals to the result. I realise sometimes this is different, but try it anyway. The reason why is that you can't control how the others are going to sail. You might have sailed very well, but the others might have been lucky, and you can't always help it. You can control how you sail yourself. If you have aims like 'I want to prepare my first beat very well and get the first beat right' or 'I want to make good mark roundings' or 'I want to sail my boat flat', then you are more or less fully under control. That's one of the reasons why somebody who wins a regatta sometimes still isn't happy, just because he knows he made some mistakes and he can do better, no matter if the others even did worse than him.

Have Fun!

Once the regatta starts, make sure you check the notice board, you know what the weather forecast is, when it is high or low tide… Be on the water in time and try to find a pattern in the wind. Try to understand what is

happening and predict what is going to happen. Keep on fighting all the time, it's not because you've lost a battle that you lost the war. Never give up. (Well, I suppose if your mast is broken, your sail is torn in three pieces and there's a big hole in your bow you might start to consider it.) Look at what the others do and try to imagine why they do it. Keep being flexible: the pattern might change, or you might have misunderstood it. You have to reconsider what to do all the time. And maybe the most important: have fun with your friends out there, if you really enjoy it, you're more likely to sail well too, and even if you don't, at least you had fun and it was much better than a day at the office.

This is about all I can say to help you with preparing your next regatta. I hope you learned something from it, even if it is only to wear sunscreen. I've got a last tip for your regatta though. Don't waste your time on jealousy. Sometimes you're ahead, sometimes you're behind. The race is long, and in the end it's only with yourself.

27. Gybe

by Garry Hoyt   Reprint from 'Go for the Gold' by Garry Hoyt

Gybing a Finn calls for a special description because it is a special experience. Whereas in most boats a gybe is normally just another routine manoeuvre, in the Finn this move assumes heroic proportions, and provides lessons in humility that have made strong men weep.

If you've never jockeyed a Finn in a breeze over 25, this will mean nothing to you, but if you have, you are automatically a soul brother. Here's a typical sequence:

You round the windward mark with a nice 90-yard lead. The wind has been coming up steadily and is now gusting to 25. Vang down, board up, cunningham off, ass out, kazoom - you're off on a screamer.

Sheets of spray and wild exhilaration as you blast out to a wider lead. And then suddenly, before you know it, there it is. "By golly hot damn, gee whiz, we better get set for the old gybe. The gybe!" Brow furrows, vision clouds, muscles stiffen, and a childlike whimper slips from your strong Nordic lips.

"Steady boy, there's nothing to this. We'll just wait for a little lull." This naive hope is quickly extinguished by a glance aft, which reveals a solid mass of hissing whitecaps racing down to join you in your moment of truth.

"Well, we'll just get the board up a bit like Elvström says, so she'll slide to leeward and not tip." So you up the board six inches - a precaution your Finn greets with a wild, sickening lurch to windward. Only a desperate jab of the tiller and a frantic yank on the main keep you from instant oblivion via the famous Finn windward wipeout, or 'death roll'.

Now the buoy is right off the port bow, and the puff hits full force. Down on your knees you plunge, neatly incising razor-like slashes on your legs from either the bailers or the hiking-strap mounting. Somehow straddling and backing into the tiller, you start the fateful arc. "The vang! The vang! Let off the vang!" (Failure to do this is a direct invitation to decapitation of the most primitive sort.)

Shredding your knuckles to the bone you manage to cast off the vang. You haul in on the sheet - "Gybe ho!" But wait, she isn't gybing, and instead she slows down to a queasy stall and hangs there, midst a sudden and unnatural silence as you haul manfully on the sheet and re jam the tiller around.

And then she comes - that malevolent boom, screeched across the deck by a thousand devils. From long practice, you deftly duck your head and bear off slightly in perfect textbook style, counteracting the momentum of the turn. Except you forget about your elbow . . . When you bore off, you quite naturally raised your elbow several inches for added leverage on the tiller - an innocent and seemingly minor oversight that would go unnoticed in most boats.

No such luck in the Finn. With unerring accuracy the boom seeks the very point of your elbow and fetches it a smash that would make Tarzan gasp. In addition to the excruciating pain, this timely blow effectively numbs the entire arm, causing a critical delay in your downward correction.

It's all over but the jeering. The boom, which has already so cruelly punished you, now seeks to bury itself in the leeward bow wave. Your noble steed slops to a stop, sail pinned to the water.

Sensing a kill, the wind shrieks its delight at a higher pitch. You hurl yourself over the windward side to save your craft. But of course you aren't Elvström, so rather than sliding

harmlessly to leeward, you dump ignominiously, quite probably fouling the mark in the process.

The rest is almost too painful to recount. Your competitors rocket by like dervishes, and since you know their control is marginal at best, moving around so as to right your boat is like stepping casually out on a California freeway.

Beyond that, your centreboard has in all likelihood retreated up the trunk, leaving you the unhappy prospect of hanging by your fingernails from the slot, till your weary craft concedes and flops back up.

Someone should make a close-up movie of Finns at the gybing mark, if only to provide drama students with a study of how a man's expression can change in a flash from stark terror (before the gybe) to mad glee (if the gybe is successfully completed). Actually the Finn gybe becomes a great equaliser, since it fells the high and mighty as readily as the tail-ender. And the saving grace is that after the Finn gybe all gybes in other classes become a piece of cake, to be executed with insolent insouciance.

28. History of the Senior European Championship

by Peter Mohilla and Robert Deaves

Reprinted from FINNLOG

At the time that the Finn became the Olympic singlehander in 1952, the IYRU used to delegate the organisation of a European Championship with a crew of one to member countries. They had the freedom to select a suitable class for the event. In those days it was customary - as it was in the Olympic Games until 1996 - that the host country supplied the boats for the European Championship and that each country is allowed to enter only one sailor.

The sailors had to qualify in a local class and then adjust to the class the host country selected and the individual boat which was assigned to them each day. Before 1954 the event was generally sailed in the O-Jolle and won by sailors unknown in the Finn class.

The 1954 IYRU European Championship for a crew of one was delegated to the Federal Republic of Germany and organised again in the 1936 O-Jolle in Berlin on the Wannsee. Interesting for us is the fact that the people who were fast in the Finn were also representing their countries in that event. The favourite, Paul Elvström, won four races but had so many collisions in others that he finally ended up only 4th. The Championship was won by Andre Nelis - silver medalist in the 1956 Olympics - without winning a single race. The silver medalist of the 1936 Olympics Werner Krogmann was second and Rickard Sarby was third.

In 1955 the Championship was delegated to Austria and the O-Jolle was selected again for the races organised on Lake Traunsee. There were 11 races with generally very little wind. The Austrian Wolfgang Erndl became the European Champion. The Finn sailor Jan de Jong from Holland was third, Andre Nelis 6th, Vernon Stratton 8th and Rickard Sarby 12th after he had left the regatta because of the poor wind conditions.

1. European Championship 1956
Loosdrechter Lakes, Holland, August 20-25
15 entries from 15 countries

Belgium should have organised the IYRU European Championship for a crew of one. However because there was no suitable sailing area the Belgians gave the organisation to the Dutch. They in turn selected a totally unsuitable sailing area themselves, although they have such fine areas. The selected site was a former peat bog near Loosdrecht with very shallow water and hundreds of little islands left over from the peat-cutting. In addition the water was crowded with about 1000 recreational spectator boats and the little islands were heavily wooded. The competitors never saw the next mark and had to decide which of the various narrows between the basins might turn out to be the most advantageous.

2. European Championship 1957
Naples, Italy, August 27-September 3
12 entries from 12 countries

The Italians selected the Finn again and provided 12 very nice brand new boats, all well and equally equipped. Racing was in Naples Bay - site of the 1960 Olympic regatta. There were 16 races scheduled, of which 10 were finally sailed. Winds were generally light and taking advantage of the tide was quite important. Andre Nelis won 8 races and became the superior winner. The battle for the runner-up was tight between Pelaschier, Vogler, and Schwarz. Sweden was represented by the nephew of Rickard Sarby, Bert Sarby.

However for the history of the Finn it is important that the Dutch selected for the first time the Finn Dinghy for that European Championship and provided 15 cold moulded boats, not all of which had self-bailers and buoyancy bags. There were very variable wind conditions so it heavily depended on the lot the sailors drew each day. Because of the unsuitable site Elvström refused to participate. The first European Champion of the Finn Class was Jürgen Vogler from the German Democratic Republic; the runner up was the Frenchman Didier Poissant, and Andre Nelis was third. In 7th place was Rickard Sarby, and in 11th Curd Ochwadt the promoter of the Finn Class in the Federal Republic of Germany. Also, at this European Championship the IFA was finally founded and had its first Annual General Meeting.

Final Results 1956

1.	Jürgen Vogler	DDR	7839
2.	Didier Poissant	F	7770
3.	Andre Nelis	B	7369
4.	Richard Murray	K	5885
5.	Y. Shavrin	SR	5868
6.	B. Markus	Z	5712
7.	Rickard Sarby	S	5680
8.	E. Rundström	N	4888
9.	Adelchi Pelaschier	I	4827
10.	S. Payne	IR	4248
11.	Curd Ochwadt	G	4204
12.	St. Rydgren	L	2926
13.	Erzin Demir	TR	2604
14.	A. Allende	D	2352
15.	Willy Pieper	H	1998

Final Results 1957

1.	Andre Nelis	B	10486
2.	Adelchi Pelaschier	I	6943
3.	Jürgen Vogler	DDR	6619
4.	Borge Schwarz	D	5924
5.	Hans Sleeswijk	H	5524
6.	Bert Sarby	S	4271
7.	Jerome Harinkouck	F	4223
8.	Czeslaw Marchaj	PZ	3891
9.	Vernon Stratton	K	3832
10.	Tonko Pivecevic	Y	3715
11.	Hans Larcher	Z	3553
12.	Erzin Demir	TK	2751

3. European Championship 1958
Cascais, Portugal, September 3-7
12 entries from 12 countries

No country was particularly interested in being entrusted by the IYRU with the organisation of the 1958 European Championship. Finally Portugal accepted without ambition, lacking experience in the Finn. For the first time, the organiser invited the participants to bring their own boats in order to save the costs in building new ones. Four sailors brought their own dinghies and had a large advantage. The 8 new boats supplied by the organiser had never

4. European Championship 1959
Silsersee, Switzerland, August 27-30
18 entries from 18 countries

For 1959 the IYRU delegated the event to Switzerland. Although this country even today still has a strong O-Jolle fleet, the Finn was selected since it was the designated singlehander for the 1960 Olympics. The Swiss choose the Silsersee south of St. Moritz with usually strong winds, where however they had never before organised a sailing regatta. The 52 year old Dutchman Jan de Jong, 1.95 m tall, weighing 100 kg, but quick as a flash and smart, won four races and was twice runner-up. In second overall, the Frenchman Pinaud, had a number of new technical gadgets on his Finn. The German Democratic Republic sent J. Vogler who came third and had won the Gold Cup before. Fourth was Kuhweide, at that time only 16 years old.

Final Results 1959

1.	Jan de Jong	H	5480
2.	Yves Louis Pinaud	F	4290
3.	Jürgen Vogler	DDR	4008
4.	Willy Kuhweide	G	3845
5.	Henning Wind	D	3816
6.	Per Jordebakke	N	3646
7.	Adelchi Pelaschier	I	3334
8.	Keith Musto	K	2886
9.	Bernhard Reist	Z	2633
10.	Peter Fürst	OE	2524
11.	Andre Nelis	B	2446
12.	E. Stadig	L	2038
13.	Bengt Hornevall	S	1786
14.	B. Oliviera	P	1723
15.	Andrzej Podolski	PZ	1298
18.	Bir	TR	1131
17.	Tolnai	M	828
18.	Perrakis	GR	191

been sailed before and were inferior. An additional problem was the launching facilities. A crane lowered and lifted the boats with the skipper on board from a 20 m high quay. So this Championship was more a test of technical skills than of sailing abilities.

Final Results 1958

1.	Adelchi Pelaschier	I	7684
2.	Karel Warburg	H	6161
3.	Bernhard Reist	Z	4021
4.	Harinkouck	F	3952
5.	Arne Baltscheffsky	L	3769
6.	Börge Schwarz	D	3518
7.	Jürgen Vogler	DDR	3427
8.	Richard Murray	K	3396
9.	Bert Sarby	S	2756
10.	Wolfgang Erndl	OE	2510

5. European Championship 1960
Ostende, Belgium, July or early August
10 entries from 10 countries

Four races between force 4 and 7 suited Paul Elvström perfectly and he won three of the races. 17 year old newcomer from the Federal Republic of Germany Willy Kuhweide won the first race, but scored never worse than 4th, and thus became runner-up. Host Andre Nelis won two races, but did not perform that well in the heavy wind and had a collision in the sixth race. In the fourth race, when it blew force 7, it is reported that Elvström in first and Kuhweide in second position did not dare to gybe. However Nelis in third position risked the manoeuvre, made it technically, but hit the mark, got entangled with the French Pinaud and lost several hundred meters.

Final Results 1960

1.	Paul Elvström	D	5074
2.	Willy Kuhweide	G	4870
3.	Andre Nelis	B	4518
4.	Yves-Louis Pinaud	F	4393
5.	Hans Sleeswijk	H	3472
6.	Jack Knights	K	2635
7.	Göran Andersson	S	2615
8.	Klaus Koop	DDR	1566
9.	Jouko Valli	L	1361
10.	Andrzej Podolski	PZ	1193

6. European Championship 1961
Warnemünde, German Democratic Republic, July 14-18, 14 entries from 14 countries

In splendid racing conditions seven races were sailed without a discard. After each race the overall lead changed. Before the last race in force 4-5 there were five competitors who could win the title. The Swede Goran Andersson won that race clearly and thought he was the champion until the last round. Chuchelov had a safe 2nd until he broke his mast step on the last beat and had to retire. So Willy Kuhweide moved into second position, which was just enough to take the championship.

Final Results 1961

1.	Willy Kuhweide	G	5456
2.	Göran Andersson	S	5326
3.	Walter Gärtner	DDR	4886
4.	Wim Maarse	H	4523
5.	Hubert Raudaschl	OE	3850
6.	Alex. Chuchelov	SR	3263
7.	Yves-Louis Pinaud	F	2787
8.	Spacek	CZ	2719

7. European Championship 1962
Kiel, Federal Republic of Germany, June 12-16, 11 entries from 11 countries

By 1962 the Finn was so well established even in the Federal Republic of Germany that it was selected (in disfavour of the 1936 O-Jolle) for the last European Championship for a crew of one under the IYRU flag. Only one mast and one sail were allowed and the reigning champ Willy Kuhweide as well as his Austrian friend Hubert Raudaschl blew their chances before the first start by selecting soft masts and flat sails. The wind turned out to be light and shifty all week. The Frenchman Francis Jammes developed a 'new' sailing technique, standing upright in his boat and pumping or gybing all the time. Jammes was leading up until the last race, but he failed to cover his only opponent and lost the title to the Swede Boris Jacobsson who had quickly picked up the art of questionable propulsion. The 3rd overall Jan de Jong and 4th Richard Creagh-Osborne despised the technique vehemently but the younger people swore to practise it.

Final Results 1962
1.	Boris Jacobsson	S 318	5098
2.	Francis Jammes	F 164	4730
3.	Jan de Jong	H 43	4700
4.	Richard Creagh-Osborne	K 7	3825
5.	Wilhelm Kuhweide	G 203	3633
6.	Hubert Raudaschl	OE 31	3378
7,	A. Schemer	M 21	2264
8.	Börge Schwarz	D 16	2232
9.	J. Kariofillis	GR 6	2072
10.	Roar Larsen	N 24	1868
11.	Dr. Fred Auer	Z 81	857

8. European Championship 1963
Lake Balaton, Hungary, September 15-22
18 entries from 10 countries

The IYRU had decided not to continue with the European Championships after 1962. So the IFA picked up the tradition and delegated the event to Hungary. From now on two entries per nation were allowed. The beginning of the regatta was postponed by one day when the British and the Norwegian entry phoned that they had a car accident but would come soon - never to arrive. Bernhard Straubinger from the Federal Republic of Germany was leading with a large margin before the last race. However as in the year before, the smart Swede Boris Jacobsson won the last two races, while Straubinger finished only 11th and 6th, and thus won the championship for the second time. The second Swedish entry Andersson won the bronze.

Final Results 1963
1.	Boris Jacobsson	S	6449
2.	Bernhard Straubinger	G	6237
3.	Bernt Andersson	S	5421
4.	Miroslav Vejvoda	CZ	4994

5.	Uwe Mares	G	4898
6.	Walter Gärtner	DDR	4764
7.	Hubert Raudaschl	OE	3955
8.	A. Neeser	Z	3647
9.	György Finaczy	M	3614
10.	B. Horák	CZ	3518

9. European Championship 1964
Oeresund, Denmark, August 26-31
32 entries from 20 countries

Six races in force 3-5 were sailed on three days and one race was abandoned when only 14 boats were still upright in force 6-8. The European Championship was the final selection for most of the participants for the Olympics soon after.

Final Results 1964
1.	Willy Kuhweide	G 503	7743
2.	Henning Wind	D 30	6245
3.	Wim Maarse	H 260	6187
4.	Bernhard Straubinger	G 416	6187
5.	Boris Jacobsson	S 318	4965
6.	Per Jordebakke	N 60	4497
7.	Miroslav Vejvoda	CZ 111	4488
8.	Bernt Andersson	S 448	4477
9.	Brian Saffery-Cooper	K 144	3740
10.	György Finaczy	M 40	3447
11.	Mike Astley	K 177	3226
12.	Miklos Tuss	M 50	3051

10. European Championship 1965
Cascais, Portugal, September 6-12
29 entries from 16 countries

As a new regulation the ruling champion in addition to his countries quota of two and overseas countries were allowed to enter. The ruling US Champion Dick Tillman entered as the only non-European. Of the seven races one was light air, two were medium, and four heavy. A burning question at that time was how much wet sweaters or sweat shirts one should use before a limitation was set by the IYRU. For the first time two boats were disqualified by the jury for infringement of rule 60 - means of propulsion.

Final Results 1965
1.	Bernd Dehmel	DDR 98	7044
2.	Valentin Mankin	SR 636	6317
3.	Willy Kuhweide	G 503	6016
4.	Jürgen Mier	DDR 2325095	
5.	Boris Jacobsson	S 318	5003
6.	J. Stutterheim	G 516	4965
7.	Henning Wind	D 82	4639
8.	Hubert Raudaschl	OE 31	3869
9.	Arne Akerson	S 321	3837
10.	Richard Hart	K 131	3510
11.	Panagiotis Couligas	GR 55	3288
12.	Rogge	B 13	3252
13.	Dick Tillman	US 419	3159
14.	Rest	H 109	3140
15.	Mike Astley	K 177	2999

Above: Willy Kuhweide

11. European Championship 1966
Attersee, Austria, September 4-12
43 entries from 25 countries

Because of the authority he had gained by winning the 1964 Gold Cup, Hubert Raudaschl managed to convince the Council at the 1965 Gold Cup, to delegate the European Championship 1966 to Austria. Since the championship was open for all the non-European countries as well, all the top helmsmen had entered with the exception of Willy Kuhweide (because he had not qualified despite winning the Gold Cup that same year) and Henning Wind (who in those days refused to sail on fresh water on principle). The first race saw a lazy drifter, a five minute thunderstorm with Bruder on a screaming reach through the finishing line, many boats capsizing, and a sudden calm again with no hope for those under water to bail their boats. In rather shifty conditions Hubert Raudaschl capitalised from his knowledge of the local conditions. He had the best speed upwind, however he lost quite a bit again on the reaches and the runs. After a poor start in the regatta Raudaschl managed to take line honours four times and won convincingly with 14.7 points against runner up Jörg Bruder with 68.0.

Final Results 1966
1.	Hubert Raudaschl	OE 81	14.7
2.	Jörg Bruder	BL 3	68.0
3.	U. Köhler	Z 208	81.4
4.	Valentin Mankin	SR 636	85.0
5.	Dick Tillman	US 419	87.4
6.	E. Altmayer	BL 25	88.7
7.	A. Rymkiewicz	PZ 42	90.4
8.	B.E. Treleaven	KZ 62	101.0
9.	Bernd Dehmel	DDR 9	107.4
10.	A. Bally	Z 145	108.0
11.	Arne Akerson	S 321	112.0
12.	Lucian Christl	OE 70	113.0
13.	Miroslav Vejvoda	CZ 111	116.0
14.	Serge Maury	F 462	116.7
15.	S. Golser	I 371	117.0
16.	B. Horák	CZ 138	120.0
17.	G. Wossala	M 77	126.0
18.	P. Lippert	DDR 3	127.0
19.	W. Erdmann	G 434	135.7
20.	György Finaczy	M 40	142.4

12. European Championship 1967
Naples, Italy, August
43 entries from 24 countries

Conditions were mainly light and fluky. The championship was in doubt up to the last leg of the last race. Van Grünewaldt from Sweden had been leading on points from the second race on. However going into the last race Willy Kuhweide was only 1.4 points behind the Swede, if both discarded their worst race - with third place a good distance behind. When Kuhweide rounded the last mark third and the Swede was around 20th everybody thought that Willy would win the title. However he made one of the few mistakes of his sailing career, tacked away from a veer and dropped to 9th. So both sailors finally discarded the last race and the Swede was the winner overall.

Final Results 1967
1.	Arnold von Grünewaldt	S 366	19.0
2.	Willy Kuhweide	G 711	21.4
3.	Jürgen Mier	DDR 3	42.8
4.	Hubert Raudaschl	OE 81	60.0
5.	Henning Wind	D 93	65.0
6.	Valentin Mankin	SR 636	73.7
7.	Fabio Albarelli	I 406	74.0
8.	Jonty Farmer	KZ 9	82.0
9.	V. Kozlov	SR 381	83.0
10.	Bernhard Reist	Z 224	85.4
11.	Bernhard Straubinger	G 416	90.0
12.	Couligas	GR 37	90.4
13.	Mauro Pelaschier	I 388	92.0
14.	Carl van Duyne	US 245	98.0
15.	Miroslav Vejvoda	CZ 111	102.0
16.	Andy Zawieja	PZ 321	107.0
17.	Sturm	OE 50	117.0
18.	Lucian Christl	OE 70	117.0
19.	J.P. Boumans	B 6	119.0
20.	Wossala	M 77	122.0
22.	Jack Knights	K 238	123.0
23.	Jose Manuel Quina	P 65	125.0
24.	Dumont	F 365	128.7
25.	B. Horák	CZ 7	129.0

13. European Championship 1968
Medemblik, Holland, August 26-31
32 entries from 19 countries

The championship was again in doubt right up to the last beat of the last race and eventually it was Arne Akerson's better consistency that pulled him just ahead of Henning Wind and Uwe Mares. Winds were predominantly from the north-east and appeared to be very steady before the start. However, during the race, slow subtle swings were invariably present. Added to this problem was the notorious Ijsselmeer chop. However, despite all the pumping that was going on, all the helmsmen restricted themselves to one pump per surfable wave. Raudaschl sails set on Bruder masts was the rig of the day. Wedges were still much in evidence and the kicking strap had still not positively demonstrated any superiority over the wedge. The outcome depended finally on tactics and it was the aggressive genius of the Swedes and their flair for going well in moderate conditions that finally proved decisive.

Final Results 1968

1.	Arne Akerson	S 321	44.0
2.	Henning Wind	D 93	48.0
3.	Uwe Mares	G 800	49.0
4.	Valentin Mankin	SR 636	56.7
5.	Andersson	S 516	60.7
6.	Bernd Dehmel	DDR 9	62.7
7.	Zawieja	PZ 321	64.7
8.	Hubert Raudaschl	OE 101	65.7
9.	Werenskiold	N 83	67.7
10.	Binkhorst	H 369	69.0
11.	Kozlov	SR 381	70.4
12.	Maury	F 496	74.7
13.	John Maynard	K 284	75.0
14.	Patrick Pym	K 274	75.7
15.	Beck	H 381	83.7
16.	Köhler	L 142	84.7

15. European Championship 1970
Dublin, Ireland, July 4-11
42 entries from 19 countries

There were three entries per country allowed, so the participation was very good. The championship was a test of stamina, determination and fitness. For the second half of the week the wind was hardly ever less than Force 4 and there were gusts of 7 or even more. After he had won the Gold Cup in 1969 Thomas Lundquist held up the Swedish flag again. Willy Kuhweide had bought back his old wooden Raudaschl boat and did much better than the previous year, finishing fourth. In the Wednesday race it was blowing so hard that Lundquist and Van Elst in first and second position wore round instead of gybing on the run. Because of fog on Tuesday there were two races scheduled on Thursday, the second of which should not have been held. Two

14. European Championship 1969
Warnemünde, German Democratic Republic
August 8-15, 39 entries from 21 countries

Measurement was too strict, indicating, that there hardly existed any genuine Finns at that time on the entire globe. Philippe Soria disregarded the 'suggestions' of Vernon Forster and was disqualified after the second race. The wind wandered aimlessly around the compass in most of the races. But Sweden's three representatives Akerson the ruling champion from 1968, Sall, and Liljegren set a record which was equalled in 1985 by the Danish but certainly can never be broken, by winning Gold, Silver and Bronze. Arne Akerson had the best speed in the difficult conditions and did not have to start in the last race in order to secure the title again.

competitors were discovered floating well away from their craft, including Gerardo Seeliger, later president of the IFA. The Canadian Phelan had his new Elvström boat sink under him. Most of the skippers wore too many wet sweaters which was unlimited by regulations at that time - and were unable to get back into their boats after a capsize. Bruder masts had taken over by 40-2.

Final Results 1970

1.	Thomas Lundquist	S 532	26.0
2.	Guy Liljegren	S 554	32.4
3.	Jürgen Mier	DDR 3	44.0
4.	Willy Kuhweide	G 711	45.7
5.	Serge Maury	F 96	50.0
6.	Hans Van Elst	H 424	50.4
7.	György Finaczy	M 40	54.0
8.	P. Mondéteguy	F 612	70.3

Final Results 1969

1.	Arne Akerson	S 321	48.7
2.	Börge Sall	S 392	58.7
3.	Guy Liljegren	S 554	74.1
4.	Jürgen Mier	DDR 3	77.7
5.	Andreas von Eicken	G 969	78.0
6.	Frits Beck	H 381	78.5
7.	György Finaczy	M 40	79.4
8.	Andrzej Zawieja	PZ 321	84.0
9.	Michel Hupin	B 90	85.0
10.	Walter Mai	G 991	102.7
11.	Valentin Mankin	SR 36	106.7
12.	Panagiotis Couligas	GR 117	106.7
13.	Jan Winquist	L 156	109.0
14.	Bernd Dehmel	DDR 9	115.0
15.	Tiemen Vries	H 418	115.0
16.	Patrick Pym	K 274	115.4
17.	Rafail Chucharov	BU 4	121.0
18.	Robert Andre	US 10	121.7
19.	Miroslav Vejvoda	CZ 111	123.0
20.	Vitall Dirdira	SR 14	124.0

9.	Bernd Dehmel	DDR 9	73.7
10.	R. Bergsten	S 557	84.7
11.	Norman Freeman	US 909	87.0
12.	B. Watson	K 233	87.7
13.	Walter Mai	G 991	93.7
14.	Oleg Shilov	SR 4	94.0
15.	Victor Potapov	SR 15	101.7
16.	Gerardo Seeliger	E 69	106.0
17.	Iain Macdonald-Smith	K 341	109.0
18.	C. Anderson	L 159	115.0
19.	Elias Hatzipavlis	GR	119.0
20.	Michel Hupin	B 90	131.0

16. European Championship 1971
Athens, Greece, August 14-22
67 entries from 27 countries

Each country was allowed to send three competitors except Sweden who had an extra quota for the ruling champion. In the pre-race measuring Gilbert Lamboley tested his 'Pendulum Method' to obtain data on the centre of gravity and weight distribution of characteristic hulls. The wind stayed in the north throughout the series and was therefore rather strong. Racing on the 4th and 5th day had to be cancelled due to winds of Force 6 and over. Thomas Lundquist from Sweden finished 3rd in the 1st race but was scored as a non-starter because he had forgotten to take out his tally. This error cost him not only the race but eventually the championship. So it was the Dutch helmsman Baudouin Binkhorst who became the new European Champion, despite the fact that he never won a race. Neither did the second overall Magnus Olin.

Final Results 1971
1.	Baudouin Binkhorst	H 454	34.0
2.	Magnus Olin	S 509	35.4
3.	György Finaczy	M 40	37.0
4.	Miroslav Vejvoda	CZ 111	49.0
5.	Victor Potapov	SR 1	55.0
6.	Fritz Beck	H 4	58.0
7.	Thomas Lundquist	S 532	59.0
8.	Serge Maury	F 7	62.0
9.	Fabio Albarelli	I 450	62.4
10.	Minski Fabris	Y 30	64.0
11.	Göran Andersson	S 516	70.0
12.	Iain MacDonald-Smith	K 347	82.0
13.	P. Mondéteguy	F 661	84.7
14.	John Clarke	KC 111	86.0
15.	Gerardo Seeliger	E 69	87.0
16.	Kees Douze	H 7	88.0
17.	Carl van Duyne	US 245	90.7
18.	Walter Bachmann	Z 267	91.0
19.	Blazy Wyskowski	PZ 179	91.0
20.	G. Asblom	S 585	93.7
21.	H. Hatzipavlis	GR 122	97.0
22.	S. Golser	I 458	99.0
23.	J. Walle Hansen	N 87	104.0
24.	Francis Jammes	F 625	106.0
25.	Kai Krüger	G 1233	107.0
26.	Richard Storer	K 360	109.0
27.	Ron Jenyns	KA 9	112.4
28.	Patrick Pym	K 274	116.0
29.	A. Rymkiewicz	PZ 174	116.0
30.	F. Schöttle	US 224	130.7
31.	Uwe Heinzmann	G 1122	132.0
32.	Ivan Hoffman	CZ 3	142.0
33.	P. Grammatikou	BU 321	142.0
34.	Andy Zawieja	PZ 321	145.0
35.	Luciano Lievi	I 417	147.0

17. European Championship 1972
Medemblik, Holland, June 14-19
47 entries from 26 countries

Wind conditions were good and from every point of the compass, ranging from light to force 7, but always shifty and demanding. Christian Schröder from the DDR won two races, was always among the top 8, and might have won even a third race when a self bailer broke while he was leading. Some of the competitors used the Mader hulls and the stiff Needlespar masts they would have to use at the Olympics, in order to become familiar with the new material. The traditional wooden masts proved to be far superior to the new aluminium masts.

Final Results 1972
1.	Christian Schröder	DDR 8	33.7
2.	Thomas Lundquist	S 532	40.7
3.	Magnus Olin	S 509	44.4
4.	Serge Maury	F 1	59.0
5.	Kees Douze	H 7	67.4
6.	Per Werenskiold	N 83	68.0
7.	Bernd Dehmel	DDR 9	73.0
8.	Alex Welter	BL 5	81.0
9.	John Bertrand	KA 113	81.0
10.	Kim Weber	L 161	82.4
11.	Blazy Wyskowski	PZ 179	85.0
12.	Walter Mai	G 1271	86.0
13.	Carl Van Duyne	US 245	91.7

18. European Championship 1973
Wladislawowo, Poland, August 5-11
48 entries from 23 countries

The ruling European Champion Christian Schröder from the DDR this time won 3 of the 7 races and had a 10th as his discard. Lennart Gustafsson of Sweden got a 2nd overall, while the German Democratic Republic also took 3rd and 4th. Sailing conditions were very difficult with medium winds but all sorts of old waves from previous wind directions. The winning sailors from the DDR used a great variety of wooden masts. They had practised weeks before the event with the help of an extraordinary support team and gathered with scientific methods the right spar for the various conditions.

Final Results 1973
1.	Christian Schroeder	DDR 8	27.7
2.	Lennart Gustafsson	S 589	37.7
3.	Jürgen Wolff	DDR 29	50.7
4.	Jochen Schümann	DDR 9	50.8
5.	Craig Thomas	US 934	61.4
6.	Ryszard Blaszka	PZ 56	72.0
7.	Magnus Olin	S 584	81.0
8.	Rolli Berdash	SR 9	89.7
9.	Jean Pasturaud	F 675	96.7
10.	Andrzej Zawieja	PZ 321	101.0
11.	David Howlett	K 341	115.0
12.	Hans Van Elst	H 424	115.4

14.	Minski Fabris	Y 30	93.0
15.	Ryszard Blaszka	PZ 56	97.7
16.	Luciano Lievi	I 417	102.0
17.	Claudio Biekarck	BL 10	103.0
18.	B.B. Barbour	SA 399	106.7
19.	P. Mondéteguy	F 6	108.0
20.	Uwe Heinzmann	G 1122	125.0
21.	K. Kruijer	H 494	127.7
22.	Baudouin Binkhorst	H 454	128.0
23.	Mauro Pelaschier	I 460	132.0
24.	A. Papaioannou	GR 165	135.0

13.	Carl van Duyne	US 245	118.0
14.	Elias Hatzipavlis	GR 162	132.0
15.	Bob Smith	US 886	137.0
16.	Uwe Heinzmann	G 1122	143.0
17.	Alex Welter	L 5	147.0
18.	Sanford Riley	KC 143	147.0
19.	Sergej Konstancki	SR 8	149.7
20.	Clive Roberts	KZ 157	152.0
21.	Andreas Haan	M 11	160.0
22.	Kees Douze	H 7	165.0
23.	Miroslav Cada	CZ 1	165.0
24.	Richard Hart	K 331	165.0
25.	Miklos Tuss	M 50	175.0

19. European Championship 1974
Niendorf, Federal Republic of Germany
June 1-7, 55 entries

Wind conditions were excellent, the organisation on the water professional, the festivities ashore disappointing. The ruling world champion Serge Maury did not participate because he had failed to qualify in the French trials. In 1974 the Needlespar B mast was reported to be the best spar, and the Swedish Marinex sails were the choice of the champion.

Final Results 1974

1.	Guy Liljegren	S	41.0
2.	Jacques Busquet	F	52.7
3.	Elias Hatzipavlis	GR	57.0
4.	Jean Grandchamp	F	76.7
5.	Kent Carlsson	S	79.0
6.	Andrei Balashov	SR	81.7
7.	Christian Schröder	DDR	89.7
8.	Jacques Rogge	B	97.4
9.	David Howlett	K	97.7
10.	Jürgen Wolff	DDR	101.0
11.	Mauro Pelaschier	I	118.7
12.	G. Ehlers	G	120.0
13.	Richard Hart	K	120.0
14.	Ryszard	PZ	122.0
15.	Palmgren	L	123.0
16.	Kees Douze	H	124.0
17.	Minski Fabris	Y	124.7

20. European Championship 1975
Palamos, Spain, May 31-June 8
49 entries from 20 countries

Every day at about 2.00 pm there was a nice sea breeze, starting with force 1, later up to force 3. The first beat was better on starboard, later you had to keep right. You had to go to the corners, tacking up in the middle was disastrous. Lanaverre and Roga boats dominated the fleet. Serge Maury won the second and the last race, and the regatta overall by a good margin.

Final Results 1975

1.	Serge Maury	F 711	33.0
2.	David Howlett	K 341	51.4
3.	Mauro Pelaschier	I 509	53.4
4.	Claudio Biekarck	BL 69	71.0
5.	Ryszard Blaszka	PZ 299	73,7
6.	Van den Broek	F 7	77.0
7.	Andrei Balashov	SR 2	77.7
8.	Gerardo Seeliger	E 99	81.0
9.	Luciano Lievi	I 517	83.0
10.	Joaquin Blanco	E 101	84.0
11.	Jonty Farmer	KZ 149	85.0
12.	Grandchamp	F 710	90.0
13.	Jörgen Lindhardtsen	D 126	90.0
14.	Jacques Rogge	B 2	91.4
15.	José Luis Doreste	E 109	102.7
16.	Jochen Schümann	DDR 9	103.0
17.	Andreas Haan	M 11	104.0
18.	Themelis	GR 49	113.0
19.	Petaja	L 161	116.7
20.	Papacannou	GR 1	120.0
21.	Baudouin Binkhorst	H 6	120.7
22.	Roberto Haas	A 42	124.0
23.	Lue van Keirsblick	B 15	129.0
24.	Hans Van Elst	H 524	132.0
25.	Richard Grönblom	L 171	133.0

21. European Championship 1976
Port Camargue, France, April 30-May 8
45 entries, from 19 countries

From the beginning the defender Serge Maury proved that he was not willing to give the title away too easily. After three races he was leading overall scoring 2-2-7. Serge was lucky when the time limit expired and his challengers Mauro Pelaschier and Andrei Balashov had only 150 meters to go and he himself was at the end of the fleet. When that race was re-sailed the wind disappeared after the first boats had finished. Nine boats failed to come in on time - including Serge. However line honours and runner-up in the two last races made everything clear in favour of Serge Maury.

Final Results 1976

1.	Serge Maury	F 721	22.0
2.	Andrei Balashov	SR 2	56.0
3.	Gus Miller	US 975	67.7
4.	Mauro Pelaschier	I 509	72.0
5.	Jochen Schümann	DDR 9	76.0
6.	Joaquin Blanco	E 101	76.0

7.	Pierre Mondéteguy	F 719	81.0
8.	José Luis Doreste	E 109	83.7
9.	Werner Sülberg	G 1611	90.7
10.	Jean J. Grandchamp	F 720	91.7
11.	Richard Grönblom	L 171	95.7
12.	John Bertrand	KA 151	96.0
13.	Guy Liljegren	S 655	96.7
14.	Andreas Haan	M 11	107.0
15.	Gerardo Seeliger	E 99	108.0
16.	Sanford Riley	KC 143	108.0
17.	Ryszard Blaszka	PZ 56	116.0
18.	J-P. Boumans	B 1	118.7
19.	Jürgen Wolff	DDR 29	119.0
20.	Anastas Boudouris	GR 176	123.0
21.	Chris Law	K 321	124.0
22.	Thomas Jungblut	G 1556	126.0

22. European Championship 1977

Istambul-Yesilyurt, Turkey, July 26-Aug 5
34 entries from 17 countries

Gilbert Lamboley as the Chairman of the IFA Technical Committee came to help the Turkish measurers to find out that there were still a lot of Finn sailers who dislike stembands. However all boats got a dispensation and from that time on the arrangement declared to be illegal in Istanbul became common practice all over the world.

Final Results 1977

1.	Joaquin Blanco	E 1	32.7
2.	Minski Fabris	Y 53	42.0
3.	Peter Vollebregt	H 535	52.4
4.	Kent Carlsson	S 677	53.7
5.	David Howlett	K 421	54.4
6.	Andrei Balashov	SR 2	60.4
7.	Jochen Schümann	DDR 9	66.7
8.	Wolfgang Gerz	G 1573	79.0
9.	Ryszard Skarbinski	PZ 28	83.0
10.	H.G. Ehlers	G 1572	88.7

23. European Championship 1978

Marstrand Sweden, August 24-September 2
54 entries, from 24 countries

The wind was strong to very strong for most of the week and the waves breathtaking even for the most experienced stalwarts. Super Skipper Howlett did not believe it, until the globe capsized below him while he claimed to remain upright. Kent Carlsson was disqualified for a too heavy weight jacket. The last decisive race had only light wind but a strong current. Minski Fabris cleared all doubts by winning this one too, after he had been superior in the heavy air previously. The Vanguard hulls were judged to be fast in the light to medium conditions and the Taylors were better in the rough weather.

Final Results 1978

1.	Minski Fabris	Y 53	16.0
2.	Joaquin Blanco	E 1	26.7
3.	Jochen Schümann	DDR 9	57.4
4.	R. Güldenpfening	DDR 21	62.7
5.	Chris Law	K 321	68.7
6.	Kent Carlsson	S 677	72.7
7.	Stewart Neff	US 1004	78.0
8.	José Luis Doreste	E 109	84.0

9.	David Howlett	K 463	89.0
10.	Wolfgang Gerz	G 1573	91.0
11.	John Bertrand	US 1007	93.0
12.	Guy Liljegren	S 516	93.7
13.	Egidio Babbi	I 619	98.0
14.	Otto Pohlmann	G 1650	101.4
15.	Jörgen Lindhardtsen	D 126	104.0
16.	Jacques Busquet	F 723	104.0
17.	Ryszard Skarbinski	PZ 122	108.0
18.	Mark Neeleman	H 555	115.0
19.	Jaques Rogge	B 2	115.0
20.	Peter Lester	KZ 191	125.7
21.	Levent Özgen	TK 71	134.0
22.	James Reynolds	KC 996	136.0
23.	Manuel Doreste	E 9	139.0
24.	Patrick Spängs	S 666	142.0
25.	August Miller	US 975	144.0

24. European Championship 1979
Malcesine, Lago di Garda, Italy, June 1-10
44 entries from 23 countries

The measurement was clouded by the start of the station 8 problem. A confusing variety of winds from all sort of strange directions, durability and force blurred the chaotic conditions. The only sailor who preserved orientation was the ruling world champion John Bertrand from the United States, winning the last three races after he had already scored 4/6/6.

Final Results 1979

1.	John Bertrand	US 1037	19.7
2.	Jochen Schümann	DDR 9	43.0
3.	Kent Carlsson	S 679	50.0
4.	Minski Fabris	Y 53	62.0
5.	Jörg Vetter	DDR 12	63.4
6.	Cameron Lewis	US 1027	66.7
7.	José Luis Doreste	E 109	77.0
8.	Magnus Liljedahl	S 589	80.7
9.	Otto Pohlmann	G 1650	86.7
10.	Ched Proctor	US 171	91.7
11.	Elias Hatzipavlis	GR 180	94.0
12.	Thomas Jungblut	G 1	95.0
13.	Jacques Rogge	B 2	103.0
14.	Josef Senkyr	CZ 303	104.0
15.	Graham Deegan	KZ 185	106.0
16.	Mark Neeleman	H 555	106.7
17.	Yves Silvestro	F 731	114.7
18.	Egidio Babbi	I 633	120.0
19.	Filip Willems	B 15	123.0
20.	Wolfgang Mayrhofer	OE 199	130.0
21.	Sergei Khoretski	SR 23	132.0
22.	Esko Rechardt	L 183	132.0
23.	Miroslav Lostak	CZ 377	134.0
24.	Andrea Roost	Z 9	138.0
25.	Boris Zakhorow	SR 3	139.0

25. European Championship 1980
Helsinki, Finland, June 10-18
37 entries from 23 countries

As the last dress rehearsal for the Olympic Games to be held shortly in Tallinn, the 1980 European Championship was sailed in Helsinki in very similar conditions. Because of the early Gold Cup in New Zealand, there was also a second extraordinary AGM of the IFA on that occasion. Chris Law tried a Vanguard and found it easier to sail and faster than his standard Taylor. He already had a big points lead when he started the 6th race in light winds. Chris finished 12th and was the sure winner. In the last race Bertrand decided the battle for the runner-up in his favour against Balashov.

Final Results 1980

1.	Chris Law	K 321	32.4
2.	John Bertrand	US 1037	50.7
3.	Andrei Balashov	SR 2	56.4
4.	Mark Neeleman	H 555	67.7
5.	José Luis Doreste	E 109	69.0
6.	Guy Liljegren	S 686	73.7
7.	Sergei Khoretski	SR 23	79.7
8.	Kent Carlsson	S 679	83.0
9.	Wolfgang Mayrhofer	OE 199	96.7
10.	Jochen Schümann	DDR 9	99.7
11.	Martin van Leeuwen	H 565	101.0
12.	Skarbinski	PZ 7	102.0
13.	Esko Rechardt	L 185	104.7
14.	Michael Nissen	G 1706	105.0
15.	Wolfgang Gerz	G 1573	107.0
16.		KZ 2	128.0
17.	Miroslav Rychcik	PZ 75	129.0
18.	Keirsblick	B 24	131.0

26. European Championship 1981
Athens, Greece, May 23-June 1
46 entries from 22 countries

Five races were sailed in southerly winds with force 3-4 and two with a north wind up to force 7. Everybody was satisfied with the organisation. The only grumbling was heard after the third race when the jury disqualified 11 boats for pumping and rocking. All of a sudden, an up to now mediocre former Laser sailor from Denmark shocked the established skippers by winning each and every race. Lasse Hjortnäs managed for the first and most likely last time to win the European Championship with a score of 0.0.

Final Results 1981

1.	Lasse Hjortnäs	D 143	0.0
2.	Jörgen Lindhardtsen	D 142	49.7
3.	Otto Pohlmann	G 1787	70.7
4.	Martin Pallson	S 684	75.4
5.	S. Khoretski	SR 23	79.5
6.	Wolfgang Gerz	G 1573	79.7
7.	Oleg Khoperski	SR 23	85.7
8.	Jochen Schümann	DDR 9	85.7
9.	Joaquin Blanco	E 1	94,7
10.	Michael Nissen	G 1795	99.4
11.	Wolfgang Mayrhofer	OE 199	105.0
12.	Mark Neeleman	H 555	107.4
13.	Martin Van Leeuwen	H 565	123.7
14.	Henryk Blaszka	PZ 6	125.0
15.	Thomas Oljelund	S 681	129.0
16.	Francisco De Angelis	I 655	137.0
17.	Miroslav Rychcik	PZ 75	139.0
18.	Lennart Persson	S 680	141.0
19.	Thomas Schmid	G 1749	143.0
20.	Paolo Semeraro	I 666	144.0
21.	Patrick Spängs	S 685	145.0
22.	José Maria v d Ploeg	E 145	146.0
23.	Istvan Rujak	M 200	154.0
24.	Peter Vollebregt	H 535	163.0
25.	Roberto Benamati	I 658	180.0

27. European Championship 1982

Masnou, Spain, September 25-October 3
67 entries from 23 countries

There was lots of wind but also a strong current and on the first day an ugly oil pollution on the water. In the third race the jury disqualified six prominent skippers because of pumping. The selection was not so much based on serious observations but rather exemplary and included Lasse Hjortnäs. After he had won the Gold Cup by a safe margin, Lasse took this European Championship with three times line honour and twice runner-up, discarding that annoying DSQ. After the magic black-top mast Lasse had used in his fabulous 1981 season had been stolen, he made the red-top presentable at court, by winning with 10% of the final score of the runner-up Mark Neeleman.

Final Results 1982

1.	Lasse Hjortnäs	D 143	6.0
2.	Mark Neeleman	H 555	65.0
3.	Thomas Schmid	G 1793	73.7
4.	Nikolai Soukhoroukow	SR 14	74.7

5.	Mike McIntyre	K 491	75.0
6.	Wolfgang Gerz	G 1573	76.0
7.	Luc Choley	F 100	91.0
8.	Henryk Blaszka	PZ 6	95.0
9.	Jochen Schümann	DDR 9	96.0
10.	Esko Rechardt	L 203	95.4
11.	Jörgen Lindhardtsen	D 142	100.0
12.	Don Nordquist	S 690	102.7
13.	Oleg Khoperski	SR 21	103.7
14.	Joaquin Blanco	E 179	105.7
15.	Otto Pohlmann	G 1787	110.7
16.	Toni Ferrer	E 170	112.0
17.	Wolfgang Mayrhofer	OE 199	116.0
18.	Stefan Myralf	D 148	119.0
19.	José Maria van der Ploeg	E 145	121.7

20.	Paolo Semeraro	I 655	128.7
21.	Patrick Spängs	S 685	129.0
22.	Juan E. Mägli	GU 1	133.0
23.	Martin Palsson	S 684	133.0
24.	Francois Le Castrec	F 888	139.0
25.	Sjaak Haakman	H 577	141.0
26.	Karsten Kaufmann	G 1706	146.0
27.	Frank Butzmann	DDR 16	147.0
28.	Andy Pimental	US 1052	151.0
29.	Miroslav Rychcik	PZ 75	151.0
30.	Kimo Worthington	US 1066	157.0

28. European Championship 1983

Neusiedlersee, Austria, June 3-11
63 entries from 24 countries

Lasse Hjortnäs came to Austria determined to defend his title as the ruling European Champion of 1981/82. There were five races with a strong shifty force 4-7 wind on three days. There would have been enough for a sixth race on the afternoon of the third day, but the race committee took pity on the worn out second half of the fleet. Lasse caught a DSQ in the second race but for the rest of them he was not content with less than the runner-up in the heavy-air races. However finally there was very little reliable wind and Hjortnäs collected 59 points, which he had to count since he had to discard his DSQ. Another second place in the last race was not enough to save him. So Jochen Schümann from the DDR won the title without ever winning a race, scoring 2/3/4/8/9/10.

Final Results 1983

1.	Jochen Schümann	DDR 9	61.7
2.	Frank Butzmann	DDR 16	70.4
3.	Lasse Hjortnäs	D 143	71.0

4.	Jörgen Lindhardtsen	D 142	74.4
5.	Mark Neeleman	H 555	78.4
6.	Kimo Worthington	US 1066	97.0
7.	Thomas Schmid	G 1793	100.1
8.	Peter Vilby	D 146	106.0
9.	Craig Healy	US 1041	108.0
10.	Nikolai Soukhoroukow	SR 14	114.0
11.	Oleg Khoperski	SR 21	114.7
12.	Larry Lemieux	KC 201	126.0
13.	Francois le Castrec	F 888	129.0
14.	Joaquin Blanco	E 179	142.0
15.	Wolfgang Mayrhofer	OE 199	144.0
16.	Sergej Khoretski	SR 23	156.0
17.	Roberto Benamati	I 658	160.0
18.	Martin Palsson	S 684	162.0
19.	Henryk Blaszka	PZ 6	162.0
20.	Tom Lehan	US 1070	164.0
21.	Sjaak Haakman	H 577	168.0
22.	Eric Bornarel	F 115	173.0
23.	Jacek Sobkowiak	PZ 7	175.0
24.	Francisco De Angelis	I 509	181.0
25.	Carl Johan Hedberg	S 697	184.0
26.	Ron Van Manen	H 616	187.0
27.	Patrick Spängs	S 685	188.0
28.	Fillip Willems	B 15	188.0
29.	Marko Prancevic	Y 90	190.7
30.	Luc Choley	F 100	191.0

29. European Championship 1984

Wladislawowo, Poland, June 5-15
35 entries from 17 countries

The entire championship was chaotic but certainly not boring. Although Andy Zawieja warned the participants to avoid a dangerous breakwater at the harbour entrance, gold-medalist Esko Rechardt and co-favourite Lasse Hjortnäs sailed right into the monsters mouth and suffered dearly. Lasse broke his best mast and returned home to look for a new one for the Olympics. Esko was seriously injured. Racing was also chaotic with shifts and holes in the wind and fog and what have you. But there was also a lot of fine wind and a deserving winner overall: Mike McIntyre from the United Kingdom. Peter Vilby as the runner-up overall with two race wins proved that Denmark had an unexhaustable supply of good sailors - with daddy-cool Lindhardtsen remaining at home, since he had not qualified.

Final Results 1984

1.	Mike McIntyre	K 491	19.0
2.	Peter Vilby	D 146	39.7
3.	Jacek Sobkowiak	PZ 7	41.0
4.	Mark Neeleman	H 555	50.4
5.	Henryk Blaszka	PZ 6	61.4
6.	Roddy Bridge	K 493	64.0
7.	Miroslav Rychcik	PZ 75	65.0
8.	Russell Silvestri	US 1074	66.0
9.	Paolo Semeraro	I 6	73.7
10.	Jochen Schümann	DDR 9	75.7
11.	Thomas Oljelund	S 700	76.0
12.	Arnoud Hummel	H 577	85.0
13.	Jaroslaw Maciuk	PZ 52	95.7
14.	Fillip Willems	B 15	96.7
15.	Roberto Benamati	I 658	100.0
16.	Chris Pratt	KA 183	108.0
17.	Ron Van Manen	H 616	108.0
18.	Tomasz Rumszewicz	PZ 77	115.7
19.	Eric Mergenthaler	MX 33	115.7
20.	Heike Birke	DDR 19	121.0

30. European Championship 1985
Athens, Greece, September 7-15
43 entries from 17 countries

Lasse Hjortnäs, usually training in cold to freezing water, obviously liked the warm Mediterranean Sea. Ever since he came into the Finn Class, whenever the Europeans are in that water, he can't be stopped. Athens was the site of his biggest victory in 1981 when he won with zero points, and in Masnou he had a mere 6.0. In 1985 again in Athens, Lasse only collected 17.0 which is not so bad in contrast to the runner-up Lindhardtsen with 35.4 and third Vilby 42.4. After Gold, Silver, and Bronze had gone to Sweden in 1969, the Danish team managed the same trick in 1985 to demoralise the rest of the world.

Final Results 1985
1.	Lasse Hjortnäs	D 143	17.0
2.	Jörgen Lindhardtsen	D 142	35.4
3.	Peter Vilby	D 156	42.4
4.	Oleg Khoperski	SR 21	45.4
5.	Peter Peet	H 630	46.7
6.	Paolo Semeraro	I 716	52.1
7.	Arnoud Hummel	H 577	62.7
8.	Stuart Childerley	K 503	78.7
9.	Thomas Schmid	G 1793	83.0
10.	Henryk Blaszka	PZ 6	86.0
11.	Jacek Sobkowiak	PZ 7	89.0
12.	Michael Luschan	OE 211	94.0
13.	Eric Mergenthaler	MX 33	95.0
14.	Ralf Kadenbach	G 1880	104.0
15.	Jaroslav Maciuk	PZ 52	109.0
16.	Josef Pirsch	G 1843	115.0
17.	Ron van Manen	H 631	115.0
18.	Marco Passoni	I 707	116.0
19.	Enrico Passoni	I 722	117.0
20.	Armando Ortolano	GR 211	120.0

31. European Championship 1986
Hyeres, France, April 29-May 7
45 entries from 21 countries

Held immediately after the pre-Olympic week in Hyeres, the Finns stayed on for another week. In the first race, the force 1-2 allowed John Hofland line honours, but caused 8 boats to be disqualified for violating rule 54. Johan Hedberg took the early lead and lead up to race 6, but a 30th in that race dropped him to second. Oleg Khoperski who performed with outstanding harmony between man and nature won races 3, 4 and 5 came 3rd in the 6th and covered Hedberg in the final race to take the Championship by 23.0 points. After the 4th race there were some scandals because of the 20 kg weight limit on wet clothing and the attempt of some sailors to secretly get rid of some of their equipment on the way home, but only one helm was disqualified.

Final Results 1986
1.	Oleg Khoperski	SR 21	37.7
2.	Johan Hedberg	S 700	60.7
3.	Heiko Birke	DDR 19	68.7
4.	Stig Westergaard	D 155	80.0
5.	Frank Butzmann	DDR 16	88.0
6.	John Cutler	KZ 234	103.0

7.	Paolo Semeraro	I 6	104.7
8.	Jacek Sobkowiak	PZ 7	113.7
9.	Jörgen Lindhardtsen	D 142	115.7
10.	Ralf Kadenbach	G 6	116.7
11.	Welf-Bodo Lixenfeld	G 1706	119.0
12.	Peter Vilby	D 156	119.7
13.	Andrei Nikandrov	SR 1	121.0
14.	Othmar M v. Blumencron	G 1835	122.0
15.	Goran Sandberg	S 698	127.7
16.	Michael Luschan	OE 211	130.0
17.	Thomas Schmid	G 1793	130.4
18.	Emanuele Vaccari	I 727	131.7
19.	Henryk Blaszka	PZ 6	133.0
20.	John Hofland	H 622	141.0
21.	Kristian Sjöberg	L 201	143.7
22.	Enrico Passoni	I 722	152.0
23.	Arnoud Hummel	H 577	155.0
24.	Hans Spitzauer	OE 218	155.0
25.	Mike Milner	KC 4	158.0

32. European Championship 1987
Rungsted, Denmark, August 3-12
48 entries

The event was sailed from the Royal Danish YC just north of Copenhagen in a mixture of conditions. After the usual measurement problems, Peter Vilby won the first two races in force 2-3. In race one the initial winner was disqualified for too carrying much weight. Stuart Childerley led race 3 in less wind until the last mark, when an incident with José Luis Doreste let him through and he had to settle for second. Lawrence Crispin won race 4 after leading the whole way, sometimes by a whole leg. After Otto Strandvig won race 5 and Michael Fisher won race 6, any of 7 helms could have won going into the last race. Arnoud Hummel won the final race but an 8th for Childerley was enough to win the series without winning a race. His lowest race was 15th in this high scoring series.

Final Results 1987
1.	Stuart Childerley	K 503	78.0
2.	Peter Vilby	D 156	97.0
3.	Otto Strandvig	D 146	97.0
4.	Lawrence Crispin	K 498	98.0
5.	Thomas Schmid	G 1903	99.7
6.	Henryk Blaszka	PZ 6	102.0
7.	Welf-Bodo Lixenfeld	G 1706	102.7
8.	José Luis Doreste	E 109	104.0
9.	Michael Luschan	OE 211	106.0
10.	Esko Rechardt	L 211	109.0
11.	Stig Westergaard	D 155	110.1
12.	Louis Verloop	US 1066	120.7
13.	Arnoud Hummel	H 577	127.0
14.	R-J Kadenbach	G 6	129.7
15.	Jacek Sobkowiak	PZ 7	132.7
16.	Hans Spitzauer	OE 218	139.0
17.	John Hofland	H 622	144.7
18.	Othmar M.v. Blumencron	G 1892	146.0
19.	Dirk Löwe	DDR 14	151.7
20.	Ruben Serra	E 106	152.0

33. European Championship 1988

Medemblik, Holland, June 5-10
50 entries from 22 countries

The event was sailed in wet conditions with a Force 2-4 wind. Most sailors had very inconsistent results throughout the week. Second placed Mergenthaler won the first and fifth race but apart from that never scored above tenth. John Cutler, Mark Neeleman, Armando Ortolano and Henryk Blaszka all won races but were not consistent enough to capitalise. Only one sailor managed a good string of results. Doreste counted a 2-6-4-4-7 and dropped his 26th in race 5 to win the Europeans, just prior to his Olympic victory in Pusan later that summer.

34. European Championship 1989

Helsinki, Finland, July 2-11
54 entries from 20 countries

Helsinki was where it had all started in 1952, and the Finns again went back in 1989. A change in the quota rule allowed the same entries as for a Gold Cup. The event belonged to Hans Spitzauer from the start after he won the first two races. Othmar Müller von Blumencron won the light weather third race and Lauri Rechardt won the fourth, with Spitzauer maintaining his points in second. The fifth race was won by Finnish Jali Makila followed by Rechardt and Mats Caap. Oleg Khoperski had worked out a good lead in the final race, but with thunderstorms around, a massive shift made a nonsense of the final beat and the race committee cancelled the race. This left Spitzauer the overall winner. On the spare day a series of match races were held. Spitzauer and Larry Lemieux reached the final tied and after one win each, no wind and rain stopped play.

Final Results 1989

1.	Hans Spitzauer	OE 218	14.7
2.	Othmar M v. Blumencron	Z 418	26.0
3.	Lauri Rechardt	L 185	32.0
4.	Mats Caap	S 718	41.7
5.	Thomas Schmid	G 1903	44.4
6.	Oleg Khoperski	SR 14	51.0
7.	Lawrence Lemieux	US 1086	57.0
8.	Lars Bergenzaun	S 698	57.0
9.	Jali Makila	L 212	59.0
10.	Emanuele Vaccari	I 727	67.7
11.	Stig Westergaard	D 155	68.0
12.	Hank Lammens	KC 19	74.0
13.	Peter Aldag	G 1993	74.0
14.	Mike Milner	KC 4	82.0
15.	Kristian Sjöberg	L 201	83.0
16.	Welf-Bodo Lixenfeld	G 1706	84.7
17.	Otto Strandvig	D 146	93.0
18.	Farkas Litkey	M 161	95.7
19.	Nick Jako	KC 13	97.0
20.	Fredrik Lööf	S 684	98.7

Final Results 1988

1.	José Luis Doreste	E 109	43.7
2.	Eric Mergenthaler	MX 33	55.0
3.	Hans Spitzauer	OE 218	58.0
4.	Stig Westergaard	D 155	60.4
5.	Chris Pratt	KA 183	61.7
6.	Luc Choley	F 100	68.0
7.	John Cutler	KZ 234	74.7
8.	Mark Neeleman	H 555	82.0
9.	Joaquin Blanco	E 179	84.7
10.	Roy Heiner	H 638	88.7
11.	Lars Bergenzaun	S 712	89.7
12.	Marco Passoni	I 710	95.7
13.	Lauri Rechardt	L 185	97.7
14.	Kristian Sjöberg	L 201	98.0
15.	Armando Ortolano	GR 211	102.0
16.	Henryk Blaszka	PZ 6	116.0
17.	Leith Armit	KZ 231	120.0
18.	Otto Strandvig	D 146	123.0
19.	John Hofland	H 622	127.7
20.	Bjorn Westergaard	D 165	128.0

35. European Championship 1990

Hayling Island, England, June 1-9
58 entries from 21 countries

The rather windy conditions seemed to suit two sailors, Stig Westergaard and Hans Spitzauer, and early on the feeling was that one of these two would win the Europeans. Westergaard was superior upwind while Spitzauer was in a class of his own on the reaches; having to catch up 100 m was just a minor problem. Second overall Spitzauer won the first race, final winner Westergaard won races 4 and 5. 3rd place overall went to Othmar Müller von Blumencron who won the 3rd race and the last one, and closed the gap on Spitzauer over the last few races. All boats had undergone thorough measurement checking by Peter Mohilla and as usual the padding manufacturers were clapping their hands! But at least all the boats ended up the same.

Final Results 1990

1.	Stig Westergaard	D 155	31.4
2.	Hans Spitzauer	OE 218	46.7
3.	Othmar M v Blumencron	Z 418	49.7
4.	Lasse Hjortnäs	D 143	72.7
5.	Jali Makila	L 212	89.0
6.	Andre Budzien	DDR 7	96.0
7.	Bjorn Westergaard	D 165	98.0
8.	Armando Ortolano	GR 211	100.0
9.	Peter Aldag	G 1920	108.7
10.	Thomas Schmid	G 1903	115.7
11.	Hank Lammens	KC 19	124.0
12.	Lawrence Lemieux	KC 201	130.0
13.	Dirk Löwe	DDR 16	135.0
14.	Bart Zielhuis	H 544	135.0
15.	Tim Tavinor	K 521	135.4
16.	Mike Milner	KC 4	136.7
17.	Brian Ledbetter	US 1080	140.7
18.	Fredrik Lööf	S 684	150.7
19.	Lars Bergenzaun	S 698	151.0
20.	Marco Passoni	I 760	153.0
21.	Richard Clarke	KC 11	153.0
22.	Enrico Passoni	I 722	160.0
23.	Kiko Villalonga	E 106	162.0
24.	Rob McMillan	K 493	179.0
25.	Jez Fanstone	K 498	179.0
26.	Toni Poncell	E 12	179.0
27.	Mark Oliver	KZ 230	193.0
28.	Emanuele Vacarri	I 727	183.0
29.	Roger Schulz	G 1984	188.0
30.	Richard Lott	K 484	188.0

36. European Championship 1991

Anzio, Italy, June 10-18
68 entries from 24 countries

The wind did not often get above 10 knots all week and only in the last race was there the wind and big waves associated with Anzio. Despite being a 'legend' Larry Lemieux had yet to win a major title - and he had been trying for 15 years. Apart from a 23rd in race 3, he never scored below 8th place, but also never won a race. José Maria van der Ploeg was leading after three races. Going into the last race, these two were tied on points and even had the same discard. Lemieux lead round the top mark and kept van der Ploeg in his sights during the race to finish third with van der Ploeg in fourth, but it was enough for Lemieux to win his first major Finn title.

Final Results 1991

1.	Lawrence Lemieux	KC 201	39.4
2.	José Maria van d Ploeg	E 105	41.4
3.	Kiko Villalonga	E 106	64.0
4.	Stuart Childerley	K 503	69.0
5.	Oleg Khoperski	SR 14	89.7
6.	Björn Westergaard	D 165	121.7
7.	Stig Westergaard	D 155	135.0
8.	Hank Lammens	KC 19	136.0
9.	Mats Caap	S 718	136.0
10.	David Himmell	US 1066	138.0
11.	Enrico Passoni	I 722	138.7
12.	André Budzien	G 70	143.7
13.	Arif Gürdenli	TK 211	144.0
14.	Yuri Tokovoi	SR 21	146.7
15.	Lasse Hjortnäs	D 143	147.0
16.	Mike Milner	KC 4	153.0
17.	Eric Mergenthaler	MX 33	155.0
18.	Alec Cutler	US 1044	157.7
19.	Joaquin Blanco	E 179	160.0
20.	Wlopz. Radwaniecko	PZ 6	165.7
21.	François Le Castrec	F 749	170.7
22.	Alexander Rinne	G 31	171.0
23.	Fredrik Lööf	S 684	173.0
24.	Pawel Pawlaczyk	PZ 7	174.0
25.	Michael Fellmann	G 1916	174.0
26.	Jeremy Fanstone	K 498	175.0
27.	Anders Lundmark	S 700	179.0
28.	Emanuele Vaccari	I 727	179.0
29.	Dirk Löwe	G 14	180.0
30.	Otto Strandvig	D 146	194.0
31.	Mark Herrmann	US 1026	200.7
32.	Philippe Presti	F 762	204.0
33.	Othmar Mv Blumencron	Z 418	207.0
34.	Hans Spitzauer	OE 218	212.0

37. European Championship 1992

Gdansk, Poland, June 6-14
51 entries from 24 countries

After two windy and wavy races, Glenn Bourke was going well with two first places but a knee injury put him out of the competition mid way through. The competition was then between Stuart Childerley, Oleg Khoperski and Dirk Löwe. Going into the last race, after the much lighter second half of the regatta, Khoperski lead Childerley by 1.3 points and Löwe was also in with a chance. But after a massive shift just after the start they were all out of it. Khoperski who had retired in the first race could not afford a bad result so struggled on to finish 23rd. This left Childerley as the winner and Löwe in second, enough to win him the German Olympic spot. However, 2 boats ahead of Khoperski were disqualified so he jumped to 0.7 points ahead of Löwe to finish as runner up and cost Löwe the German place at the Olympics. Childerley was always consistent and was the rightful winner. Philippe Presti sailed a magnificent regatta to finish 4th after winning the last two races.

Final Results 1992

1.	Stuart Childerley	K 503	56.4
2.	Oleg Khoperski	IYRU 14	63.7
3.	Dirk Löwe	G 14	64.4
4.	Philippe Presti	F 762	67.0
5.	Eric Mergenthaler	MX 33	80.0
6.	Fredrik Lööf	S 684	91.0
7.	Luca Devoti	I 789	91.4
8.	Emanuele Vaccari	I 727	93.7
9.	François Le Castrec	F 748	102.0
10.	Hans Spitzauer	OE 218	102.7
11.	Karlo Kuret	CRO 110	102.7
12.	Armando Ortolano	G 1	110.7
13.	Anders Lundmark	S 700	111.0
14.	Malte Philipp	G 25	115.7
15.	Arif Gürdenli	TK 211	116.0
16.	Yuri Tokovoi	SR 21	121.0
17.	Othmar M v Blumencron	Z 418	129.0
18.	Enrico Passoni	I 722	134.0
19.	Conrad Simpson	IR 11	141.0
20.	Atilla Szilvàssy	M 211	145.7

38. European Championship 1993

L'Estartit, Spain, June 3-12
35 entries from 20 countries

For the first time, the event was combined with the Junior European Championship, the juniors started 10 minutes after the Seniors. Stig Westergaard was the convincing winner in his new Devoti boat with a carbon fibre mast. After scoring 2,4,3,1,1,2 he did not have to sail the last race. Confusion reigned in the first race when the RC signalled a change in course direction. The top seven went to the wrong finish line while Björn and Stig Westergaard in 8th and 9th sailed to the correct finish line to take 1st and 2nd. Heiner, Presti, Devoti and van der Ploeg filed for average points. In what became known as Heiner's comedy hour, he put the mark boat's compass bearing board 60 m away outside the protest room. He then put his car with the headlights on behind it and convinced the Jury that the glare of the sun was why he hadn't been able to see the new bearing. He won the protest and the four were awarded average points!

39. European Championship 1994

Çesme, Turkey, July 5-13
34 entries from 17 countries

The '94 Europeans took place in the wonderfully warm and sunny waters of Ilica Bay, Çesme. With a NW breeze varying from 6 to 30 knots, a beautiful race course only 15 minutes outside the marina and no one else in the bay except turtles, dolphins and flying fish, this was the perfect location. And everyone loved it. The 1992 Olympic Champion was still looking to win his first Gold Cup or Europeans. He started well, had his worst race in race 5 with an 8th, then won the 6th and had the luxury of not having to sail the last race. Luca Devoti kept his cool like never before, won 3 races and came 2nd.

Final Results 1994

1.	José Maria van der Ploeg	ESP	16.0
2.	Luca Devoti	ITA	23.0
3.	Fredrik Lööf	SWE	30.0
4.	Hans Spitzauer	AUT	33.0
5.	Roy Heiner	NED	37.0
6.	Mauro Fioretto	ITA	39.0
7.	Philippe Presti	FRA	42.0
8.	Xavier Rohart	FRA	44.0
9.	Michael Maier	CZE	44.0
10.	Dirk Löwe	GER	59.0
11.	Arif Gürdenli	TUR	61.0
12.	Karlo Kuret	CRO	72.0
13.	Dominik Zycki	POL	72.0
14.	Mateusz Kusznierewicz	POL	78.0
15.	Haluk Babacan	TUR	80.0
16.	Peter Theurer	SUI	81.0
17.	Sebastien Godefroid	BEL	81.0
18.	Philippe Rogge	BEL	84.0
19.	Michael Fellmann	GER	88.0
20.	Jali Makila	FIN	100.0

Final Results 1993

1.	Stig Westergaard	DEN 155	19.7
2.	José Maria van de Ploeg	ESP 105	34.1
3.	Hans Spitzauer	AUT 1	57.6
4.	Björn Westergaard	DEN 165	63.7
5.	Luca Devoti	ITA 789	64.1
6.	Philippe Presti	FRA 762	64.8
7.	Fredrik Lööf	SWE 7	65.7
8.	Roy Heiner	NED 638	68.9
9.	Gerd Griegel	GER 71	95.7
10.	Carl Akerson	SWE 700	101.7
11.	Xavier Rohart	FRA 778	106.0
12.	Ville Aalto-Setala	FIN 2	106.0
13.	Malte Philipp	GER 25	108.0
14.	Sebastien Godefroid	BEL 7	110.0
15.	Dirk Löwe	GER 14	119.0
16.	Emanuele Vaccari	ITA 727	127.0
17.	John Driscoll	IRL 1	130.0
18.	James Lyne	GBR 503	131.0
19.	Michael Fellmann	GER 79	133.0
20.	Igor Tkachuk	UKR 105	134.0

40. European Championship 1995

Lake Balaton, Hungary, September 10-16
75 entries from 27 countries

The expected weather on Lake Balaton was light winds and big shifts. After a good start to the regatta the wind disappeared, two days were lost and only three races were sailed in the first four days. Then the wind came and two two-race days were sailed. The racing turned into a three-horse-race. Defending champion José Maria van der Ploeg started well with two second places, scored a 17th in the third race then built up a commanding points lead with a 2-7-1 to go into the final race with 13.5 points ahead of Philippe Presti with 19.75 and Fredrik Lööf with 26.75 points. In the last race Lööf needed to win, which he did, but van der Ploeg had done enough to retain his title with an 11th and Presti had slipped to third overall after finishing 20th which he had to count after an earlier 45th.

Final Results 1995

1.	José Maria v d Ploeg	ESP 105	24.75
2.	Fredrik Lööf	SWE 7	27.50
3.	Philippe Presti	FRA 762	39.75
4.	Hans Spitzauer	AUT 1	54.00
5.	Lasse Hjortnäs	DEN 143	57.00
6.	Xavier Rohart	FRA 778	65.75
7.	Richard Stenhouse	GBR 540	67.00
8.	Karlo Kuret	CRO 110	71.00
9.	Philippe Rogge	BEL 2	74.00

10.	Michael Fellmann	GER 79	84.75
11.	Sebastien Godefroid	BEL 7	85.00
12.	Oleg Khoperski	RUS 21	87.00
13.	Michael Maier	CZE 304	91.00
14.	Oth.r M v Blumencron	SUI 441	91.00
15.	Emilios Papathanasiou	GRE 6	92.00
16.	Yuri Tokovoi	UKR 21	94.00
17.	Hank Lammens	CAN 19	98.00
18.	Farkas Litkey	HUN 55	99.00
19.	Emanuele Vaccari	ITA 727	101.00
20.	Mich. Papadopoulos	GRE 11	105.75
21.	Mateusz Kusznierewicz	POL 17	108.00
22.	Igor Tkachuk	UKR 1	110.00
23.	Dirk Löwe	GER 14	121.00
24.	John Driscoll	IRL 1	122.00
25.	Roman Teply	CZE 3	143.00
26.	Michael Hruby	CZE 479	149.00
27.	Gerd Griegel	GER 71	152.00
28.	Wiebe Schippers	NED 696	153.00
29.	Peter Theurer	SUI 440	154.00
30.	Vasco Batista	POR 80	168.00

41. European Championship 1996

Hospitalet, Spain, June 7-15
36 entries from 18 countries

The Senior and Junior fleets were combined for the 1996 Championships. Some of the top sailors had already gone to train in Savannah prior to the Olympics but defending champion José Maria van der Ploeg and current World Champion Philippe Presti both decided to start. The races were sailed in light to medium winds coming from the open sea. Van der Ploeg showed his Olympic form again: he never finished worse than third and defended his title in style. He had good speed and let the others make the mistakes in the shifty winds. Runner-up and top Junior Mateusz would go on to win Gold in the Savannah Olympics later that summer.

Final Results 1996

1.	José Maria van der Ploeg	ESP	8.50
2.	Mateusz Kusznierewicz	POL	20.00
3.	Sebastien Godefroid	BEL	26.00
4.	Yuri Tokovoi	UKR	32.00
5.	Michael Maier	CZE	34.75
6.	Emilios Papathanasiou	GRE	36.75
7.	Ian Ainslie	RSA	37.75
8.	Emanuele Vaccari	ITA	39.75
9.	Philippe Presti	FRA	43.00
10.	Michael Fellmann	GER	46.00
11.	Philippe Rogge	BEL	47.00
12.	Michal Hruby	CZE	54.00
13.	Paul McKenzie	AUS	62.00
14.	Xavier Rohart	FRA	64.00
15.	Balazs Hadju	HUN	69.00
16.	Andreas Buchert	GER	77.00
17.	Manolis Marselos	GRE	77.00
18.	Vasco Batista	POR	83.00
19.	Jan Willem Kok	NED	84.00
20.	Pascal Rambeau	FRA	93.00

42. European Championship 1997

Split, Croatia, June 6-14
55 entries from 22 countries

Light winds dominated the week's racing in the picturesque Adriatic port of Split. Again the event was combined with the Juniors which boosted the numbers. The first race featured the 1978 European Champion, Minski Fabris, winning in his home town. People jumped in the water, fireworks were let off and the whole race committee was ecstatic. Hans Spitzauer was the early leader, being the only sailor to maintain a run of top 10 places. Then a second-half charge by Luca Devoti saw him win race 4 and take the lead into going race 7. Xavier Rohart won race 6 to move up to second. On the last day, the fleet waited all day for the wind to come... but it didn't come and so Luca became the new European Champion, one of the most experienced sailors in the fleet.

Final Results 1997

1.	Luca Devoti	ITA 1	19
2.	Xavier Rohart	FRA 778	25
3.	Emilios Papathanasiou	GRE 6	30
4.	Sebastien Godefroid	BEL 7	30
5.	Karlo Kuret	CRO 11	38
6.	Mateusz Kusznierewicz	POL 17	38
7.	Hans Spitzauer	AUT 1	39
8.	Richard Stenhouse	GBR 550	43
9.	Yuri Tokovoi	UKR 21	45
10.	Michael Maier	CZE 304	48
11.	Igor Tkachuk	UKR 1	63
12.	Rafael Trujillo Villar	ESP 100	63
13.	Bartul Misura	CRO 118	64
14.	Paul McKenzie	AUS 208	69
15.	Walter Riosa	ITA 55	71
16.	Nenad Viali	CRO 14	75
17.	Michal Hruby	CZE 479	79
18.	John Driscoll	IRL 1	81
19.	Michael Fellmann	GER 79	83
20.	Minski Fabris	CRO 1	85

43. European Championship 1998

Vilamoura, Portugal, June 5-13
77 entries from 25 countries

The sunny and very hot venue of Vilamoura attracted the largest entry ever seen at a Finn European Championship, which was again combined with the Junior fleet. Sebastien Godefroid who had won all the major regattas so far in 1998, added the European Championship to his list after the last race was cancelled and without winning a single race. Runner-up Michael Maier also did not win a race, but third placed Iain Percy in only his second season in the Finn won two races, but also had two bad races. Fourth placed Xavier Rohart also managed to win two races but again had some high scores to count. The British team triumphed in the final race with Jamie Lea leading a 1, 2, 3, 4 for the UK.

Final Results 1998

1.	Sebastien Godefroid	BEL 7	33
2.	Michael Maier	CZE 304	35
3.	Iain Percy	GBR 54	41
4.	Xavier Rohart	FRA 778	48
5.	Mateusz Kusznierewicz	POL 17	50
6.	Paul McKenzie	AUS 222	56
7.	Andreas Buchert	GER 6	56
8.	Fredrik Lööf	SWE 7	59
9.	Dominik Zycki	POL 4	67
10.	Rob McMillan	GBR 5	68
11.	Emilios Papathanasiou	GRE 6	68.4
12.	Jamie Lea	GBR 564	71
13.	Martijn van Muyden	NED 701	72
14.	Ian Ainslie	RSA 1	76
15.	Luca Devoti	ITA 1	77
16.	Richard Stenhouse	GBR 550	79
17.	Karlo Kuret	CRO 11	98
18.	John Driscoll	IRL 1	98
19.	Michal Hruby	CZE 479	99
20.	Javier Aguado	ESP 105	100
21.	Nenad Viali	ITA 14	100
22.	Colin Chapman	IRL 10	120
23.	Yuri Tokovoi	UKR 21	121
24.	Walter Riosa	ITA 55	121
25.	Ian Baker	NZL 242	123
26.	Rafael Trujillo	ESP 100	125
27.	Lasse Hjortnäs	DEN 143	131

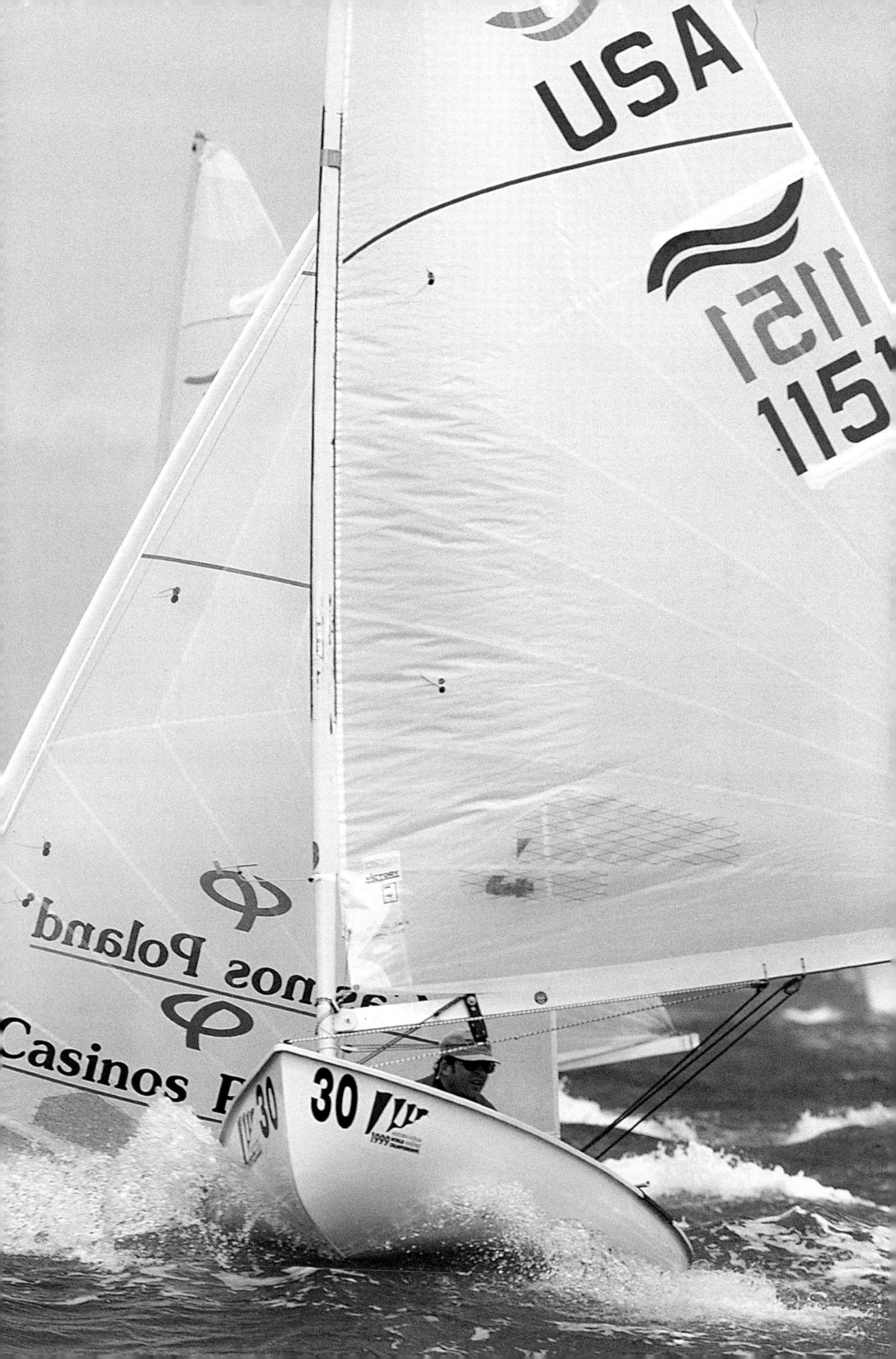
USA
1151
Casinos Poland
30
1999

29. Technical Trends

by Peter Mohilla and Robert Deaves

Based on an article by Peter Mohilla, from FINNFARE Fall 1984

The original design of the Finn featured a carvel construction in wood. The intention of Rickard Sarby was to create a boat which a skilful man could build completely by himself at home. Alternatively the sailor might have bought a wooden hull and fitted it himself according to his personal ideas. The technical development of the Finn is characterised by a steady change of three main factors: hull, mast and sail in regard with structural strength and flexibility.

The Finns in the fifties had wooden hulls in carvel, wooden masts and cotton sails. The hulls were generally leaky, the masts had a tendency to be too stiff or to break (frequently they did both), and the sails would shrink or stretch beyond measurement.

Soon the German boat builder Mader pioneered with moulded plywood hulls. These boats did not leak and were fast in flat water because of their stiffness. By the same token this proved to be a disadvantage in heavy waves. In the UK, Fairey Marine produced hot-moulded hulls for home completion.

In the early sixties a fast combination for light wind was a stiff mast with a Fritz sail, unusable in medium winds and disastrous in strong winds. If you misjudged the weather forecast you'd be better off abandoning the racing in those days. In response Paul Elvström developed triangular masts and sails with flexible leaches but no cunningham yet. You had to have a mechanism in order to control the halyard from the cockpit.

Before goosenecks were introduced, the boom was held in a slot through the mast and controlled by a wedge. Adjustment was only possible in theory on the beat. In the sixties these wedges were gradually replaced by a series of diagonal arrangements between the mast at deck height and the boom.

Sails and Masts

Cotton sails were used exclusively during the early years of the class until after the IFA authorised the use of dacron for sails in 1959, cotton sails soon faded away and dacron became the dominant cloth. In 1967, Sitka spruce from Canada was considered the best material for the mast, but was rare and very expensive in Europe. Many homemade masts were evident, some painted blue or white, but numerically superior were the stock masts from Elvström, Lanaverre, Newport, Collar etc. Many different types of sails were used: Elvström, Benrowitz, Raudaschl, North,

Wooden Raudaschl hulls dominated Finn events in the late sixties

The Wesco Finn from the USA

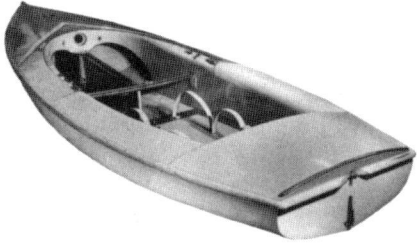

The Pearson Finn from the UK

The Mader Finn from Germany

Jongkind. Although the Elvström sails dominated numerically, the Raudaschls were considered the best looking sails.

Emergence of GRP Finns

In 1961 the IFA decided to allow reinforced polyester in the construction of hulls. The early plastic boats proved to be too soft locally and at the same time too heavy. If they had built in tanks they also turned out to be too stiff in total against torsion. Examples were the Elvström and HVM boats. The HVM Finn was moulded from the successful wooden hull of Andre Nelis (the V in HVM stands for Vliegers who later started building Finns of their own.)

In contrast Hubert Raudaschl built moulded wooden hulls. They were stiff locally but some had just the right flexibility overall in order to sag in the aft section on the reaches and runs, where they proved to be extremely fast. The best example was Willy Kuhweide's G 711. The disadvantage of these boats was that they collected a lot of water sailing in heavy air and it was difficult to sail them dry after capsizing. Attempts to build side tanks in these Raudaschl hulls proved to completely ruin their performance; the overall torsional flexibility, and thus their life, was lost. Also Raudaschl's attempts to build GRP and later sandwich hulls with the shape of his wooden boats proved to be unsuccessful. Only

Lanaverre succeeded in this direction with GRP. The secret is to produce hulls, which are stiff locally, especially in the central and lower portion, but light in the ends and especially in the deck, and flexible against torsion overall. This can only be achieved with very high technology and experience. The percentage of glassfibre material must be as high, the percentage of resin as low as possible. Only very experienced builders are able to achieve this. Less experienced builders, let alone amateurs, tended to produce heavy boats which were too flexible locally but too stiff overall against torsion.

Early Seventies

In the early seventies the most successful combination was a flexible wooden hull from Raudaschl, a mast made by Bruder of Brazil and a sail from Raudaschl. The Bruder masts had a very flexible top sideways which opened the leach of the sail in the gusts. By that time the halyards had a lock at the mast top and the sail a cunningham. This allowed the sailor to adjust his sail for a wide variety of wind

Wooden masts went out of fashion in the early seventies

forces. The best masts were the most flexible ones. Inevitably once you got into a very heavy gust or capsized they broke and you had to phone for a new one.

After Elvström retired from active Finn sailing, his sails and then his hulls carried on winning

Above: The HVM Finn developed by Andre Nelis

Below: The Elvström GRP Finn

The Roga Finn

not for the masts. Of importance for the technical development of the Finn were the 1972 Olympics in Kiel. The organisers prime aim was to provide boats as uniform as possible. Wooden hulls and wooden masts at this time, though still more successful than GRP hulls and aluminium spars, would not have been as uniform as the newer materials. In order to give equal chances to all competitors, it was decided to use GRP hulls made by Mader and aluminium spars made by Needlespar. North provided the sails.

Thus the 1972 Olympics were the basis of what the Finn class used widely for the next 20 years. The masts made by Needlespar turned out to be all equal - all equally too stiff. In the following years David Hunt turned out his M mast, which was better than the Olympia masts but still too stiff sideways. Later came the Delta, a triangular design. Both disappeared from the scene. Successful only was the Needlespar M. From the engineering point of view the Needlespar masts were crude and mediaeval. Four, later three tubes were glued together with an internal tube at the joints and should not have been a match for the ingenious aluminium masts by Bruder and Raudaschl made from one piece. But theory is not always the same as practice. In reality it proved to be prohibitively difficult to produce an aluminium spar with the changing cross section desired in one piece of uniform structure. The different cylindrical and conical parts of a Needlespar mast could be produced in the desired length and quality, carefully selected and finally joined to make a successful unity.

Later, Needlespar produced many models of the 3M mast. Each mast was distinguished by

Above: Centreboard controls, with struts to support case
Left: Typical control line system on a Vanguard
Below: Lever type kicker arrangement

internationally. He had developed his own sails whilst he sailed Finns competitively, and after that he set up in business to produce sails and hulls which dominated the Finn scene during most of the sixties and early seventies.

A popular and successful hull in the late sixties was the American Newport hull. In 1969 the Newport was used to win the Gold Cup,

Europeans, North Americans and much more with sailors such as Jörg Bruder, Arne Akerson and Thomas Lundquist using these boats to good effect.

Metal Masts
The IFA had allowed the use of aluminium for spars in 1969. In the beginning, the stiff aluminium was used only for the booms, but

its tip colours. The general guidelines were red top for stiff masts, blue tops for soft masts and black tops for average bends. There were many more colours however. The way to find a mast in the right 'ball park' was to measure the height of the first join in the mast. The higher this join, the stiffer the mast was. Good masts were between 3750 and 3780 mm measured from the heel to the join.

New Rules

After the introduction of the Lamboley pendulum test to control the distribution of weight with the hull, construction methods could be freed up and double bottoms were allowed. The first builder to take advantage of this was Peter Taylor in England. His wooden hulls had been fairly successful so far, but his GRP double-bottomed boats were used very successfully, notably at the 1976 Gold Cup where they finished 1st, 2nd and 4th. Early Vanguards were built with floorboards. Later you could buy a kit to install your own double bottom into your Vanguard Finn. Many of the older Vanguards were converted, whilst the later ones had them built in at the workshop.

Finn Development in America

In the early sixties, Fred Miller had developed the Wesco Finn for which he claimed outstanding performance. Originally there was the Newport GRP hull. Teel produced a very stiff durable hull of the highest quality. The Harken brothers took over the know-how of Teel and built and constantly improved their Vanguard boats. In 1976 they provided the know-how for the Abbott Finns of the Olympics in Kingston, and in 1980 for the Soviet builder of the Finns used in Tallinn. In 1984 and in 1992 they provided themselves the boats for the Olympics in Long Beach and Barcelona. Because of this constant input the technology of Vanguard was the highest at that time. This investment must yield a proper return and therefore the Vanguards were also the most expensive boats.

Development

The tendency was clearly towards a boat with a double bottom, which sails as dry as possible. The German Mader and Rein boats were good examples. Here an experiment of the then president of the German Finn Association Peter Kern, has to be mentioned. He got permission from the Technical Committee of

Above and Below: GRP Taylor from the UK, with full length double-bottom

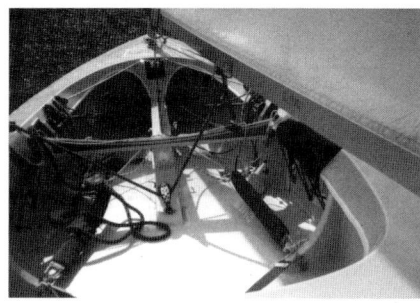

the IFA to build and race an experimental Finn with a double bottom above the waterline, thus with a self bailing cockpit. The boat contravened the rule about the height of the floorboards. The cockpit was connected with the transom and all water coming over or remaining in the boat after capsizing drained readily out without bailers. The real difficulty was tacking and mainly gybing because of the reduced height between the floor and the boom. Thus Kern gave up on that idea.

A second trend is to have no water in the bow section after a capsize. This is one of the weakest points in the Vanguard concept. In theory there is never any water in the Vanguard boats either even after turtling her over, but in reality this happens, especially in huge waves. Once you have water in the bow, you could never get her empty without outside help.

Technically the best solution was provided by the Vlieger Finn. It has a narrow slot of about 20 cm width leading from the cockpit to tile mast step which houses all the control lines. Thus the Vlieger Finn has a huge volume perfectly sealed in the front section. The problem with the Vlieger Finn is that Mark Neeleman, who promoted that boat for a while,

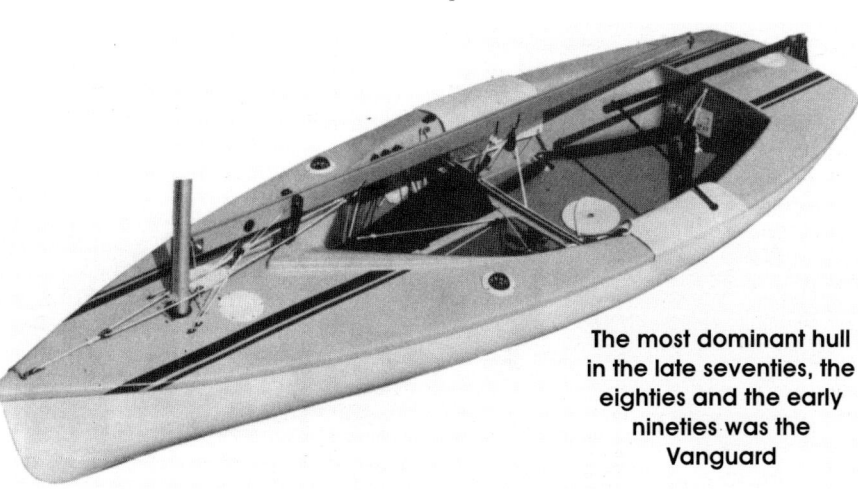

The most dominant hull in the late seventies, the eighties and the early nineties was the Vanguard

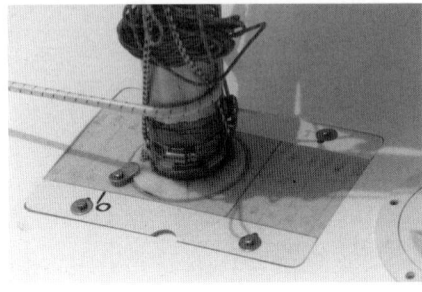

Above: An early Pata Finn
Below: Pata's solution to the adjustable mast gate

switched back to his collection of soft Lanaverres in order to qualify for the 1984 Olympics and then sailed a Vanguard in order to get accustomed to that boat. Could it be that the Vliegers were too stiff because of their construction?

Some Vanguard sailors sealed off the bow section of their boats completely and ran their control lines on deck. The mast may have a rubber collar. This provides a very dry and light bow under all circumstances. Alternatively some sailors fitted a non-return flap at the front of the centreboard case to stop water flowing forwards, but allowing it aft.

Soft Decks?
Considering the success of Lasse Hjortnäs, Wolfgang Gerz and Mark Neeleman in the mid 1980s, it is to be wondered whether one of the secrets of the winning boats might be a soft wornout deck and a good stiff old hull. Perhaps you have to sail a boat 3000 hours in heavy wind, before the deck is worn out to such a degree, that it provides the desired overall flexibility. It is known, that these three sailors used rather stiff masts in their rather flexible boats.

For the Olympics they had to adjust to stiff boats, since the Olympic Vanguards had tanks and double bottoms. In 1983 at the Gold Cup in Milwaukee there was a lot of talk and complaints, that the then new stiffer Vanguards were not as fast as the old softer ones with

The Lemieux Finn

conventional floor boards. Hjortnäs had his old boat flown over the ocean and Jörgen Lindhardtsen switched back to an old type, after testing the new type in Long Beach.

Carbon Masts
The trend to change the construction of the mast was initiated in the mid eighties. After various times of interest and disinterest, the go-ahead was finally given in 1992 and 1993 saw the first prototypes being used in serious competition. Within a very short while, they had outmoded the existing aluminium spars. Carbon masts were superior for several reasons. Firstly they could be built at a lower weight, removing both weight out of the bow and aloft. They have a faster rate of recovery characteristics which can allow carbon masts to point higher and have more power. Lastly, they enable the sailor to tailor a mast to suit his own weight and sailing style. Often, with metal masts, a sailor had to buy up 6-8 masts just to find one that was good for him. With carbon, the mast can be adjusted at much less cost to the sailor.

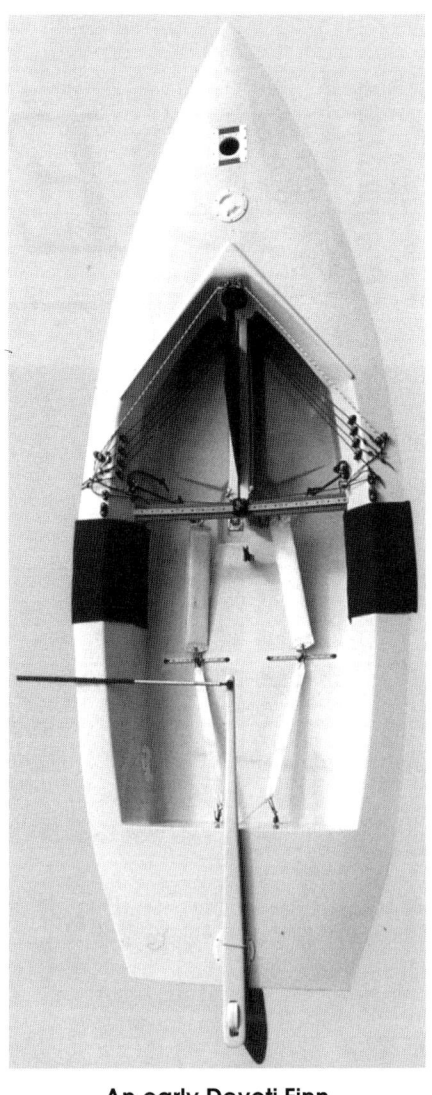

An early Devoti Finn

For the first few years when they had to carry extra weight to bring them up to the minimum weight of the existing aluminium masts. Carbon booms were discussed, but never implemented. Early on in the carbon mast

development phase, many sailors would top their original metal mast with a carbon top section. This gave the mast a large percentage of the characteristics of a totally carbon mast, but they never really flourished, probably because with a totally carbon mast a much more even bend could be manufactured - the joins in metal masts always provided hard spots along the mast.

Modern Hulls
As opposed to some points in the class history, there is not the wide choice of builder available to the Finn sailor at the present time to that which was available in the sixties and seventies, but certainly more than were available during the eighties with the Vanguard domination. This may be because certain builders gained a monopoly on fast Finns and swamped the market with their boats, thus limiting development of construction and shape by other builders.

The Vanguard monopoly was effectively broken in 1993, when for the first time in many years there were four different boat builders in the top five at the Gold Cup. Philippe Presti sailed the then new Devoti Finn to its first Gold Cup win, Hans Spitzauer sailed the Pata Finn into 5th place whilst Richard Clarke sailed the new Lemieux Finn into 3rd. Since the introduction of these hulls, Vanguards are hardly ever seen at the front of an International fleet.

Plastic Sails
At the start of 1998, plastic sails started to gain rapid acceptance in Finns. It soon became apparent that these sails, made from a variety of materials (such as Kevlar, Mylar, monofilm, polyester), were superior to the standard Dacron sails which had been around for 29 years. The hard sails allowed far more power to be held by the sailor, so masts became slightly stiffer again.

Finns Then and Now
Above: Paul Elvström in the 1950s
Below: José Maria van der Ploeg in 1996

The Future
What else might be the trend in the future of Finn development? One of the interests of IFA is to keep the price of the Finn lower, The best instrument to achieve this is to encourage competition, by allowing experiments with new materials, combinations, or designs. From 1952 up until 1996, the Finns at the Olympic Games were supplied by the organisers (as were rigs until 1972). Will the fact that competitors can now bring all their own equipment to the Olympics (including the hull) change the development process of the Finn?

Left: Devoti Finn under construction
Below: Completed Boat

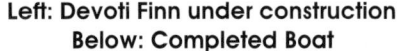

30. Downwind Finn Sailing

by Robert Deaves and Peter Mohilla

While most races are won and lost on the upwind legs of the course, it has to be said that distance lost (or gained) offwind is much harder to regain upwind. Downwind speed is mainly dependent on good concentration and balance in light airs but is much more dependent on strength, technique and coordination in strong winds. Sailing a Finn offwind in a strong breeze can be a rewarding experience. The exhilaration of the acceleration and power, slicing through the water with spray flying over your head is something that has to be experienced first hand in order to be fully appreciated.

Balance and Steering

When sailing the Finn upwind in a breeze, vigorous steering is often needed to get the best performance. When sailing offwind, the opposite is usually the case, the rudder acting as a brake every time it is used. You should aim to use the rudder as little as possible, because every time you use it you will be slowing down the boat. Instead, steer by balancing the boat and by continuous trimming of the mainsheet. When there is a good breeze the boat should be kept level, but when there is very little it should be heeled to windward on a run and to leeward on a reach.

Heeling the boat helps you with steering the boat. The boat can be made to change course, gybe and tack faster just by using a combination of boat heel and sheet tension. Obviously the rudder is going to have to be used at some point but when you do use it, use it gently and smoothly so as to maintain boat speed. One final point is to make sure that your rudder system has no play in it at all. All joints should be tight fitting so that the boat responds immediately the helm is moved and not a few seconds afterwards.

Laminar Flow on a Run

What you should try to achieve on the run is as much of a steady laminar flow along the sail as possible, from the boom to the leach and from the mast to the leach upward. A laminar flow from across the boom upward is only possible in very light air and flat water, because it requires a rather unstable position of the hull. A second possibility is a laminar flow from the leach to the mast, which is possible and advantageous in medium wind, especially if you sail slightly by the lee. Whenever you want a laminar flow downwind, have your kicker fairly loose. In both cases lift up your centreboard completely, in order to reduce the wetted surface. Downwind the

centreboard is only a disadvantage from the point of view of maximum speed, and only necessary from the safety point of view in order not to capsize.

In stronger wind you do not want to have a laminar flow. Therefore have your kicker tight. If your kicker is tight, the boat will have less tendency to death roll to windward.

Sheeting

As soon as you are sailing free such that the boom is a few feet out from the gunwhale the sail can be sheeted directly from the boom using the last purchase of the mainsheet. This gives a much better feel on the sail. You can feel the puffs and lulls as they arrive and can respond to a change in direction much more quickly. Also, pumping is far more effective. As the wind increases you may have difficulty holding onto the single sheet unless you are strong enough. There are various ways that the sail can be sheeted - other than through the floor block with three purchases or directly from the boom.

1. Cleat the sheet in the sidedeck cleat or let the sheet run through the bottom block until it reaches the stopper knot (the latter is not practical on a close reach). Pick up the purchase from the traveller to the block on the boom and then sheet from the block on the boom. You will then be sheeting with one block in the system. The only problem with this method is when you have to change back to a normal sheeting method and the breeze has picked up. You then have to hold the purchase direct from the boom for a moment while you pick up the loose end and take up the slack. This can be problematical if you are sailing tight to the wind.

2. Alternatively, take the sheet from the other side of the floor block and then sheet straight from the block on the boom. You will then be sheeting with two blocks in the system.

When sailing in medium to strong winds, sheeting from the boom through less purchases gives an advantage when the sail is pumped because the pump will be sharper and therefore more effective in accelerating the boat. You will also have more 'range' through which the sail can be pumped. However this can take great strength and stamina and needs a strong arm and a good technique to be able to execute it effectively.

Light Winds

Below force 1 there is little danger of capsizing, so even the beginner can risk sailing fully for speed. One of the major objectives for going fast in light airs is to reduce the wetted surface area of the hull. All areas in contact with the water cause friction and hence induce drag on the hull. When on a run sit well forward, sometimes even in front of the traveller so as to bring the wide transom area out of the water. At the same time heel the boat to windward. This reduces the overall area of hull surface which is immersed in water. This extreme technique is only used in very light winds. As soon as the wind increases, body weight will have to be brought aft again so that the rudder has enough grip on the water to be effective in steering the boat. Body motion in the boat should be kept to a minimum as every movement will shake what little wind there is from the sail. A steady flow of air over the sail is important at all times. When on a beam reach or tighter, the boat should again be

trimmed bow down, but it should also be heeled to leeward so that the sail takes up its natural shape.

The centreboard should be fully retracted when on a run, and only slightly down when on a reach. As a general rule only put enough down to keep the boat moving in a straight line. If too little is down, the boat will tend to skid sideways. The centreboard still causes frictional drag so use as little as possible. Another important device is a strong JC strap to hold the boom out. Without one, the boat cannot be heeled to windward on a run or broad reach without the boom falling back to the centreline.

In light airs the sail needs to be flat with an open leech. Little or no kicker tension is ever required. A tight kicker would give a hooked leech and would kill boatspeed and cause the sail to fold in on itself, making it very difficult to fill and produce drive. Ease the inhaul to produce depth in the foot of the sail and continually adjust the sheet.

Increasing the Safety Margin

If the wind and the waves are building up, the helm position at the thwart without any centreboard is too dangerous. You have to make up your mind how to increase the safety margin. This can be done in different ways. You can sit further aft, you may lower the centreboard, you may tighten the kicker, you can avoid capsizing by holding the sail on one part only or on two parts of sheet instead of three, if you feel strong enough to do so, and pull before you capsize to weather. It is a question of your skill and strength, the wind

force, the wave characteristics and their direction. Generally it boils down to a compromise between speed and safety. Lowering the centreboard gives better steering control and reduces the tendency for rocking, but increases the wetted surface drag. Pulling the kicker flattens the sail and reduces the danger of a death roll to weather, but reduces also the possibility for a laminar flow behind the sail. Sitting further aft reduces the danger of cutting under a wave and increases stability, but also increases the danger of whirls at the transom.

Medium Winds

As the wind increases when on a run, more kicker tension is required to keep the leech behind the mast. If the leech is allowed to go in front of the mast, a twisting force is set up which can roll the boat into windward. However if the rolling can be controlled, this technique, combined with sailing slightly by the lee, can be fast. You must have twist in the sail to make sailing by the lee effective. To induce twist in the sail ease the kicker so that the leech moves out or forward. To reduce twist in the sail, tension the kicker to move the leech in or back. When sailing by the lee the wind flow along the sail reverses and flows from the leech towards the mast.

In the increased wind move your weight further aft to gain rudder control and to bring the bow out of the water (essential when it is windy enough to start planing). The sail may need to be flattened slightly when reaching otherwise the boat might prove hard to control. Play the gusts and the waves. Continually adjust the mainsheet. Ease it until the sail just luffs then haul in until the telltales stream, then ease until the sail just luffs and then do it again and again.

Experts

The experts sail with as little centreboard as possible, hardly use the tiller, but keep balance by holding one part of the sheet. If the boat heels to weather they pull, if it heels to leeward they slacken. Thus they imitate the boat with the sail. In addition they try to stay on the face of a wave in order to sail as long as possible down the wave and as little as possible up the wave.

It needs a lot of physical strength and practice to do this, but it is fast as long as you do not capsize. One of the difficulties is to terminate that technique, either at the leeward mark, in case you have to gybe, or worst in case the gust gets too strong. In this case try to grab the loose sheet with your tiller hand and pull in the loose parts of the sheet until you achieve a three rope purchase again. But sometimes a two rope purchase is the better than a single purchase if you are not strong enough.

Sail Shape on a Reach

On a reach the fundamental requirement is an even angle of entry of the wind at the luff. Set up the fullness of the sail to match the wind conditions and then adjust the kicker such that all of the luff tell tales are flowing together - that they all lift together at the same time. If the wind eases, there will be less force on the leech and consequently it will start to hook and the sail will stall. Ease the kicker to open up the leech a bit until the tell-tales are streaming together again. If the wind increases, the extra pressure in the sail will cause the leech to open up more (giving the sail more twist). As a result the luff will not be aligned. Tension the kicker to bring the sail back into line, closing the leech and straightening the luff. Whereas too loose a kicker can be seen by the fluttering luff, too tight a kicker can be seen by the leech tell-tales looking lifeless and not streaming. It can thus be seen that on a offwind leg, the kicker needs to be adjusted almost as much as the mainsheet in order to maintain optimum sail shape.

Playing the Gusts

Special considerations apply, if the wind is changing direction and strength on the run. If you know from the last beat of frequent shifts, apply the following techniques. You have to distinguish clearly between light wind without and strong wind with the possibility of planing. In light wind you bear off in the relative gusts, in order to stay as long as possible in the ribbons of stronger wind and luff in the lulls. Either go straight down with the wind, applying the principles of running with no or very little centreboard, or go on a proper low reach with proper centreboard and a laminar flow in your sail. Which of the two alternatives you choose when, depends on the other competitors. Look back over your shoulder and try to have clean air. As long as the wind does not change

direction, it does not pay on the Finn to gybe downwind.

On the Run

In a steady medium wind it is fast to have a reversed steady flow along the sail from the leach to the mast, by totally slackening the cunningham, the outhaul and the inhaul, loosening the kicker and pulling in the sheet a little bit. The actual danger of an involuntary gybe is by far not as bad as the beginner always assumes.

In medium to strong wind a good indication of a fast down wind run is the amount of pressure on the tiller. The less pressure you have, the fewer and more gentle movements you do with the rudder, the better. Control your balance with the sheet instead - as described by imitating the boat. If it heels away slacken, it it heels towards you pull tight. Whenever possible have the cunningham, the inhaul and the outhaul slackened on the run and the kicker fairly loose, but reset these controls on the last meters of the run and not on the first meters of the beat.

Waves

As the wind increases there will no doubt be waves around and the helm that can use them well can make big gains over those helms that cannot. Basically the technique consists of watching for a wave to come, steering (by trimming, balance and perhaps a little rudder) to catch the wave, surfing down the wave, loosing it and then picking up another. Always head for the troughs, and you will always be heading downhill. If you head for the crests you will always be heading uphill, which is slow. When on a wave, steer down for the lowest point that you can see so that you are always moving down a wave. If it is very windy you may find yourself ploughing into

will be way above the deck and your head, and there will be little power left in it. Also beware of too tight a kicker on reach. A gust catching you unaware can heel the boat just enough to dip the boom end in the water and flip you in. Try to keep the boat dead level or heeled slightly to windward and ease the kicker slightly if you find the boom starting to skim the water. Waves just make the matter worse of course.

In very windy conditions, centreboard position is very much personal choice. As a rough guideline, a 'safe' point to have it is when the top upper most corner is just going into the case. More than this is usually unnecessary and less than this may make the boat hard to control in the waves and gusts, but will most likely be faster if you are in control of the boat.

Downwind Speed

When sailing upwind, the boat that reaches the windward mark first is normally the boat that has taken the best route up the beat as dictated by wind shifts, tide etc - in short, by taking the shortest route possible. Offwind, the speed of the boat has more importance than distance sailed. Always steer for clear water and clean wind. Disturbed water and wind can completely destroy downwind performance, so a route should be steered clear of all other boats and obstructions. You may find yourself taking a very roundabout route to the leeward mark but if you can maintain full speed all the way while others are only travelling at 50% speed you will obviously get there quicker. Always try to sail fast as possible, by powering up the sail, by sailing by the lee, easing kicker and reversing flow, raising the centreboard and reducing wetted surface area and by watching the gusts and playing the waves.

the wave in front. Head up or bear away and pick up the next wave just before you hit the wave in front. Hitting waves not only slows you down considerably, but you also run the risk of a broach. If the wind is not quite strong enough for you to keep up with the wave, you will eventually find the wave overtaking you, the crest moving underneath the boat. Pump hard to maintain position on the wave for as long as possible, steering for the lowest point of water around you, so that you are always moving fast. When you eventually fall off the the wave head up a little and look for the next one on which a catch a ride, and then bear away again once on it, pumping hard to initiate surfing. However try to stay on the same wave for as long as possible, as this is faster than a continual sequence of catching and losing waves.

Strong Winds

In stronger winds when you can plane in the gusts you can get your boat planing on a low reach but not on a run. In this case you point higher in the gusts and bear off in the lulls, exactly the opposite of what you would do in light winds, when you cannot plane even on a reach in a relative gust. Have frequent careful looks over your shoulder. If you see the water getting darker, lower your centreboard and get ready to hike out harder. Once the gust hits, luff suddenly, hike out very hard, pull in the sheet and bear of again carefully once you hit the downward face of a wave.

In very strong winds you again apply a similar techniques as in very light wind. Bear off in the gusts straight down wind, because then the apparent wind is not so strong and you have more of a chance of surviving. Point higher in the weaker periods when you have more of a chance to manage the sudden changes of laminar and turbulent flow, when

the danger of capsizing to leeward and windward is about even. On the low reaches you should sail with a fairly tight kicker as well, while the dead runs you negotiate best with full centreboard and tight kicker.

Sailing a Finn offwind in strong winds requires strong arms and quick reflexes. Your primary task is to stop the bow burying into waves because not only will this slow you down somewhat it also runs the great risk of causing a capsize. So sit well back in the boat to bring the bow up. Play the sheet constantly either from the boom or more probably direct from the floor block. The gusts need to be played on the reach and the run. On a reach bear off to stay with the area of stronger wind for longer; come up in the lulls to find the incoming gusts. When on a run it may pay to come up slightly to promote planing in the gusts and bear off in the lulls.

When gybing use minimum kicker and a flat sail to survive. With no kicker on, the boom

31. Gybing the Finn

by Robert Deaves

Gybing the Finn is one of those manoeuvres that requires much practice but is easy to improve with practice. However it is essential to 'visualise' what you are trying to achieve during the gybe - where you should be in the boat and what you should be doing at all times into the gybe, during the gybe and out of the gybe. How you go into the gybe and how you come out of the gybe is probably more important than actually doing the gybe as this is where the mistakes are more frequently made. There are many techniques for gybing the Finn. Pick one that you can get along with and perform confidently in all conditions.

Boat Set-up

A number of aspects apply to all methods of gybing. The idea is to perform the gybe without losing any boat speed, doing it smoothly and with the minimum of fuss. To allow adequate space underneath the boom the kicker should be slackened a touch. In strong winds this is essential, as is sheeting in the boom slightly so that the leech does not extend forward of the mast. If it does then the resulting force will try to roll the boat into windward. A tighter kicker (and hence a tighter leech) will

give you more acceleration out of the gybe, but has the disadvantage of a lower boom. A looser kicker will provide a safer gybe but with less speed out the other side because of the loss of power in the now open leech. With

the centreboard, a compromise has to be reached between having too much down so that the boat may trip over itself and having so little showing that the boat skids sideways, possibly rolling you in in the process if you are not quick enough to respond on the helm. The experts generally tend to have the centreboard all the way up in all conditions. In general, to be safe, set its position such that the corner on the aft face of the board is just showing out of the case. This gives an extension of about ten inches below the hull. The mainsheet system should be free flowing and must not catch on any fittings or jam up in its own blocks.

When to Gybe

There is only really one moment to gybe, if you have the luxury of time. Gybe when the boat is going fastest down the biggest wave that you can find. This will ensure that there is hardly any pressure on the sail and it will be easier to haul over. Also when the boom extends out to the new leeward side there will be very little force on it (providing you are still moving down the wave that is), and the boat will therefore be much easier to control while you sort out your position in the boat. On the larger waves you may find that the boom is reluctant to actually take up position and the sail flaps along the centreline. This

3. Move your forward foot over, swivel your body and then sit on the sidedeck. Drop the tiller extension (or sit on it), change hands on sheet and pick up the tiller extension again. (In light airs the change can be made while standing up after the gybe.) Finally, tension the kicker again, let the sheet out and adjust your course.

The main advantage of this method is that you can see the boom coming and can time your movements and actions much more precisely.

Not Facing the Boom
This method is very different from that just described. First of all you change hands on the sheet and the tiller extension before the gybe is commenced. This means that as you come out of the gybe you are ready to start sailing properly immediately and have little sorting out to do. As a result your speed out of the gybe can be faster. Kicker and sheet adjustments are the same as above.

1. Holding the sheet straight from the boom, bring your tiller hand across to grab it and then turn your back to the boom and pick up the tiller extension from behind your back. Keep the tiller extension pointing at the current windward side.

2. Bear away into the gybe and then pull the sheet hard and duck down so that the boom passes over your head and across the boat.

3. Flip the tiller extension to the new windward side as soon as the boom has passed overhead. Then move backwards onto the new sidedeck, sit down and assume the correct course.

As soon as the boom has passed overhead you have effectively completed the manoeuvre. All you then have to do is sit down and carry on sailing. This gybe has often been dubbed 'the experts gybe' in that it can look cleaner and done properly can produce a better result. However it is much more difficult to get right and can cause problems in windy weather because the boat has to be kept dead level throughout, while you are facing the wrong way and unable to sit on the sidedeck. It is also much easier to make a mistake and harder to recover from one because your hands are effectively crossed.

In training always visualise the technique you are going to practice - practice in your mind before you do it on the water. However you end up gybing though, one thing cannot be disputed: practice makes perfect!

happens because you are moving faster down the wave than the wind is blowing. Watch out for when you slow down and make sure the boom is hovering on the side of the boat that you want it to end up on.

Steering
Steering is a very important part of the gybe. In strong winds how you steer into and out of the gybe can determine how successful it is - i.e. if you capsize or not. You must steer positively (and occasionally aggressively in strong winds) through the gybe. Don't hesitate or back out - this will invariably cause a capsize in windy weather or a significant loss of speed in light airs. Sometimes it can pay to steer a 's' shape into and out of the gybe when on a run. Bear away hard into the gybe, swing round through the gybe and bear away again to resume your original course.

Ways to Gybe
There are two principle ways to gybe a Finn. In one method you are facing the boom as it passes through the wind, and in the other method you have your back to the boom. The method you choose to gybe can be changed depending on the situation you are in, although it is far better to stick to one method and excel at that. However you may have to change technique occasionally, for example in extreme windy weather or when crash gybing to avoid another boat or an obstruction.

Gybing Facing the Boom
If you are sheeting through the block on the floor (and not direct from the boom) then when gybing grab hold of at least one, if not all, of the mainsheet purchases to pull the boom over. Don't try to gybe by giving the sheet a sharp tug through the floor block (except in survival conditions). Because of the length of the boom it can take a long time to react to your pull and come across too slowly- taking it straight from the boom produces a more positive action which is more reliable. In lighter winds, when gybing from a reach to a reach, the boat can be rolled to windward going into the gybe, thus making the boom fall down. Once the boom has passed through the wind, roll the boat the other way, to the new windward side. As the wind increases you will need to keep the boat flat at all times. Only try to pull the boom across the boat once you have steered round so that the wind is blowing onto your lee quarter. The technique is therefore:

1. Sheet in, ease the kicker and point the tiller extension towards the new windward (old leeward) side. Then bear away until the wind is off the lee quarter. Hold the sheet directly from the boom, give it a positive tug, and pull it as far across the boat as your reach permits

2. As soon as the boom passes overhead move your aft foot across the boat, with your body facing forwards. The tiller extension is now being held behind your back. Steer the opposite way out of the gybe to the way the boat is trying to go - you will then follow a straight course. If the boat is trying to spin into the wind (more usual), then you must bear away hard to counteract it

32. Plastic Fantastic - a new chapter in sail development

by Mickey Ickert

The Finn Dinghy has been at the fore front of development and new technology from its earliest days and always kept pace with new yachting technology. The sails are an example of how a class 50 years old can be stringed in one-design rules although be avante-garde in development. The rule for specific sailcloth has been relaxed since 1981 in the hay days of 3.8 oz soft Dacron Finn specs. The early '80s showed some new fabrics appearing and the class didn't see a threat in allowing any fabric into the rule as the specific needs for the Finn did not see any of those fabrics making a big change in performance. At the time I myself worked at North Sails in Germany and we built a Finn sail out of the early kevlar scrims. The sail was dismissed very early on and it seemed to prove the point that you have to use a soft sleazy fabric to build Finn sails. I remember using the discarded sail on a training run and it was so bad the Finn didn't

sail up wind at all and I had to reach back and forwards to get home like a wind surfer. . .the new type fabrics were dead for the next 14 years or so.

During the 1994-95 America's Cup, Craig Monk approached me and asked us if we would be interested in building him a Finn sail. As the 1992 Olympic Bronze Medalist he was interested in working with a team of people which proved to be able to design the fastest America's Cup sails. The initial reaction from our side was pretty subdued. We believed there was not much point in building a Dacron sail as there were plenty of sailmakers which did a good job at the time, all using sails which had somehow been derived from the early '70s John Bertrand (the Australian) design. Those sails and the design concept were very refined and had been developed over the last 20 years or more. However, we looked at the Finn dinghy rule regarding sails again to see how much scope there was to do something different. And to my surprise 15 years later the fabric for the sails was still open and unused.

What Cloth to Use ?

We decided to build a sail for Craig using a Mylar scrim of some sort, but what is the right fabric? Over the years through our involvement in various America's Cups, Whitbread campaigns and other level rated events we had come across all sorts of fabrics which have been used for reaching gennakers in particular. Looking through the files and the cloth stock we came across a very promising fabric we with a bit of history. . .

During the 1993-94 Whitbread the US entry Winston used a gennaker fabric based on .75 mil Mylar with a Vectran wrap and fill yarn. The fabric first appeared on the 1992 Stars and Stripes AC yacht. The Whitbread 60 rule at the time was not accommodating any aramid fibres for the gennaker and the sailmaker and the yacht argued that Vectran is a form of Polyester. The ruling from the Whitbread measurers allowed the fabric in and then banned it unexpected for the second leg. As the first leg was being sailed we ordered plenty of the fabric to use throughout the race. Bang, we owned a lot of a very specified fabric, very light compared to 3.8 oz soft Dacron and up to 5 times stronger with the same bias to warp ratio as a 3.8 oz soft Dacron. In 1995 the fabric seemed perfect and was used for Craig Monk's first Mylar Finn sail. The same sail was used by one of the competitors in the 1999 sail Auckland regatta.

The Race Began

The early results with two boat testing between Craig Monk and Joe Spooner showed surprisingly early that the sail was right on the pace in some conditions. Extensive testing showed a huge potential and Craig won the New Zealand nationals the same year. At the same time more and more Finn sailors used Carbon wing masts which certainly moved the development even further. The finished sail weight was half of that of a Dacron sail.

Rubber Boats and very close N.Z Trials

Leading up to the New Zealand trials things got a bit heated as Craig's very different sail was very obvious. But due to the fact that we had an exclusive contract with Craig Monk we were unable to pass any of the information or fabric on to others. However, the first run of sails trying to look similar to the first Mylar appeared and the radial Mylar sails became more and more a figure here in N.Z. Craig was trying to guard it as best as he could. However the pressure increased and more and more and rubber boats started following him around taking photographs. The whole sailing situation and rumours sounded more like an America's Cup campaign than a Finn sailor preparing for the N.Z trials. The tension and expectations led to an absolute thriller in which Craig Monk won the trials in N.Z using a Vectran sail beating Dean Barker in the last race to qualify for the Olympics in 1996.

During all this time one of our biggest concerns was that Craig had to race against a fleet of soft Dacron sails which sit very nicely in the lighter breeze without too much adjustment and obviously were being used with the knowledge of the previous 20 plus years.

Masts are Still Important

Leading up to the Atlanta Olympics Craig had a very good result at the Hilton Head regatta. At times he sailed through the fleet with good speed and he was looking forward to the Games. With one week to go his wing masts started breaking and in the period of two or 3 days he was down to his last mast. Craig than decided to use a round mast and a Dacron sail for the Games using what every other competitor would use. The frustration with the mast program made it a very difficult regatta for him. The Finn fleet must have thought this was the end of the Mylar sails and the point seemed to be proven once more that you need to build soft sails to win regattas.

The design and fabric got put away for the next 18 months with only a few people using the sails overseas and a very skeptical Finn fraternity. However, some of the younger Kiwi sailors used some of Craig's old sails with some success and later in 1997 the bubble was finally about to burst.

Both Sebastien Godefroid and Mateusz Kusznierewicz ordered a sail in December '97 and combined, won all the events leading up to the middle of 1998. Sebastien won the European Championships with a Vectran sail very similar to Craig Monk's last sail and most Finn sailors took notice from then on. The ball got rolling and the worlds in Athens saw mainly Mylar sails. The class completely changed from the 1997 Gold Cup to the 1998 Gold Cup.

Today there are more and more sail makers picking up the radial Mylar sail in different versions and trying new fabric and panel layouts based on the original 1995 sail. Looking through a fleet of Finn Dinghies today, the boats look a lot more modern and most people enjoy the new sails.

Micket Ickert works as a Sail Designer for North Sails New Zealand and Team New Zealand.

50 Years of Finn Sail Development
Top: Cotton sails at the 1952 Olympics
Middle: A typical Dacron sail
Lower: An early plastic sail in 1997

33. Campaign Management

by Gus Miller   Adapted from the Talk Notes for a Lecture Gus Miller gave in New Zealand in 1994

If you do an Olympic campaign, make certain that you make a commitment to excellence and then this will carry you through. Win or lose it will be one of the greatest things you have done in your life. Enjoy the competition and the people you meet. These are things you will remember for a long time. Success will come though from hard work, effort, discipline and joy. Don't leave any stone unturned.

Also, it is important to have other goals that continue past the Olympics. Otherwise you can burn out. Sport is an end in itself, not the means to satisfy any individual or group vanity. Any trace of jealousy or animosity has no place. In the long run, whoever turns out to be the victor or the vanquished makes little difference. What is remembered is the participation and the effort to do your best along the way. Character and not complaints in the face of adversity are what is important.

John Wooden never preached winning, what he sought was effort which is something a little less tangible. "Cervantes said it is better to travel hopefully than to arrive. I always, from the beginning, enjoyed planning my practices and conducting my practices more than I did the games. My definition of success is peace of mind. That can be obtained only in self satisfaction."

One of the wonderful things about sailboat racing is that most racing fleets have a range of levels in them and the randomness of the wind allows those at the rear of the fleet an occasional chance to be up front. For many, it is a joy just to be part of the race, playing with the wind. For others, as the exploration of excellence in sailing works to higher levels of competition, eventually the question comes, "How does a sailor achieve the possibility of a high finish in a World Championship Regatta or an Olympic Regatta?" Part of the answer to this question is that old saw, "Proper prior preparation prevents poor performance".

This chapter will examine some important preparation areas that include: Boat Handling, Boat Preparation and Technology, Boat Speed, Physical Fitness, Psychological Fitness, Racing Savvy, Strategy, Tactics and Training Techniques. The elusive other part is indicated by remembering that the best prepared, the smartest, the strongest, the most talented and the fastest are not inherently the winners.

The intangible is 99% mental at the highest level. The winner at this level will have a consistent, centred focus of concentration and this chapter will also examine the challenges of that kind of concentration.

Proper Prior Preparation
Hard work usually beats talent. Make a commitment and strive for excellence; keep a professional approach and identify and work on your weaknesses.

Some of sailing is luck, but in the end it is the foundation of fundamentals that counts. It is not just what is right, but what is wrong in your repertoire: finding out what you don't do well and eliminating the weakness. It is easy to train to your strengths, but they will take care of themselves. Most find their weak points uncomfortable, unenjoyable and because they are difficult and ego deflating, they shirk them in training. If you don't overcome this and practise weak areas, then in tough competition and when under pressure you'll come apart and self destruct. Every great Finn sailor has had a period where he lived in the cockpit of his Finn. It has to fit like a shoe. After strapping on your hiking pants, you strap on the boat.

Get Organised - Have a Plan
Sailboat racing is a complex game. It makes a difference if you take the time to write goals down.

These might be:
• Major - central - wish Goals
• Objective - task Goals
• Implementation - action Goals

Arrange milestones to reevaluate your goals to check on your progress at various stages. Keep a diary or a log. This is the only reliable way to keep track of all the details. At milestones or before major regattas, review the record and evaluate your diary and look for patterns and then work on your weaknesses.

Whenever you pick the brains of some smart sailor, write it down because he probably said some things you won't understand for six months or more. The act of writing will make you reflect and develop a deeper understanding of the game.

Boat Preparation and Technology

Details, details, details and more tiny details. Have the finest gear that you can possible get. Every part of the boat is optimal, so make sure it is tested and proven. Does your racing machine really measure in or is it just another good looking dinghy? There is no excuse for breakdowns. Make boat preparation check lists - all the big and the little things. Don't commit to or favour one sailmaker but respect their wishes. Thorough testing in tuning and combat - rational, unemotional testing. Consider: centreboard fairness and alignment, rudder cord, length & depth legal? Make sure the rudder isn't cocked and that the fittings are tight and fluid. Is the tiller length right for your arm and body size? Put calibration marks on all sail controls: outhaul, cunningham and inhaul etc. so you can accurately evaluate sail setting positions and record and reproduce fast settings.

Boat Handling

Drills, drills and more drills. These should be rigorously rehearsed and consistently done.

Things like:
• Little Piggy in the Middle,
• Pandora's Box
• Tacking & Gybing Drills
• Two buoy tacking and gybing chase drill
• Ten minute crusher drill - who can work the hardest all out the longest. (Your goal is to win on every exchange: gybes, tacks, mark roundings.)
• Starting technique
• Rabbit Starts
• Acceleration starts

• Stalling, slowing and manoeuvring around other boats.
• 720°s beating & running
• Righting from a capsize quickly. (José Doreste was capsized by a huge breaking wave in 25 knots of wind on the last reach of the last race in the 1988 Olympic Regatta, but still won the Gold.)

Boat Speed

Learn about sail and rig trim and what to do to coax speed out of the boat, especially in wave and wind transitions. The boat set-up transitions between different winds should be automatic. Also learn the differences in the boat set-up for different tactical situations and steer to that setup. Remember that most boat speed comes from training sessions with a better partner.

Concentrate on
• Steering
• footing speed and pointing speed
• Waves offwind, Waves pointing
• Kinetics and pumping technique

Physical Fitness

Sports science has made a five component contribution to boat speed and mental stamina. This requires daily preparation, especially in the run-up to competitions.

The Five components are:
Cardiovascular endurance - be aerobic, anaerobic and alactic specific. Rowing, running, bicycling, swimming, climbing, skiing, games.
Flexibility and stretching - movement and injury prevention.
Muscle - Strength, power, endurance and balance.
Resistance training - Variables are: Exercise choice, order of exercise, load or resistance used, rest period between sessions and sets, number of sets.
Nutrition - Fluid/electrolyte replacement drink, etc.

Make sure that you also get proper rest - "If a lot is good, even more is better" can be bad.

Psychological Fitness

This includes joyfulness and having fun in racing, courage, goal setting, training evaluation and diary keeping, relaxation training to deal with stress, anxiety, fear, doubt, emotional roller coasters, motivation, peaking, self image, visualisation and mental rehearsal or practice. This also requires daily preparation - molecular restructuring of the mind takes time. Stress and pressure can have a detrimental effect on performance. Use centred Relaxation Techniques such as progressive relaxation, relaxation on cue, relaxation anywhere, letting go of thoughts relaxation.

Reduce stress - learn to manage your life style. "It's not the situation that's causing your stress, buddy; it's your thoughts, and you can change that right here and now." Be confident and think positive thoughts rather than being self defeating with negative thoughts.

Joseph Brodsky in his December, 1988 University of Michigan commencement address said: "No matter how abominable your condition may be, try not to blame anything or anyone: history, the state, superiors, race, parents, the phase of the moon, childhood toilet training, etc Be precise with your language, be kind to parents and do not set too much store by politicians."

The most successful of all sailors from the Former Soviet Union was Viktor Potapov. He won a Bronze Medal in 1972 at Kiel in a Finn, was fourth in 1976 in a 470, was Gold Medalist and World Champion in 1980 in a Tornado. He was also the best Flying Dutchman and Star sailor in the Former Soviet Union. He was thrown off the National team because he only trained hard enough to be the best Soviet.

He was more interested in a Ph.D. in psychology than in the Soviet style of continuous training. It is indicative that this greatest of all Soviet racing sailors wrote his Ph.D. thesis on the psychology of competing at the top for world championships and Olympic medals.

In a word - What some want to think: "No pressure I can go just for fun.", "Try not to lose your head.", "Your anxiety is your opponent.", "Be able to rely on your instincts, conscious thinking is too slow.", "Be confident and attack.", "Don't lose composure.", "Don't have to hang your head.", "Timing is everything."

José Maria Van der Ploeg said, "Thinking with a clear head was the key to my consistency and a Gold Medal."

Training Techniques
Practice, Practice, Practice. Practice like you race: well planned and intense. Quality, not quantity is important. Use training partners. In the end, they want you to know as much as them; having a superb training partner or small group that you can be open, honest and candid with is critical. Being willing to talk pays off when others think of things you didn't or their questions open up new ideas. Training partners should also try to 'kill' each other in practice.

Also use coaches. In the end, they want you to know more (than they do). They are usually excellent observers and should be cultivated. Eventually you have to make their ideas your own. However ups and downs will occur with a disciplined, rational, unemotional training outlook.

Training sessions with a partner(s) should have an agreed focus and goals. A coach can help by giving these. At the end of each practice, it is important to evaluate what you have done and achieved. A training and racing diary is very helpful but it takes effort to keep your log entries up-to-date.

It is important to have periodization in your training. It is very difficult to maintain the highest level of preparation and competitive intensity over a long period of time. You have to point toward some future period, about a month long, where you will be at your best and on the path to that period you have to train

to your weak points. Get out of your boat and watch it in gory detail working against other boats. Experiment with different sailing styles. Be radical, sometimes do counter intuitive things.

Racing Savvy and Overseas Racing
Have a vision of the entire race from start to finish and where the critical points are. Make sure that you have had lots of recent time around the buoys so that your moves are intuitive, automatic and you never out think yourself. Don't experiment and stray from what makes you successful in a major competition.

Develop competitive maturity. Going overseas can be disorienting, so understand that and be ready, and learn to overcome problems. Plan 50% of your time exploring distractions away from the boat, then concentrate totally and hard on the racing. Don't let anything get in the way of racing hard and with full commitment.

Consider
• Regatta strategy and goals. Race game plan.
• Weather - is it accurate?
• Currents and local conditions.
• Consistency and high percentage moves.
• Overall race and regatta plan based on large scale understanding of the wind, course and one's competitors.

Tactics
Consider
• Small scale playing off the immediate wind, waves, competitor's positions and mark locations.
• Starts and everything associated with them.
• Mark roundings.
• Controlling other competitors.
• Get a good start with clear air so you are inside the first shift.

Rules, Respect and Sportsmanship
• What game are you playing?
• Tactical considerations.
• Eat, drink, relax and sleep rather than argue all night, if possible.
• Paul Elvström's focus: let them go because I'll destroy them on the next leg.
• Protests and the 50:50 rule - Get witnesses.

Budgets, Funding, and Logistics
Make a detailed budget with cash flow needs. Logistics includes vehicles, housing, parts, stocks, tools, clothes, insurance, credit cards, passports, tickets, especially timing, etc. When you need some money - 'Look 'em in the eye and ask for their help'. Politics is an intriguing game on its own but it is a distraction; whining doesn't help. When the pressure is on - remember mental training, eliminate distractions, keep centred.

Public Relations and Sponsorship
No one ever does it alone so make it fun for your supporters. Have a press release w/day phone number - for reporters, supporters and sponsors. Produce a self promotion brochure: describe the boat, your results, your campaign, contribution mechanisms. Describe what a potential sponsor gains from involvement with you: Local, National and International Exposure, Image Enhancement, Advertisement availability and cost: Hull, sail, boom, clothes. Have a contractual agreement and arrangement. Have a mailing list to keep everyone abreast of your successes, trials and the experience. Even produce a newsletter to make others feel a part of it. Keep a file of newspaper clippings, obtain photos (get a pro but keep the rights and include his credit line), or take a reporter sailing.

Thank yous - Most important! Give back. Maybe a quarter of what you get.

Finally...
Enjoy it yourself, enjoy others and never give up.

34. History of the Junior European Championships

by Peter Mohilla and Robert Deaves   Reprinted from FINNLOG

The idea of a Junior Championship was born at the 1966 IFA AGM. The Council was discussing the problem that eastern European countries were willing to pay IFA Fees, able to collect funds in local currencies, but unable or hampered to transfer these funds to the IFA account in a capitalist bank. Hungary proposed to use up the credit already accumulated for the organisation of IFA regattas and added that substantial financial support can be expected from the corresponding state organisations, if such regattas are earmarked as 'Junior Events' limited to competitors up to the age of 21 years. So the 1966 AGM decided to create the 'Junior European Championship' and delegated the organisation of the first event to Hungary as an experiment. As far as the main intention was concerned - to transfer funds from one economic system to another circumventing the official difficulties - the idea did not work out. However as a sporting and social event these Junior European Championships turned out to be very successful and therefore the tradition was kept up.

1. Junior European Championship 1967
Balatonfüred, Hungary, July 23-29
24 entries from 10 countries

Unfortunately there was hardly any wind for the whole week of the regatta. The competitors spent more time waiting for wind on the water and swimming than actual sailing. Nevertheless 7 races were completed.

Final results:

1.	Serge Maury	F 496	38.4
2.	Andreas von Eicken	G 567	40.4
3.	G. Chabaud	F 440	46.0
4.	Andreas Haan	M 64	56.4
5.	B. Posposil	CZ 12	59.7
6.	Mikael Brandt	S 545	63.7
7.	T. Izsak	M 40	74.7
8.	G. Hoffmann	DDR 7	82.0

2. Junior European Championship 1968
Maubisson, France, July 26-August 1
21 entries from 9 countries

The defender Serge Maury was now too old to compete again. So he, with the help of his father and brother organised the second Junior European Championship on a lake near Bordeaux. The Maurys have been producing barrels for the famous Bordeaux wine for centuries. Medium winds favoured the light helmsmen.

Final results:

1.	Fritz Geis	G 656	36.7
2.	Luciano Lievi	I 410	41.0
3.	Andreas van Eicken	G 567	44.7
4.	Mauro Pelaschier	I 388	51.4
5.	Blazy Wyskowski	PZ 179	52.0
6.	Jamiz Knasiecki	PZ 335	52.7
7.	Pieter Keyser	H 321	66.0
8.	Martin Mitterer	G 116	73.4
9.	Jacques Manifre	F 425	81.7
10.	Walter Bachmann	Z 12	83.1

3. Junior European Championship 1969
Lake Garda, Campione, Italy
July 27-August 2, 27 entries from 14 countries

There was a standard pattern. A morning race in medium north winds faded away in a dying breeze, and an afternoon race in a fresh southerly turned into a procession along the cliff. At the end the Swede Liljegren tied with the Pole Skarbinski in points but took the title by his two firsts.

Final results:

1.	Guy Liljegren	S 554	26.7
2.	Ryszard Skarbinski	PZ 28	26.7
3.	Luciano Lievi	I 417	27.4
4.	Claudio Biekarck	BL 9	29.7
5.	Pieter Keyzer	H 404	48.0
6.	Mauro Pelaschier	I 433	48.7
7.	Fritz Geis	G 1030	65.1
8.	Walter Bachmann	Z 12	70.0
9.	Lennart Gustafsson	S 558	75.7
10.	Bock	G 505	77.0
11.	Blazy Wyskowski.	PZ 179	78.0
12.	Saija	I 426	81.7
13.	B. Horák	CZ 14	86.0
14.	Fages	F 594	91.7
15.	W. Kolb	G 604	94.0

4. Junior European Championship 1970
Lake Orava, CSSR, August 2-8
31 entries from 11 countries

In 1970 the event was organised in the CSSR and well attended. However it suffered from poor wind conditions and only 4 races were scored.

Final results:

1.	Luciano Lievi	I 417	18.7
2.	Petr Chlebek	CZ 225	48.0
3.	Leo Lolic	Y 10	48.7
4.	Bo Rogberg	S 442	51.0
5.	Reinhard Bauer	DDR 1	54.0
6.	Ryszard Skarbinski	PZ 404	55.7
7.	Gilles Cuccurullo	F 650	56.7
8.	Alex Balakirev	SR 36	59.0
9.	Ernst Seidl	OE 12	59.0
10.	Bogdan Walusz	PZ 391	59.7
11.	Jean J.Grandchamp	F 587	62.0
12.	Jevgenij Belousov	SR 1	65.0
13.	Björn Stenberg	S 549	66.7
14.	Axel Kördt	G 867	72.0
15.	Ath. Papaioannou	GR 113	73.0

5. Junior European Championship 1971
Athens Greece, August 6-13
27 entries from 18 countries

The win of the Greek Boudouris was clouded by a protest from the French, that he was sailing without the lead he had in his boat during measurement. The jury did not hasten to check the boat up until the next evening when his downwind speed had decreased considerably and the lead was found in place.

Final results:

1.	Anastas Boudouris	GR 144	29.0
2.	Jean Grandchamp	F 641	46.7
3.	Jevgenij Belousov	SR 4	47.4
4.	Claudio Biekarck	BL 10	47.4
5.	Chris Law	K 321	48.0
6.	Gerd Hübner	G 1096	54.0
7.	D. Sarikavazis	GR 150	54.4
8.	Jacques Busquet	F 496	55.7
9.	Romould Knasiecki	PZ 321	61.7
10.	Ath Papaioannou	GR 147	65.7
11.	Ryszard Blaszka	PZ 174	67.4
12.	W. Kolb	G 1094	70.0
13.	A. Cherdnichenko	SR 1	71.0
14.	Luciano Lievi	I 417	84.0
15.	Danny Thompson	US 169	89.0

6. Junior European Championship 1972
Neusiedl, Austria, July 9-15
36 entries from 16 countries

In the practice race with hardly any wind at all a storm warning caused the race committee to abandon sailing. The dashing young heros grumbled at the funky race committee. But after six races with never less than 5 Beaufort they changed their attitude towards sailing on Lake Neusiedl. The 36 competitors together had about 150 capsizes and broke 50 masts. In 1972 none of the Juniors had an aluminium spar.

Final results:

1.	Ryszard Blaszka	PZ 56	8.7
2.	Claudio Biekarck	BL 10	9.0
3.	Romould Knasiecki	PZ 13	34.1
4.	Jacques Busquet	F 496	36.4
5.	Sanford Riley	KC 143	53.7
6.	Paul Phelan Jr.	KC 104	55.7
7.	Bela Bankuthy	M S	58.7
8.	Anastas Boudouris	GR 144	63.0
9.	Demetrios Sarikavazis	GR 163	82.7
11.	Guy Grossmith	KA 28	85.0
12.	Levent Özgen	TK 61	90.0
13.	Borislav Loukota	CZ 11	91.0
14.	Theodor Georgiadis	GR 120	91.7
15.	Gille Didier	F 9	92.0
16.	Kajetan Glinkiewicz	PZ 595	92.0
17.	Miroslav Kouril	CZ 111	100.0
18.	Gabor Regoczy	M 41	112.0
19.	Jan Zetzeija	H 453	117.0
20.	Wolfgang Kolb	G 1094	122.0

7. Junior European Championship 1973
Wladislawowo, Poland, August 12-18
42 entries from 16 countries

In 1973 the Polish organised the European Juniors right after the Seniors. 13 boats with 7 identical helmsmen participated in both events. Winds in the Juniors were not so strong. Twenty year old Moscow sailor Vitali Zaroslav scored 1/2/3/4/5 in that order in the light weather races and took the championship. However his victory seemed shaky when, after the 5th race, the DDR sailors and the race committee protested him for pumping. However after consultation with their coach the sailors withdrew their protest.

Final results:

1.	Vitali Zaroslav	SR 8	50.7
2.	Chris Law	K 1	57.0
3.	Ath Papaioannou	GR 165	59.4
4.	Alex Welter	BL S	62.7
5.	Detlef Schreiber	DDR 6	78.0
6.	Patrice Charee	F 675	89.0
7.	Manfred Kaufmann	BL 7	92.0
8.	Jochen Schümann	DDR 9	94.4
9.	Craig Thomas	US 934	96.7
10.	Jacques Busquet	F 496	98.7
11.	Robert Holbrook	K 351	100.0
12.	Tzvetain Pentchev	BU 11	103.7
13.	Bob Smith	US 886	126.0
14.	Miroslav Kouril	CZ 435	128.4
15.	Janusz Frackowiak	PZ 216	128.7
16.	Alex Norkine	SR 1	132.0
17.	Jozsef Hillier	M 1	144.0
18.	George Costas	GR 156	145.0
19.	Bernt Jonsson	S 581	146.0
20.	Romould Knasiecki	PZ 13	158.0
21.	Jiri Kmonicek	CZ 111	160.0
22.	Guido Salvi	I 474	160.0
23.	Didier Gille	F 9	161.0
24.	Leonard Eriksson	S 473	162.0
25.	Erich Offermanns	G 1256	164.0

8. Junior European Championship 1974
Port Camargue, France, June 25-30
27 entries from 12 countries
This time the Juniors were scheduled right after the Veteran Gold Cup in the same club. Jochen Schumann scored four wins in reliable wind conditions.

Final results:

1.	Jochen Schümann	DDR	18.0
2.	Patrice Charee	F	24.7
3.	R. Güldenpfening	DDR	27.4
4.	Jacques Busquet	F	30.7
5.	Alex Welter	BL	42.7
6.	Klug	G	60.4
7.	Anastas Boudouris	GR	60.4
8	Manfred Kaufmann	BL	61.7
9.	Bieberitz	DDR	65.0
10.	José Luis Doreste	E	65.7
11.	Issakov	SR	86.0
12.	Keep	SR	89.0
13.	Hellbrügge	G	91.0
14.	D. Sarikavazis	GR	92.7
15.	Van der Veen	H	97.0

9. Junior European Championship 1975
Port Barcares, Perpignon, France
September 20-27, 16 entries from 8 countries

A great variety of difficult sailing conditions required flexibility and experience. Changes in the weather conditions, wind direction, wave pattern and current about every half an hour taught a lesson for most of the juniors about half an hour too late.

Final results:

1.	Jochen Schumann	DDR 9	21.7
2.	R. Güldenpfening	DDR 21	37.1
3.	Josef Senkyr	CZ 105	41.0
4.	Tomasz Rumszewicz	PZ 379	41.8
5.	Alex Hellbrügge	G 1513	45.7
6.	Jean-Marie Marteau	F 702	50.0
7.	Bjorn Maartenson	S 550	57.4
8.	Andrzej Smigelski	PZ 21	57.4
9.	Reyis Beringuier	F 714	63.7
10.	Joaquin Blanco	E 1	71.0

10. Junior European Championship 1976
Port Barcares, Perpignon, France, May 1-8
19 entries from 11 countries

Every day there was a reliable sea breeze in the morning from 7 to 11 a.m. However who wants to sail in the middle of the night? Therefore the races were scheduled at 11 and started at 12. The surprising variety of conditions did not at all impress the Russians. Most of the juniors behind them sailed just as well but were prevented from winning by storms, calms, shifts, currents, fogs, and most of all by the decisions of the race committee.

Final results:

1.	A. Mudrichenko	SR 19	18.7
2.	Boris Zakhorow	SR 11	29.7
3.	R. Güldenpfening	DDR 21	36.0
4.	Y. Silvestro	F 727	38.7
5.	A. Rumszewicz	PZ 379	40.7
6.	T. Yntema	H 526	47.1
7.	P. Liljeberg	S 625	55.7
8.	A. Hellbrügge	G 1513	63.4
9.	J. Fiquemont	F 710	70.7
10.	N. Peters	G 191	78.0

11. Junior European Championship 1977
Balatonfüred, Hungary, September 25-October 3, 40 entries from 16 countries

The weather was unusually cold for the time of the year and the wind rather weak. Most of the races were sailed in Force 1-2. On October 1 the fleet was towed in search of wind to the other shore to be trapped in even more of a calm. The young skippers were invited to a club there. When a good wind came up but too late for a full race, a fun race was announced. On the way home everybody would be disqualified not seen pumping at least once. Most of the boys worked so hard, that they capsized several times. On the last day the seventh race was sailed in 6-7 Beaufort. Only Spängs and Khoretski still had chances to win the title. Patrick finished as runner-up behind Pohlmann, but a third was good enough for Serge to become Champion.

Final results:

1.	Serge Khoretski	SR 23	41.7
2.	Patrick Spängs	S 66	46.7
3.	Nicolai Korichkin	SR 22	65.4
4.	Victor Soliviev	SR 11	81.4
5.	Otto Pohlmann	G 6	83.0
6.	Luc Choley	F 1	83.0
7.	Alexander Hellbrügge	G 1513	84.7
8.	Wolfgang Mayrhofer	OE 191	91.0
9.	Istvan Rujak	M 187	95.0
10.	Eckhard Drephal	DDR 10	98.7
11.	Krasimir Krastev	BU 114	100.0
12.	Klaes Mattson	S 662	105.0
13.	Graham Scott	K 437	111.7
14.	Egidio Babbi	I 487	116.7
15.	Miklos Sulyok	M 50	122.0
16.	Georg Kostas	GR 12	123.7
17.	William Masterman	K 417	126.0
18.	Jean-Jan Marteau	F 702	129.0
19.	Jörg Vetter	DDR 12	135.0
20.	Bo Carlsson	S 591	137.7

12. Junior European Championship 1978
Nessebar, Bulgaria, September 22-30
39 Entries from 16 countries

Shifty, generally weak winds, a strong current, an inflexible race committee, never correcting a crooked starting line or a sloping beat by fighting frivolously with DSQs, gnawed at the nerves of the spoiled young skippers. That regatta saw the Finn debut of Lasse Hjortnäs, who twice had flashes of genius but two DSQ as well, and therefore does not show up in the upper part of the final results.

Final results:

1.	Viktor Soliviev	SR 19	42.7
2.	Alexander Avdeev	SR 2	44.0
3.	Mario Turazza	I 517	45.4
4.	Wolfgang Mayrhofer	OE 191	57.0
5.	Jose van der Ploeg	E 109	70.0
6.	Klaes Mattson	S 526	78.7
7.	Vesselin Prokopov	BU 4	83.7
8.	Egidio Babbi	I 619	90.0
9.	Martin Palsson	S 664	107.0
10.	Boncho Nikolov	BU 114	109.0

13. Junior European Championship 1979
Athens, Greece, August
41 entries from 15 countries

Generally with very strong wind conditions, however sometimes rather shifty, Frank Butzmann in the former boat of Jochen Schumann turned out to be superior, taking five times line honours.

Final Results:

1.	Frank Butzmann	DDR 19	13.0
2.	Wolfgang Mayrhofer	OE 199	51.1
3.	Luc Choley	F 729	56.7
4.	Klaes Mattsson	S 526	69.7
5.	Istvan Rujak	M 199	76.4
6.	C. Lizancos	E 9	81.4
7.	Jose Maria v. d. Ploeg	E 145	88.0
8.	Francois Le Castrec	F 741	88.0
9.	Mario Turazza	1517	94.4
10.	Patrick Spängs	S 666	102.7
11.	F. Bisztray	M 13	103.0
12.	Oleg Khoperski	SR 21	105.0
13.	R. Völker	DDR 13	106.4
14.	B. Oliviera	BL 73	120.0
15.	A. Migliaccio	I 628	122.0
16.	A. Simoneschi	I 646	126.0
17.	M. Hofmann	G 1510	147.0
18.	M. Knospe	DDR 10	148.0
19.	A. Sailer	OE 196	148.0
20.	Joaquin Blanco	E 10	151.0

16. Junior European Championship 1982
Malmö, Sweden, July 5-11
33 entries from 14 countries

As usual in Malmö the current was more of a problem than the wind. On the first three days with medium winds Andrej Nikandrov collected twice line honour and three times runner-up. Two more races with wind between force 5-8 saw Nikandrov in 11th and 6th, which was easily enough for the title.

Final results:

1.	Andrei Nikandrov	SR 14	20.7
2.	V. Gurov	SR 22	46.7
3.	Tom Jungell	L 200	48.0
4.	J. Rosengren	S 699	51.4
5.	Karsten Kaufmann	G 1706	67.4
6.	S. Pichugin	SR 30	74.7
7.	H. Webbink	H 585	79.2
8.	A. Räder	DDR 27	84.0
9.	Heike Birke	DDR 19	92.7
10.	M. Eliasson	S 666	94.0
11.	Paolo Semeraro	I 666	96.7
12.	R. Edens	H 607	104.5
13.	R. Polaczyk	PZ 7	115.0
14.	F. Favini	I 672	122.0
15.	Björn Österreich	DDR 21	122.7
16.	M. Ickert	G 1734	127.0
17.	Marco Di Natale	I 654	136.0
18.	T. Janka	G 1747	140.7
19.	M. Byrien	S 655	144.0
20.	Ruben Serra	E 106	144.7

14. Junior European Championship 1980
Vilassa de Mar, Barcelona, Spain
August 5-14, 24 entries from 9 countries

All races enjoyed fine wind between force 2 and 5. In a report it can be read, that the same problems as five years later plagued the competitors. Cars were forced open in broad daylight with money and passports stolen by the dozen, the launching facilities were scandalous but the people in the club so cordial and the racing on the water fabulous.

Final results:

1.	Francisco de Angelis	I 633	40.0
2.	Mats Nyberg	S 657	44.7
3.	Joaquin Blanco	E 10	47.4
4.	Jacek Sobkowiak	PZ 7	48.7
5.	J. Sadowski	PZ 56	57.7
6.	Klaes Mattson	S 688	59.7
7.	A. Migliaccio	I 654	62.7
8.	Francois Le Castrec	F 741	78.4

17. Junior European Championship 1983
Porto San Giorgio, Italy, July 14-20
37 entries from 15 countries

Wind were light to absent and therefore only 4 races were finally scored. At the first mark Heiko Birke (DDR) was frequently leading, however during the race the clever Dane Peter Vilby, a newcomer from the Laser, passed him and finally scored 1/4/1/1.

Final results:

1.	Peter Vilby	D 146	8.0
2.	Heiko Birke	DDR 19	26.7
3.	Andre Nikandrov	SR 35	36.7
4.	Dirk Löwe	DDR 14	47.4
5.	Ralf Rainer Lixenfeld	G 1734	49.0
6.	Lauri Rechardt	L 185	54.0
7.	Kristian Sjöberg	L 195	61.0
8.	Konstantin Gordeiko	SR 20	62.4

15. Junior European Championship 1981
Hoorn Ijsselmeer, Holland July 17-22
37 entries from 13 countries

Fine weather conditions but difficult waves characterised the regatta. After Jacek Sobkowiak was leading overall and Paolo Semeraro had some good score in the middle phases, Tinu Tootsy took line honours and the final win.

Final results:

1.	Tinu Tootsy	SR 31	43.4
2.	Jacek Sobkowiak	PZ 7	51.1
3.	Paolo Semeraro	I 666	54.0
4.	Nikolai Soukhoroukow	SR 21	55.8
5.	Andrei Nikandrov	SR 23	66.0
6.	Francois le Castrec	F 741	73.0
7.	De Angelis	I 655	75.0
8.	Ron van Manen	H 616	79.0
9.	Rauder	DDR 10	82.0
10.	Kristian Sjöberg	L 198	93.0
11.	Roberto Benamati	I 658	94.7
12.	Gerd Golatowski	DDR 11	95.4

9.	Jörgen Rosengren	S 699	67.0
10.	Hans Spitzauer	OE 218	73.7
11.	Marco Passoni	I 689	77.0
12.	Paolo Semeraro	I 655	81.7
13.	Bob Edens	H 607	83.0
14.	Michael Fischer	OE 223	86.0
15.	Viali Nenad	Y 87	90.0
16.	Makjanic Mladen	Y 88	91.0
17.	Flavio Favini	I 672	94.0
18.	Stanislaw Mickiewicz	PZ 4	104.0
19.	Hendrik Heiden	G 1808	105.0
20.	Beat Stegmeier	Z 394	110.0

18. Junior European Championship 1984
Helsinki, Finland, August 22-26
34 entries from 14 countries

The first race with a force 5 caused quite a number of capsizes. The second day with light winds saw the Jury busy to record infringements of rule 60 - means of propulsion - on tape recorder. 11 boats were disqualified and the sailing techniques of these and ten more changed considerably. The rest of the regatta enjoyed constant winds of force 3-5.

Final results:
1.	Björn Österreich	DDR 21	22.7
2.	Dirk Löwe	DDR 14	49.4
3.	Henry Herrman	DDR 31	51.7
4.	Armando Ortolano	GR 211	56.0
5.	Mikhael Apukhtin	SR 4	60.7
6.	Hans Spitzauer	OE 218	60.7
7.	Vilhelm Roberts	L 201	61.0
8.	Jali Makila	L 208	71.0
9.	Peter Peet	H 555	73.0
10.	Bart Zielhuis	H 544	79.7
11.	Benedetto Allotta	I 9	80.7
12.	D. Orlov	SR 1	81.7
13.	L. Lachi	I 712	95.0
14.	M. Skibski	PZ 52	102.7
15.	K. Manthos	GR 194	109.0
16.	T.Vadnai	M 156	110.0
17.	H. Aronsson	S 679	114.0
18.	M.Pentti	L 195	118.0
19.	Aare Taveter	SR 8	120.0
20.	Nick Jako	KC 22	120.0

19. Junior European Championship 1985
Vilassa de Mar, Spain, August 5-11
30 entries from 11 countries

The launching facilities were as bad or as spectacular - depending whether you were a participant or an onlooker - as five years before. In the first race the windward mark and the gybe mark drifted and so the race had to be abandoned despite wonderful sailing conditions. For the rest of the week the wind was medium, racing great and the mood high.

Final results:
1.	Yuri Tokovoi	SR 32	21.7
2.	Dirk Löwe	DDR 14	25.7
3.	Peter Peet	H 630	30.7
4.	Armando Ortolano	GR 211	34.7
5.	Mikhael Apukhtin	SR 4	41.4
6.	Hans Spitzauer	OE 218	48.7
7.	Eric Mergenthaler	MX 33	55.7
8.	Eman. Vaccari	I 69	65.7
9.	Michael Luschan	OE 211	72.7
10.	Vit. Bergamaschi	I 710	73.4
11.	Ruben Serra	E 106	77.0
12.	Kons. Manthos	GR 21	84.0
13.	Henry Herrmann	DDR 3	90.0
14.	Elmer Henrik	D 148	97.0
15.	Ola Sonesson	S 705	100.0

20. Junior European Championship 1986
Balatonfüred, Hungary, July 19-21
43 entries from 16 countries

The event was characterised by shifting winds and thunderstorms, typical of Lake Balaton. Armando Ortolano won the first two races. W-B Lixenfeld won the third and Hans Spitzauer the fourth. After Peter Aldag won the fifth, any of six boats could have won overall going into the last race. It looked lost for Spitzauer after two successive sixths in previous years, as he rounded the last leeward mark in 20th, but a huge cloud changed things. With nothing to lose, he split from the fleet and caught a tremendous shift in his favour and finished on a screaming reach in first place, to take the title in his last year as a junior.

Final results:
1.	Hans Spitzauer	OE 218	24.7
2.	Armando Ortolano	GR 211	32.7
3.	Michael Luschan	OE 211	47.1
4.	Peter Aldag	G 1893	51.0
5.	W-B Lixenfeld	G 1706	51.4
6.	Emanuele Vaccari	I 727	52.7
7.	A Poncell-Vich	E 12	55.0
8.	H Hermann	DDR 3	68.7
9.	Farkas Litkey	M 161	69.0
10.	Par Dahllof	S 704	74.7
11.	V Mekhanikov	SR 2	81.0
12.	H Weichert	DDR 21	84.0
13.	Attila Szilvàssy	M 200	87.0
14.	R Serra-Merckens	E 106	88.7
15.	Torsten Bahr	DDR 9	92.0
16.	S Blaszka	PZ 6	93.7
17.	Igor Bychkov	SR 35	102.0
18.	G Zapalskyi	SR 23	104.0
19.	B Falkenberg	S 684	118.0
20.	Leonardo Lachi	I 655	121.0
21.	I Tsavdaridis	GR 12	122.0
22.	Andras Tovisi	M 12	133.0
23.	Jozsef Csomai	M 158	140.0

21. Junior European Championship 1987
Çesme, Turkey, September 5-12
17 entries

The event was sailed in strong winds, normally around Force 4-5 and was dominated by the sailors from Russia and East Germany. Imre Taveter narrowly beat his fellow countryman Tammo Otasoo.

Final results:
1.	Imre Taveter	SR 31	23.4
2.	Tammo Otasoo	SR 13	27.4
3.	Ingo Khon	DDR 10	28.0
4.	Emanuele Vaccari	I 727	29.0
5.	Matthias Mier	DDR 13	32.4
6.	Farkas Litkey	M 161	40.1

22. Junior European Championship 1988
Athens, Greece, July 31-August 8
21 entries

All starts were arranged at 3 pm to correspond to the peak of the wind strength. Villalonga won the first race while Malte never caught up after restarting because of a PMS. Rohart won the second. Malte then won the next two with Villalonga winning another in race 5. Malte won the sixth and Chivikov the last, but Malte had done enough to win the regatta.

Final results:

1.	Philipp Malte	DDR	26.0
2.	Kico Villalonga	E	37.0
3.	Matthias Mier	DDR	49.4
4.	Tkachuk	SR	62.7
5.	Imre Taveter	SR	63.7
6.	Chivikov	SR	65.7
7.	Kryszcryiski	PZ	65.7
8.	J. Knuth	DDR	69.7
9.	Jure Orel	Y	80.0
10.	Xavier Rohart	F	82.7

23. Junior European Championship 1989
Club Nautico Arenal, Spain, August 5-15
15 competitors from 10 countries

J Knuth dominated the event in all conditions, scoring 1 win, 4 second places and discarding a 5th. Malte Philipp in second place also won two races and completed the DDR supremacy. Xavier Rohart in 3rd showed the advantages and disadvantages of weighing 102 kg with excellent beats in the breeze but suffering offwind.

Final results:

1.	J. Knuth	DDR 11	9.0
2.	Malte Philipp	DDR 25	27.1
3.	Xavier Rohart	F 748	38.1
4.	Xavier Garcia	E 109	40.4
5.	A Rinne	G 1912	40.7
6.	Jure Orel	Y 97	74.1
7.	John Driscoll	IR 1	80.8
8.	Yannick Adde	F 760	82.0
9.	Richard Kouveras	GR 195	85.0

24. Junior European Championship 1990
Quiberon, France,
20 entries from 12 countries

Fredrik Lööf was consistently the best sailor winning the shortened series by 13.3 points, Second placed Xavier Garcia won two races, against Lööf's one win, but lost control in the middle of the series in two windy races. Third placed Uwe Thielemann won the first race and was still leading after a 3rd in the second, but likewise picked up two bad results in the windy races. In contrast, fourth placed Michael Fellmann, scored a 1st and 4th in the windy races and higher scores in the light winds.

Final results:

1.	Fredrik Lööf	S 684	11.7
2.	Xavier Garcia	E 109	25.0
3.	Uwe Thielemann	DDR 11	36.7
4.	Michael Fellmann	G 1916	38.0
5.	Richard Kouveras	GR 195	39.4
6.	David Drappeau	F 758	45.1
7.	Andreas Buchert	DDR 6	45.7
8.	Zsombor Majthenyi	M 159	46.7
9.	Karlo Kuret	Y 53	47.7
10.	Jure Orel	Y 97	51.0
11.	Yannick Adde	F 760	55.0
12.	Ville Aalto-Setala	L 198	58.0

26. Junior European Championship 1992
Caprilo, Italy, July 3-13
27 entries from 11 countries

Sailed in generally light and very shifty conditions, the week provided very difficult sailing conditions made worse by the arrival of thunderstorms during two of the races. Sebastien Godefroid led from the second race, (which he won) on and by the last race was only threatened by Emilios Papathanasiou who had closed the gap by winning the sixth race. Sebastien won the final race as well to win the championship.

25. Junior European Championship 1991
Gdansk, Poland, August 18-25
28 entries from 11 countries

The wind ranged from Force 2-5 with excellent weather conditions. Xavier Garcia led from the start and won the first 4 races. Then a DSQ in race 5 for rocking put the pressure on. Going into the last race a 17th would have been good enough but he held out for a 5th and won by 20 points ahead of second overall Carl Akerson. Garcia was sailing José Doreste's old Roga Finn.

Final results:

1.	Xavier Garcia	E	15.7
2.	Carl Akerson	S	35.4
3.	Sebastien Godefroid	B	41.7
4.	Karlo Kuret	Y	43.7
5.	Thomas Wallis	G	63.1
6.	Zsombor Majthenyi	M	73.0
7.	Ville Aalto-Setala	L	73.7
8.	Marek Krause	PZ	88.0
9.	Diego Negri	I	92.0
10.	Andreas Buchert	G	97.7
11.	Dominik Zycki	PZ	105.7
12.	Dmitri Bakunovich	SR	107.4
13.	Andrzej Mackiewicz	PZ	114.0
14.	Stefan Wenzel	G	115.7
15.	Laszlo Gelley	M	120.0

Final results:

1.	Sebastien Godefroid	B 7	31.7
2.	Emilios Papathanasiou	GR 6	39.4
3.	Diego Negri	I 779	57.1
4.	Daniele Giuntoli	I 716	59.0
5.	Carl Akerson	S 703	61.1
6.	Torsten Faass	G 1755	66.0
7.	Wiebe Schippers	H 592	82.7
8.	Luigo Masturzo	I 787	84.4
9.	Jaroslaw Gorsky	PZ 75	88.0
10.	Richard Kouveras	GR 201	89.7
11.	Dominik Zycki	PZ 86	100.0
12.	Sven Heilmann	G 28	101.0

27. Junior European Championship 1993
L'Estartit, Spain, June 3-12
16 entries

For the first time, the event was combined with the Seniors, the two fleets using different marks. Most people were tipping Andreas Buchert from Germany, but the convincing winner was Dominik Zycki from Poland. His 10-3-4-3-2-1-9 eventually gave him a 12.6 point lead over Andreas. The bronze also seemed destined to go to Poland but Mateusz Kusznierewicz lost a protest in the last race, which meant that third place went to Italian Simone Cercello.

Final results:
1.	Dominik Zycki	POL 4	37.4
2.	Andreas Buchert	GER 6	50.0
3.	Simone Cercello	ITA 794	53.7
4.	Mateusz Kusznierewicz	POL 5	57.0
5.	Michal Hruby	CZE 479	60.7
6.	Emilios Papathanasiou	GRE 6	62.0
7.	Petr Hyza	TCH 6	65.0
8.	Michael Lundh	S 1	66.7
9.	Pascal Rambeau	F 748	68.4
10.	Kai Naef	I 622	82.0

28. Junior European Championship 1994
Çesme, Turkey, July 5-13
17 entries from 8 countries

The weather was mainly light and Ali Kemal Tüfekçi from Turkey dominated the week, winning races 2-6 in the mainly light conditions. Michal Hruby won the first race and the last to finish as runner up.

Final results:
1.	Ali Kemal Tüfekçi	TUR	9.0
2.	Michal Hruby	CZE	16.0
3.	Odysseas Papadopoulos	GRE	23.0
4.	Ugo Grande	ITA	26.0
5.	John Gochberg	USA	27.0
6.	Loizos Vassillis	GRE	31.0
7.	Petr Hyza	CZE	41.0
8.	Marek Valasek	SVK	42.0
9.	Serdar Oskay	TUR	51.0
10.	Peter Palmaj	SVK	58.0

29. Junior European Championship 1995
Lake Balaton, Hungary, September 10-16

The 1995 event was combined with the seniors.

Final results:
1. Mateusz Kusznierewicz POL 17
2. Misura Bartul CRO
3. Dominik Zycki POL 4

32. Junior European Championship 1998
Vilamoura, Portugal, June 5-13
18 entries from 9 countries

Combined with the Senior fleet, many of the Juniors put in good performances, mixing well with the Seniors and getting top ten results in the combined fleet of 77 boats. In the closest competition for several years, Clifton Webb from New Zealand clinched the title.

Final results:
1.	Clifton Webb	NZL 27
2.	Vladislav Aleinikov	RUS 2
3.	David Burrows	IRL 8
4.	Christos Chionas	GRE 11
5.	Stefan de Vries	NED 733
6.	Alexandros Dragoutsis	GRE 8
7.	Paulo Leandro	POR 81
8.	Georg Kodogouris	GRE 1
9.	Rudolf Lidarik	CZE 13
10.	Marcin Wojtonia	POL 1
11.	Adam Cowling	GBR 537
12.	Manolis Marselos	GRE 2

30. Junior European Championship 1996
Hospitalet, Spain, June 7-15
10 entries from 9 countries

The ten Juniors combined with the senior fleet and Mateusz Kusznierewicz dominated the juniors and finished runner-up in the seniors too, beating second placed junior Balazs Hadju by 47 points.

Final results:
1.	Mateusz Kusznierewicz	POL
2.	Balazs Hadju	HUN
3.	Manolis Marselos	GRE
4.	Rafael Trujillo	ESP
5.	Jiri Hyza	CZE
6.	Henrique Anjos	POR
7.	Sinan Sumar	TUR
8.	Armando Battaglia	ITA
9.	Zsolt Meszaros	HUN
10.	Liviu Brighidau	ROM

31. Junior European Championship 1997
Split, Croatia June, 6-14
14 entries from 10 countries

Combined with the Senior fleet again, Manolis Marselos was the clear winner, taking the lead after the second race and maintaining it in the generally light winds.

Final results:
1.	Manolis Marselos	GRE 2
2.	Georg Kodogouris	GRE 1
3.	Rafal Szukiel	POL 7
4.	Henrique Anjos	POR 8
5.	Vladislav Aleinikov	RUS 2
6.	Clifton Webb	NZL 27
7.	Christos Chionas	GRE 11
8.	Massimo Gherarducci	ITA 71
9.	Arando Battaglia	ITA 25
10.	Erwan Taulois	FRA 760

35. Finn National Champions of the World

Over the 50 year history of the class, National Finn Associations have been recognised in the following countries:

Angola, Argentina, Antigua, Algeria, Australia, Austria, Bahamas, Belarus, Belgium, Bermuda, Botswana, Brazil, Bulgaria, Canada, Chile, China, Columbia, Costa Rica, Croatia, Cyprus, Czech Republic (forner Czechoslovakia), Denmark, Egypt, Estonia, Fiji, Finland, France, Germany (formerly East and West), Guatemala, Greece, Holland, Hong Kong, Hungary, Iceland, India, Italy, Israel, Japan, Lithuania, Luxembourg, Mexico, Monaco, Morocco, New Zealand, Northern Ireland, Norway, Pakistan, Panama, Peru, Philippines, Poland, Portugal, Puerto Rico, Romania, Russia, Slovakia, Slovenia, South Africa, South West Africa, Spain, Sweden, Switzerland, Thailand, Trinidad and Tobago, Tunisia, Turkey, UAR, USA, former USSR, US Virgin Islands, Yugoslavia, Zambia, Zimbabwe (Rhodesia).

The absence of results for any country and any gaps in the results for any country is either because these could not be tracked down or they were not contributed.

Argentina

1961	Ricardo Boneo
1962	Ricardo Boneo
1966	Adrián Obarrio
1967	Enrique Alurralde
1970	Alberto Obarrio
1973	Roberto Haas
1974	Roberto Haas
1977	Alejandro Caviglia
1979	Alberto Carrea
1980	Alberto Larrea
1981	Alberto Larrea

Ricardo Boneo and Juan Carlos Firpo travelling to the 1964 Gold Cup

Australia

1957/58	Colin S Ryrie
1958/59	Ron Jenyns
1959/60	Ron Jenyns
1960/61	Ron Jenyns
1961/62	Ron Jenyns
1962/63	Ron Jenyns
1963/64	Ron Jenyns
1964/65	Colin S Ryrie
1965/66	Ron Jenyns
1966/67	Ron Jenyns
1967/68	Ron Jenyns
1968/69	Tony James
1969/70	Ron Jenyns
1970/71	P Burford
1971/72	John Bertrand
1972/73	Steve Kiely
1973/74	Tony James
1974/75	Tony James
1975/76	John Bertrand
1976/77	C Proctor
1977/78	C Proctor
1978/79	Geoff Davidson
1979/80	Geoff Davidson
1980/81	Geoff Davidson
1981/82	Geoff Davidson
1982/83	Chris Pratt
1983/84	Larry Kleist
1984/85	Chris Pratt
1985/86	Chris Pratt
1988/89	Simon Gorman
1989/90	Simon Gorman
1990/91	Glenn Bourke
1991/92	Glenn Bourke
1992/93	Mark Bulka
1993/94	Simon Gorman
1994/95	Dean Barker NZL
	(1st AUS Paul McKenzie)
1995/96	Paul McKenzie
1996/97	Paul McKenzie & Carl Schmidt
1997/98	Ian Ainslie RSA
	(1st AUS Paul McKenzie)
1998/99	Mateusz Kusznierewicz
	(1st AUS Paul McKenzie)

Austria

1959	P. Stern
1960	Hans Peter Fürst
1961	D. Mayr
1962	Gerhard Huska
1963	Gerhard Huska
1964	Wernfried Türr
1965	Hubert Raudaschl
1966	Hubert Raudaschl
1967	Hubert Raudaschl
1968	Lucian Cristl
1969	Hubert Raudaschl
1970	Hubert Raudaschl
1971	Florian Granzer
1972	Florian Granzer
1973	Gerhard Gfreiner
1974	Florian Granzer
1975	Albert Sturm
1976	Albert Sturm
1977	Herbert Houf
1978	Wolfgang Mayrhofer
1979	Wolfgang Mayrhofer
1980	Wolfgang Mayrhofer
1981	Bernd Moser
1982	Wolfgang Mayrhofer
1983	Wolfgang Mayrhofer
1984	Michael Luscan
1985	Michael Luscan
1986	Michael Luscan
1987	Michael Fischer
1988	Hans Spitzauer
1989	Hans Spitzauer
1990	Hans Spitzauer
1991	Arno Gsell
1992	Hans Spitzauer
1993	Hans Spitzauer
1994	Hans Spitzauer
1995	Hans Spitzauer
1996	Hans Spitzauer
1997	Hans Spitzauer
1998	Michael Gubi

Belgium

1951	Andre Nelis
1952	Andre Nelis
1953	Andre Nelis
1954	Andre Nelis
1955	Andre Nelis
1956	Andre Nelis
1957	Andre Nelis
1958	Andre Nelis
1959	Andre Nelis
1960	Andre Nelis
1961	Andre Nelis
1962	Andre Nelis
1964	Jacques Rogge
1965	Eric Serranne
1966-92	Unknown

Austrian National Championshp 1980

1995 Sebastien Godefroid
1996 Sebastien Godefroid
1997 Sebastien Godefroid
1998 Philippe Rogge

Brazil

1964 Jörg Bruder
1965 Jörg Bruder
1966 Jörg Bruder
1967 Jörg Bruder
1975 Claudio Biekarck
1983 Christoph Bergmann
1990 Jorge Zarif Neto
1993 Bruno Prada
1994 Christoph Bergmann
1995 Guilherme de Almeida
1996 Christoph Bergmann
1997 Bruno Prada
1998 Bruno Prada

Canada

1963 Dr John Clarke
1964 Tim Clarke
1965 Hank Hornidge
1966 Dave Smalley
1967 Norm Freeman
1968 Norm Freeman
1969 John Clarke
1970 Carl van Duyne
1971 John Eastwood
1972 John Clarke
1973 Paul Seidenberg
1974 Brian Todd
1975 Bruce Brymer
1976 Sandy Riley
1977 Sandy Riley
1978 Larry Lemieux
1979 Paul Van Cleve, USA
1980 Larry Lemieux

Terry Neilson (Canada)

1981 Terry Neilson
1982 Larry Lemieux
1983 Terry Neilson
1984 Derek Mess
1985 Derek Mess
1986 Lawrence Lemieux
1987 Lawrence Lemieux
1988 Lasse Hjortnäs, DEN
1989 Craig Monk, NZL
1990 Hank Lammens
1991 Mike Milner
1992 Richard Clarke
1993 Hank Lammens
1994 Lawrence Lemieux
1995 Richard Clarke

1996 Tyler Bjorn
1997 Lawrence Lemniex
1998 Mike Deyett, USA

Croatia

1990 Luksa Cicarelli
1991 Karlo Kuret
1993 Karlo Kuret
1994 Karlo Kuret
1995 Emil Tomasevic
1996 Karlo Kuret
1997 Karlo Kuret

Czech Republic
(Formerly Czechoslovakia)

1958 Miroslav Vejvoda
1959 Miroslav Vejvoda
1960 Miroslav Spacek
1961 B.Horak
1962 Not sailed
1963 Miroslav Vejvoda
1964 Miroslav Vejvoda
1965 Miroslav Vejvoda
1966 Miroslav Vejvoda
1967 Ivan Hoffmann
1968 Miroslav Vejvoda
1969 I.Racek
1970 Miroslav Vejvoda
1971 Miroslav Vejvoda
1972 Miroslav Cada
1973 Ivan Hoffmann
1974 Václav Cintl
1975 Ivan Hoffmann
1976 Miroslav Cada
1977 Josef Senkyr
1978 Josef Senkyr
1979 M.Lostak
1980 Josef Senkyr
1981 Josef Senkyr
1982 Josef Senkyr
1983 Roman Teply
1984 R.Pridal
1985 Jiri Outrata
1986 Michael Maier
1987 Michael Maier
1988 Michael Maier
1989 Roman Teply
1990 Michael Maier
1991 Roman Teply
1992 Michael Maier
1993 Roman Teply
1994 Roman Teply
1995 Michael Maier
1996 Michael Maier
1997 Michael Maier
1998 Michael Maier

Denmark

1963 Henning Wind
1964 Henning Wind
1966 Henning Wind
1967 Henning Wind
1968 Henning Wind
1969 Peter Malm

Danish National Championships 1996

1970 Peter Malm and
Peter Vienberg
1971 Henning Wind
1972 Steen Kjølhede
1973 Not sailed
1974 Jørgen Lindhardtsen
and Torben S. Olsen
1975 Poul Kirketerp
1976 Jørgen Lindhardtsen
1977 Jørgen Lindhardtsen
1978 Jørgen Lindhardtsen
1979 Jørgen Lindhardtsen
1980 Lasse Hjortnäs
1981 Jørgen Lindhardtsen
1982 Jørgen Lindhardtsen
1983 Lasse Hjortnäs
1984 Jørgen Lindhardtsen
1985 Jørgen Lindhardtsen
1986 Lasse Hjortnäs
1987 Not sailed
1988 Peter Vilby
1989 Stig Westergaard
1990 Stig Westergaard
1991 Not sailed
1992 Not sailed
1993 Björn Westergaard
1994 Jørgen Lindhardtsen
1995 Lasse Hjortnäs
1996 Jørgen Lindhardtsen
1997 Jørgen Lindhardtsen
1998 Jørgen Lindhardtsen

Estonia

1959 Alexander Chuchelov
1962 A. Bukovski
1963 A. Bukovski
1964 R. Berdasch
1965 V. Kose
1966 Vitali Dyrdyra
1967 Vitali Dyrdyra
1968 Jüri Saraskin
1969 A. Bukovski
1970 Jüri Saraskin
1971 Aare Kööp
1972 A. Bukovski
1973 Jevgeni Petchonkin
1974 Aare Kööp
1975 Aare Kööp
1976 Aare Kööp
1977 Tynu Tootsi

1978 Aare Kööp
1979 E. Smiltenieks
1980 Aare Kööp
1981 Aare Kööp
1982 Vaiko Vooremaa
1983 Aare Taveter
1984 Aare Taveter
1985 Aare Taveter
1986 Aare Taveter
1987 Meelis Männik
1988 Meelis Männik
1989 Tammo Otsasoo
1990 Jaak Jõgi
1991 Tammo Otsasoo
1992 Imre Taveter
1993 Tammo Otsasoo
1994 Imre Taveter
1995 Imre Taveter
1996 Imre Taveter
1997 Imre Taveter
1998 Imre Taveter

France

1954 Didier Poissant
1955 Thimoté Baudoin
1956 Didier Poissant
1957 Didier Poissant
1958 Yves-Louis Pinaud
1959 Yves-Louis Pinaud
1960 Yves-Louis Pinaud
1961 Francis Jammes
1962 Jean-Claude Jammes
1963 Francis Jammes
1964 Gérard Devillard
1965 Franck Poullain

1966   Serge Verneuil
1967   Jacques Lemanissier
1968   Jean Lapalu
1969   Serge Maury
1970   Serge Maury
1971   Serge Maury
1972   J.G. Pasturaud
1973   Serge Maury
1974   Serge Maury
1975   Daniel Chedeville
1976   Pierre Mondeteguy
1977   Alain Maury
1978   Pierre Mondeteguy
1979   Yves Silvestro
1980   Francois Le Castrec
1981   Francois Le Castrec
1982   Francois Le Castrec
1983   Francois Le Castrec
1984   Jean Paul Gaston
1985   Jean Paul Gervaiseau
1986   Jacques Martin
1987   Jean Paul Gaston
1988   Pierre Le Chatelier
1989   Jean Paul Gaston
1990   Francois Le Castrec
1991   Loic Le Helley
1992   Loic Le Helley
1993   Xavier Rohart
1994   Jean Paul Gaston
1995   Regis Baumgarten
1996   Jean Paul Gaston
1997   Jean Paul Gaston
1998   Erwan Taulois

Germany
West Germany (1958-1989)

1958   Bernhard Straubinger
1959   H Kammerer
1960   Bernhard Straubinger
1961   no championship
1962   Bernhard Straubinger
1963   Bernhard Straubinger
1964   J.v.Alt-Stutterheim
1965   Bernhard Straubinger
1966   Willy Kuhweide
1967   Willy Kuhweide
1968   Bernhard Straubinger
1969   Richard Hart (GBR)
(1st GER Willy Kuhweide)
1970   Iain Macdonald-Smith K
(1st GER T Jungblut)
1971   Willy Kuhweide
1972   Werner Sülberg
1973   Werner Sülberg
1974   H Jåger
1975   no championship
1976   Deegan (NZL)
(1st GER Roland Balthasar)
1977   Roland Balthasar
1978   Otto Pohlmann
1979   Wolfgang Gerz
1980   José Luis Doreste
1981   Wolfgang Gerz
1982   M Nissen
1983   Lutz Patrunky

1984   Ivor Ganahl (SUI)
1st GER Othmar M v Blumencron
1985   Rob McMillan (GBR)
1st GER Wolfgang Gerz
1986   John Hofland (NED)
1st GER Othmar Mv Blumencron
1987   W B Lixenfeld
1988   M Hofmann
1989   W B Lixenfeld

East Germany (1957- 1989)
1957   Jürgen Vogler
1958   Jürgen Vogler
1959   Walter Gärtner
1961   Manfred Ernst
1962   Walter Gärtner
1963   Bernd Dehmel
1965   Horst Herrmann
1967   Herbert Raben
1968   Christian Schröder
1969   Jürgen Mier
1970   Christian Schröder
1971   Bernd Dehmel
1972   Detlef Gehreiber
1973   Jochen Schümann
1974   Jürgen Wolff
1975   Jürgen Wolff
1976   Eckard Drefahl

1977   Jochen Schümann
1978   Jochen Schümann
1979   Jochen Schümann
1980   Jochen Schümann
1981   Frank Butzmann
1982   Jochen Schümann
1983   Frank Butzmann
1984   Jochen Schümann
1985   Frank Butzmann
1986   Frank Butzmann
1987   Andre Budzien
1988   Heiko Burke
1989   Heiko Burke

Germany (1990-1998)
1990   Malte Philipp
1991   L Bolle
1992   Dirk Löwe
1993   Malte Philipp
1994   Michael Fellmann
1995   Dirk Löwe
1996   Fredrik Lööf (SWE)
       1st GER Andreas Buchert
1997   Andreas Buchert
1998   Michael Fellmann

Hungary
1957   Kalman Tolnai
1958   Kalman Tolnai
1959   Bela Kovacs
1960   Kalman Tolnai
1961   Miklos Tuss
1962   Andras Schomer
1963   Gyogy Finaczy
1964   Gyorgy Wossala
1965   Gyogy Finaczy
1966   Miklos Tuss
1967   Gyogy Finaczy
1968   Gyogy Finaczy
1969   Gyogy Finaczy
1970   Andras Haan
1971   Gyula Scharbert
1972   Andras Haan
1973   Miklos Tuss
1974   Andras Haán
1975   Andras Haán
1976   Andras Haán
1977   Andras Haán
1978   Andras Haán
1979   Andras Haán
1980   Andras Haán
1981   György Wossola
1982   Andreas Haán
1983   Antal Szekely
1984   Antal Szekely
1985   Istvan Rujak
1986   Farkas Litkey
1987   Attila Szilvàssy
1988   Antal Szekely
1989   Farkas Litkey
1990   Attila Szilvàssy
1991   Attila Szilvàssy
1992   Attila Szilvàssy
1993   Attila Szilvàssy
1994   Farkas Litkey
1995   Farkas Litkey
1996   Farkas Litkey
1997   Balazs Hadju
1998   Attila Szilvàssy

Mexico

1963	Mario Colligon Jr
1964	Fernando Ortiz Monasterio
1965	Dico Kristianson
1966	Michal Kun
1967	Michal Kun
1968	Diego Mujica
1969	Alfredo Vazquez
1970	Lloyd Sloane
1971	Lloyd Sloane
1972	Lorenzo Villasnor
1973	Roberto Colliard
1974	Roberto Colliard
1975	not sailed
1976	Guillermo Tapio
1977	Angel Franco
1991	Guillermo Tapia Jr

Netherlands

1980	Mark Neeleman
1981	Mark Neeleman
1982	Jorgen Lindhardsten
	(1st NED Sjaak Haakman)
1984	Wilhelm Roberts
	(1st NED Bart Zielhuis)
1985	Jorgen Lindhardtsen
	(1st NED Peter Peet)
1986	Stig Westergaard
1987	Mark Neeleman
1988	Bart Zielhuis
1989	Bart Zielhuis
1990	Jaap Zielhuis
1991	Bart Zeilhius
1992	Gert Kwikkers
1993	Philippe Rogge
1994	Sebastien Godefroid
1995	Sebastien Godefroid
1996	Sebastien Godefroid
1997	Sebastien Godefroid
1998	Martijn van Muyden

New Zealand

1956	P Spencer
1957	P Spencer
1958	Ralph Roberts
1960	Ralph Roberts
1961	Peter Mander
1962	Ralph Roberts
1963	Ralph Roberts
1964	Peter Mander
1965	N.R. Everett
1966	Bret De Thier
1967	N.R. Everett
1968	Jonty Farmer
1969	Bret De Thier
1970	Bruce Watson
1971	Bret De Their
1972	Bret De Their
1973	Jonty Farmer
1974	Bret De Thier
1975	Clive Roberts
1976	Jonty Farmer
1977	Jonty Farmer
1978	M. Thom
1979	Graham Deegan
1980	T Dodson
1981	T Dodson
1982	B Deegan
1983	Rick Dodson
1985	John Cutler
1986	John Cutler
1987	John Cutler
1988	John Cutler
1989	Craig Monk
1990	Craig Monk
1991	Craig Monk
1992	Craig Monk
1993	Craig Monk
1994	Craig Monk
1995	Craig Monk
1996	Craig Monk
1997	Ian Baker
1998	Sebastien Godefroid BEL
	1st NZL Ian Baker

Poland

1953	J. Sieradzki
1954	W. Szraj
1955	W. Szraj
1956	Z. Twardowski
1957	Z. Twardowski
1958	A. Podolski
1959	J. Szloser
1960	Wl. Fischer
1961	T. Zero
1962	B. Knasiecki
1963	M. Skalisz
1964	L. Poklewski
1965	T. Zero
1966	M. Skalisz
1967	A. Rymkiewicz
1968	M. Skalisz
1969	Andreij Zawieja
1970	W. Braclaw
1971	Andreij Zawieja
1972	A. Rymkiewicz
1973	Andreij Zawieja
1974	Ryszard Blaszka
1975	Andreij Zawieja
1976	R. Knasiecki
1977	T. Rumszewicz
1978	Ryszard Skarbinski
1979	Henryk Blaszka

1980	Henryk Blaszka
1981	Henryk Blaszka
1982	Henryk Blaszka
1983	Miroslav Rychcik
1984	Miroslav Rychcik
1985	Miroslav Rychcik
1986	Henryk Blaszka
	and Jaroslav Maciuk
1987	Jacek Sobkowiak
1988	Henryk Blaszka
1989	Pawel Pawlaczyk
1990	Maceij Skibski
1991	Wlopz Radwaniecki
1992	Maceij Skibski
1993	Mateusz Kusznierewicz
1994	Dominik Zycki
1995	Mateusz Kusznierewicz
1996	Mateusz Kusznierewicz
1997	Mateusz Kusznierewicz
1998	Mateusz Kusznierewicz

Romania

1969	G. Nicolcioiu
1975	Vasiliu Alexandru
1977	G. Nicoliciou
1992	Dumitru Fratila
1993	Dumitru Fratila
1994	Dumitru Fratila
1995	Vladescu Ctin
1996	Dumitru Fratila
1997	Dumitru Fratila
1998	Dumitru Fratila

Russia

Championship of the USSR (1955-1991)

1955	Yuri Shavrin
1956	Evgeni Gorshkov
1957	Peter Gorelikiov
1958	Anatoli Yn Sun
1959	Valentin Mankin
1960	Evgeni Kuznetsov
1961	Valentin Mankin
1962	Valentin Mankin
1963	Valentin Mankin
1964	Alexander Chuchelov
1965	Viktor Kozlov
1966	Viktor Kozlov
1967	Valentin Mankin
1968	Rolland Berdash
1969	Vitali Dirdiara
1970	Viktor Potopov
1971	Viktor Potopov
1972	Rolland Berdash
1973	Andrei Balashov
1974	Andrei Balashov
1975	Andrei Balashov
1976	Andrei Balashov
1977	Nicholai Koryachkin
1978	Andrei Balashov
1979	Sergei Khoretski
1980	Andrei Balashov
1981	Sergei Khoretski
1982	Sergei Khoretski

1983 Nikolai Sukhorukov
1984 Oleg Khoperski
1985 Oleg Khoperski
1986 Oleg Khoperski
1987 Nikolai Sukhorukov
1988 Oleg Khoperski
1989 Yuri Tokovoi
1990 Oleg Khoperski
1991 Dmitri Orlov
Championship of the UIS
1992 Michail Apukhtin
Championship of Russia
1993 Michail Apukhtin
1994 Yuri Tokovoi
1995 Oleg Khoperski
1996 Oleg Khoperski
1997 Oleg Khoperski
1998 Evgeni Chernov

South Africa

1958 Paul Elvström
1959 Ernie Morrison
1960 Helmut Stauch
1961 P. Barker
1963 George Burn-Wood
1964 Bruce McCurragh
1964 Harvey Blogg
1965 Harvey Blogg
1966 Peter Barrett
1967 Ernie Morrison
1968 Paul Elvström
1969 Hubert Raudaschl
1970 Bruce McCurrach
1971 Nigel Sharples
1972 Stuart Donkin
1973 Jorge Bruder
1975 Ernie Shaw
1976 Ali Serritslev
1977 Stuart Donkin
1978 Dick Leeksma
1979 Ali Serritslev
1980 Alan Tucker
1981 Alan Tucker
1982 Barry Barbour
1983 Klaus Weixelbaumer
1984 Ali Serritslev
1985 Roy Heiner
1986 Roy Heiner
1987 Bruce Savage
1988 Greg Davis
1989 Dave Collins
1990 Ant Steward
1991 Greg Davis
1993 Greg Davis
1994 Greg Davis
1995 Ali Serritslev
1996 Ian Ainslie
1997 Ian Ainslie
1998 Ian Ainslie

Spain

1960 J. Olavarri
1961 Phil Barker
1964 G. Arion
1968 J.I. Sirvent

1970 Gerardo Seeliger
1971 Gerardo Seeliger
1972 Gerardo Seeliger
1973 Joaquin Blanco
1984 Antonio Ferrer
1986 José Luis Doreste
1987 José Luis Doreste
1988 José Luis Doreste
1989 Eric Merganthaler
1991 Francisco Villalonga
1992 José Maria van der Ploeg
1993 José Maria van der Ploeg
1994 José Maria van der Ploeg
1998 Rafael Trujillo

Switzerland

1960 Bernhard Reist
1961 Louis Schiess
1962 Louis Schiess
1963 Louis Schiess
1964 Louis Schiess
1965 L. Albarelli
1966 Bally Alexis
1967 Bernhard Reist
1970 Peter 'Sam' Gubelmann
1971 Walter Bachmann
1972 Walter Bachmann
1973 Walter Bachmann
1974 Walter Bachmann
1975 Walter Bachmann
1977 George Hatzipavlis
1978 Marcel Wunderli
1979 Karl Schmid
1980 Ivor Ganahl
1981 Ivor Ganahl
1982 Eric Bornarel FRA
1983 Ivor Ganahl
1984 J Senkyr
1985 H Fratzer
1988 Othmar M v Blumencron
1989 Alexander Rinne
1990 Alexander Rinne
1991 Othmar M v Blumencron
1992 Othmar M v Blumencron
1993 Othmar M v Blumencron
1994 Peter Theurer

1995 Othmar M v Blumencron
1996 Gerd Griegel
1997 Hajdu Balazs
1998 Peter Theurer

Turkey

1957 Erzin Demir
1958 Erzin Demir
1959 Erzin Demir
1960 Erzin Demir
1961 Erzin Demir
1962 Erdal Berkay
1963 Kemal Kayin
1964 Ziya Ergün
1965 Haluk Kakis
1966 Haluk Kakis
1967 Haluk Kakis
1968 Haluk Kakis
1969 Haluk Kakis
1970 Haluk Kakis
1971 Haluk Kakis
1972 Levent Ozgen
1973 Levent Ozgen
1974 Levent Ozgen
1975 Levent Ozgen
1977 Levent Ozgen
1978 Levent Ozgen
1979 Levent Ozgen
1980 Levent Ozgen

1981 Levent Ozgen
1982 Levent Ozgen
1983 Levent Ozgen
1984 Levent Ozgen
1985 Levent Ozgen
1986 Levent Ozgen
1987 Haluk Babacan
1988 Arif Gürdenli
1989 Haluk Babacan
1990 Arif Gürdenli
1991 Haluk Babacan
1992 Arif Gürdenli
1993 Yilmaz Canözer
1994 Arif Gürdenli
1995 Haluk Babacan
1996 Yilmaz Canözer
1997 Ali Kemal Tüfekci
1998 Sinan Sümer

United Kingdom

1956 Richard Creagh-Osborne
1957 Vernon Stratton
1958 Richard Creagh-Osborne
1959 Vernon Stratton
1960 Richard Creagh-Osborne
1961 Richard Creagh-Osborne
1962 Richard Creagh-Osborne
1963 Jack Knights
1964 Brian Saffrey-Cooper

1965 Richard Hart
1966 John Maynard
1967 Jack Knights
1968 John Maynard
1969 Jack Knights
1970 Iain Macdonald-Smith
1971 Iain Macdonald-Smith
1972 Robert Holbrook
1973 Robert Holbrook
1974 David Howlett
1975 Chris Law
1976 David Howlett
1977 David Howlett
1978 Chris Law
1979 Chris Law
1980 Chris Law
1981 Mike McIntyre
1982 Mike McIntyre
1983 Roddy Bridge
1984 Roddy Bridge
1985 Roddy Bridge
1986 Lawrence Crispin
1987 Stuart Childerley
1988 Stuart Childerley
1989 Rob McMillan
1990 Rob McMillan
1991 No Championship
1992 Richard Lott
1993 Richard Lott
1994 Rob McMillan
1995 Richard Stenhouse
1996 Richard Stenhouse
1997 Richard Stenhouse
1998 Iain Percy

USA

1959 Jack Knights (GBR)
    (1st US Richard Rowan)
1960 Glen Foster
1961 Glen Foster
1962 Peter Barrett
1963 Henry Sprague
1964 Henry Sprague
1965 Dick Tillmann
1966 Peter Barrett
1967 Fred Miller

1968 Jorg Bruder (BRA)
    (1st US Henry Sprague)
1969 Jorg Bruder (BRA)
    (1st US Norm Freeman)
1970 Bob Andre
1971 Bod Andre
1972 Edward Bennett
1973 Fred Cook
1974 Henry Sprague
1975 Sanford Riley (CAN)
    (1st US Bill Allen)
1976 John Bertrand (AUS)
    (1st US Ed Bennett)
1977 Tony Herrmann
1978 John Bertrand
1979 Cam Lewis
1980 John Bertrand
1981 Terry Neilson CAN
    (1st US Andy Pimental)
1982 Craig Healy
1983 Larry Lemieux CAN
    (1st US Andy Pimental)
1984 Terry Neilson CAN
    (1st US Craig Healy)
1985 Brian Ledbetter
1986 Brian Ledbetter
1987 Brian Ledbetter
1988 Brian Ledbetter
1989 Alec Cutler
1990 Brian Ledbetter
1991 Hank Lammens
    (1st US Brian Ledbetter)
1992 Brian Ledbetter
1993 Will Martin
1994 John Porter
1995 Sam Kerner
1996 John Porter

1997 Darrell Peck
1998 Darrell Peck

Yugoslavia

National Champions include:
Minksi Fabris (15 times)
Luksa Cicarelli (3 times)
Marin Mrduljas (2 times)
Marko Prancevic
Tonko Pivecic
Miro Balov
Pasko Kolomatovic

1981 D Righi
1983 Makjani
1985 Nenad Viali
1994 Branimir Banovac
1995 Branislav Erac
1996 Branislav Erac
1997 Branislav Erac
1998 Srdjan Volarevic

Zimbabwe

1961 R. G. Rich
1962 Hemlmut Stauch RSA
1963 Mike McFadden
1965 Mike McFadden
1966 Anthony Crossley
1967 Barry Dixon
1968 Mike McFadden
1969 John Chadwick
1970 John Skinner
1971 John Chadwick
1973 John Chadwick
1974 John Chadwick
1975 John Chadwick

1976 Peter Wilson
1977 Don Scott
1978 John Skinner
1979 John Chadwick
1980 Mike Fisher
1981 Archie Wilson
1982 Guy Grossmith
1983 Nicholas Wingfield
1984 Archie Wilson
1985 Guy Grossmith
1986 Guy Grossmith
1987 Guy Redmile
1988 Guy Grossmith
1989 Guy Grossmith
1990 Derek Grossmith
1991 Guy Grossmith
1992 Archie Wilson
1993 Guy Grossmith
1995 John Skinner

36. Planning Your Sailing Season

by Mateusz Kusznierewicz

My own sailing calendar is the most important thing in my preparation for the season. Without it I can't imagine how I would manage (especially in terms of organisation) and do well in any regatta.

In order to keep getting better and to continue achieving your aims you must go through certain steps in your career. It takes some time to get to the top and how long it will take you to get there will depend only on you and the plans that you make.

I am going to tell you how I plan my sailing season. I'm sure it is still not a perfect plan, but at least you can have something to start with or can use it to make your existing plans even better. You will see a lot of dates taken from the system that have around been for ages. I reckon it works very well, but every sailor is different and that's why I've changed it for my own use a little bit after a couple of years. Right now I'm preparing my own especially designed diagram to make my schedule more clear and exact.

The first time I stepped onto the Finn was when I became the member of Polish Olympic Preparation Team. I was still far away from even thinking about going to the Olympics, but the first thing I noticed was a very well prepared schedule of the sailing calendar for the following season made by specially designated people in the Polish Yachting Association. Everyone in the Polish team has his own sailing calendar. It is made especially for him/her and is personally adjusted to the current level of his/her skills.

I remember that myself, my coach and those people I told you above, would spend whole

days on deciding which and how many regattas and what training camps I should go to in order to succeed in the coming sailing season.

We used some custom designed computer software to make it easier to write down (draw) and read our plans. Apart from this I made my own big paper calendar which I put on the wall in my room. I still do it every year to be able to see easily what is going to happen in the future. I suggest you should do the same. Especially in the beginning when you want to make many changes to the plan and add a lot of information to it - that helps a lot.

It is very important to learn in advance all the information and dates and finally make your personal schedule before the beginning of the

season. I always start to plan my schedule in November - two months before the next sailing season actually begins.

Nowadays it is very easy when we are able to get all of regatta dates from the internet and ISAF annual books. Also our great FinnFare contains information on all major regattas for at least one year in advance.

But regattas are not everything you need to know before you start to plan your season. You have to think also about your pure sailing techniques and some training camps. I'm sure you agree with me that every Finn sailor is open minded and very keen to train with other Finn sailors.

At the very beginning of designing my sailing calendar we wrote down my goals for the season. In 1992 I was a very young and fresh sailor who just jumped from the OK-Dinghy class into the Olympic Sailing Heroes Dynasty. I was very small and so my goals were also very small. I had to keep in mind the fact that my National Association wanted me to satisfy certain requirements, but more important for me was to see whether I was getting ahead, and if so, whether I could do it any faster.

As you're getting closer to the Olympics you have to change your plans and the contents of your calendar.

Therefore we divided my sailing calendar into four smaller periods. The first one usually starts at the beginning of the year and ends in late April just after the big regatta in Hyeres.

After two weeks of rest we start the second period in the middle of May and finish it at the Kieler Woche regatta in June. Then, most of us are having holidays and everything slows down. But we are still sailing so the third period: July, August and September we spend training. During that time we have many small regattas in our countries and none of the World Cup series.

The last period begins in October and ends at the end of the year. It all changes a bit when you are sailing all the year and it also depends a lot on the dates of the Finn Gold Cup, Europeans or (every four years) the Olympics.

In each period I'm looking for some time for sailing, on-shore body and equipment preparations and, of course, for some rest from it all. It is very important to find time for everything otherwise your sailing development may go a completely wrong way.

I divide my calendar in vertical rows. The first one contains only the names and dates of all regattas, training camps and holidays I'm going to go to this time.

I think you should write it in different colours to mark by yourself which regattas and training camps are the most important for you, which ones are not so important i. e. when you should push a lot and when simply take it easy. You will notice later that it makes your sailing and winning easier when you know what the expectations of your performance are.

In the next row I write my own expectations about the work I'm going to do there (in the time and place indicated in the first row). For example when I'm going to such a regatta like SPA in Holland I'm usually coming with some new gear which I'm thinking to try on this regatta. It can be any new part of your equipment but it is important to write in your calendar much earlier when and where you are going to get (buy) a new mast or a sail and where and with whom is the best to test it.

The next row in my calendar contains information about my physical training and preparations. It is also important to monitor separately your cardio and strength training and try to be at the top of your athletic possibilities close to the most important regattas in your calendar. For one month you can concentrate more on the strength of your legs and arms and then the next month focus on your flexibility. It all depends on you and your feelings. You can talk about it with the specialist or your physio.

Another row should contain information on your gear shopping. Lately we have had to wait quite a long time to get any piece of equipment from the manufacturer. I reckon that you should also mark it on the calendar when you should order everything. Make sure you know (at least approximately) what your budget for the next year will be and spend your money in the right way. It was my mistake for many years that I was buying everything in the beginning of the year and at the end I was out of the game, having nothing to work and develop with.

And after all of this you should leave one row for a summary. Leave it clear to write your opinions and thoughts. It is important to write there your feelings, what you missed in the previous periods and on what you think you should focus more. It could help to ask somebody (like your personal coach or a friend who is following your sailing), their opinion about these things and write them down too.

Never throw away your calendars from previous years. You can use them while planning your next ones. After all, we are all learning from our past mistakes. Your own and other people's too.

To sum up: your sailing calendar should help you know what you're doing and what you're going to do and avoid making too many mistakes. It should play the same role as your personal or business schedule.

37. Finn Racing Maxims

by Larry Lemieux (LL), Richard Lott (RL), Simon Stonehouse (SS), Philippe Rogge (PR), Paul Elvström (PE), Darrell Peck (DP), Richard Stenhouse (RS), Iain Percy (IP), Sebastien Godefroid (SG), Wolfgang Mayrhofer (WM), Robert Deaves (RD), Oleg Khoperski (OK), Valentin Mankin (VM), Gus Miller (GM) and from FINNFARE (FF)

Starting

You don't have to win the start to have a good one, you only have to be able to do what you want. LL

If the tide is pushing you over the line, the pin end on starboard is not the place to plan to start. Go late for the boat end (if there's not too much line bias). There should be a decent gap there created by the boats pushed down by the tide. RL

As a Finn has a relatively large rudder the boat can be held on the line in the correct position by rapid movements of the tiller. Practice by staying as close to a marker buoy as possible, for as long as possible. SS

Don't be over afraid of being early or you'll never start well. RD

If you are late for the start, the rule is not to get too nervous but go on racing in the usual style. VM

Buy a stopwatch with small buttons on the side. It may be harder to start when the ten minute gun goes but you won't turn it off accidentally when you're bending your wrist whilst steering in the pre-start. RL

Always try to ensure that you keep a gap to leeward, this will allow you to bear away and pick up speed a few seconds before the gun. SS

Get it moving early. DP

Clear air after the start is 40% of your race! PR

Get a transit, choose the biased end and go. RS

Beating

When in marginal conditions (comfortable hiking but not over-powered) bear away slightly to pick up speed, then slowly bring the boat back up to close hauled course until the speed begins to drop, then repeat. This can be a very effective method of increasing VMG to windward, particularly in choppier conditions, but be warned you have to hike hard to make it pay. SS

Sail it flat. DP

The faster you go in the wrong direction the farther behind you'll be. LL

Make sure you learn from the previous beats. PR

Due to inefficient foil shape of the centreboard and the oversized rudder, it is usually recommended to sail with about 5° of weather helm. Having the tiller slightly angled to windward helps the rudder to generate lift to windward, improving the overall VMG. Be careful not to overdo the weather helm, which will create too much drag and although lift generated will be high overall VMG will be poor. As with much in sailing getting the right balance is crucial. SS

If you are able to walk up the beach after a windy race, you haven't worked hard enough! RL

Take the shortest route and hike hard. RS

Read Stuart Walker's (ancient 14 sailor) old book on racing. There is an excellent explanation of shift mastering. RL

Reaching

If you decide to go low, go low. Don't try to slowly fade away, you won't get clear air. PR

It's better maintain a fast average speed rather than flying down a wave only to stop at the bottom and have to waste time getting back up to surfing speed. Get off the wave before you loose it. LL

In surfing conditions, but not planing, the emphasis is on pumping. This is the most physically demanding aspect of Finn sailing. Pumping should be a combination of large pumps, using the back and arm, and shorter 'jerky' type pumps using only the arm. IP

Luffers and stuffers - not generally found at the front of a fleet as most sailors there have learnt that trying to luff over a boat who is sailed by a sailor of similar ability and speed, is pointless. At best you might pass one or two boats but half the fleet will have sailed underneath you. If you really want to pass a boat in front, follow on their transom but do not luff. If they make a mistake then that's your chance to luff over the top of them, if they never make a mistake then you might just sneak water at the next mark. SS

Concentrate on good trim and balance and always have the sail well trimmed. RS

The secret of fast reaching is balance. Don't pump really hard and then let the boat fall over on top of you. It is imperative to keep the power in the sail all the time. FF

Go down in the gusts and up in the lulls. The people who constantly seem to be able to sail lower and faster than you on a broad reach are surely using this technique. Also use the waves to get down. FF

Downwind

The best preparation you can possibly have for downwind sailing in strong winds is to go

out in heavy weather and sail a lot. Do everything. Fool with your vang. Experiment with your position on the deck. And finally, gybe, gybe, gybe. Even capsize and practice righting your boat for time. This will be tough and you will then see why getting into shape is also good preparation. The key is to get so you are comfortable with the boat and the conditions as you are screaming downwind in a race. FF

Because you are unable to pump in light winds, being smooth around the boat is most important factor. Sail trim should concentrate on keeping the leeward tell tale flying. IP

Never go straight down, Either sail by the lee or broad reach to keep the speed up. RS

Learn to run by the lee. RL

In any breeze sail large angles to avoid hitting the wave in front, sometimes heading up the wave when speed is needed and also diving down the wave when you are too high. IP

Good downwind speed can turn a throwout into a keeper. It is essential. LL

Your run ends two lengths from the mark, not ten. PR

When running in strong winds, think of it as an escalator of waves. The only way to jump to the next step is to surf along the wave, either up or down looking for a break to jump through. It is not a problem to sail off-course as once on a wave you can sail to the right or left without falling off and therefore without losing distance. IP

Keep a careful watch on the boats behind to ensure they are not stealing your wind, if they are head up or gybe off until you can find clear air. SS

Remember that the hook in the leach of a deep Finn sail is much more than that in a Laser sail. It's therefore much more difficult to get a reversing of the flow on the sail. RL

Downwind is like slow dancing with a gorgeous woman - just let yourself go but stay in control. SG

All the good guys know when to use their rocking skills. Just when you need to make/break the overlap at the mark. RL

Steer a lot (be afraid). DP

Mental Fitness / Psychology

Major events like world championships or Olympic Games are won or lost in the psychological realm. GM

By recognising your individual preferences and aversions you are able to create an environment which supports your psychological comfort or at least is not detrimental to your ease. WM

All the top guys have educated themselves about it, why not you? PR

First of all you have to be a fighter who never gives up, even when your legs fall off and your arms are not listening to your mind anymore. Pain is just some electricity that runs through your body. You can ignore it if you really have too. SG

Play scrabble and do the crossword every day. RL

You have to admit that some people are better than you, but that's not a reason to give up. It's just another challenge to work on. Learn from your masters. Sailing well is contagious, so if you sail a lot, automatically (this is if you really want) you'll slowly get a little better. But it takes plenty of time !!! SG

Focus of the things you have to do rather than the mistakes you have made. RS

A positive contribution to the psychological environment is possible through the recognition of individual differentiations between the actual and the optimal level of activity, and the creation of a mechanism of compensation like a ritualised behavioural pattern. WM

Just because you know a lot about sailing does not mean that you also know a lot about the human brain. That's why you shouldn't be afraid to consult a sports psychologist if you think you have a problem or you might get a problem in the future. SG

You must also be TOUGH mentally and physically. You can be the fittest person out there but if you're not tough the fitness doesn't matter. You have to be fit enough so you can still think straight when you're tired. LL

Be honest about your performance. Know your strengths and weaknesses. Be analytical. SS

It is surprising how important events leading up to a major regatta can be to one's performance. Obviously a good journey, accommodation etc are vital but events a few days before can also have a negative or a positive influence: event management, entries, packing, avoiding stress etc. SS

By recognising your individual performance patterns, the psychological specifics of a long competition, and by proper counter-steering of your own reactions you are able to promote your psychological output and gain stamina and staying power. WM

Read the book. 'Tennis, the inner game'. RL

Never consider that you have a best sailing condition, eg. light winds, flat water. If the forecast for the event is strong winds and heavy seas, what frame of mind will you be in travelling to the event? SS

Mental rehearsal really works and it's a damn sight warmer in the middle of winter. You can also do it anywhere. RL

At critical moments on the race course learn to concentrate only on generating maximum speed. Most people know to do this off the start line but how many sailors are busy retuning the rig, adjusting the centreboard etc just after a mark rounding. Valuable seconds can be gained by an ability to block out external influences. One method for this is to look and focus at a particular aspect of the boat, always use the same focal point and learn to switch into this 'super fast mode' almost without thinking. SS

Be patient. DP

Never be afraid to approach and ask the top sailors, whether this be at Club, National or International level. The world champion might not tell you his exact rig settings but he will generally provide useful information which will aid your improvement. SS

For mental training I like to smile a lot. OK

Sailing is like darts. There are times when you can't miss and times when you can't hit the board. FF

Physical Fitness
You can never be too fit. RL

In all but the lightest winds - the fitter you are the faster you will sail. There are many methods of getting fit for sailing but by far the best is time in the boat. Not only are you working all the required muscles, you are also gaining by learning and improving in other key areas. SS

If you don't want to invest in this, buy a catamaran. PR

You need to be far fitter to sail fast than you think. Always train on the water at maximum intensity. One hour of good quality work is worth five of slacking!!! RL

Work hard. DP

Time on the water is best, but if you're in the gym don't forget suppleness as well as power. RS

In my opinion cycling is the best possible fitness work for sailing, probably better than sailing itself because it's easier to get intensity (stay in a big gear up hill) and thus get HUGE thighs. RL

Boat Speed
The sail should fit the mast. (Seek advice off top sailors. They will be happy to help you.) RS

Two or three boat tuning is the best way of learning how to improve your rig settings. When selecting potential partners try to pick sailors whose ability and equipment are a close match to you and yours. Instead of joining club racing one afternoon try some tuning runs, it's surprising how much fun it is. SS

Boat speed is everything. Don't underestimate the cost and there is no substitute for measured, time consuming two boat work, but make sure you choose the best training partner you can find (preferably faster than you). RL

When deciding on a mast three things need checking first. The weight (minimum), the centre of gravity (minimum height) and the bend. The best bend test is the cantilever test, although this is sometimes difficult to achieve in practice for sideways bend. What mast bend will be fast for you is mainly dependent on your weight. Ideally you want a different mast for each condition: light - more bend fore and

aft to get correct leech tension; medium - stiffer to get more power; windy - softer sideways to allow the mast to depower. As this is impractical you need to find one all round mast. The bigger you are the nearer to the medium ideal this mast will be, so that you have more power. Lighter helms should opt for a mast that is more suitable for windy conditions. RS

In all sailing, preparation and checking prior to a race can locate problems that can make the difference between smoothly executed moved and time lost due to a foul up. There is not much room for error, so preparation is even more valuable in strong winds. FF

Tune with a method. Don't change all parameters at the same time. And don't kid yourself about how fast you are. PR

Steering

When going up a wave and you see that you will bang into the next wave, then point up more to take the speed off. You will gain on pointing and won't bounce into the next wave, but will sail over it - so you will make better speed. PE

When going up wave, point high and when going down wave, bear off.

The most important control on the whole boat is the tiller. Everything else is just along for the ride. LL

Practice your rudderless sailing skills on a medium wind day far from shore. You will appreciate it the first time you attend a major event and find you have to launch into an onshore wind, shallow water and a breaking sea. Even if you can't win the race, you can look cool on the slipway (and save your very expensive carbon rudder from major damage!) RL

Boat Handling

Analyse your mistakes/manoeuvres. Visualise doing it correctly and practice a lot to make it smooth and fast. RS

There is nothing to it in a Finn. The rudder is huge and great for paddling around on the start line. Practice that skill a lot. In light airs, there's nothing quite like canoeing off the start line. RL

Live in the boat. DP

The main thing in balance at sea is that the weight must be in the middle of the boat. You must have a light bow and a light stern and therefore it is important to stay in the middle of the boat. PE

Hours and hours on the water in between regattas. PE

Go sailing a lot. DP

The only way to learn it is to do it. You have to get to the point where you can feel everything about the boat. Then the answers become obvious. LL

Gybing

The fatal thing with gybing in strong winds is any steering delay or hesitancy, particularly in a by-the-lee position. FF

The object is to remove gybing of its terrors. The best way to do this is to find the easiest way and then to practice doing it this way until it becomes mere routine. FF

The two greatest dangers during the gybe while planing are over steering and diving the boat under the wave. FF

When gybing - grab the mainsheet straight from the boom and physically pull it over your head. This helps to remove the worry about the boom hitting your head. SS

Finn Philosophy

You don't have to be light to do well in light airs . . . but you do have to be patient and philosophical. Get interested in light air sailing, get to enjoy it as an end in itself. Do not look upon it as a boring nuisance, as something to be endured. It is as much a part of Finn sailing as planing amidst salt spray in a Force 7 wind and in many ways a great deal more difficult. Jack Knights

The most important thing about beating is practice. Reading articles does not help much - it might even confuse you. Get out on the water in any conditions, until beating is a motion like walking on the land. You must not feel any pain and should do it subconsciously, then you will be able to concentrate on tactics and strategy. Peter Mohilla

A beginner in the Finn needs no 'special abilities'. He should however be heavy enough and athletic. He should first learn to master the Finn, then to tune it well, to develop an effective hiking technique and finally to become a good tactician. Jochen Schümann

Plan your training with great objectivity, and at the same time with high energy and flexibility. And after that, the most important thing is to have high hopes and a strong desire to win. José Maria van der Ploeg

Whatever you do, don't waste your time on jealousy. Sometimes you're ahead, sometimes you're behind, but the race is long and in the end it's only with yourself Sebastien Godefroid

In other classes, there is very little difference in speed between the good and the very good. But in the Finn, the very good can always leave distance between himself and all others. If you really love competitive sailing, want to work hard, race hard and enjoy the fruits of your efforts then the Finn Class is for you. Paul Elvström

38. History of the Finn World Masters

by Peter Mohilla and Robert Deaves

Reprinted from FINNLOG

The first suggestion for a special Finn Veteran Gold Cup for sailors over 40 years of age was presented by Dr. Fred and Heidi Auer at the 1969 AGM in Bermuda. The Auers - in those days the most active force in the Finn Class - also organised the first Veteran Gold Cup on the Silvaplana See close to St. Moritz in Switzerland. Even Rickard Sarby sailed in the regatta to represent Sweden. When the first race was scheduled it was raining and very cold. So most of the veterans would have preferred not to sail. But the Dutch Mel Oskamp declared to be eager to sail, and so the race was started. When the sun came, the wind grew even stronger. It always paid to sail very close to the shore along the Ho-Tschi-Minh-path. Finally Mel Oskamp won and therefore had to organise the next event in Holland. From this time stems the tradition, that the winner has the right to decide the place of the next Veteran Gold Cup.

1. Veteran Gold Cup 1970

St. Moritz, Silvaplana See, Switzerland,
18 entries from 8 countries

1.	Mel Oskamp	H 396	5.6
2.	Othmar Reich	Z 183	9.9
3.	Worn Clark	SA 393	12.9
4.	Jakob Janich	G 945	16.0
5.	Åke Sätre	S 272	19.0
6.	Rickard Sarby	S 517	20.6
7.	Louis Schiess	Z 217	22.0
8.	Marc Lambelet	Z 221	25.0
9.	Jacques Gillard	B 77	25.6

In 1971, Mel Oskamp invited the veterans to Medemblik. Menoni from Italy won and therefore took the Cup to Lake Garda. where Mel Oskamp won it back in 1972. However, since Mel already knew how much work it was to organise such a regatta, he declined the honour to do it again and delegated it back to Switzerland. In 1973, 14 participants met at Lac de Neuchatel. De Yong from Holland arrived, looked around and declared that on that lake there would be no wind and left again the same hour, without even having unpacked his boat. He was right. since only one race

was sailed in very poor wind conditions and the title was not assigned.

2. Veteran Gold Cup 1971

Medemblik, Holland, September 17-19
13 entries from 6 countries

1.	Andreino Menoni	I 447	9.0
2.	Othmar Reich	Z 183	14.4
3.	Mel Oskamp	H 396	20.4
4.	W. Heisch	G 1050	54.7
5.	Jacques Gillard	B 77	39.4
6.	Martin Quadfass	Z 136	60.7
7.	P. Hakker	H 63	63.0

3. Veteran Gold Cup 1972

Gargnano, Lago di Garda, Italy, July 29-31
14 entries from 6 countries

1.	Mel Oskamp	H 396	5.7
2.	Andreino Menoni	I 447	19.0
3.	Beda Zingg	Z 271	22.4
4.	Gino Filippini	I 417	26.7
5.	Jean Gillard	B 77	35.4
6.	Franco Ciresa	I 338	37.7
7.	Othmar Reich	Z 290	43.0

4. Veteran Gold Cup 1973

Neuchatel, Switzerland
Because of poor weather conditions the title was not assigned.

In 1974 twenty competitors from eight countries met in Port Camargue. Racing was tough with two heats in Force 4 on the first day. which Vernon Stratton won both. When the wind got weaker every day. Stratton faded out. Andre Mevel took over and had difficulties to beat Mel Oskamp.

5. Veteran Gold Cup 1974

Port Camargue, France, June 19-23
20 entries from 8 countries

| 1. | Andre Mevel | F | 12.0 |
| 2. | Mel Oskamp | H | 35.7 |

3.	Vernon Stratton	K	48.0
4.	P. Goujon	F	53.7
5.	Catalano	I	61.7
6.	R. Gorchon	F	68.4
7.	J. Goujon	F	73.7
8.	Lebois	F	77.7
9.	Reich	Z	81.4
10.	Lombard	SA	85.7

Mevel kept the Cup in Port Camargue for 1975. Regular winds from force 1-3 ensured perfect racing with Philippe Soria as the chairman of the race committee. Andre Mevel, in those days the French Finn Secretary, was able to beat Othmar Reich from Switzerland in a 7 boat fleet.

6. Veteran Gold Cup 1975

Port Camargue, France, June 24-28
7 entries from 4 countries

1.	Andre Mevel	F 629	17.7
2.	Othmar Reich	Z 290	19.4
3.	Erich Kaspareth	I 368	24.4
4.	Louis Schiess	Z 217	33.7

Andre Mevel won again in 1976 with Laszlo Zsindely runner-up and Othmar Reich third, who had been participating since the first event in 1970.

7. Veteran Gold Cup 1976

Port Camargue, France, June 13-19

1.	Andre Mevel	F
2.	Laszlo Zsindely	Z
3.	Othmar Reich	Z

The 1977 event had very good participation with 27 skippers from 7 countries. The newcomer Georg Oser, who had learned the basics of sailing just a few years before managed to beat them all, starting a sparkling career in the Veteran Gold Cup regattas. After the race, Georg declined the privilege to

organise the next event on the spot and asked the Centre de Yachting Mediterranean, personified in Robert Laban, to organise it again in 1978.

8. Veteran Gold Cup 1977
Port Camargue, France, June 11-17
28 entries from 7 countries

1.	Georg Oser	Z 1	38.0
2.	Heinz Reiter	G 1594	39.7
3.	Andre Mevel	F 629	40.0
4.	Laszlo Zsindely	Z 347	41.7
5.	B. L. Morley	KZ 12	42.0
6.	H. Sellschopp	G 523	47.4
7.	P. Lebois	F 713	60.7
8.	Mel Oskamp	H 1	63.7
9.	E. Kaspareth	I 368	66.0
10.	C. Sturm	Z 352	66.7
11.	H.Wildhagen	G 1518	72.7
12.	Louis Schiess	Z 217	78.0
13.	J.P. Auzas	F 647	81.0
14.	Othmar Reich	Z 290	86.7
15.	Gilbert Lamboley	F 588	90.0

By this time the Germans had taken over the majority of participants and so it was only a question of statistics when one of them would win the Cup. In 1978 Heinz Reiter won the Veteran Gold Cup by never winning a race but scoring 3/5/2/2/4 and discarding a 12th.

9. Veteran Gold Cup 1978
Port Camargue, France, June 11-17
37 entries from 8 countries

1.	Heinz Reiter	G 1594	29.7
2.	P. Lebois	F 713	31.7
3.	Georg Oser	Z 1	39.4
4.	Laszlo Zsindely	Z 347	52.7
5.	Karel Hruby	CZ 26	61.7
6.	Othmar Reich	Z 364	64.0
7.	Andre Mevel	F 629	69.4
8.	Hans Chiochetti	I 506	72.0
9.	Erich Kaspareth	I 627	79.0
10.	G. Schilling	G 1310	82.0
11.	Hans Dieter Faass	G 1298	83.0
12.	Gilbert Lamboley	F 588	84.0
13.	Mel Oskamp	H 544	84.4
14.	J.P. Auzas	F 647	84.7
15.	Sturm	Z 352	86.0

When he offered to organise the Veterans for 1979. a committee was formed to override his ambitions and to retain the event in sunny Port Camargue in the experienced hands of Philippe Soria and Robert Laban. When Karel Hruby was the winner in 1979 he turned out to be

more stubborn than Reiter the previous year and nobody could convince him not to take the organisation along.

10. Veteran Gold Cup 1979
Port Camargue, France, June 4-9
29 entries from 7 countries

1.	Karel Hruby	CZ 26	9.0
2.	C. Sturm	Z 352	28.0
3.	Andre Mevel	F 629	38.1
4.	Othmar Reich	Z 364	41.0
5.	Georg Oser	Z 2	44.7
6.	J. Termoz	F 736	45.5
7.	Eric Larsson	S 596	50.0
8.	Hans Dieter Faass	G 1298	50.0
9.	J. Ask	S 419	60.0
10.	J. Martin	F 717	63.7
11.	Hanno Wildhagen	G 1518	65.7
12.	Roland Wenz	G 1696	67.0
13.	Orounet Lagrange	F 682	68.7

So in 1980 the veterans had to go to Czechoslovakia to Lake Lipno. 30 skippers from 7 countries made the trip. The organisation was of highest standard. Seven races were sailed. Whenever the defending champion Karel Hruby was in front. the wind died. When Georg Oser was lucky the races were counted. So, finally Oser won his second title far ahead of defender and runner-up Karel Hruby.

11. Veteran Gold Cup 1980
Lake Lipno, CSSR, June 21-27
30 entries from 7 countries

1.	Georg Oser	Z	17.0
2.	Karel Hruby	CZ	31.7
3.	Jiri Maier	CZ	49.0
4.	Dr. Egbert Vincke	G	53.7
5.	Walter Schuster	OE	55.4
6.	Václav Hudec	CZ	66.1
7.	Othmar Reich	Z	74.7
8.	Milo Splitek	CZ	74.7

9.	Werner Oberheidt	G	81.7
10.	Klaus Schulze	G	91.7
11.	Erich Kaspareth	I	102.0
12.	Helmut Junker	G	102.0
13.	Miroslav Vejvoda	CZ	103.7
14.	Antonin Vachek	CZ	106.0
15.	Elmer Rist	G	109.0

According to his habit Oser again delegated the organisation to southern France. Good-natured Robert Laban took the full load once again. 38 skippers from 10 nations came after the sun and some exciting sailing. Gy Wossala had superior speed in good winds and won four races, then finished second behind Georg Oser and did not sail in the final heavy wind race.

12. Veteran Gold Cup 1981
Port Camargue, France, June 7-13
38 entries from 10 countries

1.	Gy Wossala	M	3.0
2.	Georg Oser	Z	21.7
3.	Frank Roth	Z	31.4
4.	O. Burger	Z	42.4
5.	Peter Bohland	G	52.4
6.	Erich Kaspareth	I	62.0
7.	Jiri Maier	CZ	63.7
8.	Bernd Haller	G	67.0
9.	Peter Kron	G	72.0
10.	Karel Hruby	CZ	77.7
11.	Eric Larsson	S	78.7
12.	P. Gellert	G	82.0
13.	C. Sturm	Z	93.0
14.	Othmar Reich	Z	96.0
15.	J. Martin	F	97.0
16.	Werner Orth	G	111.0
17.	Peter Mohilla	OE	111.7
18.	Hans Dieter Faass	G	112.0
19.	Roland Wenz	G	113.0
20.	E. Holub	CZ	119.0

Gy Wossala was not able or willing to stage the next Championship in his home waters Lake Balaton and therefore delegated it to Austria. Nice gentle winds for the skippers and sun for the ladies were the predominant features of the 1982 Veteran Gold Cup. Ivan Hoffmann was leading most of the time up until the last beat of the last race, and everybody was thinking of sailing in the CSSR again. However smart Georg Oser won that last race and the title for the third time to ring up Robert Laban for help once more.

13. Veteran Gold Cup 1982
Lake Neusiedl, Austria, May 31-June 4
51 entries from 7 countries

1.	Georg Oser	Z 1	21.0
2.	Ivan Hoffmann	CZ 93	25.7
3.	Friedrich Müller	G 1683	34.0
4.	G. Wossala	M 7	34,4
5.	Klaus von Packowski	G 1756	56.0
6.	Peter Mohilla	OE 1	60.0
7.	Erich Kaspareth	I 665	64.0
8.	Karel Hruby	CZ 262	66.0
9.	G. Schilling	G 7	67.0
10.	Horst Klein	G 1687	67.0
11.	Adalbert Wiest	G 1336	67.4
12.	Erich Baumgartner	OE 222	72.7
13.	Gerhard Gfreiner	OE 158	73.0
14.	Klaus Schulze	G 1704	73.0
15.	Peter Bohland	G 1562	75.0
16.	Jiri Maier	CZ 654	75.0
17.	Elmer Rist	G 998	78.7
18.	Dieter Ottlik	G 1798	86.0
19.	Werner Oberheidt	G 1810	86.0
20.	V. Chalupnik	CZ 371	90.7

And Robert Laban was kind enough to grant it. However the wind in Port Camargue was already bored by the constant visits of the old boys. Seven times is fine, but eight is too much and so it was determined to expel the veterans from that paradise. Therefore it blew a lot in 1983; for some too much. The favourite, Georg Oser, collected two wins but also twice a PMS and dropped to 10th overall. The unexpected winner was Heini Unterhauser from German speaking northern Italy.

14. Veteran Gold Cup 1983
Port Camargue, France, May 21-28
48 entries from 8 countries

1.	Heini Unterhauser	I 651	24.4
2.	Frank Roth	Z 334	47.7
3.	H. Herwig	G 1682	52.4
4.	Werner Oberheidt	G 1810	53.0
5.	Friedrich Müller	G 1683	55.1
6.	Erich Kaspareth	I 665	55.7
7.	Andrea Roost	Z 9	56.0
8.	Peter Bohland	G 1562	68.4
9.	U. Gut	Z 409	79.0
10.	Georg Oser	Z 2	87.0
11.	Bernd Gunther	G 1565	88.0
12.	Bernd Haller	G 1853	93.0
13.	Dieter Ottlik	G 1798	97.0
14.	C. Sturm	Z 352	110.0
15.	Elmer Rist	G 998	111.0
16.	Eric Larsson	S 596	118.0

17.	Rolf Lehnert	G 1815	113.0
18.	Hendrik Vincke	G 1312	115.0
19.	Karel Hruby	CZ 26	118.0
20.	Hans Dieter Mölls	G 1509	125.0

15. Veteran Gold Cup 1984
Lago di Caldaro/Kalterersee, Italy
June 11-15, 103 entries from 8 countries

1.	Walter Mai	G 1818	6.0
2.	Palle-Steen Larsen	D 147	6.0
3.	Friedrich Müller	G 1683	28.4
4.	Klaus Stuffer	I 506	35.7
5.	Jürgen Bärwind	G 1790	41.0
6.	Jürgen Oberheidt	G 1810	48.4
7.	G.J. van der Werf	H 615	50.7
8.	Heinrich Unterhauser	I 651	52.7
9.	Peter Bohland	G 1562	54.0
10.	Bernd Gunther	G 1565	56.4
11.	Walter Schuster	OE 208	56.7

12.	H. Herwig	G 1682	59.1
13.	Georg Oser	Z 1	59.7
14.	Laszlo Zsindely	Z 347	61.0
15.	Alan Tucker	OE 490	63.7
16.	Václav Hudec	CZ 10	69.0
17.	B. Burton Barbour	OE 504	69.0
18.	Frank Roth	Z 334	69.4
19.	Horst Klein	G 1687	72.7
20.	Klaus v. Packowski	G 1756	75.0
21.	Erich Kaspareth	I 665	76.0
22.	Franz Steib	G 1676	82.0
23.	Fabio Albarelli	I 516	83.7
24.	Dieter Ottlik	G 1798	84.7
25.	Adalbert Wiest	G 1836	86.0
26.	O. Andergassen	I 662	87.0
27.	Günter Kellermann	G 1589	87.0
28.	Herbert Sondermann	G 1 774	98.0
29.	Klaus Weixelbaumer	OE 219	100.0
30.	Rolf Lehnert	G 1815	101.0
31.	Elmar Rist	G 998	101.7
32.	Erich Baumgartner	OE 222	103.0
33.	Riccardo Grande	I 147	103.0
34.	Berthold Hailer	G 1853	105.7
35.	Cornel Mayrgündter	I 694	107.0

In 1984 they had to divide the fleet into two groups, otherwise it would not have been possible to get the more than 100 boats across the line, already hitting the shores on both sides. Old hand Walter Mai and newcomer Palle-Steen Larsen were equal in overall points before the last race, which was not sailed because there was no wind. So they gave the title to Mai, because he was second in the first race when Palle-Steen ended up 25th.

In 1985, an even larger number of veterans gathered in Bavaria. Lake Chiemsee offered not too much wind, but it was good enough for four races. The veterans were no challenge for the professional Jorgen Lindhardtsen who won with four straight line honours. The 110 amateurs behind him enjoyed the event very much.

16. Veteran Gold Cup 1985
Seebruck, Chiemsee, Federal Republic of Germany, May 28-31
111 entries from 10 countries

1.	Jörgen Lindhardtsen	D 142	0.0
2.	Klaus Stuffer	I 506	27.0
3.	Henning Wind	D 157	50.9
4.	Georg Oser	Z 1	59.0
5.	Heini Unterhauser	I 651	70.9
6.	Berthold Hailer	G 1853	74.6
7.	Peter Weichel	G 1869	74.6
8.	Adalbert Or. Wiest	G 1836	81.0
9.	Jürgen Bärwind	G 1790	100.0
10.	Friedrich Müller	G 1846	102.0
11.	Palle-Steen Larsen	D 147	106.9
12.	Karel Hruby	CZ 26	110.0
13.	Peter Mohilla	OE 1	110.0
14.	G.-J van der Werf	H 615	115.0
15.	Wilfried Balthasar	G 1671	115.0
16.	Louie Nady	US 1009	117.0
17.	Jiri Maier	CZ 304	118.0
18.	Hans Wölke	G 1767	122.0
19.	Egbert Vincke	G 1705	124.0
20.	Herbert Sondermann	G 1774	125.0
21.	Georg Rieperdinger	C 1876	125.6
22.	Martin Quadfass	Z 406	126.0
23.	Herbert Herwig	G 1682	130.0
24.	Erich Kaspareth	I 665	134.0
25.	H.P. Schobert	G 470	135.0
26.	Peter Bohland	C 1562	136.0
27.	Horst Klein	C 1687	139.0
28.	Gerhard Gfreiner	OE 158	153.0
29.	Günter Plinke	C 1733	155.0
30.	Hans Dieter Faass	C 1 298	158.0
31.	Gerhard Benz	Z 398	162.0
32.	Dieter Ottlik	C 1803	164.0
33.	Antonin Vachek	CZ 311	168.0
34.	Klaus P. Schulze	C 1704	171.0
35.	Gerhard Kohlwig	C 1 724	177.0
36.	Bernd Günter	C 1565	177.0
37.	Laszlo Zsindely	Z 347	179.0
38.	Jürgen Koch	G 1066	180.0

17. Veteran Gold Cup 1986
Lago di Bracciano, Italy, May 18-23
83 entries from 7 countries
Four boats dominated the top of the fleet in the mainly light wind regatta, those of Heini Unterhauser, Klaus Stuffer, Václav Hudec and Georg Oser. After a postponement most days due to lack of wind, the breeze filled in early in the afternoon and the fleet managed to complete five of the schedules six races.

1.	Heini Unterhauser	I 651	20.7
2.	Klaus Stuffer	I 508	26.4
3.	Georg Oser	Z 1	36.7

4.	Václav Hudec	CZ 10	47.0
5.	Peter Weichel	G 1869	53.7
6.	Cintl Václav	CZ 7	58.0
7.	Franz Steib	G 1667	58.7
8.	Jürgen Bärwind	G 1790	61.0
9.	Hans-Dieter Faass	G 1298	6.7
10.	Karel Hruby	CZ 26	67.0
11.	G J van der Werf	H 615	72.7
12.	Horst Klein	G 1687	73.0
13.	Dieter Ottlik	G 1803	75.7
14.	Erich Kaspareth	I 665	78.7
15.	Laszlo Zsindely	Z 347	88.0
16.	Hendrik Vincke	G 1559	90.0
17.	Elmar Rist	G 998	91.0
18.	Frank Roth	Z 334	96.0
19.	H Duckerhoff	G 1805	99.0
20.	K von Packowski	G 1866	99.0
21.	Herbert Herwig	G 1682	103.0
22.	H Drexelius	G 1684	103.0
23.	Riccardo Grande	I 698	107.0
24.	Rodney Cobb	K 510	111.0
25.	V Chalupnik	CZ 252	113.0
26.	Marcel Haegler	Z 410	119.0
27.	Antonin Vachek	CZ 28	120.0
28.	Petr Topiarz	CZ 126	127.0
29.	Cornel Mayrgündter	I 694	129.0
30.	Hans Wölke	G 1767	130.0
31.	Georg Rieperdinger	G 1876	130.0
32.	Hans-Dieter Mölls	G 1509	136.0
33.	Bernd Gunther	G 1565	139.0
34.	Jürgen Puchert	G 1801	153.0
35.	Jürgen Koch	G 1066	153.0
36.	Howard Mitchell	K 373	154.0
37.	Jiri Maier	CZ 5	157.7
38.	Peter Atzwanger	I 648	158.0
39.	H-P Schobert	G 470	158.0
40.	O. Andergassen	I 662	164.0

18. Veteran Gold Cup 1987

Les Embiez, France, June 7-12
94 entries
Before the event the wind either blew a mistral
or there was none at all. So the first race started
in no wind and large waves with the wind
gradually increasing up to a force 6. Tuesday's
race was abandoned due to too much wind,
but then they caught up with two races on the
next two days. Peter Raderschadt from
Germany won his first Veteran Gold Cup with
a 1,1,2,2,3 scoreline.

1.	Peter Raderschadt	G 1470	13.7
2.	Walter Mai	G 1525	23.1
3.	Ivor Ganahl	Z 393	33.0
4.	Jiri Outrata	CZ 8	44.4

5.	Friedrich Müller	G 1846	54.7
6.	Roland Balthasar	G 1665	55.0
7.	Louie Nady	US 1009	65.0
8.	Henning Wind	D 154	71.0
9.	Kurt Schimitzek	OE 2	73.4
10.	Rodney Cobb	K 491	80.0
11.	Mikael Brandt	S 366	82.7
12.	Herbert Herwig	G 1682	103.0
13.	Martin Mitterer	G 875	104.0
14.	Herbert Sondermann	G 1774	110.0
15.	Han van Vierssen	H 632	110.0
16.	Peter Malm	D 1	120.0
17.	Dieter Ohlik	G 1803	128.0
18.	Heinrich Unterhauser	I 726	130.0
19.	Horst Klein	G 1889	138.0
20.	Rolf Lehnert	G 1815	139.0

19. Veteran Gold Cup 1988

Lido degli Estensi, Italy, May 21-28
100 entries from 10 countries
The big and heavy favourites were excluded
this year and a Swiss, named Hans Fatzer,
who had not been paid much attention to before
was the great surprise. He dominated early on
with a 2nd, 1st and 2nd in the light conditions
and the strong current, but later in the week
Schimitzek, Ottlik and König each won a race.
The jury was very strict, disqualifying five
boats in the first race.

1.	Hans Fatzer	Z 386	11.7
2.	Jiri Outrata	CZ 8	21.7
3.	Kurt Schimitzek	OE 2	36.7
4.	Friedrich Müller	G 1846	53.0
5.	Dieter Ottlik	G 1883	59.0
6.	Goerg Oser	Z 1	63.0
7.	Goerg Rieperdinger	G 1987	72.4
8.	Laszlo Zsindely	Z 347	74.0
9.	Leek Neve	B 28	79.0
10.	Jürgen Barwind	G 1790	81.0

20. Veteran Gold Cup 1989

Torbole, Garda, Italy, May 15-20
101 entries from 10 countries
Fickle and light winds plagued the event as a
low pressure system sat on top of the Alps
and refused to move. The result was that there
was very little wind and the famous southerly
wind, the Ora, failing to come up. Peter
Raderschadt won for a second time.

1.	Peter Raderschadt	G 1470
2.	Kurt Schimitzek	OE 2
3.	Mikael Brandt	S 681
4.	Jiri Outrata	CZ 8
5.	Louie Nady	US 1009
6.	Gerd Hufner	G 1500
7.	Walter Mai	G 1928
8.	Werner Beuck	G 1772
9.	Friedrich Müller	G 1846
10.	Adalbert Wiest	G 1836
11.	Andi Lochbrunner	G 1476
12.	Horst Klein	G 1489
13.	Heinrich Unterhauser	I 742
14.	Roland Balthasar	G 66
15.	Jack van Hellehond	H 650
16.	Kees Kruyer	H 538
17.	Handi Hittmer	G 875

18.	Coppi Herwig	G 1632
19.	Hans-Gunther Ehlers	G 35
20.	Franz Steib	G 1667
21.	Manfred Immler	G 4
22.	Herbert Gondermein	G 55
33.	Henk de Jäger	H 665
34.	Olaf Burger	Z 350
35.	Han van Vierssen	H 632

21. Finn World Masters 1990

Altenrhein, Lake Boden, Switzerland
103 entries from 11 countries
Only four races were managed to be sailed in
1990 and the rain was incessant. Mikael Brandt
won the first race, came 3rd in the second and
held on to his points to win. During the week,
the sailors forced Georg Oser (Old Joe) to
organise an 'Oldie-AGM'. During this
meeting, it was agreed that the event would
be know from now on as the FINN WORLD
MASTERS and to have a regular meeting
during the event at which new ideas can be
discussed.

1.	Mikael Brandt	G
2.	Friedrich Müller	G
3.	Jiri Outrata	CZ
4.	Roland Balthasar	G
5.	G Hübner	G
6.	Herbert Herwig	G
7.	Laszlo Zsindely	Z
8.	Heini Mai	G
10.	Jürgen Kraft	DDR
11.	Rodney Cobb	K
12.	Peter Raderschadt	G

22. Finn World Masters 1991

Port Camargue, France May 18-25
97 entries
Only four races were managed as the 'Mistral'
wind whipped up a very rough Mediterranean.
And when it was possible to sail there were
huge shifts in the wind. However Kurt

Schimitzek managed to work them out and won the regatta by a large margin.

1.	Kurt Schimitzek	OE 2	14.0
2.	Jochen Lollert	G 72	31.0
3.	Hermann Heide	G 51	37.0
4.	Jiri Outrata	CZ 8	40.0
5.	Coppi Herwig	G 1682	66.0
6.	Heinz Stammnitz	G 40	69.0
7.	Peter Raderschadt	G 47	73.0
8.	Louis Nady	US 1009	73.0
9.	Henk de Jäger	H 559	82.0
10.	Walter Schuster	OE 210	83.0
11.	Herbert Sondermann	G 55	97.0
12	Heinrich Unterhauser	I 749	98.0

23. Finn World Masters 1992

Uppsala, Sweden, June 6-12
85 entries 10 countries
In 1992 Roland Balthasar sailed consistently well and chose the correct side enough times such that he didn't have to sail the last race.

1.	Roland Balthasar	G 66
2.	Hermann Heide	G 51
3.	Peter Vollebregt	H 708
4.	Dieter Borges	G 34
5.	Jiri Outrata	CZ 8
6.	Kurt Schimitzek	OE 2
7.	Andi Lochbrunner	G 1478
8.	Mikael Brandt	S 682
9.	Axel Kettler	G 14
10.	Peter Bohland	G 1562
11.	Jurgen Kraft	G 42
12.	Henk de Jäger	H 665
13.	Wilfried Balthasar	G 68
14.	Jochen Lollert	G 72
15.	Arne Akerson	S 703
16.	Bernd Gunther	G 1669
17.	Hennie Van Den Brink	H 600
18.	Jan Björnberg	S 681
19.	Friedrich Müller	G 1846
20.	Manfred Immler	G 4
21.	Manfred Poschl	G 48
22.	Alfred Blum	G 1941

24. Finn World Masters 1993

Lake Bracciano, Italy, May 29 - June 4
127 entries
Races were won by old Finn cracks such as Kurt Schimitzek, Walter Mai, Roland Balthasar, Jan Björnberg and Peter Vollebregt. With the title still up for grabs the last race was cancelled because of too much wind. In race 4 Competitor Joseph Thermoz from France died of a heart attack and the organisers wanted to stop the regatta, but his relatives wanted them to continue. "Old Joe" Goerg Oser, long time organiser of the event, retired as Masters Supreme Organiser and handed

the reigns over to Rolf Lehnert.

1.	Peter Vollebregt	H 708
2.	Walter Mai	G 3
3.	Jan Björnberg	S 690
4.	Roland Balthasar	G 66
5.	Jiri Outrata	CZ 8
6.	Kurt Schimitzek	OE 2
7.	Hans-Gunther Ehlers	G 35
8.	Hermann Heide	G 51
9.	Bruno Catalan	I 784
10.	Chris Frydal	H 664
11.	Peter Raderschadt	G 47
12.	Henk de Jäger	H 665
13.	Lucio Nodari	H 644
14.	Wilfried Balthasar	G 68
15.	Axel Kettler	G 171
16.	Walter Schuster	OE 210
17.	Dieter Borges	G 34
18.	Andi Lochbrunner	G 14
19.	Friedrich Müller	G 146
20.	Moreno Brunori	I 802
21.	Manfred Immler	G 4
22.	Daniele Daneri	I 701
23.	Dieter Ottlik	G 1803
24.	Jürgen Kraft	G 42
25.	Heinrich Unterhauser	I 1
26.	Klaus Stuffer	I 761
27.	Horst Klein	G 49
28.	Rodney Cobb	K 503
29.	Bernd Gunther	G 1669
30.	Rolf Lehnert	G 1815
31.	Laszlo Zsindely	Z 347
32.	Adalbert Wiest	G 96
33.	Manfred Poschl	G 48
34.	Herbert Sondermann	G 55

25. Finn World Masters 1994

Diessen, Ammersee, Germany, May 21-27
140 entries
The 140 Masters had every sort of wind condition from 0-6 and after 6 races minus discard both Roland Balthasar and Jiri Outrata both had results of 1, 2, 3, 4, and 5 and therefore exactly the same score of 14.75. Under the scoring system the scores remained tied, so there were two Masters World Champions.

1.	Roland Balthasar	GER 66	14.75
1.	Jiri Outrata	CZE 8	14.75
3.	Walter Mai	GER 3	25.75
4.	Wolfgang Gerz	GER 168	25.75
5.	Hans-Günter Ehlers	GER 35	31.75
6.	Peter Raderschadt	GER 47	42.0
7.	Andreas Lochbrunner	GER 44	42.0
8.	Bruno Catalan	ITA 784	45.0
9.	Pat Healy	CAN 15	45.0
10.	Mikael Brandt	SWE 682	53.0
11.	Lucio Nodari	NED 644	59.0
12.	Werner Beuck	GER 1	73.0

13.	Horst Klein	HER 49	73.0
14.	Hans Fatzer	SUI 427	83.0
15.	Detlev Guminski	GER 92	89.0
16.	Ulrich Matthiesen	GER 110	91.0
17.	Eberhard Bieberitz	GER 10	113.0
18.	Gerhard Gfreiner	AUT 4	113.0
19.	Wilfried Balthasar	GER 68	114.0
20.	John van Altena	NED 670	115.0
21.	Laszlo Zsindely	SUI 347	115.0
22.	Walter Schuster	AUT 210	130.0
23.	Jan Björnberg	SWE 690	132.0

26. Finn World Masters 1995

Malcesine, Lake Garda, Italy
132 entries from 14 countries
At SPA, a week before the start of the Masters, Larry Lemieux found out that you don't have to be 40 to sail the Finn World Masters, as long as you promise to turn 40 that year. That wasn't a problem so Larry drove down to Lake Garda. Larry Lemieux, and not unexpectedly won the regatta, winning races 1,3 and 4. Roland Balthasar won race 2, Bruno Catalan won race 4 and Klaus Stuffer won race 6.

1.	Lawrence Lemieux	CAN	8.25
2.	Kurt Schimitzek	AUT	22.0
3.	Wolfgang Gerz	GER	23.0
4.	Bruno Catalan	ITA	24.75
5.	Roland Balthasar	GER	31.75
6.	Minski Fabris	CRO	37.0
7.	Walter Mai	GER	
8.	Peter Raderschadt	GER	
9.	Chris Frydal	NED	
10.	Paul Phelan	CAN	
11.	Hans-Günter Ehlers	GER	70.0
12.	Horst Klein	GER	72.0
13.	Andi Lochbrunner	GER	74.0
14.	Luksa Cicarelli	CRO	85.0
15.	Jan Björnberg	SWE	100.0
16.	Jiri Outrata	CZE	100.0
17.	Lucio Nodari	NED	103.0
18.	Hain Wladimir	GER	117.0
19.	Wilfried Balthasar	GER	118.0
20.	Hendrik Vincke	GER	118.0
21.	Klaus Stuffer	ITA	119.75
22.	Adalbart Wiest	GER	120.0
23.	John van Altena	NED	120.0
24.	Andrea Roost	SUI	123.0
25.	Henk de Jäger	NED	133.0
26.	Dieter Borges	GER	138.0
27.	Walter Schuster	AUT	140.0
28.	Dieter Ottlik	GER	145.0
29.	Han v Vierssen	NED	151.0
30.	Michael Pandler	GER	151.0

27. Finn World Masters 1996
La Rochelle, France, May 1-10
120 entries from 14 countries
For the first time ever the Finn World Masters was combined with the 'real' Finn Gold Cup. A scoreline of 17-2-2-1-9-1 was enough for Roland Balthasar to take the Masters title for the third time. Fifi Ehlers lead at the beginning of the regatta but faded towards the end. Wolfgang Gerz won the 5th race to take second overall.

1.	Roland Balthasar	GER 66
2.	Wolfgang Gerz	GER 12
3.	Walter Mai	GER 3
4.	Henk de Jäger	NED 665
5.	Hans-Gunther Ehlers	GER 35
6.	Chris Frydal	NED 664
7.	Andi Lochbrunner	GER 44
8.	Bruno Catalan	ITA 784
9.	Eberhard Biebritz	GER 10
10.	Hermann Heide	GER 51
11.	Jiri Outrata	CZE 8
12.	August Miller	USA 975
13.	Jean Paul Gaston	FRA 772
14.	Sergei Chtmerbalcon	UKR 21
15.	Kurt Schimitzek	AUT 2
16.	Lucio Nodari	NED 644
17.	Wilfried Balthasar	GER 68
18.	Jochen Lollert	GER 72
19.	Hannes Diefenbach	GER 85
20.	Mikael Brandt	SWE 682
21.	Hans Fatzer	SUI 306
22.	Sten Waldo	SWE 711
23.	Erich Scherzer	NED 711
24.	Jiri Maier	CZ 304
25.	Bill Bell	A 10
26.	Franz Steib	GER 1837
27.	Georg Siebeck	GER 293
28.	Carsten Niehusen	GER 17
29.	Per Nilson	SWE 688
30.	Jan Björnberg	SWE 6
31.	Claude Vauthier	FRA 764
32.	John Van Altena	NED 670
33.	Karl-Heinz Erich	GER 39
34.	Manfred Poschl	GER 48
35.	Jurgen Kraft	GER 42
36.	Horst Klein	GER 49
37.	Michael Till	GBR 536
38.	Patrick Moore	GBR 533

28. Finn World Masters 1997
Cervia, Italy, May 18-24
131 entries from 13 countries
The regatta was a battle between the 1995 champion Larry Lemieux and 1981 Gold Cup winner Wolfgang Gerz. Four times each had

top three results, but a couple bad races in the middle for both of them, including a DSQ for Lemieux meant the title went to Gerz.

1.	Wolfgang Gerz	ITA 1	24
2.	Lawrence Lemieux	CAN 1	29
3.	Minski Fabris	CRO 1	42
4.	Bruno Catalan	ITA 784	44
5.	Peter Raderschadt	GER 47	48
6.	Walter Mai	GER 3	50
7.	Gabor Antal	HUN 177	52
8.	R. Bosetti	ITA 82	59
9.	Jiri Outrata	CZE 8	62
10.	Kurt Schimitzek	AUT 2	62
11.	Jan Björnberg	SWE 6	67
12.	Jean Paul Gaston	FRA 78	69
13.	Hermann Heide	GER 51	78
14.	Henk De Jäger	NED 713	81
15.	Eberhard Biebritz	GER 10	86
16.	K. Erich	GER 39	89
17.	A. Schippers	NED 717	93
18.	M. Plecity	CZE 318	104
19.	Andi Lochbrunner	GER 44	116
20.	Lucio Nodari	NED 644	117
21.	M.V. Damir	CRO 111	118
22.	Mikael Brandt	SWE 7	122
23.	L. Koepnick	GER 77	127
24.	B. Van Den	NED 600	129
25.	Andrea Roost	SUI 445	131
26.	Walter Schuster	AUT 210	135
27.	Luksa Cicarelli	CRO 110	135
28.	Michael Pandler	GER 63	140
29.	Horst Klein	GER 49	141
30.	Wilfried Balthasar	GER 68	142
31.	Roland Balthasar	GER 66	154
32.	E. Scherzer	NED 711	155
33.	Josef Senkyr	CZE 2	160
34.	Rodney Cobb	GBR 534	165
35.	Vaclav Cintl	CZE 7	166
36.	R. Boeckelt	GER 2071	180
37.	Herbert Sondermann	GER 55	190
38.	Heinz Stammnitz	GER 40	191
39.	Hans Fatzer	SUI 438	193
40.	Per Nilson	SWE 688	206
41.	Sten Waldo	SWE 711	207
42.	M. Poeschl	GER 48	207
43.	K. Kruyer	NED 712	209
44.	R. Baumann	SUI 430	210

29. Finn World Masters 1998
Castelleto di Brenzone, Lake Garda, Italy
May 30-June 5, 128 entries from 13 countries
1998 saw the total domination of Larry Lemieux who won the first 5 races, although in race 2 he was awarded first place after the two boats ahead of him at the finish were scored OCS. Minski Fabris was the only sailor close on points with a scoreline of 2-2-5-2-1 which would be enough to win in most years. The defending champion, Wolfgang Gerz, could only manage third overall.

1.	Lawrence Lemieux	CAN 1	5
2.	Minski Fabris	CRO 1	12
3.	Wolfgang Gerz	ITA 1	33
4.	R. Bosetti	ITA 82	42
5.	Walter Mai	GER 3	50
6.	Jan Björnberg	SWE 6	52
7.	Haluk Beverwijk	NED 724	56
8.	Gabor Antal	HUN 113	60
9.	Andi Lochbrunner	GER 44	62
10.	H. Wuhn	GER 12	83
11.	Kurt Schimitzek	AUT 2	84
12.	Henk De Jäger	NED 713	99
13.	Andrew Cooper	GBR 7	104
14.	M. Poschl	GER 48	104
15.	Roland Balthasar	GER 66	106
16.	Bruno Catalan	ITA 784	110
17.	P. Sipos	HUN 14	116
18.	K. Kruijer	NED 712	117
19.	M. Plecity	CZE 318	120
20.	Jiri Outrata	CZE 8	124
21.	Horst Klein	GER 49	125
22.	D. Vrdoljak	CRO 111	133
23.	Mikael Brandt	SWE 701	140
24.	Lucio Nodari	NED 7	145
25.	A. Schippers	NED 717	146
26.	B. Van Den	NED 600	149
27.	K. Suffer	ITA 3	156
28.	Rodney Cobb	GBR 534	161
29.	Hans Fatzer	SUI 438	164
30.	Walter Schuster	AUT 210	168
31.	Michael Pandler	GER 63	172
32.	Eberhard Biebritz	GER 10	183
33.	Herbert Sondermann	GER 55	184
34.	L. Köpnick	GER 77	187
35.	Jürgen Kraft	GER 42	189
36.	Luksa Cicarelli	CRO 110	191
37.	V. Altena	NED 716	194
38.	Laszlo Zsindely	SUI 711	198
39.	Sten Waldo	SWE 711	198
40.	Wilfried Balthasar	GER 68	199
41.	Claude Vauthier	FRA 784	199
42.	J. Lalanne	FRA 785	207
43.	N. Boot	NED 630	211
44.	G. Dufner	GER 87	212

The only problem with the Finn World Masters is that each year a new group of sailors qualify without merit simply by getting older than 40, so the numbers sailing get bigger all the time. Since 1984 the Masters has regularly attracted over 100 boats, with the highest turnout in 1994 with 140 entries.

Each helm has his countries letters next to his name. To avoid confusion and to standardise the listings, the new national letters, which were introduced in 1992 are used throughout. The only exceptions to this is when the country in question did not exist after 1992 where the older letters are used.

Athens Eurolymp

1994	Vasilis Iliopoulos	GRE
1995	Michalis Papadopoupos	GRE
1996	Michalis Papadopoupos	GRE
1997	Emilios Papathanasiou	GRE
1998	Karlo Kuret	CRO

Balkan Championship

1970	Minski Fabris	Y
1971	Anastasios Boudouris	GRE
1974	Minski Fabris	Y
1975	Elias Hatzipavlis	GRE
1976	Elias Hatzipavlis	GRE
1977	Elias Hatzipavlis	GRE
1981	Neno Viali	Y
1983	N.B. Vassilev	BUL
1987	Mihail Kopanov	BUL

Cannes Ski Yachting

1961	Herbert Reich	GER
1962	S. Verneuil	FRA
1963	J. Lemanissier	FRA
1968	Alexis Bally	SUI
1969	Serge Maury	FRA
1970	Fabio Albarelli	ITA
1971	Henning Wind	DEN
1972	Iain Macdonald-Smith	GBR
1976	Serge Maury	FRA
1977	Silvestro	ESP
1980	Sergei Khoretski	SR
1981	Joaquin Blanco	ESP
1982	Sergei Khoretski	SR
1983	Henrik Blaszka	POL
1984	Oleg Khoperski	SR
1985	Thomas Oljelund	SWE
1986	Frank Butzmann	DDR
1987	Stuart Childerley	GBR
1988	Hans Spitzauer	AUT
1989	Hans Spitzauer	AUT
1990	Jeremy Fanstone	GBR

CORK

1969	Gordy Bowers	USA
1970	Carl van Duyne	USA

1971	John Eastwood	CAN
1972	not sailed	
1973	Henry Sprague	USA
1974	Henry Sprague	USA
1975	David Howlett	GBR
1976	not sailed	
1977	Sandy Riley	CAN
1978	Dave Buemi	USA
1979	Paul Van Cleve	USA
1980	Larry Lemieux	CAN
1981	Terry Neilson	CAN
1982	Larry Lemieux	CAN
1983	Paul Van Cleve	USA
1984	Derek Mess	CAN
1985	Lawrence Lemieux	CAN
1986	Scott MacLeod	USA
1987	Larry Lemieux	CAN
1988	Lasse Hjortnäs	DEN
1989	Craig Monk	NZL
1990	Hank Lammens	CAN
1991	Alec Cutler	CAN
1992	Richard Clarke	CAN
1993	John Porter	USA
1994	Lawrence Lemieux	CAN
1995	Richard Clarke	CAN
1996	Tyler Bjorn	CAN
1997	Larry Lemieux	CAN
1998	Mike Deyett	USA

Right: Notice of Race from first ever South American Championship in Buenos Aires, Argentina in 1964

Goodwill Games

1986			
1	Oleg Khoperski	SR
2	Dirk Pittlekov	DDR
3	Buzz Reynolds	USA

1990			
1	Brian Ledbetter	USA
2	Stig Westergaard	DEN
3	Peter Holmberg	ISV

North American Finn Championship

1957	Oyster Bay, New York	11 entries	Glen Foster USA	Mark Coholen USA	Jack Knights GBR
1958	Marion, Massachusetts	11 entries	Jack Knights GBR	Mark Coholen USA	George O'Day USA
1959	Not sailed due to Pan-Am Games in Chicago				
1960	Marion, Massachusetts	13 entries	Glen Foster USA	Peter Barrett USA	Ian Bruce CAN
1961	Long Beach, California	32 entries	Fred Miller USA	Roland Whitaker USA	Larry Wood USA
1962	Nassau, Bahamas	15 entries	Fred Miller USA	Henry Sprague USA	Dick Prince USA
1963	Quebec, Canada	45 entries	Henry Sprague USA	Dave Smalley USA	Dick Prince USA
1964	New Orleans, Louisiana	47 entries	Dan Hurley USA	O J Young USA	Fred Miller USA
1965	Warwick, Bermuda	37 entries	Dick Tillman USA	Glen Foster USA	Peter Barrett USA
1966	Tawas Bay, Michigan	53 entries	Peter Barrett USA	Bob Andre USA	Paul Henderson CAN
1967	Miami, Florida	32 entries	Ralph Conrad USA	Jörg Bruder BRA	Garry Hoyt PUR
1968	Long Beach, California	40 entries	Carl van Duyne USA	Peter Barrett USA	Clive Roberts NZL
1969	CORK, Kingston, Canada	40 entries	Gordy Bowers USA	Andy Schöttle USA	Hubert Raudaschl AUT
1970	Atlantic Highlands, New Jersey	64 entries	Carl van Duyne USA	Andy Schöttle USA	Norm Freeman USA
1971	Toronto, Canada	59 entries	Jörg Bruder BRA	Bret De Thier NZL	Carl van Duyne USA
1972	San Francisco, California	47 entries	Henry Sprague USA	Edward Bennett USA	Jeff Lenhart USA
1973	Valle de Bravo, Mexico	45 entries	Jeff Lenhart USA	Randy MacLaren USA	Lou Nady USA
1974	Toronto, Canada	49 entries	Peter Conrad USA	Sanford Riley CAN	Gordy Bowers USA
1975	New Orleans, Louisiana	32 entries	John Bertrand AUS	Ron Dougherty USA	Bill Allen USA
1976	Mantoloking, New Jersey	21 entries	Gus Miller USA	Lee Morrison USA	Dan Hurley USA
1977	Manzanillo, Mexico	19 entries	Henry Sprague USA	Randy MacLaren USA	Tom Bissell USA
1978	CORK, Kingston, Canada	39 entries	Dave Buemi USA	Larry Lemieux CAN	Sandy Riley CAN
1979	Milwaukee, Wisconsin, USA	52 Entries	Paul Van Cleve USA	Kurt Miller USA	Jamie Richardson CAN
1980	Nassau, Bahamas	29 Entries	Peter Commette USA	Buzz Reynolds USA	Carl Buchan USA
1981	New Orleans, Louisiana, USA	11 Entries	Craig Healy USA	Monty Spindler USA	Larry Lemieux CAN
1982	Kingston, Canada	18 entries	Buzz Reynolds USA	Peter Quigley USA	Jim Hahn USA
1983	San Diego, USA	51 entries	Tim Lihan USA	Terry Neilson CAN	Paul Van Cleve USA
1984	Gulfport, USA	46 Entries	Larry Lemieux CAN	Kimo Worthington USA	Russ Silvestri USA
1985	San Diego, USA		Russ Silvestri USA	Kimo Worthington USA	Lou Nady USA
1986	Marblehead, USA	34 Entries	Scot MacLeod USA	Buzz Reynolds USA	Mark Lammens CAN
1987	San Francisco, USA	19 Entries	Russ Silvestri USA	Peter Truslow USA	Louis Verloop USA
1988	Halifax, Nova Scotia		Russ Silvestri USA	Scott MacLeod USA	Lawrence Lemieux CAN
1989	Marblehead, USA		Rich Byron USA	Peter Tanscheit BRA	Jere White USA
1990	Seattle, Washington, USA	26 Entries	Brian Ledbetter USA	Rich Byron USA	Mark Herrmann USA
1991	Wilmette, USA	26 Entries	Richard Clarke CAN	Rich Byron USA	Dave Himmell USA
1992	Marblehead, USA		John Porter USA	Will Martin USA	Darrell Peck USA
1993	Dorval, Quebec, Canada		Hank Lammens CAN	John Porter USA	Brian Huntsman USA
1994	Santa Cruz		Larry Lemieux CAN	Eric Oetgen USA	Richard Clarke CAN
1995	Toronto, Ontario, Canada	39 Entries	Hank Lammens CAN	Richard Clarke CAN	Craig Monk NZL
1996	Hilton Head Island, USA	28 Entries	Fredrik Lööf SWE	Chris Bergmann BRA	Craig Monk NZL
1997	San Francisco, USA	13 Entries	Richard Clarke CAN	Russ Silvestri USA	Darrell Peck USA
1998	St Margarets Bay, Nova Scotia	17 entries	Richard Clarke CAN	Larry Lemieux CAN	Mike Deyett USA

Pan Am Games

1959	Chicago, USA	Kenneth Alburg BAH	E. Berisso ARG	William McLean USA
1963	Sau Paulo, Brazil	H. Bomshke BRA	Peter Barrett USA	P Garra URU
1967	Winnipeg, Canada	Jörg Bruder BRA	Carl van Duyne USA	John Clarke CAN
1971	Cali, Columbia	Jörg Bruder BRA	Carl van Duyne USA	Roberto Haas ARG
1975	Valle de Bravo, Mexico	Bill Allen USA	Claudio Biekarck BRA	Daniel Mugica MEX
1979-87		Finn not used		
1991	La Habana, Cuba	Larry Lemieux CAN	Christoph Bergmann BRA	Eric Mergenthaler MEX
1995	Finn not used			

South American Championship

1964	Buenos Aires, Argentina	Jörg Bruder BRA	H. Domscke BRA	M. Kojima JPN
1968	Vina del Mar, Chile	Adrian Obarrio ARG	Jörg Brecht GER	Jorge Sanjurjo ARG
1974	San Pablo, Brazil	Claudio Biekarck BRA	Roberto Martins BRA	Juan Carlo Firpo ARG
1975		Manfred Kaufmann BRA	Roberto Martins BRA	Peter Scheel BRA
1981		Jorge Zarif BRA		

Hyeres

1970	Guy Liljegren	SWE
1971	Serge Maury	FRA
1972	Serge Maury	FRA
1973	M. Busquet	FRA
1975	Mauro Pelaschier	ITA
1976	David Howlett	GBR
1977	Chris Law	GBR
1978	Jochen Schümann	FRG
1979	Guy Liljegren	SWE
1980	Joaquin Blanco	ESP
1981	Francois Le Castrec	FRA
1982	Wolfgang Gerz	GER
1983	Jorgen Lindhardtsen	DEN
1984	Oleg Khoperski	SR
1985	Oleg Khoperski	SR
1986	Paolo Semeraro	ITA
1987	Hans Spitzauer	AUT
1988	Hans Spitzauer	AUT
1989	Armando Ortolano	GRE
1990	Jali Makila	FIN
1991	Jali Makila	FIN
1992	Dirk Löwe	GER
1993	Roy Heiner	NED
1994	José Maria van der Ploeg	ESP
1995	José Maria van der Ploeg	ESP
1996	Sebastien Godefroid	BEL
1997	Fredrik Lööf	SWE
1998	Sebastien Godefroid	BEL
1999	Mateusz Kusznierewicz	POL

Interunfall Lakes Week

1997	Emilios Papathanasiou	GRE
1998	Michael Maier	CZE

Kiel Week

1952	Dr. Enelli	
1956	Paul Elvström	DEN
1957	Paul Elvström	DEN
1958	Börge Schwartz	DEN
1959	Willy Kuhweide	FRG
1960	Paul Elvström	DEN
1961	Bruce McCurrach	RSA
1962	J C Jammes	FRA
1963	Uwe Mares	GER
1964	Willy Kuhweide	GER
1965	Willy Kuhweide	GER
1966	Willy Kuhweide	GER
1967	Willy Kuhweide	GER
1968	Uwe Mares	GER
1969	Andreas von Eicken	GER
1970	Willy Kuhweide	GER
1971	Thomas Jungblut	GER
1972	Thomas Lundquist	SWE
1973	Uwe Heinzmann	GER
1974	Serge Maury	FRA
1975	David Howlett	GBR
1976	Chris Law	GBR
1977	Ryszard Skarbinski	POL
1978	Joaquin Blanco	ESP
1979	John Bertrand	USA
1980	Liljegren	SWE
1981	Lasse Hjortnäs	DEN
1982	Lasse Hjortnäs	DEN
1983	Lasse Hjortnäs	DEN
1984	Lasse Hjortnäs	DEN
1985	Brian Ledbetter	USA
1986	Lasse Hjortnäs	DEN
1987	Oleg Khoperski	SR
1988	Stig Westergaard	DEN
1989	Mats Caap	SW\E
1990	Hans Spitzauer	AUT
1991	Anders Lundmark	SWE
1992	José Maria van der Ploeg	ESP
1993	Fredrik Lööf	SWE
1994	Hans Spitzauer	AUT
1995	Xavier Rohart	FRA
1996	Michael Maier	CZE
1997	Hans Spitzauer	AUT
1998	Mateusz Kusznierewicz	POL

Miami Olympic Classes Regatta

1990	Mike Milner	CAN
1991	Lawrence Lemieux	CAN
1992	Brian Ledbetter	USA
1993	Richard Clarke	CAN
1994	Jose Maria van der Ploeg	ESP
1995	Brian Ledbetter	USA
1996	Philippe Presti	FRA
1997	Sebastien Godefroid	BEL
1998	Larry Lemieux	CAN
1999	Rodrigo Meireles	BRA

Palamos Christmas Race

1979	José Luis Doreste	ESP
1981	Jaques Hartmann	
1983	Mark Neeleman	NED
1984	Passoni	ITA
1985	José Luis Doreste	ESP
1986	Stuart Childerley	GBR
1987	Hans Spitzauer	AUT
1988	José Maria van der Ploeg	ESP
1989	Eric Mergenthaler	MEX
1990	Stig Westergaard	DEN
1991	José Maria van der Ploeg	ESP
1992	José Maria van der Ploeg	ESP
1993	Fredrik Lööf	SWE
1994	Joaquin Blanco	ESP
1995	José Maria van der Ploeg	ESP
1996	Fredrik Lööf	SWE
1997	Emilios Papathanasiou	GRE
1998	Rafael Trujillo	ESP

Nordic / Scandinavian Championship

1951	Rickard Sarby	SWE
1952	Paul Elvström	DEN
1953	Paul Elvström	DEN
1954	Paul Elvström	DEN
1955	Paul Elvström	DEN
1956	Börge Schwartz	DEN
1957	Paul Elvström	DEN
1958	Paul Elvström	DEN
1959	Paul Elvström	DEN
1960	Paul Elvström	DEN
1961	Börge Schwartz	DEN
1966	Boris Jacobson	SWE
1967	Arnold van Grünewaldt	SWE
1970	Arne Akerson	SWE
1976	Kent Carlsson	SWE
1977	Kenneth Palmgren	FIN
1979	Stewart Neff	USA

1980	Lasse Hjortnäs	DEN
1981	Lasse Hjortnäs	DEN
1983	Lasse Hjortnäs	DEN
1984	Peter Vilby	DEN
1985	Peter Vilby	DEN
1988	Lauri Rechardt	FIN

Olympicsail

1981	Richard Dodson
1985	John Cutler
1989	Craig Monk
1995	Dean Barker
1997	Ian Baker
1998	Craig Monk

Princessa Sofia Trophy

1981	Lasse Hjortnäs	DEN
1983	Jorgen Lindhardtsen	DEN
1984	Lasse Hjortnäs	DEN
1985	Joaquin Blanco	ESP
1986	Thomas Schmid	GER
1987	José Luis Doreste	ESP
1988	Stuart Childerley	GBR
1992	Eric Mergenthaler	MEX
1994	Fredrik Lööf	SWE
1995	Fredrik Lööf	SWE
1996	Mateusz Kusznierewicz	POL
1997	Mateusz Kusznierewicz	POL
1998	Xavier Rohart	FRA
1999	Mateusz Kusznierewicz	POL

Roma Sail Week

1982	Wolfgang Gerz	GER
1983	Bengtsson	SWE
1984	Mark Neeleman	NED
1985	Thomas Oljelund	SWE
1987	Arnoud Hummel	NED
1988	Othmar Müller v Blumencron	GER
1989	Armando Ortolano	GRE
1991	Eric Mergenthaler	MEX
1993	Luca Devoti	ITA
1994	Emanuele Vaccari	ITA
1995	Hank Lammens	CAN
1996	Oleg Khoperski	RUS
1997	Emilios Papathanasiou	GRE
1998	Mateusz Kusznierewicz	POL
1999	Emilios Papathanasiou	GRE

Sail Auckland

1993	Craig Monk	NZL
1994	Fredrik Lööf	SWE
1996	Dean Barker	NZL
1997	Sebastien Godefroid	BEL
1999	Mateusz Kusznierewicz	POL

Sail Melbourne

1996	Paul McKenzie	AUS
1998	Sebastien Godefroid	BEL

Schaumburg-Lippische Nesselblatt Steinhude

1964	Wim Maarse
1965	W. Erdmann
1966	W. Erdmann
1967	Uwe Mares
1968	Uwe Mares
1969	Michael Hupin
1970	W. Gerlinger
1971	Willy Kuhweide
1972	Magnus Olin
1973	Lennart Gustafsson
1974	Andreas von Eicken
1975	Serge Maury
1976	Uwe Heinzmann
1977	Jacques Rogge
1978	Otto Pohlmann
1979	Michael Nissen
1980	Kent Carlsson
1981	Jörgen Lindhardtsen
1982	Thomas Schmid
1983	Mark Neeleman
1984	Miroslav Rychcik
1985	Miroslav Rychcik
1986	H.W. Lixenfeld
1987	M. Hofmann
1988	M. Hofmann
1989	W.B. Lixenfeld
1990	Gerd Griegel
1991	Malte Philipp
1992	H. Winkler
1993	Heike Birke
1994	Andre Budzien
1995	Michael Maier
1996	J. Eiermann
1997	Andreas Buchert
1998	Andreas Buchert

SPA Regatta

1985	Jörgen Lindhardtsen	DEN
1986	Stig Westergaard	DEN
1987	Oleg Khoperski	SR
1988	Mark Neeleman	NED
1989	Oleg Khoperski	SR
1990	Stig Westergaard	DEN
1991	Oleg Khoperski	SR
1992	Fredrik Lööf	SWE

1993	Stig Westergaard	DEN
1994	Fredrik Lööf	SWE
1995	Fredrik Lööf	SWE
1996	Will Martin	USA
1997	Xavier Rohart	FRA
1998	Sebastien Godefroid	BEL

Weymouth Olympic Week

1973	John Arthur	GBR
1974	Richard Hart	GBR
1975	Chris Law	GBR
1976	David Howlett	GBR
1977	David Howlett	GBR
1978	Graham Deegan	NZL
1979	Chris Law	GBR
1980	Chris Law	GBR
1981	Mike McIntyre	GBR
1982	Nigel Walbank	GBR
1983	Roddy Bridge	GBR

1984	Mike McIntyre	GBR
1985	Stuart Childerley	GBR
1986	Lawrence Crispin	GBR
1987	Hans Spitzauer	AUT
1988	Stuart Childerley	GBR

ISAF World Sailing Rankings

May 1991	Lawrence Lemieux	CAN
Sep 1992	Stuart Childerley (tied)	GBR
	Fredrik Lööf (tied)	SWE
Feb 1993	Fredrik Lööf	SWE
Apr 1993	Richard Clarke	CAN
Jun 1993	Xavier Rohart	FRA
Sep 1993	Philippe Presti	FRA
Jan 1994	Xavier Rohart	FRA
Jan 1994	Fredrik Lööf	SWE
Feb 1994	Philippe Presti	FRA
Jun 1994	Fredrik Lööf	SWE
Feb 1998	Sebastien Godefroid	BEL
Feb 1999	Mateusz Kusznierewicz	POL

40. History and Evolution of the Finn Mast

by Gus Miller and Andy Zawieja   Reprinted from Solo and FINNFARE June 1994

The Finn is famous for having an extremely powerful rig. At first it was overpowering - so overpowering that many thought it was impossible to sail a Finn in more than 12 knots of wind. The original masts were stiff, like solid telephone poles, although the original design competition specifications called for a hollow mast with a luff groove.

Original masts
Jack Knights said that the original masts looked as if they had been felled in a forest. They just rotated and did not bend. There was a hole for the boom. Sailing a boat with such a mast was very difficult. No one ever claimed to have mastered the boat in heavy winds.

Developments
Over the years, sailors (especially Paul Elvström) found that smaller diameter, bendier masts allowed them to adjust and change the sail's shape and extend the rig's wind range. This requirement to change a full sail into a flat sail really changed the mast's profile. One problem discovered was that when the sail flattened, the draft moved backwards. This resulted in the incorporation of a second tack grommet in the late 1950s to pull the draft back forward. This second tack grommet came to be called the Cunningham.

Evolvement
The mast has continued to evolve so that at the 1992 Gold Cup in Cadiz, Spain, a fleet of 94 Finns were racing in 40+ knot winds without many problems. The mast handled such wind by bending so the sail flattened, twisted and depowered automatically. The same mast and sail combination also has to be very effective in light winds. One of the attractions of the Finn is the possibility of

adjusting the mast, boom and sail to the particular weight, sailing style and ideas of the sailor.

In 1952, no one expected that a rotating mast could make such an evolution. Many experienced sailors and sailmakers say that more time, thought and experimentation have gone into developing the Finn rig than any sailboat in history. It is easy to build a sail for an America's Cup boat because the crew will find out where it is good and use it happily in that condition. It is very difficult to build a single sail that will be completely competitive in the range from 1 to 41 knots.

IFA
The other important element in this evolution has been the International Finn Association's Technical Committee that writes and oversees the measurement rules. The guiding principle and tradition has been that the class be open to progress, modernisation and the development of better performance provided that any change would not outdate the present fleet. Changes must be implementable in the existing fleet of boats. This has meant that 10 to 17 year-old boats have been able to win a World Championship. It has also meant that for four decades the Finn has been the first to

develop many concepts and techniques now common in high-performance dinghy sailing.

Wooden mast developments
Over the years there were many wooden mastmakers. In England, Collar masts were very popular. The Soviets used Siberian Spruce. North American sailors used aircraft grade Sitka Spruce. Elvström wooden masts had a period of great popularity. There were many secrets. For instance, what kind of glue should be used, because there were many different glues available. The bend characteristics of wooden masts changed with sunny days and rainy days. It required considerable knowledge to know how to change the mast to match weather conditions. Another problem was breakage at the weak place caused by the boom hole. This was solved by reinforcement with oak or other strong wood.

It was important for masts to bend down low, because the fullness of the sail was mainly in the lower half. Many broke if the sailor made the front too soft. Elvström always said they were fastest just before they broke. Masts were softer up high to depower the upper sail first. The Polish fluid dynamist and author of Theory of Sailing, Czeslaw Marchaj, said the sail

should change shape evenly and not look like a pear, but without dacron, and having only cotton, which was unstable, this did not work. The ideal sail at the time was flat at the top and full at the bottom. As the masts got smaller in the upper section, the rule requiring a 40 mm top had to be changed at a Gold Cup to get rid of the top knob most masts had to meet the letter of the rule.

Dacron

Dacron sail cloth was approved for use after January 1 1960, and initiated new directions for the mast. By 1963 dacron sails could be set on even more bendy masts. This had given lighter helmsmen the ability to compete well upwind and a dramatic advantage offwind. Austrian Hubert Raudaschl won the Finn Gold Cup in 1964 with a new home-made wooden mast and a dacron sail.

Bruder masts

By 1968, Brazilian Jörg Bruder and Hubert Raudaschl had designed a mast and dacron sail combination where the mast was much stiffer at the top with an even bend. Bruder had found that one mast at his home club was faster than any other and he measured it carefully to find out why. The base of his new mast met the rule that the mast had to be 100 mm at the deck but the mast became an ellipse sideways just above deck. Masts commonly bent 22 cm in the middle. Bruder's new mast bent only 15 cm. The key change was the small fore and aft elliptical shape of the top meter of the mast. The small tip bent sideways easily and coupled to the upper leach to allow it to twist off automatically. In the next few years, Bruder did not glue the front of the mast in order to make it even softer down low. He eliminated the boom hole on his wooden masts and made a metal gooseneck. He also used Parana Pine, which he claimed was superior.

**Wooden masts made by
Jörg Bruder (below) dominated the
Finn scene in the late sixties**

Halyards

The sailor could adjust the halyard in the beginning. Up to 1966 the halyard came into the cockpit and the sailor could release it when off the wind. Masts had wooden grooves or small 'V' blocks to keep the halyard in front of the mast. Sailors found that this halyard arrangement often resulted in too much mast compression. After 1968 the halyard changed to a halyard hook.

Vangs

The first masts had no vangs. Then some newer masts began to have a wedge that rode over the top of the boom in the mast's boom hole to keep the boom down. That resulted in the same boom position for the full race. Then came arrangements to adjust a wedge under the boom during the race. Next came wheel vangs in the late 1960s. In the early 1970s sailors started using metal levers and multiple blocks. A favourite game was to invent new fittings for masts. The most popular has been the double-lever vang designed and made originally by Art Diefendorf for Vanguard. The outhaul had knots to adjust and come around the end of the boom. There was no inhaul. Russian Valentin Mankin used a wire outhaul. After a while, he feared that the wire would decapitate him on a jibe. He finally had to break it with his paddle.

Aluminium masts

Many were dreaming of metal masts in order to eliminate all the variables and problems of wood. They never imagined the metal mast would make so many problems of its own.

In 1967 the Class asked the IYRU for permission to experiment with glass and aluminium spars. In 1968 several spars of aluminium or glass were produced and tested and the IYRU approved the use of these materials for racing. In 1969 Jack Knights brought an aluminium mast to use at the Gold Cup in Bermuda. Competition between builders was really good in the beginning. Boyce, Bruder and Z-Spars all built one-piece aluminium masts with early success. Stromeyer, a Swede in Austria, built a stainless steel mast. Needlespar built a mast with different size tubes glued together over sleeves. By 1972 about one-third of the Finn sailors were using aluminium masts. Bruder won the Gold Cup in 1972 with one. Bruder's winning the Gold Cup using his own aluminium mast convinced many of the top helmsmen that aluminium masts were better.

Many early aluminium masts broke at the deck or the gooseneck and had to have wooden poles or metal tubes inside the lower section to keep them from getting permanent bends at the gooseneck or from breaking.

Masts, masts and more masts!

1972 Olympics

At this time, the host country for the Olympics supplied both the hulls and the rigs for the Olympics. Many were surprised when the IYRU directed the Germans to provide aluminium masts for the Finn class, as many sailors had never used aluminium masts. Needlespar (England) won the order for 100 of their 2B masts for the Kiel Olympics after David Hunt promised that all masts would be perfectly identical. The supplied rigs at previous Olympics had never been really identical. This order helped kill off the other aluminium builders.

Needlespar

The 3B came in 1973 as a development of the 2B with constant wall thickness and a wide elliptical base. The 3M came in 1974 at the Finn Gold Cup with a smaller lower section of variable wall thickness, a three-piece top and took over. In 1975 Needlespar produced a delta-shaped lower section and single-piece top that was very good in light air but too soft at the deck for heavy air. In 1975 Needlespar also produced the 4B that incorporated a two-piece top over a wide elliptical base but it never was as good an all-round mast as the 3M. Since 1974 the 3M has been the most successful aluminium mast with many different tips. Every time Needlespar's designer David Hunt needed a new car, he came with a new tip design for the 3M with a different colour tip. The sailors would buy a new spar, hoping to find a superior coupling of mast top to upper sail leech. At latest count there are black, blue, silver, gold, red, green and purple coloured tips located in Finn fleets around the world. However, the development of the aluminium mast ended up eliminating many light small

guys, who were 1/3 of the fleet, because the aluminium masts never developed the tip release of the wooden mast.

Many masts?

Everyone needs something a little different from their masts. Many would buy as many as 6 to 10 masts to find the one with the bend that was best for them. There are stories of a sailor selling one of his rejects only to have the buyer come back and beat him with it. Many cut their tracks to change the bend characteristics. 1976 Olympics. For the 1976 Olympics in Kingston, Canada, the IYRU allowed participants to use their own rigs (but they had to use the hull furnished by Canada). At the Regatta, Mike Fletcher, the great Australian coach, told Australian Finn sailor John Bertrand that if he saw a hacksaw in John's hand one more time, he was going to take a hammer and break John's fingers.

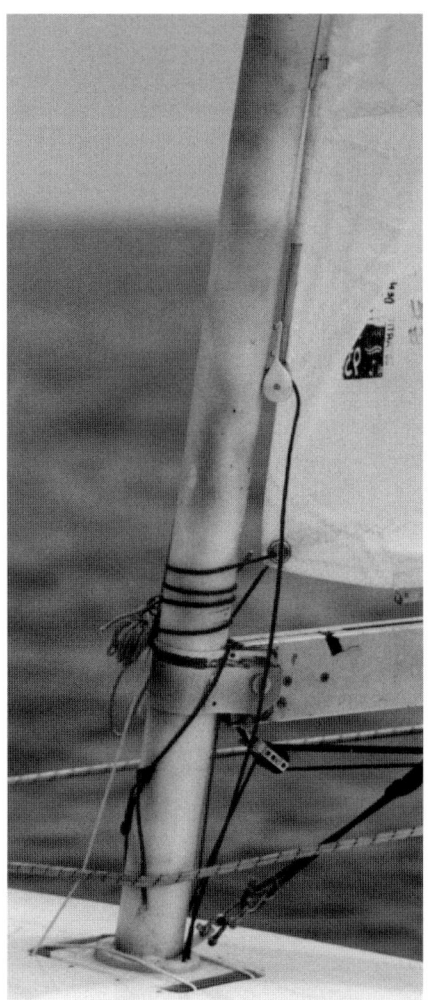

Allowing the competitors to bring their own rigs resulted in the closest boat speeds up to that point. The East Germans cut slots in their mast tracks with washers under the rivets' heads so the track could slide relative to the mast. This resulted in a mast that was soft in light air and stiff in heavy air. Later on, the Danes, Bjorn and Stig Westergaard had a variety of tiny shims that they taped into the track cuts to adjust their masts for the day's conditions.

Measuring bend

There have been at least a dozen different methods of measuring a mast's bend characteristics, each of which has advantages and disadvantages.

• The Elvström, Bruder, Russian, Polish, Swedish and German methods all use carpenter's horses to support the mast either at the ends or at the black bends, hang a calibrated weight somewhere in the middle and measure offsets sideways and fore and aft.

• The Photographic method used large photos taken up the axis of the boom or perpendicular to it. The Henry Sprague or Guy Liljegren Shake Test is done by holding two masts to be compared by the tips at shoulder height and shaking them vertically to see the fore and aft side modes of vibration. This requires calibrated eyeballs and is not very reliable.

• The Strain Gauge Dynamic method places pairs of strain gauges at preselected points along the mast and measures deflections as a function of time.

• The Horizontal Cantilever and Vertical Cantilever methods both pin the mast at the butt and deck ring and load the tip with either with a hanging weight or spring scale. John Bertrand used the Horizontal Cantilever with the mast about four feet off the ground in order to get the fanned luff curve for a sail off the mast.

• Another method is to hoist a sail with a standard luff curve and closely observe where the inversion appears when the sail is slowly sheeted in. This is not a very reliable method.

Lamboley's mast
In 1977, IFA Technical Committee Chairman Gilbert Lamboley, France, built probably the most sophisticated aluminium mast. It was a single-tempered aluminium sheet wrapped around in an ellipse so that a flange along each side could be bolted to a track. The bolt tension could be changed so that the degree of upper twist could be controlled. It was a great mast, but Gilbert never went into production and today the mast is only seen on the Rhone river outside Lyon.

Miller Glass mast
In the same year the late Fred Miller from Newport Beach, California, tried to build a competitive glass mast. It was never accepted because they were a larger diameter at the top than the aluminium masts. Between 1980 and 1984 Gus Miller built a dozen S Glass masts about the same size as aluminium. They were fast in smooth water and especially off the wind. However, the dynamics of the material were not as good as aluminium in waves. Today they are still sailing but with new carbon coats.

Carbon masts
In 1981 it was proposed to the IFA that carbon masts be allowed. Many were against the idea because they feared the development of an aerodynamically superior mast would be too expensive. By 1983, only England was against the idea. IFA decided to allow masts of any material for one year after the 1984 Games in Long Beach, California.

Peter Quigley of Larchmont, New York, made a couple of experimental carbon masts for the USOYC in 1985. Peter used one of them to come in second at the US National Championship. They were taken to the Finn Gold Cup in Palma de Mallorca for the IFA to see, but no one was willing to try them out.

Polish system
At the time of the 1992 Olympic Regatta, the ideal range of measurements for a successful mast under the Polish system were as follows:

Fore/aft deflection at 1/2	135-145 mm
Fore/aft Black Band	31-32% of 1/2 F/A deflection
Fore/aft at 3/4 point	89-91% of 1/2 F/A deflection
Side deflection at 1/2	175-180 mm
Side at Black Band	28-30% of 1/2 side deflection
Side at 3/4 point	90-91% of 1/2 side deflection

Correctors on a carbon mast

In the late 1980s, Wisconsin's Bob Guidinger built a carbon mast over a plastic mandrel like an ice boat mast. He raced it in Miami until it broke at the deck.

The carbon mast idea languished for the next few years. The restrictions on minimum diameter were kept because of fears that an aerodynamically superior mast would make obsolete every aluminium mast in the world.

Opened up
At the 1990 IFA Annual Meeting in Greece the Technical Committee was instructed to open things up so that modern material could be used once the 1992 Olympics were over. The expectation was that while a carbon mast might be slightly more expensive, a sailor would only need two, because they would be so easy to modify. The class wanted experience with carbon masts and felt they were not taking advantage of an opportunity. It was also expected that with carbon, some of the advantages for small light sailors that were lost when the aluminium mast took over, could be regained. This is very important because many developing countries felt they did not have anyone big or strong enough to race a Finn competitively. Certainly in the US there are many good Laser sailors who are blown away by the Finn's power with an aluminium mast.

Experiments
In 1991, Lawrence Lemieux of Canada and Needlespar both experimented with carbon tips for Needlespar 3M aluminium bottom tubes. After many months of working in Sweden with Swedish Olympic Finnster Fredrik Lööf in 1993, the Swede Kurt Anderson produced a successful S Glass/Carbon mast with the same wet lay-up

technique Gus Miller had used ten years earlier. Previous prototype masts had a number of breakage problems.

Success
This new-type mast had great success in the hands of great sailors during their first season and during the 1993 Europeans and Gold Cup. The mast was especially good off the wind but it did not outmode all the aluminium masts overnight. The success of these Anderson masts inspired Luca Devoti to start building masts in Italy and others in Europe to begin building their own carbon masts. The development continued throughout 1994 with more and more carbon masts becoming successful, although the cost and availability of some of them became a problem. At the time it was expected that market forces would eradicate these problems in the medium term.

Early carbon masts had to conform to the old weight rule, so many had to have correctors attached to them to bring them up to weight. This all changed for the 1995 Gold Cup in Melbourne when the minimum weight of the mast was reduced to 8 kg from 10.5 kg, although many masts still needed correctors. Almost everyone had carbon masts in Melbourne and the development of Finn masts had turned full circle with everyone sanding carbon off or adding carbon onto the mast to find the perfect bend, which was reminiscent of the old days of wooden mast shaping. Also in Melbourne, Hans Spitzauer introduced the first wing mast into Gold Cup scenery and won the Gold Cup in the process.

(R)evolution - 1999
It was great to return to the Finns and the 1999 Finn Gold Cup after nearly two and a half years away. The top sailors seem to keep getting more professional each year. Some things don't change though. New gear appears and Finnsters are buying everything in sight but haven't figured out how to use it. They call it having analysis paralysis.

Plastic sails have been making appearances since at least 1985. In most cases they were interesting experiments in the eternal search for Finn speed. As racing sails they were usually quite good in one condition, but steps backwards in all other conditions. When the wind dropped below their optimum condition they became too full and when the wind increased above their optimum, they became too flat.

The current revolution in Finn rigs started with Craig Monk having exclusive use of Team New Zealand sail material that they were using for gennakers. That was the first plastic to be suitable for a competitive Finn sail. The New Zealand effort for the Finn Olympics amounted to something like

$500,000 NZD split between two competing camps. Last year the top Europeans went to NZ to train for the Sail Down Under series and had access to the Team New Zealand material which is lighter than dacron and stretchy enough for a Finn rig. Then the (r)evolution sped up and is still going on.

Special material is now being manufactured just for Finn sails. One type of sail at the 1999 Gold Cup cost $2,600 because of material costs. Most are using wing masts that are too stiff for a 3.8 oz dacron sail but match the new material's stiffness. Wing masts can out point round masts probably because of their greater inherent twist which is being accentuated by making them relatively softer fore and aft in the top. The only condition where the old round mast rigs seem to have a chance is in light air and flat water. This points toward the dynamics of the stiffer wing mast being better in phase with the waves. When a puff hits now, the rig doesn't distort as much and more energy goes into driving the boat forward.

The new rigs are faster if you can keep them trimmed in a groove for the conditions but they are slower if you haven't put a lot of time in learning how to use them. They are not as good a combat sail for amateurs because they are not as forgiving as the old rigs. It is the case where the top group of highly funded professionals have fine tuned the use of a more sensitive rig. It is similar to high performance fighter planes which are inherently unstable and require a huge investment in training the pilot's skills. When they have the training, they are awesome.

Another element in the new rigs is the lighter, weight-jacket-less sailors. They are evolving new styles in steering and using the rig. This has been the history of the Finn. The biggest opportunity for increased speed has usually been the rig.

41. Downwind Speed

by Larry Lemieux

Whenever you can catch a wave without pumping the sail, you automatically give yourself more options as to what you can do with the wave. Because the sail is out and pulling all the time you don't have to 'reload' it. You are powered up the whole time, so this allows you to keep control of the 'windward rock', which makes the boat more stable, makes it easier to steer the course that you want to and you also always have a 'reserve' if you need it. Here is the technique that works for me.

Downwind speed is a function of three things: 1 - the direction and amount you steer; 2 - the range you play your sail in; 3 - controlling the rock to windward.

You can't control how much you steer if you can't control the rock to windward. You can't control the rock to windward unless you're playing the sail in the right range and you can't play your sail in the right range if you're steering all over the place. They are all related.

The ideal course to steer is just a couple degrees either side of directly down wind. The boat is always more 'lively' when you're close to being square to the wind. You have to take advantage of this. When everything is balanced you should be able to feel added pressure on the main sheet when you let the boat rock up to windward. If not, then your sail is too far out. The amount you let the boat heal to windward depends on how far you want to bear away.

In order to control the windward rock you need to be playing the sail in the right range. The right range is when you let your main sheet out the length of your arm so that the boat starts to roll over on top of you. When you reach the desired angle you then pull in the sheet to flatten the boat. If you rock too far and consequently bear off too much then

you will steer out of the effective trimming range of the length of your arm. It is very important not to steer too far away from dead down wind. This way, when you get in the groove it will be easier to keep it there.

To put this all together here is the sequence of movements. While sailing just a couple degrees from dead down wind you first let the sail out slightly which causes the boat to rock to windward. When the boat reaches the desired angle you 'catch it' by pulling the sail back in enough to stop the rock and maintain the desired angle. The desired angle is determined by how much you want to bear away as a result of the rock.

Now the boat is on the wave, sailing slightly by the lee, heeled to windward. Because you haven't pumped in the sail to catch the wave it is still out and pulling as the boat bears away to sailing by the lee. This is very important because now the boat is going to rock back the other way, and because you're slightly by the lee, the flow across the sail is reversed and you get a second push from the sail as the boom comes down. As the boat flattens out it rounds up slightly putting you back to where you started from, ready for the whole routine to begin again.

When all three components of this technique are done properly then none of them need to be extreme. The rock doesn't have to be a big one, the boat doesn't have to bear away very far and the sail trimming range is only the length of your arm. When done correctly this technique is like the difference between paddling a canoe or a kayak. In a canoe you only use one end of the paddle. This is like giving the sail one big pump. In a kayak you use both ends of the paddle. This is the same as what I've described.

When you're set up correctly, you can not only get a push from the sail when the boat rolls over to windward but also when it rolls back. All the movements of the boat can therefore propel you forwards when you are set up properly.

42. The Best Finn Sailors of all Time

In FINNLOG, Peter Mohilla worked out the best Finn sailors of all time by looking at the Olympics, the Finn Gold Cup and the Finn Europeans and scoring 6 points for Gold, 3 for Silver and 1 for Bronze. To conclude this book marking 50 Years of the Finn, that earlier table is here updated and it might well be changed to read 'The Best Finn Sailors over the first 50 Years of the Finn'. In the 14 years since Peter Mohilla's list, three sailors have moved into the top ten of the list. Note also that Lasse Hjortnäs has moved up to joint first and that there are only two current sailors inside the top 20 who have a chance to move up the list in the future. Combining the sailors points to find the best country, Denmark comes out on top with 119 points, then Sweden with 110 and Germany with 85.

1. Willy Kuhweide GER   43

1. Lasse Hjortnäs DEN   43

3. Paul Elvström DEN   39

4. Andre Nelis BEL   35

5. Fredrik Lööf SWE   32

6. José Maria van der Ploeg ESP 31

7. Jörg Bruder BRA   28

8. Serge Maury FRA   25

9. John Bertrand USA   24

10. Stig Westergaard DEN   24

11. Jose Luis Doreste ESP   22

12. Hans Spitzauer AUT   21

13. Arne Akerson SWE 18   13. Joaquin Blanco ESP 18   13. Boris Jacobsson SWE 18   13. Mateusz Kusznierewicz POL 18   17. Jochen Schümann GER 16

18. Hank Lammens CAN 15   18. Thomas Lundquist SWE 15   18. Hubert Raudaschl AUT 15   21. Oleg Khoperski RUS 14   21. Guy Liljegren SWE 14

21. Philippe Presti FRA 14   21. Jürgen Vogler GER 14   25. Eric Mergenthaler MEX 13   25. Magnus Olin SWE 13   25. Henning Wind DEN 13

28. Stuart Childerley GBR 12   28. Christian Schröder GER 12   28. Luca Devoti ITA 12   28. Chris Law GBR 12   28. Cam Lewis USA 12

28. Valentin Mankin RUS 12   34. Sebastien Godefroid BEL 10   34. Brian Ledbetter USA 10   34. Larry Lemieux CAN 10   34. Adelchi Pelaschier ITA 10

Index of Names

A

Aalto-Setala, Ville 75, 77, 147, 172
Aare Kööp 175
Aasblom, G 63, 65, 139
Adde, Yannick 172
Aguado, Javier 148
Ahlback, Torbjorn 67
Ainslie, Ian 78, 79, 95, 148, 174, 178
Akerson, Arne 60, 61, 62,63 64, 66, 93, 137, 138, 190, 195
Akerson, Carl 147, 172
Akerson, Kalle 77
Akerson, P 65, 66
Albarelli, Fabio 62, 63, 65 67, 93, 137, 139, 188, 192
Albarelli, L 178
Alburg, Kenneth 91, 193
Aldag, Peter 75, 76, 95, 145, 171
Aleinikov, Vladislav 173
Alexandru, Vasiliu 177
Allen, Bill 179, 193
Allende, A 134
Allotta, Benedetto 72, 171
Almeida, Guilherme de 175
Altena, John Van 91, 190, 191
Altmayer, E 137
Alurralde, Enrique 174
Andergassen, O 189
Andersen, J J 89
Anderson, C 138
Anderson, Gordon 73, 74, 75
Anderson, Tom 68
Andersson 138
Andersson, Bernt 60, 61, 65, 136
Andersson, Bo Steffan 75
Andersson, Goran 60, 62, 63, 64, 66, 68, 135, 139
Andersson, Gunnar 61
Andersson, H 58, 60, 63
Andre, Robert 63, 65, 66, 138, 179, 193
Angelis, Francisco De 71, 142, 143, 170
Anjos, Henrique 173
Antal, Gabor 191
Appel 63
Apukhtin, Mikhael 78, 171, 178
Arion, G 178
Armit, Leith 70, 78, 145
Aronsson, H 171
Arthur, John 196
Arvidsson, Ulf 67
Ask, J 187
Asklund, Hans 61
Astley, Mike 62, 63, 136, 137
Atzwanger, Peter 189
Auclair 59
Auzas, J P 187
Avdeev, Alexander 169

B

Babacan, Haluk 75, 147, 178
Babbi, Egidio 141, 142, 169
Bachmann, Walter 93, 139, 167, 178
Bahr, Torbjorn 171
Baird, Ed 69
Baker, Ian 78, 79, 148, 195
Baker, Richard 177
Bakunovich, Dmitri 172
Balakirev, Alex 167
Balashov, Andrei 69, 93 140, 141, 142, 177
Balazs, Hadju 148, 173176, 178
Balcells, R 91
Bally, Alexis 63, 93, 137, 178, 192
Balov, Miro 179
Balthasar, Roland 176, 189, 190, 191
Balthasar, Wilfried 188, 190, 191
Baltscheffsky, Arne 58, 135
Banks, Bruce 58
Bankuthy, Bela 168
Banovac, Branimir 179

Barbour, Barry 139, 178, 188
Barker, Dean 78, 174, 195
Barker, Phil 178
Barrett, Peter 65, 91, 178, 179, 193
Barton 59
Bartul, Misura 173
Barwind, Jürgen 188, 189
Batista, Vasco 147, 148
Battaglia, Armando 173
Baudoin, Thimoté 175
Bauer, Reinhard 167
Baumann, R 191
Baumgarten, Regis 176
Baumgartner, Erich 188
Beck, Frits 65, 138, 139
Beck, Rolf 67
Beda Zingg 186
Behr, Edgar 89
Beisen, A. van der 89
Bell, Bill 191
Belousov, Jevgenij 167, 168
Benamati, Roberto 72, 142, 143, 170
Bengtsson 195
Bengtsson, Ingvar 72, 73, 95
Bennett, Ed 63, 66, 67, 68, 69, 179, 193
Benz, Gerhard 188
Bercht, A F 91
Berdasch, R 175
Berdash, Rolland 139, 177
Bergamaschi, Vit. 171
Bergenzaun, Lars 75, 145
Bergmann, Christoph 73, 76, 95, 95, 175, 193
Bergsten, B 65
Bergsten, R 63, 64, 138
Beringuier, Reyis 169
Berisso, E 193
Berkay, Erdal 178
Bertrand, John AUS 66, 67 68, 93, 139,140, 141, 171 179, 193
Bertrand, John USA 69, 70 95, 142, 179, 194, 202
Beuck, Werner 189, 190
Beverijk, Haluk 71, 191
Beyn, Egon 89
Bieberitz, Eberhard 168, 191, 190
Biekarck, Claudio 67, 68, 69, 70, 93, 139, 140 167, 168, 175, 193
Binkhorst, Baudouin 63, 64 65, 67, 68, 138, 139, 140 179, 193
Bir 135
Birke, Heike 73, 75, 143, 144, 170, 196
Bissell, Tom 193
Bisztray, F 170
Björkman, Svante 68
Bjorn, Tyler 175, 192
Björnberg, Jan 190, 191
Blanco, Joaquin 69, 70, 71 73, 75, 95, 140, 141, 142, 143 145, 146, 169, 170, 178, 192 194, 195, 203
Blaszka, Henryk 71, 72, 73 74, 142, 143, 144, 145 177, 192
Blaszka, Ryszard 139, 139, 140, 168, 177
Blaszka, S 171
Blogg, Harvey 178
Blum, Alfred 190
Blumencron, Othmar Müller von 74, 75, 76, 77, 78, 95 145, 146, 147, 176, 178, 195
Bock 167
Boeckelt, R 191
Bohland, Peter 187, 188, 189, 190
Bolle, L 176
Bomshke, H 193
Boneo, Ricardo 62, 174
Bongers, Eric 91
Boot, N 191
Borges, Dieter 190
Bornarel, Eric 143, 178
Bosetti, R 191
Boudouris, Anastas 93, 140, 168, 192
Boumans, Chris 69

Boumans, J P 65, 67, 68, 137, 140
Bourke, Glenn 76, 174
Bowers, Gordy 65, 66, 192, 193
Braathen, Erik 70
Braclaw, W 177
Brandt, Mikael 67, 68, 167, 189, 190, 191
Branislav Erac 179
Brecht, Jörg 63, 193
Breitenstein, Derek 68, 69
Breitenstein, L 70
Bridge, Roddy 72, 73, 143, 179, 196
Brighidau, Liviu 173
Brink, Hennie Van Den 190
Broek, Van den 140
Broman, Berth 89
Brown, Ian 65
Bruce, Ian 91, 193
Bruder, Jörg 62, 63, 64, 65, 66, 67, 91, 93 137, 175, 178, 179, 202
Brunori, Moreno 190
Brymer, Bruce 175
Buchan, Carl 69, 70, 193
Buchert, Andreas 78, 79 148, 172, 173, 176, 196
Budzien, Andre 77, 78, 145, 146, 176, 196
Buemi, Dave 69, 192, 193
Bueno, Mauricio 79
Bukovski, A 175
Bulka, Mark 174
Burford, P 174
Burger, Olaf 187, 189
Burghardt 63
Burke, Heiko 176
Burn-Wood, George 178
Burrows 63
Burrows, David 79, 173
Bush, Daniel 79
Busquet, Jacques 67, 68, 140, 141, 168
Busquet, M 194
Butler, Robert 68
Butzmann, Frank 70, 73, 143, 144, 176, 192
Bychkov, Igor 171
Byrien, M 170
Byron, Richard 76, 193

C

Caap, Mats 75, 76, 145, 146, 194
Cada, Miroslav 139, 175, 179
Canham, Peter 60, 61, 62
Canözer, Yilmaz 178
Cansino, Santl. 89
Carlsson, Bo 169
Carlsson, Kent 67, 68, 69, 70 93, 140, 141, 142, 195, 196
Carrea, Alberto 174
Carver, Tim 79
Castellanos, F S 89
Castrec, Francois Le 71, 76 143, 146, 170, 176, 194
Catalan, Bruno 186, 191, 190
Caviglia, Alejandro 174
Cercello, Simone 173
Chabaud, G 167
Chadwick, John 179
Chalupnik, V 188, 189
Chapman , Colin 148
Charee, Patrice 67, 168
Chatelier, Pierre Le 176
Chedeville, Daniel 67, 176
Cherdnichenko, A 168
Chernov, Evgeni 179
Childerley, Stuart 73, 74, 76 95, 144, 146, 179, 192 195, 196, 203
Chiochetti, Hans 187
Chionas, Christos 173
Chivikov 172
Chlebek, Petr 167
Choley, Luc 71, 72, 143, 145, 169, 170
Christensen 89
Christianson, Roy 67
Christl, Lucian 63, 64, 137
Chtmerbalcon, Sergei 191

Chucharov, Rafail 138
Chuchelov, Alexander 59, 61, 62, 91, 135, 165, 177
Cicarelli, Luksa 175, 179, 190, 191
Cintl , Václav 175, 189, 191
Ciresa, Franco 186
Clark, Worn 186
Clarke, John 65, 66, 67,139, 175, 193
Clarke, Richard 75, 76, 77 78, 79, 95, 145, 175 192, 194, 196
Clarke, Tim 175
Cleve, Paul Van 72, 175, 192, 193
Cobb, Rodney 189, 190, 191
Coccoloni, L 64
Coholen, Mark 193
Cole 63
Colliard, Roberto 177
Colligon, Mario Jr 177
Collins, Dave 178
Commette, Peter 93, 193
Conrad, Peter 65, 67, 193
Conrad, Ralph 193
Conrad, Reinaldo 91
Cook, Fred 179
Cooper, Andrew 191
Cordshagen, F 62
Costas, George 168
Couligas, Panagiotis 137, 138
Coutts, Russell 72, 95
Cowling, Adam 173
Creagh-Osborne, Richard 58, 59, 60, 61, 62, 136, 178
Crispin, Lawrence 74, 144, 179, 196
Cristl, Lucian 174
Crossley, Anthony 179
Csomai, Jozsef 171
Ctin, Vladescu 177
Cuccurullo, Christian 67
Cuccurullo, Gilles 167
Cumbley, Charlie 79
Currey, Charles 91
Cutler, Alec 75, 76, 146, 179, 192
Cutler, John 73, 74, 95, 144, 145, 177, 195
Czapski, Andrej 148

D

Dahlgaard, Gunnar 61, 62
Dahllof, Par 171
Dahlstrom, G 64, 66
Damir, M V 191
Danby, Peter 59, 60
Daneri, Daniele 190
Davidson, Geoff 70, 174
Davis, Greg 178
De Angelis 170
de Jong 59
Deegan 176
Deegan, Bruce 70, 177
Deegan, Graham 69, 70, 142, 177, 196
Dehmel, Bernd 62, 63, 64 65, 137, 138, 139, 176
Delfs 69
Demir, Erzin 134, 178
Devillard, Gérard 61, 63, 91, 175
Devoti, Luca 76, 77, 78 95, 146, 147, 148, 195, 203
Deyett, Mike 175, 192, 193
Didier, Gille 168
Diefenbach, Hannes 191
Dijkors 58
Dirdiara, Vitali 60, 65, 138, 177
Dittmar, Hans 89
Dixon, Barry 179
Dixon, Reginald 89
Dodson, Richard 70, 195
Dodson, Rick 177
Dodson, Tom 70, 72, 177
Domscke, H 193
Donkin, Stuart 178
Dordora, V 168
Doreste, José Luis 69, 73 74, 93, 95, 140, 141, 142, 144 145, 168, 176, 178, 195, 202

Doreste, Manuel 141
Dotsch, Bill 59
Dougherty, Ron 67, 193
Douglas, John 68, 70
Douze, Kees 65, 67, 68, 139, 140
Doyle, Robbie 66
Dragoutsis, Alexandros 173
Drappeau, David 75, 172
Drefahl, Eckard 169, 176
Drexelius, H 189
Driscoll, John 77, 78, 79, 147, 148, 172
Duckeroff, Heilmut 67, 189
Dufner, G 191
Dumont 137
Duyne, Carl Van 63, 66 93, 137, 139, 175, 192, 193
Dyrdyra, V 175

E

Eastwood, John 175, 192
Edens, Bob 170
Eggers, J 65
Ehlers, Hans-Günter 65, 67 68, 140, 141, 189, 190, 191
Ehrnrooth, Mats 71
Eicken, Andreas van 64, 65, 67, 138, 167, 194, 196
Eiermann, J 196
Ek, Lars 67
Ekes, Albert 190
Eliasson, M 170
Elst, Hans Van 63, 67, 138, 139, 140
Elvström, Paul 58, 59, 65 89, 91, 135, 174, 178 194, 195, 202
Enelli, Dr 194
Erdmann, W 137, 196
Ergün, Ziya 178
Erich, Karl-Heinz 190, 191
Eriksen, Harald Bredo 58, 59, 60, 61
Eriksson 89
Eriksson, Leonard 168
Eriksson, Peter 71
Erndl, Wolff 91
Erndl, Wolfgang 135
Ernst, M 176
Evans, R 89
Everett, N R 62, 177

F

Faass, Hans Dieter 187, 188, 189
Faass, Torsten 172
Fages 167
Fago, Guiseppe 89
Fago, Nicolino 60
Falkenberg, B 171
Fanstone, Jeremy 75, 76, 145, 146, 192
Farmer, Jonty 63, 65, 67 68, 93, 137, 140, 177
Fatzer, Hans 189, 190, 191
Fauroux, J 61
Favini, Flavio 170
Fellmann, Michael 76, 77, 78 79, 146, 147, 148, 172, 176
Ferguson, John 68, 70
Ferrer, Antonio 72, 178
Ferrer, Toni 143
Filippini, Gino 186
Finaczy, György 62, 91 93, 136, 137, 138, 139, 176
Fioretto, Mauro 75, 77, 147
Fiquemont, J 169
Firpo, Juan Carlo 193
Fischer, Michael 74, 170, 174
Fischer, Wl. 177
Fisher, Mike 179
Fleckenstein, S 73
Fletcher, M 61
Flint, Hans Gerhard 59, 61
Fogh, Hans 60, 61, 62, 66
Fonseca, Teixeira da 135
Foster, Glen 61, 179, 193
Fowler, G 89
Frackowiak, Janusz 168
Franco, Angel 177
Frändestam, R 58, 59

Fratila, Dumitru 177
Fratzer, H 178
Fravezzi, A 68
Fred Auer, Dr 136
Freeman, Norman 138, 175, 179, 193
Frijdal, Chris 71, 191, 190
Frimansson, B O 62, 63, 64, 65
Fritze, Hans Joachim 64, 65
Fürst, Hans Peter 91, 135, 174

G

Ganahl, Ivor 71, 176, 178, 189
Garcia, Xavier 172
Garra, P 193
Gärtner, Walter 135, 136, 176
Gaston, Jean Paul 176, 191
Gaydon, H R 89
Gebhart, Antonin 190
Gehreiber, Detlef 89
Geis, Fritz 67, 167
Gelder, Van 62
Gellert, P 187
Gelley, Laszlo 172
Georgiadis, Alfis 71
Georgiadis, Theodor 168
Gerhards, Leo 58, 59
Gerlinger, W 196
Gervaiseau, Jean Paul 176
Gerz, Wolfgang 68, 70, 71 72, 74, 141, 142, 143 176, 190, 191, 194, 195
Gfreiner, Gerhard 174, 188, 190
Gherarducci, Massimo 79, 173
Ghiglia 63
Gillard, Jacques 59, 186
Gillard, Jean 186
Gille, Didier 168
Giuntoli, Daniele 172
Glinkiewicz, Kajetan 168
Gochberg, John 173
Godefroid, Sebastien 77, 78 79, 95, 147, 148, 172 175, 177194, 195, 196, 203
Golatowski, Gerd 170
Golser, S 62, 63, 64, 65, 137, 139
Gondermein, Herbert 189
Gorchon, R 186
Gordeiko, K. 73
Gordeiko, Konstantin 170
Gorelikiov, Peter 59, 60, 91, 177
Gorla, Giorgio 67
Gorman, Simon 75, 174
Gorshkov, Evgeni 177
Gorsky, Jaroslaw 172
Goujon, J 186
Goujon, P 186
Grammatikou, P 139
Grandchamp, Jean J 67, 69, 140, 167, 168
Grande, Riccardo 188, 189, 190
Grande, Ugo 173
Granzer, Florian 174
Greenwood, John 72, 73
Gretsch, Martin 190
Griegel, G 196
Griegel, Gerd 75, 147, 148, 178
Grönblom, Richard 68, 140
Gros, B 68
Grossmith, Derek 179
Grossmith, Guy 168, 179
Grünewaldt, Arnold van 61, 62, 63, 65, 137, 195
Gsell, Arno 174
Gubelmann, Peter 178
Gubi, Michael 174
Güldenpfening, R 141, 168, 169
Gull-Burnay, F 89
Guminski, Detlev 196
Gunther, Bernd 188, 189, 190
Gürdenli, Arif 75, 95, 146, 147, 178
Gurov, V 170
Gustafsson, Lennart 65, 66 67, 68, 69, 139, 167, 196

Gustavsson, P O 64
Gut, U 188

H

Haakman, Sjaak 71, 72, 143
Haan, Andreas 139, 140, 167, 176
Haas, Roberto 140, 174, 193
Haeghen, P von der 89
Haegler, Marcel 189
Hagan, Ulrich 61
Hahn, James 67, 68, 71, 193
Haller, Bernd 187, 188
Hailer, Berthold 188
Hakker, P 186
Hambrouck, Willy 70
Hammag, Clar. 89
Hammelso, Henrik 73
Hanbrook 69
Hansen, Chr. 61
Hardy, Brian 190
Hardy, D 63, 64
Harinkouck 135
Harinkouck, Jerome 58, 59, 134
Harinkouck, Philippe 59
Hart, Richard 61, 62, 63, 64, 67, 137, 139, 140, 176, 179, 194
Hartmann, Jaques 195
Hatzipavlis, Elias 65, 67, 69, 93, 138, 139, 140, 142, 192
Hatzipavlis, George 178
Healy, Craig 69, 71, 143, 179, 193
Healy, Pat 190
Hedberg, Carl Johan 72, 73, 143, 144
Heide, Hermann 190, 191
Heiden, Hendrik 170
Heilmann, Sven 172
Heiner, Roy 72, 74, 77, 78, 95, 145, 147, 178, 194
Heinrich, von 89
Heinzmann, Uwe 65
Heisch, W 186
Hellbrügge, Alex 69, 168, 169
Hellehond, Jack van 189
Helley, Loic Le 176
Helm
Henderson, Paul 193
Henrik, Elmer 171
Herbulot, J 89
Hermann, Anthony 65, 69, 70 , 179
Herrman, Henry 62, 171
Herrmann, Horst 176
Herrmann, Mark 76, 77, 146, 193
Herwig, Coppi 189, 190
Herwig, Herbert 188, 189
Heselius, Lennart 69
Hewitt, Rick 69
Higgins, Paul 69
Higgins, Peter 69
Hiles, Paul 93
Hillier, Jozsef 168
Himmell, David 76, 146, 193
Hin, Johannes 89
Hittmer, Handi 189
Hjortnäs, Lasse 71, 72, 73, 74, 75, 76, 79, 95, 142, 143, 144, 145, 146, 147, 148, 175, 192, 194, 195, 202
Hoffman, Ivan 139, 175, 188
Hoffmann, G 167
Hoflan, John 176
Hofland, A A 63, 64
Hofland, John 73, 74, 75, 144, 145
Hofmann, M 170, 176, 196
Holbrook, Robert 67, 68, 168, 179
Holmberg, Peter 72, 95, 192
Holmstrom, Bill 67
Holub, E 187
Horák, B. 136, 137, 167, 175
Hornevall, Bengt 58, 135
Hornidge, Hank 175
Houf, Herbert 174
Hoyt, Garry 193
Hruby, Karel 187, 188, 189
Hruby, Michal 147, 148, 173

Huber, F 65
Hübner, G 189
Hübner, Gerd 68, 69, 168, 169
Hudec, Václav 187, 188, 189
Hummel, Arnoud 73, 74, 143, 144, 195
Huntsman, Brian 193
Hupin, Michael 65, 138, 193
Hurley, Dan 193
Huska, Gerhard 61, 63, 174
Huybrechts, L 89
Hyt 93
Hyza, Jiri 173
Hyza, Petr 173

I

Ickert, M 170
Iliopoulos, Vasilis 192
Immler, Manfred 189, 190
Irvine, John 74
Issakov 168
Izsak, T 167

J

Jacobsson, Boris 61, 62, 63, 91, 136, 137, 195, 203
Jäger, Harro 68, 176
Jäger, Henk De 189, 190, 191
Jako, Nick 75, 145, 171
James, Tony 67, 174
Jammes, Francis 63, 136, 139, 175
Jammes, Jean-Claude 61, 175, 194
Janich, Jakob 186
Janka, T 170
Jannich 59
Jenyns, Ron 68, 91, 93, 139, 174
Jewett 89
Jõgi, Jaak 175
Johannussen, O M 60
Johnsson, Bernt 67, 68, 168
Jong, Jan de 135, 136
Jongh, Koos de 89, 91
Jordbakke, Per 60, 61, 62, 91, 135, 136
Jornmark, U 60
Josephsen, P 60
Jungblut, Thomas 65, 66, 67, 68, 70, 140, 142, 194
Jungell, Tom 71, 170
Junker, Helmut 187

K

Kadenbach, Ralf 73, 74, 144
Kagchelland, D 89
Kakis, Haluk 178
Källström, K H 58
Kammerer 59
Kammerer, H 176
Kariofillis, J 136
Kaspareth, Erich 186, 187, 188, 189
Kaufmann, Karsten 71, 143, 170
Kaufmann, Manfred 168, 193
Kayin 178
Keep 168
Keirsblick, Lue Van 70, 140, 142
Kellermann, Günter 188
Kellner, Hakan 61, 62
Kennedy, Fred 74
Kerner, Sam 179
Ketelaar, R 64
Kettler, Axel 190
Keyser, Pieter 65, 167
Khon, Ingo 171
Khoperski, Oleg 73, 75, 76, 78, 79, 95, 142, 143, 144, 145, 146, 147, 170, 178, 192, 194, 195, 196, 203
Khoretski, Sergei 70, 142, 143, 169, 177, 192
Kiely, Steve 174
Kiepa 69
Kirby, Bruce 91
Kirketerp, Poul 175
Klug 168
Kjølhede, Steen 175
Klein, Horst 188, 189, 190, 191
Kleist, Larry 72, 174

Kmonicek, Jiri 168
Knasiecki, B 177
Knasiecki, Jamiz 65, 167
Knasiecki, Romould 68, 168, 177
Knights, Jack 135, 137, 178, 179, 193
Knospe, M 170
Knuth, J 172
Koch, Jürgen 188, 189
Kodogouris, Georg 173
Koepnick, L 191
Köhler 138
Köhler, U 137
Kohlwig, Gerhard 188
Kolb, Wolfgang 167, 168
Kojima, M 61, 62, 193
Kok, Jan Willem 148
Kollock, D R 65
Kolomatovic, Pasko 179
Konstancki, Sergej 139
Kontogouris, George 79
Koop, Klaus 135
Koopmans, Rinze 58
Kopanov, Mihail 192
Kördt, Axel 167
Korichkin, Nicolai 169
Koryachkin, Nicholai 177
Kose, V 175
Kostas, Georg 169
Kouligas, P 65, 91, 93
Kouril, Miroslav 168
Kouveras, Richard 172
Kovacs, Bela 176
Kozlov, Viktor 63, 64, 137, 138, 177
Kraft, Jurgen 189, 190, 191
Krastev, Krasimir 169
Krause, Marek 172
Kristianson, Dico 177
Krogmann, W 89
Krüger, Kai 63, 65, 139, 191
Kruyer, Kees 189, 190
Kryszcryiski 172
Kuhwede, Willy 60, 61, 63, 64, 65, 91, 93, 135, 136, 137, 138, 176, 194, 196, 202
Kun, Michal 177
Kuret, Karlo 78, 79, 146, 147, 148, 172, 175, 192
Kusznierewicz, Mateusz 77, 78, 79, 95, 147, 148, 173, 174, 177, 194, 195, 203
Kuznetsov, Evgeni 177
Kwikkers, Gert 177

L

Lachi, Leonardo 171
Ladendorf, Kurt 60
Lagrange, Orounet 187
Lalanne, J 191
Lambelet, Marc 186
Lamboley, Gilbert 62, 187
Lammens 72
Lammens, Hank 75, 76, 77, 78, 95, 145, 146, 147, 175, 192, 193, 195, 203
Lammens, Mark 71, 73, 77, 193
Lapalu, Jean 176
Larcher, Hans 134
Larsen, Palle-Steen 188
Larsen, Roar 61, 136
Larsson, Eric 187, 188
Larsson, Mats 61
Law, Chris 65, 66, 68, 69, 70, 140, 141, 142, 168, 179, 194, 196, 203
Law, Tim 71, 72
Lea, Jamie 79, 148
Leandro, Paulo 173
Lebois, P 186, 187
Lebrun, Jaques 89, 91
Ledbetter, Brian 73, 74, 75, 76, 95, 145, 179, 192, 193, 194, 203
Leeksma, Dick 178
Leenstra, A 65
Leeuwen, Martin Van 71, 72, 142
Lehan , Tom 143
Lehnert, Rolf 188, 189, 190
Leistikow 65
Lemanissier 63
Lemanissier, J 192

Lemanissier, Jacques 176
Lemieux, Lawrence 69, 70, 71, 72, 73, 74, 75, 76, 77, 78, 143, 145, 146, 174, 177, 190, 191, 192, 193, 194, 196, 203
Lemoine 59
Lenhart, Jeff 193
Lester, Peter 141
Letcher, P 62
Leverland, Gerald 60, 61
Lewis, Cameron 69, 70, 142, 179, 203
Liandier, J 64
Libor, Ulrich 61
Lidarik, Rudolf 173
Lidholm, M 68
Lidholm, Magnus 67
Lievi, Luciano 67, 68, 139, 140, 167, 168
Lihan, Tim 193
Liljeberg, S 169
Liljedahl, Magnus 70, 142
Liljegren 194
Liljegren, Guy 65, 66, 67, 68, 69, 70, 138, 140, 141, 142, 194, 203
Lindahl, Lennart 61
Lindhardtsen, Jörgen 68, 70, 71, 72, 73, 75, 93, 140, 141, 142, 143, 144, 75, 177, 188, 194, 195, 196
Lippert, P 63, 137
Litkey, Farkas 145, 147, 171, 176
Littlejohn, Mark 74
Lixenfeld, H W 196
Lixenfeld, Ralf Rainer 196
Lixenfeld, Welf-Bodo 73, 74, 75, 144, 145, 171, 176, 196
Lizancos, C 170
Lochbrunner, Andi 69, 191, 189, 190
Lolic, Leo 167
Lollert, Jochen 190, 191
Lombard 186
Lööf, Fredrik 75, 76, 77, 78, 79, 95, 145, 146, 147, 172, 176, 193, 194, 195, 196, 202
Lostak, Miroslav 142, 175
Lott, Richard 76, 145, 179
Loukota, Borislav 168
Löwe, Dirk 73, 75, 76, 77, 78, 144, 145, 146, 147, 170, 171, 176, 194
Lückner, S 58
Lundh, Michael 173
Lundmark, Anders 73, 75, 76, 77, 146, 194
Lundquist, Thomas 62, 63, 64, 65, 66, 67, 68, 93, 138, 139, 194, 203
Luschan, Michael 144, 171, 174
Luttgart, P 62
Lyne, James 77, 147

M

Maarse, Wim 58, 59, 60, 62, 63, 135, 136, 196
Maartenson, Bjorn 169
Maas, Adriaan 89
MacDonald-Smith, Iain 65, 67, 138, 139, 176, 179, 192
Maciuk, Jaroslav 73, 143, 144, 177
Mackiewicz, Andrzej 172
MacLaren, Randy 67
MacLaverty, Kevin 67
MacLeod, Scott 192, 193
MacLoud, Steve 73
Mägli, Juan 70, 71, 72, 143
Mai, Heini 189
Mai, Walter 63, 64, 65, 66, 68, 71, 93, 138, 139, 188, 189, 190, 191
Maier, Jiri 187, 188, 189, 191
Maier, Michael 75, 77, 78, 79, 95, 147, 148, 175, 194
Majthenyi, Zsombor 172
Makila, Jali 73, 75, 76, 77, 78, 95, 145, 147, 171, 194
Makjani 179
Malm, Peter 63, 175, 189
Mander, Peter 91, 177

Manen, Ron van 72, 143, 144, 170
Manifre, Jacques 167
Mankin, Valantin 61, 62, 63, 64, 93, 137, 138, 177, 203
Männik, Meelis 175
Manthos, Kons. 171
Marchaj, Czeslaw 134
Mares, Uwe 61, 63, 64, 65, 136, 138, 172, 194, 196
Markus, B 134
Marselos, Manolis 148, 173
Marteau, Jean Marie 69, 169
Marteau, Jean-Jan 169
Martensson 69
Martin, Jacques 176, 187
Martin, Will 77, 179, 193, 196
Martins, Roberto 193
Marvin, John 91
Masterman, William 169
Masturzo, Luigo 172
Matsyuama, Kazuoki 196
Matthiesen, Ulrich 190
Mattson, Klaes 169, 170
Maury 138
Maury, Alain 63, 176
Maury, Serge 64, 65, 66, 67, 68, 93, 137, 138, 139, 140, 167, 176, 192, 194, 196, 202
Maynard, John 63, 64, 138, 179
Mayr, Dieter 61, 174
Mayrgündter, Cornel 188, 189, 190
Mayrhofer, Wolfgang 71, 93, 142, 143, 169, 170, 174
McCurrach, Bruce 60, 62, 63, 178, 194
McFadden, Mike 179
McIntyre, Mike 70, 71, 72, 95, 143, 179, 196
McKenzie, Paul 77, 78, 79, 95, 148, 174, 196
McLaughlin, Paul 89, 91
McLean, William 193
McMillan, Rob 145, 148, 176, 179
Meireles, Rodrigo 194
Mekhanikov, V 171
Mellor, Dave 79
Menkart, Andrew 70
Menoni, Andreino 186
Mergenthaler, Eric 75, 76, 143, 144, 145, 146, 171, 178, 193,195, 203
Mess, Derek 72, 73, 175, 193
Meszaros, Zsolt 173
Mevel, Andre 186, 187
Mickiewicz, Stanislaw 170
Mier, Jürgen 63, 64, 65, 93, 137, 138, 176
Mier, Matthias 171, 172
Migacz, Dariusz 78
Migliaccio, A 170
Miller 63
Miller, August 68, 69, 140, 141, 191, 193
Miller, Fred 60, 179, 193
Miller, Kurt 193
Milner, Mike 74, 75, 76, 144, 145, 146, 175, 196
Minski, Fabris 67, 68, 69, 70, 93, 139, 140, 141, 148, 190, 191, 192
Misura, Bartul 79, 148
Mitchell, Howard 189
Mitterer, Martin 167, 189
Mladen, Makjanic 170
Mohilla, Peter 187, 188
Mölls, Hans Dieter 188, 189
Monasterio, Fernando Ortiz 177
Mondeteguy, Pierre 67, 68, 138, 139, 140, 176
Monk, Craig 76, 77, 95, 175, 177, 192, 193, 195
Moore, Patrick 190, 191
Morley, B L 187
Morrison, Ernie 178
Morrison, Lee 193
Moser, Bernd 174
Moshkvin, Igor 61
Mrduljas, M 179
Mudrichenko, A. 169

Mugica, Daniel 193
Mujica, Diego 177
Müller, Friedrich 188, 189, 190
Murray, Richard 58, 60, 134, 135
Musto, Keith 59, 60, 135
Muyden, Martijn Van 79, 148, 177
Myralf, Stefan 71, 143

N

Nady, Lou 67, 69, 72, 188, 189, 190, 193
Naef, Kai 173
Natale, Marco Di 170
Neeleman, Mark 70, 71, 72, 74, 95, 141, 142, 143, 145, 177, 195, 196
Neeser, A. 136
Neff, Stewart 70, 141, 195
Negri, Diego 172
Neilson, Terry 71, 72, 73, 95, 192, 193
Nelis, Andre 58, 59, 60, 61, 91, 134, 135, 174, 202
Neudoeffer, V 66
Neve, Leek 189
Newell, D 61
Nicolcioiu, G 177
Niehusen, Carsten 191
Nielsen 59
Nikandrov, Andrei 144, 170
Nikolov, Boncho 169
Nilsen, Per 71, 191
Nilsson 63
Nissen, Michael 70, 71, 142, 176, 196
Nodari, Lucio 190, 191
Noguer, Miguel 73
Noordt, I R W van 60
Nordio, Tito 89
Nordquist, Don 71, 143
Norkine, Alex 168
Nossiter, Anthony 79
Nyberg, Mats 170
Nyman 89
Nyren, Tony 71, 73

O

O'Day, George 193
O'Hara 95
Obarrio, Adrián 93, 174, 193
Obarrio, Alberto 174
Oberbauer, Josef 71
Oberheidt, Jürgen 188
Oberheidt, Werner 187, 188
Ochwadt, Curd 58, 134, 135
Oetgen, Eric 193
Offermanns, Erich 168
Ohlik, Dieter 188, 189, 190
Olavarri, J 178
Olin, Magnus 65, 66, 67, 68, 69, 139, 196, 203
Oliver, Mark 145
Oliviera, B 135, 170
Oliviera, H. de 91
Oljelund, Thomas 72, 73, 142, 143, 192, 195
Orel, Jure 172
Orlov, Dmitri 171, 178
Orth, Werner 187
Ortolano, Armando 74, 75, 76, 95, 144, 145, 146, 171, 194, 195
Oser, Georg 187, 188, 189
Oskamp, Mel 186, 187
Oskay, Serdar 173
Österreich, Björn 170, 171
Oswald, A. 89
Otasoo, Tammo 171
Oundjian, Nick 68
Outrata, Jiri 175, 189, 190, 191
Özgen, Levent 141, 168, 178

P

Packowski, Klaus von 188, 189
Page, Mark 72
Pallson, Martin 71, 72, 142, 143, 169
Palmaj, Peter 173
Palmgren, Kenneth 140, 195

Pampaloni, F 62
Pandler, Michael 190, 191
Papacannou 140
Papadopoulos, Michalis 147, 192
Papadopoulos, Odysseas 173
Papaioannou, Ath 67, 139, 167, 168
Papantoniou, A 75
Papathanasiou, Emilios 78, 79, 147, 148, 172 173, 192, 194, 195
Passoni, Enrico 73, 75, 76, 144, 145, 146
Passoni, Marco 73, 75, 144, 145, 170
Pasturaud, Jean 67, 139, 176
Patrunky, Lutz 71, 72, 176
Pawlaczyk, Pawel 146, 177
Payne, S 134
Peck, Darrell 77, 78, 179, 193
Peet, Peter 73, 144, 171
Pelaschier, Adelchi 59, 61, 62, 91, 134, 135, 203
Pelaschier, Mauro 64, 67, 69 93, 137, 139, 140, 167, 194
Pentchev, Tzvetain 168
Pentti, M 171
Percy, Iain 78, 79, 148, 179
Perrakis 135
Persson, Lennart 71, 142
Petaja 140
Petchonkin, Jevgeni 175
Peter Conrad 65
Peter Kron 187
Peters, N 169
Petersen, Ole G 61
Phelan Jr, Paul 168, 190
Phelan, Paul 65
Philipp, Malte 75, 76, 146 147, 171, 172, 176, 196
Pichugin, S 170
Pieper, Willy 89, 91, 134
Pimental, Andy 71, 72, 143, 179, 193
Pinaud, Yves-Louis 59, 91, 135, 175
Pirsch, Josef 144
Pittlekov, Dirk 192
Pitts-Pitts, Derrick 58
Pivecevic, Tonko 91, 134, 179
Plecity, M 191
Plinke, Günter 188
Ploeg, Jose Maria van der 76, 77, 78, 95, 142, 143 46, 147, 148, 169 170, 178, 194, 195, 202
Podolski, Andrzej 135, 177
Poeschl, M 191
Pohlmann, Otto 70, 71 141, 142, 143, 169, 176, 196
Poissant, Didier 134, 175
Poklewski, L 177
Polaczyk, R 170
Poncell, Toni 75, 145
Poncell-Vich, A 171
Porter, John 179, 192, 193
Poschl, Manfred 190, 191
Posposil, B 167
Potapov, Victor 65, 93, 138, 139, 177
Poullain, Franck 63, 175
Poullain, Pierre 59, 63
Prada, Bruno 79, 175
Prancevic, Marko 143, 179
Pratt, Chris 95, 143, 145, 174
Prenat 67
Presti, Philippe 76, 77, 78, 95 146, 147, 148, 194, 196, 203
Pridal, R 175
Prince, Dick 193
Proctor, C 174
Proctor, Ched 142
Prokopov, Vesselin 169
Prost 59
Puchert, Jürgen 189
Pym, Patrick 63, 64, 65, 66, 93, 138, 139

Q

Quadfass, Martin 186, 188
Quass, E 64
Quigley, Peter 72, 193
Quina, Jose Manuel 93, 137

R

Raben, Herbert 176
Racek, I 167, 175
Räder , A 170
Raderschadt, Peter 189, 190, 191
Radwaniecko, Wlopz. 146, 177
Rambeau, Pascal 148, 173
Randy MacLaren 69, 193
Raphalen 67
Ratsey, Colin 89
Raudaschl, Hubert 61, 62 63, 65, 66, 91, 93, 135 136, 137, 138, 174, 193, 203
Rauder 170
Rechardt, Esko 70, 71, 93, 95, 142, 143, 144
Rechardt, Lauri 73 74, 75, 95, 145, 170, 195
Redmile, Guy 179
Regoczy, Gabor 168
Reich, Herbert 60, 192
Reich, Othmar 186, 187
Reist, Bernhard 60, 61, 63 67, 135, 137, 178
Reiter, Heinz 187
Remien, A 61
Reynolds, Buzz 69, 70, 71, 72, 192, 193
Reynolds, James 141
Ribbhagen, Bjoern 65
Rich, R G 179
Richardson, Jamie 193
Rieperdinger, Georg 188, 189
Righi, D 179
Riley, Sanford 67, 68, 69 93, 139, 140, 168, 175 179, 192, 193
Rinne, Alexander 75, 76, 146, 172, 178
Riosa, Walter 78, 79, 148
Rist, Elmer 187, 188, 189
Robert, Henrik 89
Roberts, Clive 63, 91, 139, 177, 193
Roberts, Ralph 61, 177
Roberts, Vilhelm 72, 73, 171, 177
Rogber , Bo 67, 167
Rogge, Jacques 60, 65, 68, 70 93, 140, 141, 142, 174, 196
Rogge, Philippe 77, 78, 79, 147, 148, 175, 177
Rohart, Xavier 76, 77 78, 79, 95, 147, 148 172, 176, 194, 195, 196
Roost, Andrea 191, 142, 188, 190
Rosen, Bjorn 58, 60, 61
Rosengren, Jörgen 71, 170
Ross, Willi 190
Roswell, Brian 58
Roth, Frank 187, 188, 189
Rowan, Richard 179
Rudling, Paul 69, 70
Rudolphi, Thomas 71
Rudström, Erik 59
Rujak, Istvan 93, 142, 169, 172, 176
Rumszewicz, A 137, 139, 169
Rumszewicz, Tomasz 69, 143, 169, 177
Rundström, Erik 58, 134
Rychcik, Miroslav 70, 71 72, 73, 142, 143, 177, 196
Rydgren, St. 134
Rymkiewicz, A 177
Rymkiewicz, J 167
Ryrie, Colin 91, 174

S

Sadowski, J 170
Saffery-Cooper, Brian 61, 62, 136, 178
Saija 167
Sailer, A 170
Sall, Börge 62, 63, 64, 65, 138
Salvi, Guido 168
Sandberg, Goran 144
Sandberg, Tom 67, 68
Sanjurjo, Jorge 193
Santroch, Jim 67, 69
Saraskin, Jüri 175
Sarby, Bert 58, 59, 134, 135
Sarby, Rickard 58, 89, 91, 134, 186, 195
Sarikavazis, Demetrios 168
Sätre, Åke 186
Savage, Bruce 178
Scharbert, Gyula 176
Scheel, Peter 193
Schemer, A. 136
Scherzer, Erich 191
Schiess, Louis 178, 186, 187
Schilling, G 187, 188
Schimitzek, Kurt 71, 189, 190, 191
Schippers, A. 191
Schippers, Wiebe 147, 172
Schmid, Karl 178
Schmid, Thomas 71, 72, 73 74, 75, 76, 78, 95, 142 143, 144, 145, 195, 196
Schmidt, Carl 174
Schmidt, David 67, 68, 70
Schmidt-Grael, T 71
Schobert, H P 188, 189
Schomer, Andras 176, 190
Schöttle, F 139
Schreiber, Detlef 168
Schröder, Christian 65, 93, 139, 140, 176, 203
Schuldt 60
Schulz, Roger 75, 145
Schulze, Klaus 187, 188
Schümann, Jochen 93 139, 140, 141, 142, 143 168,169, 176, 194 203
Schuster, Walter 187, 188, 190, 191
Schwan 63
Schwarz, Borge 59, 58 59, 134, 135, 136, 194, 195
Schwarz, G 62
Scott, Don 179
Scott, Graham 169
Scott, Peter 89
Seeliger, Gerardo 138, 139, 140, 178
Seidenberg, Paul 175
Seidl, Ernst 167
Sellschopp, H 187
Semeraro, Paolo 71, 72, 73 74, 142, 143, 144, 170, 194
Senkyr, Josef 142, 169, 175, 178, 191
Serra, Ruben 74, 144, 170, 177
Serra-Merckens, R 171
Serranne, Eric 174
Serritslev, Ali 178
Sharples, Nigel 64, 178
Shavrin, Yuri 134, 177
Shaw, Ernie 65, 178
Shelton, David 77
Shilov, Oleg 65, 138
Shope, Peter 74
Siebeck, Georg 191
Sieradzki, J 177
Silvestri, Russ 71, 73, 79, 143, 193
Silvestro, Yves 142, 169, 176, 192
Simoneschi, A 170
Simpson, Conrad 146
Sipos, P 191
Sirvent, J I 178
Sjöberg, Kristian 73, 74, 144, 145, 170
Skalisz, M 61, 62, 63, 177
Skarbinski, Ryszard 69, 93 141, 142, 167, 177, 194
Skaugen, M 191
Skibski, Maciej 75, 171, 177
Skinner, John 179
Sleeswijk, Hans 58, 59, 60, 134, 135
Sloane, Lloyd 177
Smalley, Dave 175, 193
Smigelski, Alex 70, 72
Smigelski, Andrzej 169
Smiltenieks, E 175
Smith, Bob 139, 168
Sobkowiak, Jacek 71, 72, 73, 143, 144, 170, 177
Soliviev, Victor 169
Somers Payne, J 91
Sondermann, Herbert 188, 189, 190, 191
Sonesson, Ola 171
Soria, Philippe 62, 65, 93
Soukhoroukow, Nikolai 143, 170
Spacek, Miroslav 135, 175
Spängs, Patrick 70, 71 72, 141, 142, 143, 169, 170
Spencer, P 177
Spindler, Monty 71, 193
Spitzauer, Hans 73, 74, 75 76, 77, 78, 95, 144, 145, 146 147, 148, 170, 171, 174 192, 194, 195, 196, 202
Splitek, Milo 187
Spooner, Joe 79
Sprague, Henry 63, 64 65, 66, 67, 179, 192, 193
Stadig, E 58, 135
Stammnitz, Heinz 189, 190, 191
Stauch, Hemlmut 178, 179
Stegmeier, Beat 170
Steib, Franz 191, 188, 189, 190
Steiner, H 167
Stenberg, Björn 167
Stenhouse, Richard 78, 79, 95, 147, 148, 179
Stern, P 174
Steward, Ant 178
Storer, Richard 66, 139
Stork, Jan Olov 59
Stork, S 63
Strandvig, Otto 75, 76, 144, 145, 146
Stratton, Desmond 60, 61, 64
Stratton, Vernon 58, 59 60, 61, 65, 91, 134, 178, 186
Straubinger, Bernhard 59, 60 61, 63, 65, 136, 137, 176
Stuffer, Klaus 188, 190
Stulcken, Peter 60
Sturm 137, 187
Sturm, Albert 174
Sturm, C 187, 188
Stutterheim, J.v.Alt 64, 137, 176
Suchorokov, Nicolai 74
Suffer, K 191
Sukhorukov, Nikolai 178
Sülberg, Werner 67, 68, 69, 71, 140, 176
Sulyok, Miklos 169
Sumar, Sinan 173, 178
Sun, Anatoli Yn 177
Sundelin, Per 68
Svenson, A 58
Szekely, Antal 176
Szilvàssy, Atilla 75, 146, 171, 176
Szloser, J 177
Szraj, W 177
Szukiel, Rafal 173

T

Tallberg, H 63
Tallberg, Peter 63, 65
Tammo Otsasoo 175
Tanscheit, Peter 74, 193
Tapio, Guillermo 177
Taulois, Erwan 173, 176
Taveter, Aare 171, 175
Taveter, Imre 171, 172, 175
Tavinor, Timothy 73, 75, 145
Teply, Roman 147, 175
Termoz, J 187
Terry Neilson 175, 179
Themelis 140
Theodis 69
Theurer, Peter 78, 79, 147, 178
Thielemann, Uwe 172
Thier, Bret De 66, 65, 68, 93, 177, 193
Thom, Barry 68, 73, 64, 75, 76, 145, 171
Thom, M 177
Thomas, Craig 67, 68, 139, 168
Thompson, Danny 67, 168
Thorell, Sven 89
Thorwaldsen 89
Till, Michael 191
Tillman, Dick 63, 137, 179, 193
Tkachuk, Igor 77, 78, 147, 148, 172
Todd, Brian 67, 69, 175
Tokovoi, Yuri 75, 76, 78 79, 95, 146, 147 148, 171, 178
Tolnai, Kalman 135, 176
Tomasevic, Emil 175
Tootsy, Tinu 170, 175
Topiarz, Petr 189
Tovisi, Andras 171
Trani, Bruno 61, 91
Treleaven, B E 63, 68, 137
Trujillo Villar, Rafael 78, 148, 173, 178, 195
Truslow, Peter 73, 193
Tsavdaridis, I 171
Tucker, Alan 178, 188
Tüfekçi, Ali Kemal 173, 178
Turazza, Mario 169, 170
Türklitz, Achim 65, 67
Türr, Wernfried 174
Turro, Jesus 69
Tuss, Miklos 62, 136, 139, 176
Twardowski, Z 177
Twist 63

U

Ugelstad, Rudolf 60, 61
Unterhauser, Heinrich 188, 189, 190
Uwe Heinzmann 139, 139, 194, 196

V

Vacarri, Emanuele 74, 75, 76, 78, 95, 144 145, 146, 147, 148, 171, 195
Vachek, Antonin 187, 188, 189
Václav, Cintl 189
Vadnai, T 171
Valasek, Marek 173
Valli, Jouki 60, 61, 135
Van Den, B 191
Vassilev, N B 192
Vassillis, Loizos 173
Vauthier, Claude 191
Vazquez, Alfredo 177
Veen, Van der 168
Vejvoda, Mirek 190
Vejvoda, Miroslav 62, 63 64, 65, 67, 93, 136, 137 138, 139, 175, 187
Verloop, Louis 74, 144, 193
Verneuil, Serge 176, 192
Vetter, Jörg 142, 169
Viali, Nenad 78, 79, 148, 170, 179, 192
Vienberg, Peter 175
Vierssen, Han van 189, 190
Vilby, Peter 72, 73 74, 143, 144, 170, 175, 195
Villalonga, Francisco 75, 76, 145, 146, 172, 178
Villasnor, Lorenzo 177
Vincke, Egbert 68, 187, 188
Vincke, Hendrik 188, 189, 190
Vogler, Jürgen 58, 59, 91, 134, 135, 176, 203
Volarevic, Srdjan 179
Völker, R 170
Vollebregt, Peter 68, 69, 71, 141, 142, 190
Vooremaa, Vaiko 175
Voorhis, Ch. van 73
Vrdoljak, D 191
Vries, Stefan de 173
Vries, Tiemen de 64, 67, 138
Vries, Wm. de 89

W

Walbank, Nigel 71, 72, 196
Waldo, Sten 191
Wall, Per Erik 75
Walle Hansen, J 139
Wallin, Lennart 60, 61
Wallis, Thomas 172
Walusz, Bogdan 167
Warburg, Karel 58, 59, 135
Watson, Bruce 138, 177
Wayboer, D 60
Webb, Clifton 79,, 148, 173
Webb, Robin 61
Webbink, H 170
Weber, Kim 65, 67, 93, 139
Wegener, K H 58
Weichel, Peter 188, 189
Weichert, H 171
Weixelbaumer, Klaus 178, 188
Welter, Alex 67, 139, 168
Wenz, Roland 187
Wenzel, Stefan 172
Werenskiold 138
Werenskiold, Per 60, 61, 62, 63, 65, 139
Werenskiold, Werner 61
Werf, G J van der 188, 189
Westergaard, Bjorn 76, 145, 147, 175
Westergaard, Stig 73, 75, 76 77, 95, 144, 145, 146, 147, 175 177, 192, 194, 195, 196, 202
Whitaker, Roland 193
White, Jere 69
Wiest, Adalbart 188, 189, 190
Wildhagen, Hanno 187
Willems 91
Willems, Filip 71, 142, 143
Willems, Hans 61, 63
Wilson, Archie 179
Wilson, Peter 179
Wind, Henning 59, 61 62, 63, 64, 91, 135, 136 137, 138, 175, 188 189, 192, 203
Wingfield, Nicholas 179
Winkler, H 196
Winquist, Jan 63, 93, 138
Wirchmann-Harbeck 89
Wladimir, Hain 190
Wojtonia, Marcin 173
Wolff, Jürgen 68, 139, 140, 176
Wölke, Hans 188, 189
Wood, Larry 193
Woodbury, Rob 70, 71
Woodroffe, Graeme 68, 70
Worthington, Kimo 71, 72, 143, 193
Wossala, Gyorgy 137, 176, 187, 188
Wuhn, H 191
Wunderli, M 178
Wyskowski, Blazy 139, 167

Y

Yamada, T 62
Yannick Adde 172
Yntema, T 169
Yong, J M de 58, 61
Young, O J 193

Z

Zachariassen, Hans Werner 63, 64, 65, 66, 68, 69
Zakhorow, Boris 69, 142, 169
Zapalskyi, G 171
Zarif, Jorge 72, 95, 175, 193
Zaroslav, Vitali 168
Zawieja, Andrzej 65, 66, 68, 93, 138, 139, 177
Zero, T 177
Zetzeija, Jan 168
Zielhuis, Bart 72, 73, 177
Zielhuis, Jaap 177
Zsindely, Laszlo 186, 187, 188, 189, 190, 191
Zycki, Dominik 77, 78 79, 147, 148, 172, 173, 177

Epilogue - Why The Finn?

So there it is. This is the Finn: fifty years of innovation, fifty years of development, and fifty years of great racing. The Finn, simply put, is the ultimate singlehanded sailing machine. Its design, though over half a century old, remains so perfectly balanced that it still ranks as the fastest non-trapeze International singlehander despite the introduction of a host of other classes.

The fact that the boat is powerful means that it requires a true athlete to get the most out of it. In strong winds the boat rewards those who are fit and able to discipline themselves to perform the exhausting task of driving the boat full out while managing the tactical and psychological aspects of the race and with very close performances, the Finn is an intensely tactical boat.

Overall the Finn is one of the few boats that requires one athlete to be at the same time exceptionally fit and strong, outstanding in tactics and familiar with the techniques of sail and rig tuning. It is for that reason that many Finn sailors have performed so well in other boats upon leaving the class.

The Finn's simple rig limits the variables to be tuned. The evolution of class rules have remained prudent over the last fifty years so that the nature of the boat has remained the same, but has allowed the class to move with the times and embrace new technologies that make the boast faster, safer, more economic and easier to sail. The Finn also achieves the dual objectives of allowing enough flexibility to test knowledge, and allows adaption of the rig to suit sailor weight and size, whilst also being standard and affordable enough to be accessible to all.

After fifty years the Finn is still a thoroughly modern boat and remains one of the most challenging high performance singlehanded dinghies, testing all aspects of a sailor's skill and awakening the skills of the winners of the future. After fifty years of progess and development, mastery of the Finn is still one of sailing's ultimate challenges and will hopefully long remain so.

The Finn is the true embodiment of all things great about sailing. It is to be hoped that this book, written on the verge of a new millennium, has portrayed what the Finn is truly about: a group of like minded athletes, pushing the limits of endurance and technology, making worldwide sailing friendships and sailing and racing a great boat - that is the Finn.

Index of Advertisers

Devoti Sailing Ltd	IBC
Latini Wing Masts	96
Lemieux Boats	113
Marina Dellas	113
North Sails New Zealand	113
Pata Boats	96
Sailcoach	96
Segel von Broen	113, 208

The International Finn Association wishes to thank all these organisations for supporting this project through advertisments in this book.